The Art of Jewish Children · Germany 1936 – 1941

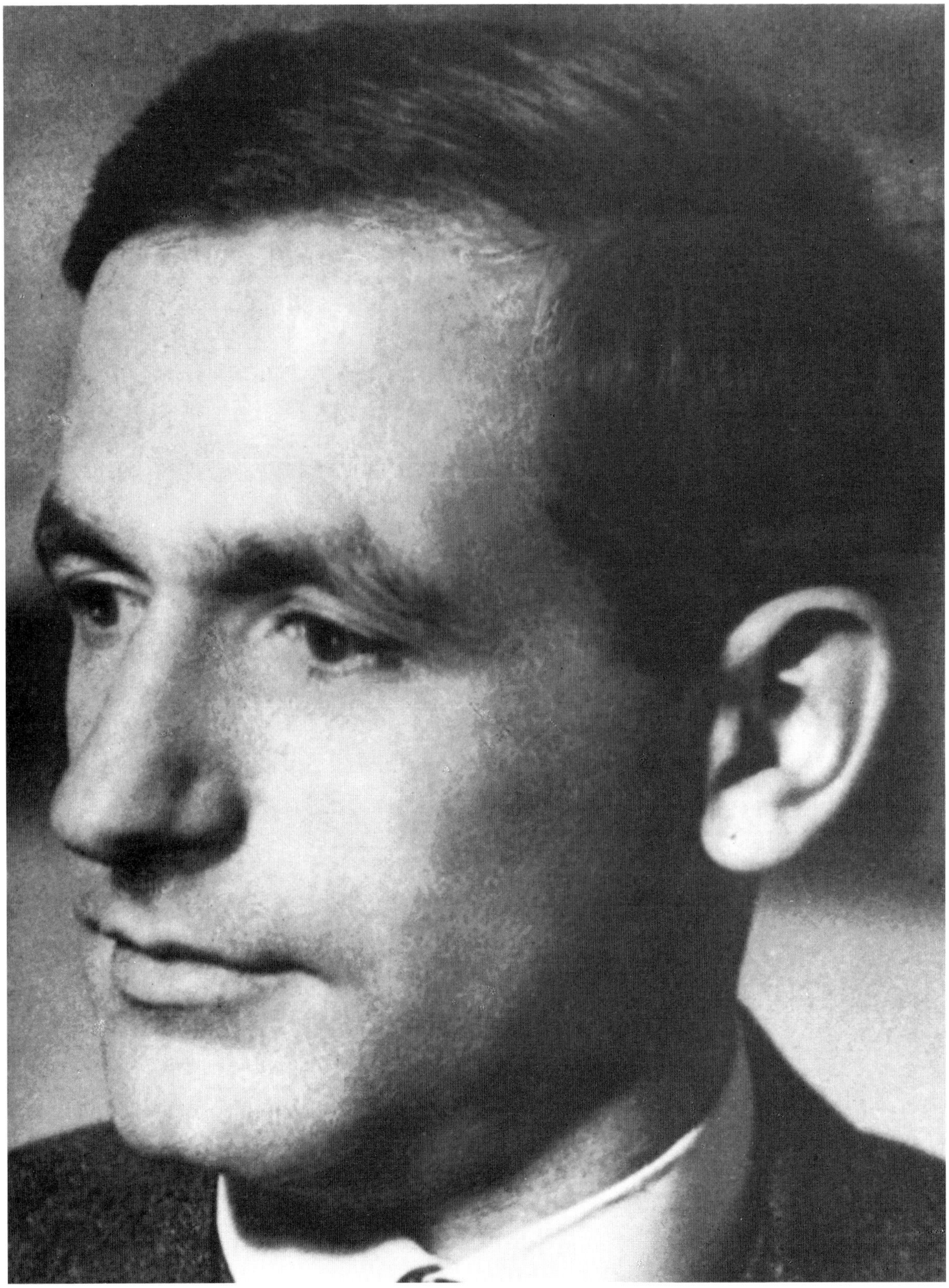

Julo Levin in the early 1930s (Private Collection)

The Art of Jewish Children

Germany 1936–1941

Innocence and Persecution

Edited and translated
by Sybil Milton

PHILOSOPHICAL
LIBRARY

Library of Congress Cataloging-in-Publication Data

Art by Jewish children in Nazi Germany, 1936–1941,
from the collections of the Düsseldorf City Museum.

1. Children's art – Berlin (Germany) – Catalogs.
2. Children's art – Germany (West) – Düsseldorf – Catalogs.
3. Stadtmuseum Düsseldorf – Catalogs.
4. Jews – Germany (West) – Düsseldorf – Persecutions.
5. Holocaust, Jewish (1939–1945) – Germany (West) – Düsseldorf.
6. Jewish children – Germany (West) – Düsseldorf.
7. Jewish day schools – Germany (West) – Düsseldorf.
I. Milton, Sybil. II. Stadtmuseum Düsseldorf.
N352.2.G3A78 1988 741.9'088054 88-12600
ISBN 0-8022-2558-6 (U.S.)

ISBN 0-8022-2558-6

Translation by Sybil Milton of the German volume
Verjagt, ermordet: Zeichnungen jüdischer Schüler 1936–1941
ed. Landeshauptstadt Düsseldorf, Stadtmuseum (Düsseldorf:
Claassen, 1988).

Printed in Germany

Contents

Introduction

Sybil Milton

This book and the exhibition it documents have the daring, even impertinent, title: *Verjagt, ermordet: Zeichnungen jüdischer Schüler, 1936–1941*, which can be literally translated as *Hunted and Murdered: Drawings by Jewish School Children, 1936–1941.* Although such bluntness is unusual, it is clear that the Düsseldorf City Museum *(Stadtmuseum Düsseldorf)* has no taboos in exploring Germany's traumatic past in order to illuminate the present. Using the artistic record created by the victims – racially and politically persecuted professional artists as well as Jewish school children – the City Museum has created what the survivor Jean Améry has called "a spiritual frame of reference in the widest sense."

It is a powerful story about blatant and escalating persecution, using the vehicle of 105 drawings made by German Jewish schoolchildren created in art classes in Jewish schools in Düsseldorf and Berlin. These drawings represent only a fragment of the 1,200 works collected by the artist and teacher Julo Levin (born 1901 in Stettin – murdered 1943 in Auschwitz). This book tells us about Levin's circle of friends, and contains memoirs by Mieke Monjau and Carl Lauterbach about the circumstances in which the children's art collection was created, how it survived, and how it was donated to the Düsseldorf City Museum. It also includes paintings by Julo Levin and his circle.

It shows the dreams and fears of Jewish children inside Nazi Germany: the transmission of Jewish traditions and biblical themes from Purim, Passover, and Hanukkah stories. These motifs are sometimes directly connected with daily life inside Nazi Germany and the hope for rescue by emigration. There are drawings of foreign countries and also of Blacks and Roma and Sinti Gypsies. The language of art reveals the success of a conscious Jewish "education for life." It is this latter theme that connects the drawings of German Jewish schoolchildren from 1936 to 1941 with the art made by children incarcerated in Theresienstadt. This volume tries to demystify the Holocaust by making it concrete and comprehensible, presenting the diverse stories of the victims with a common geographical connection to Düsseldorf after 1933.

The last aspect of this book and exhibition is a series of twenty-four paintings about children and childhood in Germany from the 1920s to the present. These works of art serve to link the past with the present, affirming the fact that the Holocaust also illuminates our contemporary concerns and human values.

The rich selection in this book says something about the Düsseldorf City Museum, which houses one of the largest and most significant collections of Holocaust art in the world. The Museum has used these resources over the past decade to tell the individual stories of the persecuted artists between 1933 and 1945. These works of art affirm the importance of this documentary art as a form of communication. It is my personal privilege to have worked with the *Stadtmuseum Düsseldorf*; its director, Dr. Koenig; and the survivors and colleagues who brought this project to fruition. It is an honor to introduce this collection to a wider American audience.

Sybil Milton
Co-curator of *Verjagt, ermordet*

Foreword

A past that doesn't disappear or "dissipate with the wind" can be a burden for the living. Germans, however insecure or confused when contemplating this past, cannot escape its burden. However, as we recall the past, we gain political and human strength in the present and this enables us to think with humanity and brotherhood now and for the future.

It was with these thoughts as well as with hope and gratitude that I greeted this exhibition of drawings by Jewish children in Nazi Germany. Developed under the auspices of the *Stadtmuseum Düsseldorf,* it opened at the North Rhine Westphalian State Building in Bonn in 1988 and will subsequently travel to Jerusalem, Paris, Los Angeles, Washington, D. C., and New York.

Most of these children's drawings were created between 1936 and 1938 in classes taught by the Jewish artist Julo Levin at the Jewish elementary school in Düsseldorf. They document Jewish life in those difficult years. They also remind us that despite persecution and deprivation of rights, Jewish life still existed amongst our parents and grandparents. How those children understood, discovered, and depicted this life in their drawings should touch us even at a distance of fifty years. But this exhibition is also a contribution to twentieth century German history, which we cannot view only through the eyes of a new generation.

In 1988, we commemorate not only the fiftieth anniversary of those November days when synagogues were burned, Jewish businesses destroyed and looted, Jewish communal offices demolished, and Jewish fellow citizens taunted and abused. The expression *Reichskristallnacht* is without doubt a cynical euphemism. Our use of language must not obscure the fact that this was an organized and directed pogrom to make Jews inside the Third Reich submissive, prepared to emigrate, and conscious of their loss of rights. I cannot chronicle here the persecution of Jews between 1933 and 1938. We know that those five years were but the first chapter in the Nazi policy of extermination, marked by racism and the determination to establish the "master race" as the goal of a nationalist German history.

This dictatorial policy of inhumanity was an insane and illegitimate vision of German history. Far too many watched in silence, went along, and also obeyed orders. Although this was not only true for Germany, it certainly does not – nor can it – diminish our responsibility as Germans.

This exhibition of drawings by Jewish children will be a reminder for us in Germany and later also remind others in Europe, Israel, and the United States, of what once happened in Germany. We must and want to see these drawings not only as part of a fiftieth anniversary commemoration of the November 1938 pogrom, but as historical documents and as a warning now and in the future for us to live together without exclusion, hatred, racism, or delusions of power. Freedom and human rights cannot be restricted.

Johannes Rau
Minister-President of the
State of North Rhine-Westphalia

Not Only Pictures: Instead of a Preface

For Lili and Ephraim Eylon

Not strangers, but fellow Germans, even fellow Düsseldorfers, excluded them from public schools and sent them to separate Jewish schools, then robbed them of their homes, their friends, and their roots, finally exiling and murdering them. This also happened to their teacher Julo Levin, who was murdered in Auschwitz in 1943. We are still close enough to these crimes to label them explicitly for what they were. More than 1,000 drawings, hidden from the Gestapo by Mieke Monjau and Carl Lauterbach, have survived and been donated to the *Stadtmuseum Düsseldorf*. This exhibition consists not only of works by German Jewish children, but also includes the works of professional artists depicting the lives of children in Germany during the Weimar Republic, World War II, and today. This extension of the subject enables us to place the children's art in a broader context and thus to view it as an ongoing aspect of our confrontation with German history.

How did these artists depict the lives of these Düsseldorf children before 1933?: working-class children from Düsseldorf-Flingern painted by Mathias Barz in 1926 (Fig. 1); middle-class infants portrayed by Gerhard Keller in 1928 (Fig. 2); intimidated youths like Karlrobert Kreiten – later hanged in Plötzensee Prison in 1943 – painted by Willem Stocké in 1925 (Fig. 3); or even children representing the hopes of militaristic pan-German philistines shown in Adolf Uzarski's *German Family* in 1932 (Fig. 5).

In emigration, the German Jewish artist Bernhard Sopher completed a series of sculptures entitled *Motherhood in War*, showing women trying to protect their children from the horrors of war (*Chinese Mother*, Fig. 9). Similarly, Paul Loskill entitled his 1943 painting *The Madonna of the Bombs*, depicting a woman with her dying child in burning Düsseldorf (Fig. 10).

Mathias Barz worked on a large canvas entitled *Inferno* (Fig. 11) from 1945 until his death; he was never able to finish this painting because of tormenting questions about the guilt of his own nation. Barz was also haunted by the thought of the children murdered in concentration camps. He thus created the work *SS Man* in 1979, also included in this exhibition (Fig. 12).

And today? In 1951, Peter August Böckstiegel painted a refugee youth. In 1985, Matthias Koppel painted a young man admiring the mountains, while behind his back a concatenation of the old and the new was created (*Looking Backward: Hitler's Tea House at Berchtesgaden*, Fig. 14).

Even Düsseldorf has its own such local sites, shown in Lothar Spinn-Conradt's 1985 photographs *Deported from Here: The Düsseldorf-Bilk Train Station* (Fig. 18) and *Mühlenstrasse: The Maidanek Trial*, the locale of the Düsseldorf District Court (Fig. 19).

The question "Is Mengele still alive?" inspired the Israeli artist Youval Yariv, resident in Düsseldorf, to create a cycle of paintings, two of which are included in this exhibition: *The Artist on his Way to Work*, from the series *In Homage to Dinah Gottliebova, No. 1* (1985; Fig. 15) and No. 4 (1986–1987; Fig. 16).

Wieland Koenig
Director, *Stadtmuseum Düsseldorf*

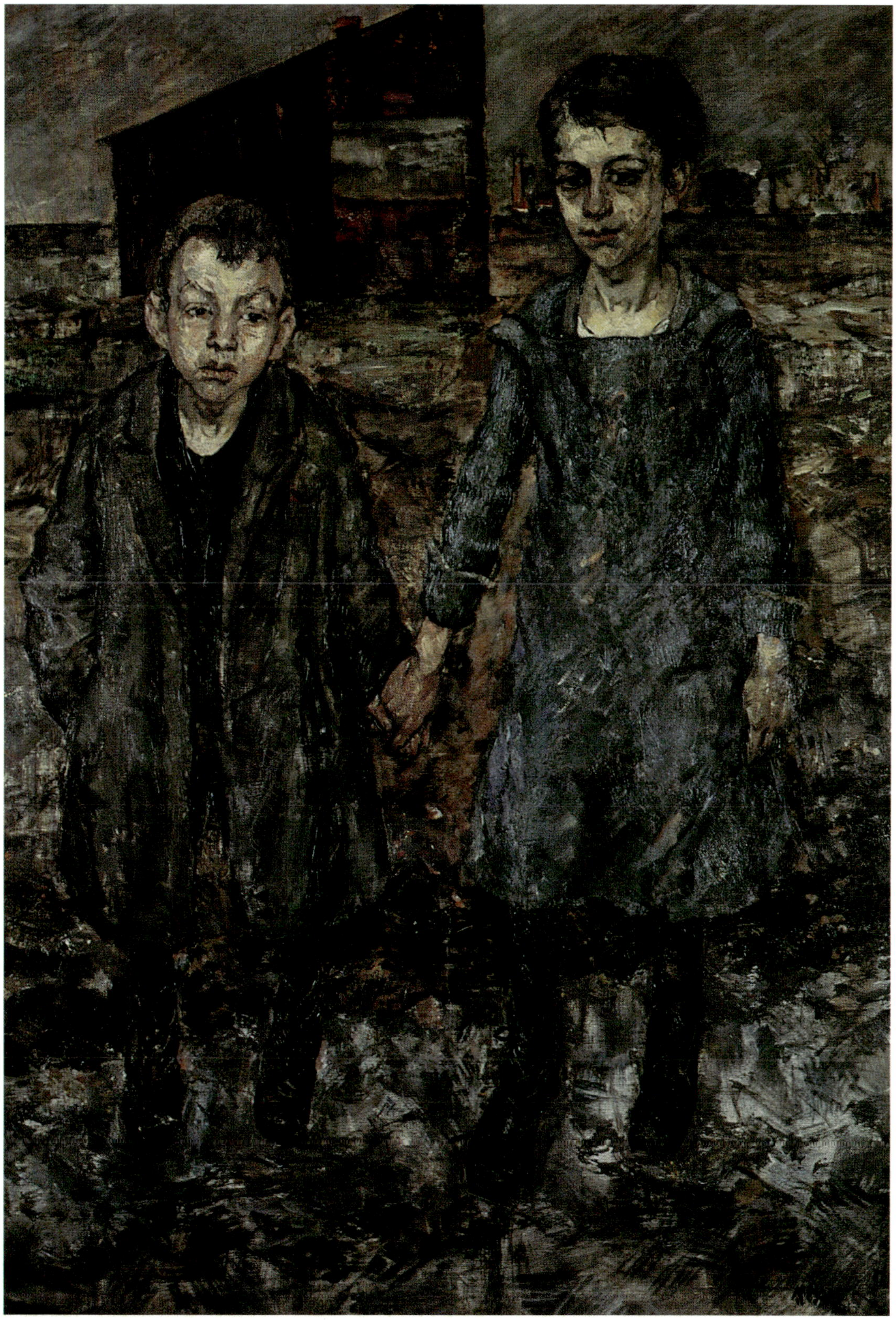

1 Mathias Barz, *Working-Class Children*, 1926 (Cat. 108)

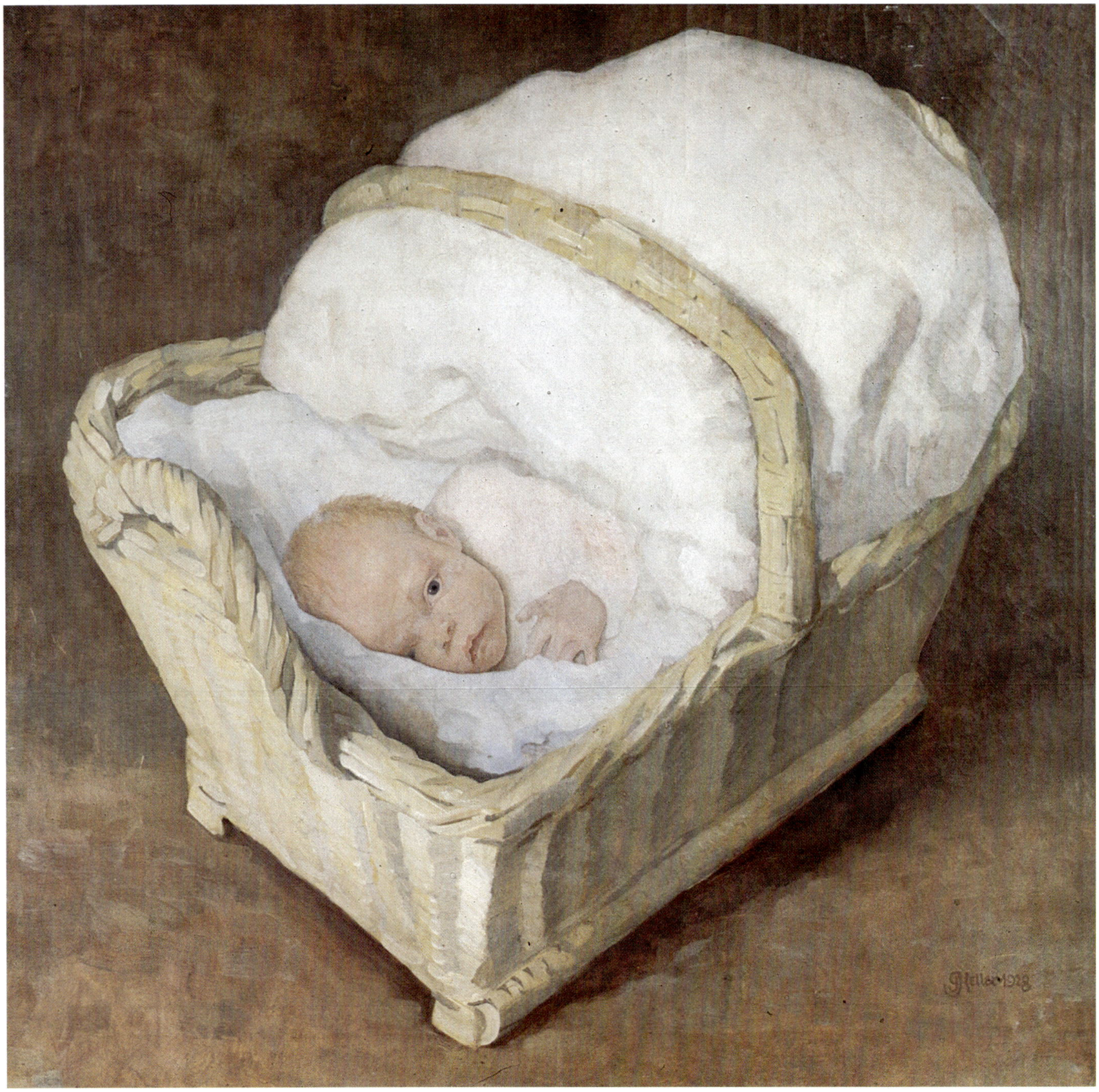

2 Gerhard Keller, *Portrait of Childhood (Ilse Studemund)*, 1928 (Cat. 109)

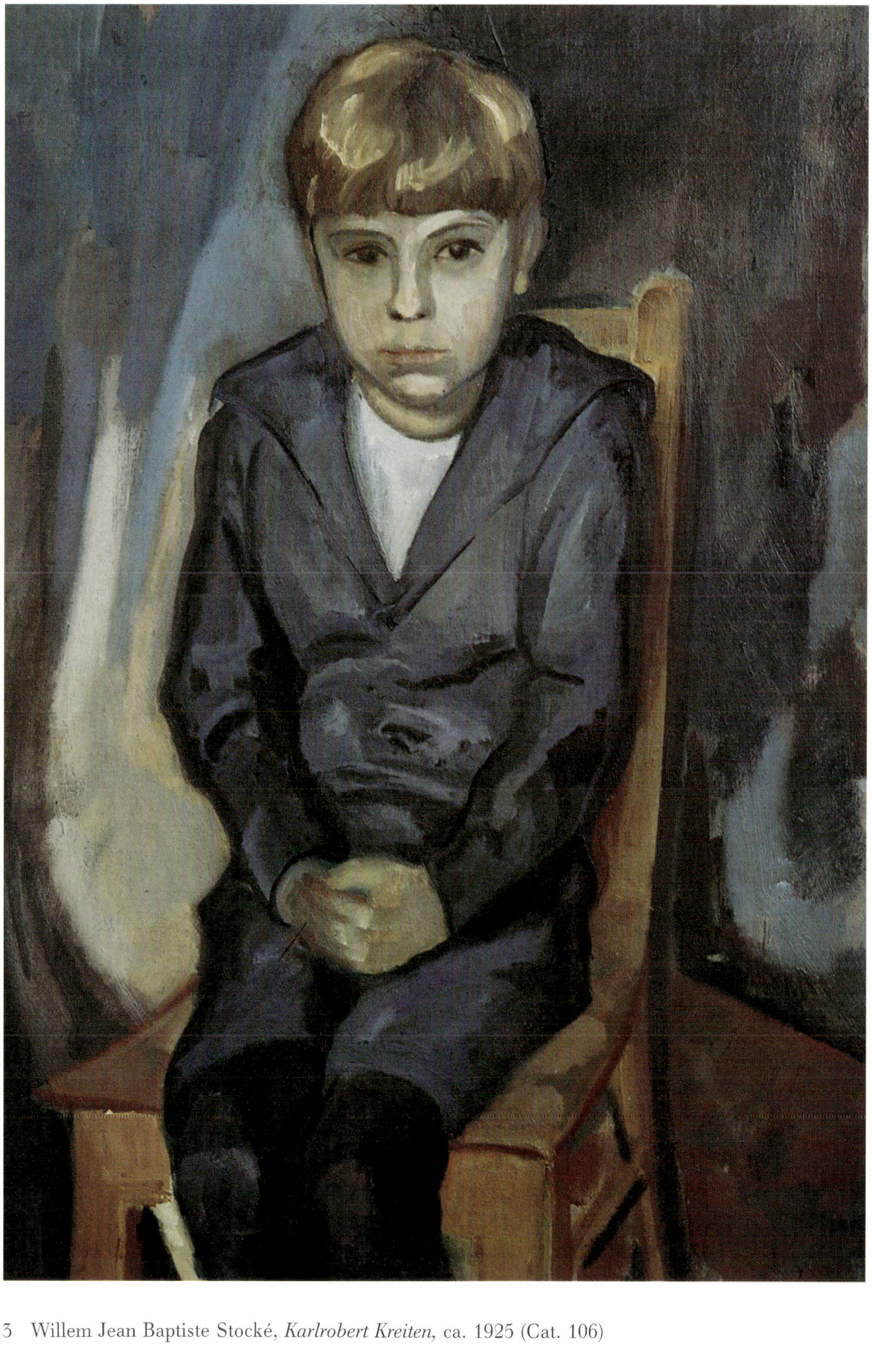

3 Willem Jean Baptiste Stocké, *Karlrobert Kreiten*, ca. 1925 (Cat. 106)

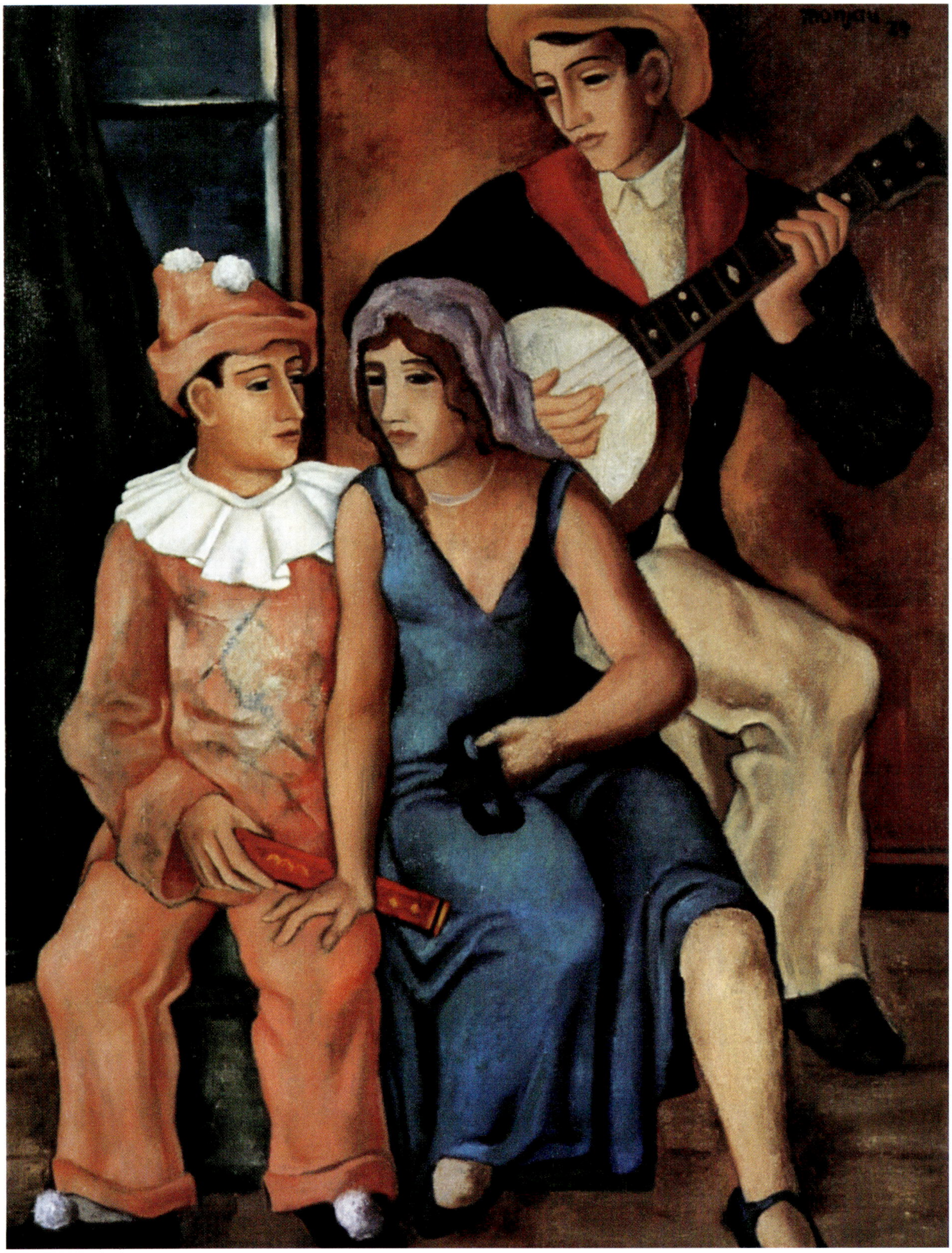

4 Franz Monjau, *Carnival*, 1929 (Cat. 110)

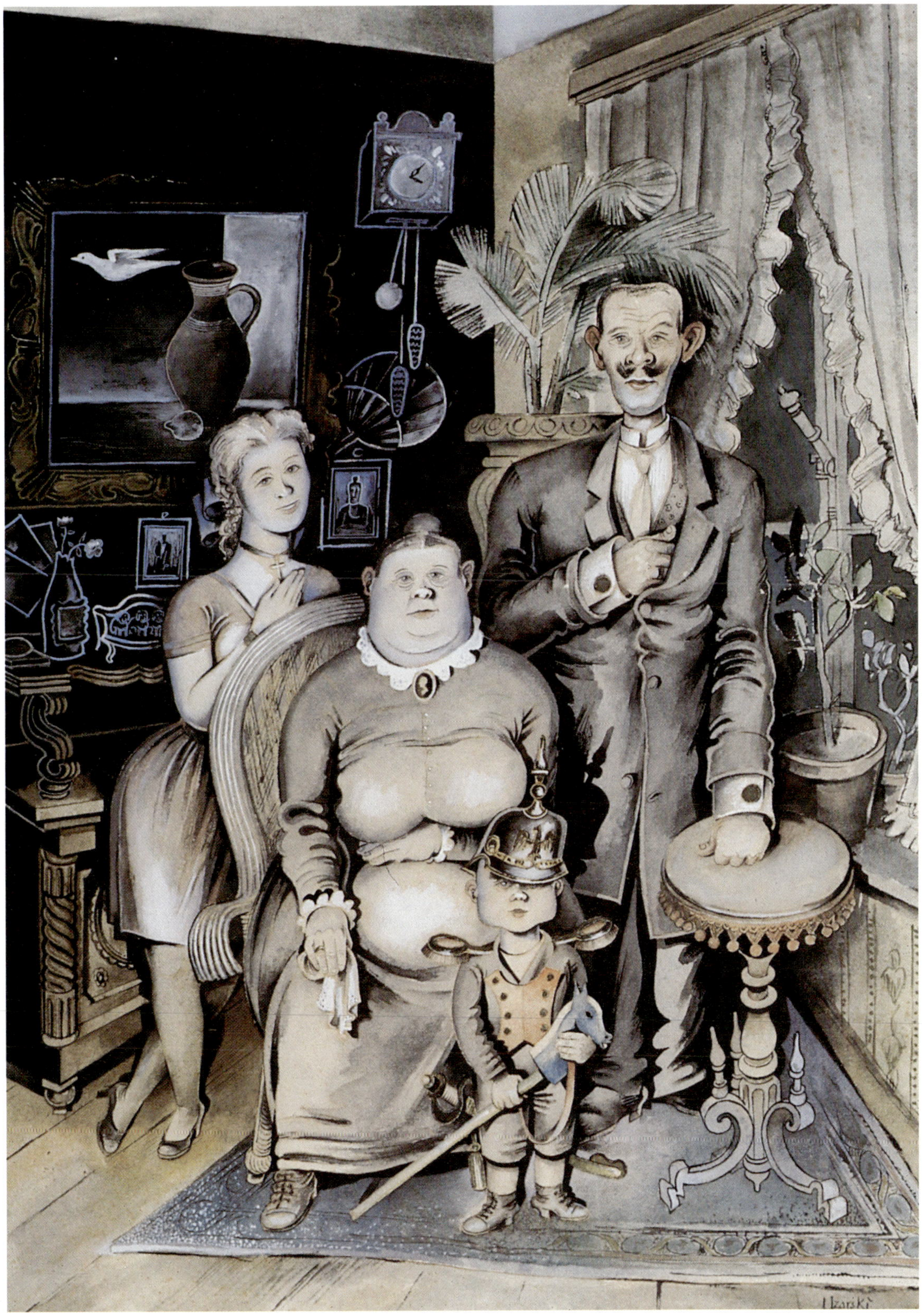

5 Adolf Uzarski, *German Family*, 1932 (Cat. 111)

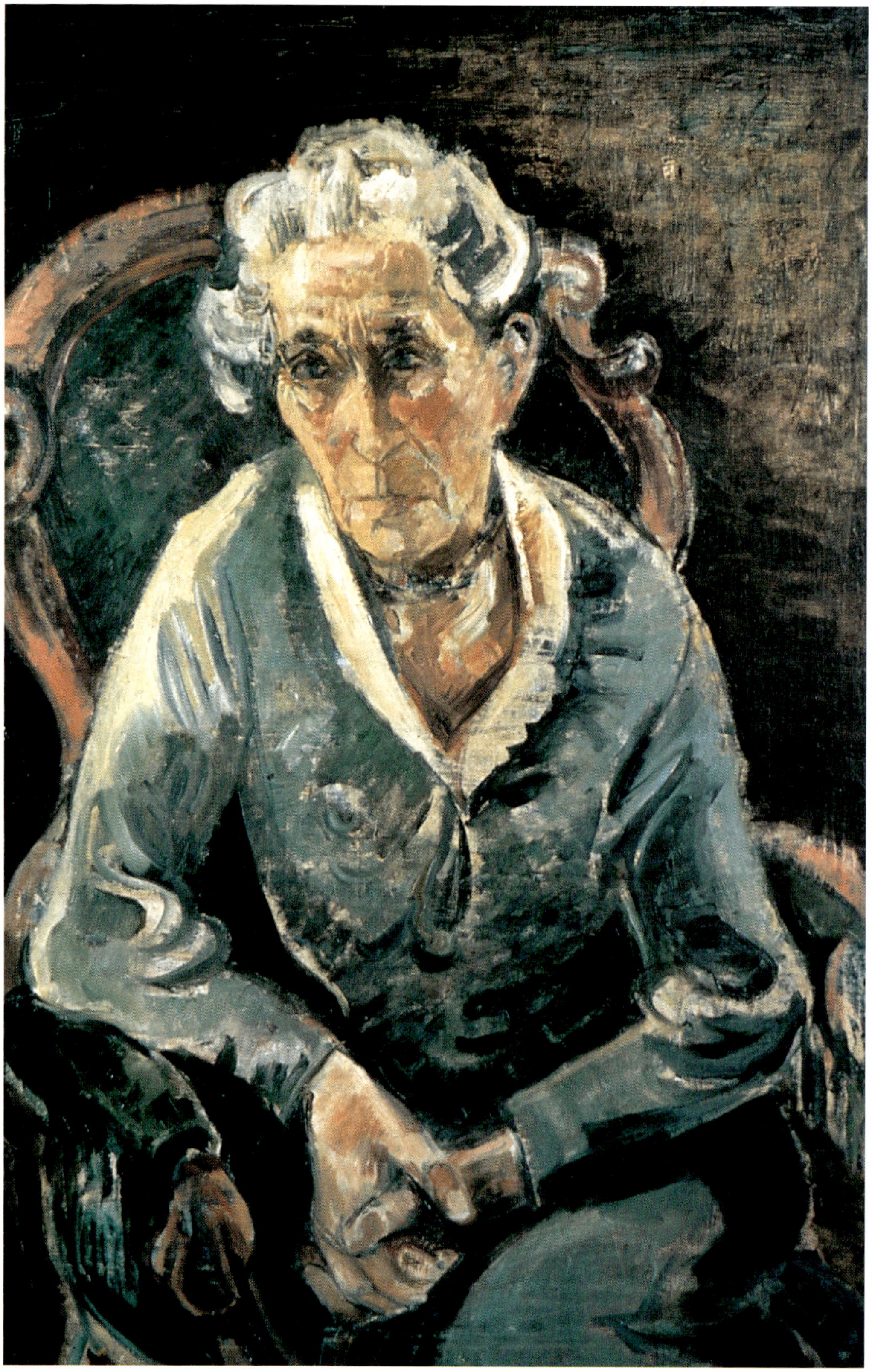

6 Julo Levin, *My Mother*, 1939–1940 (Cat. 115)

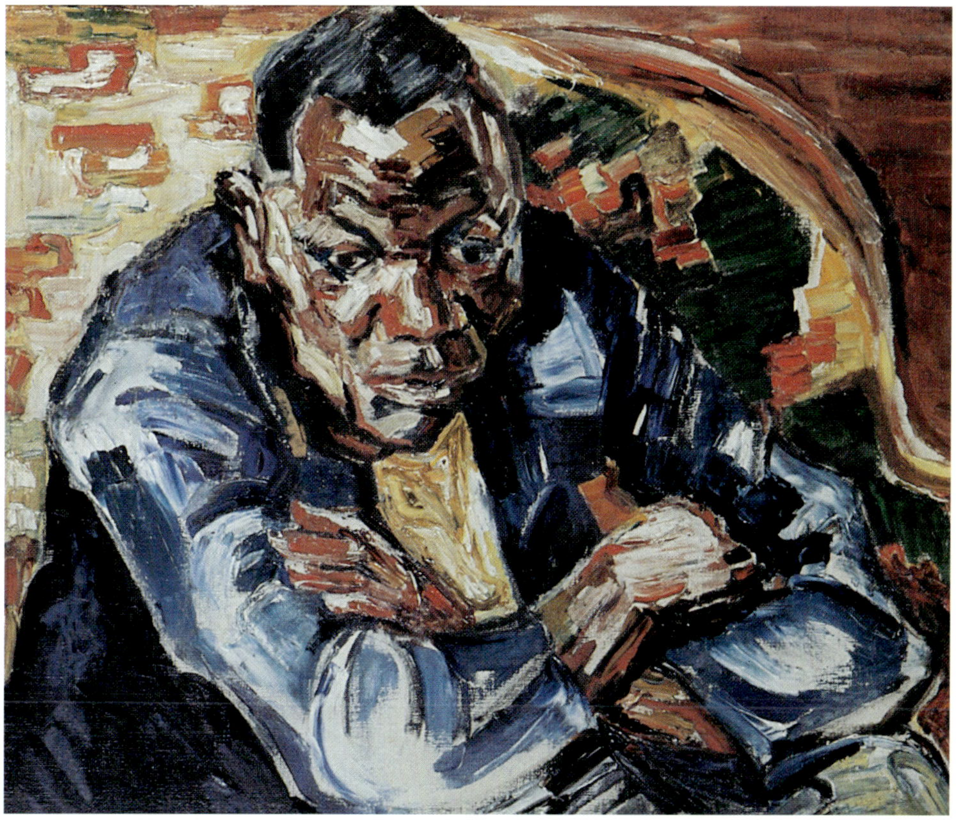

7 Julo Levin
My Friend Ibrahim,
1931
(Cat. 113)

8 Julo Levin,
Job,
1933–1934
(Cat. 114)

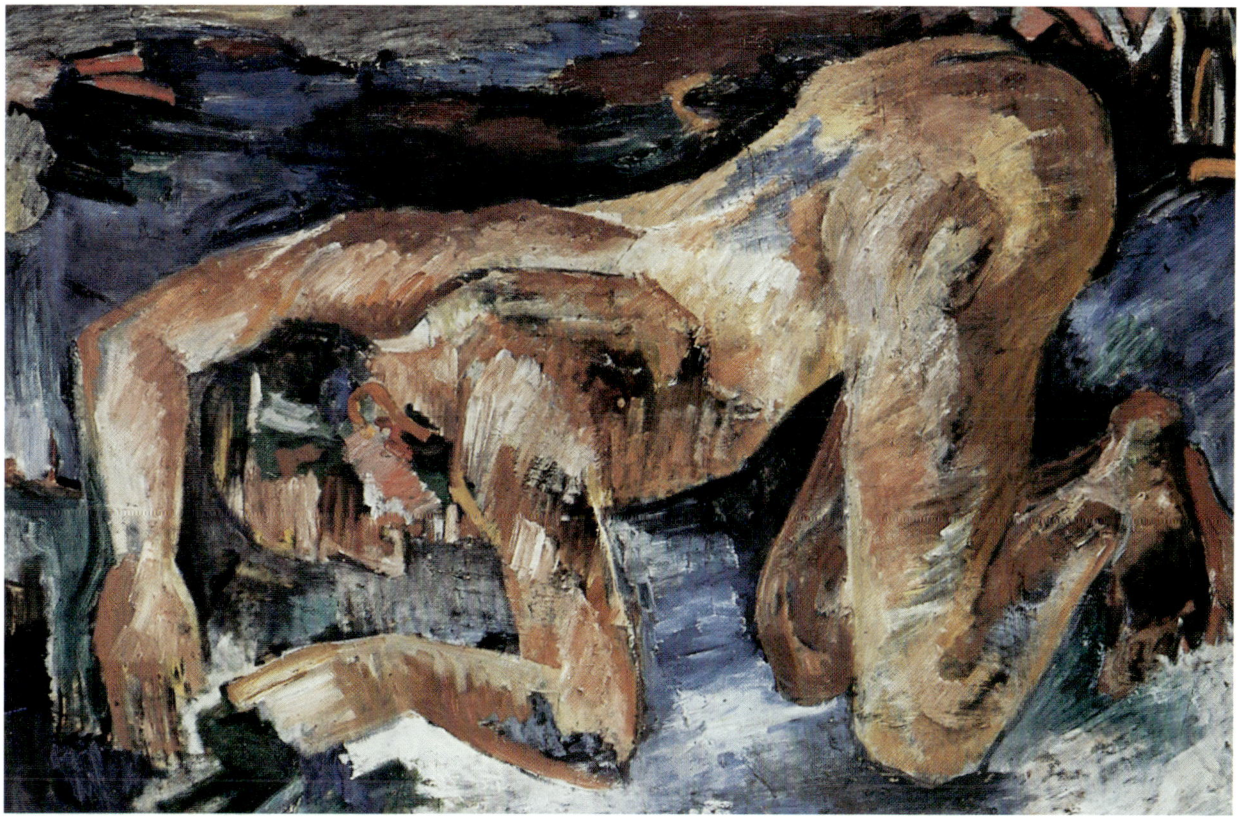

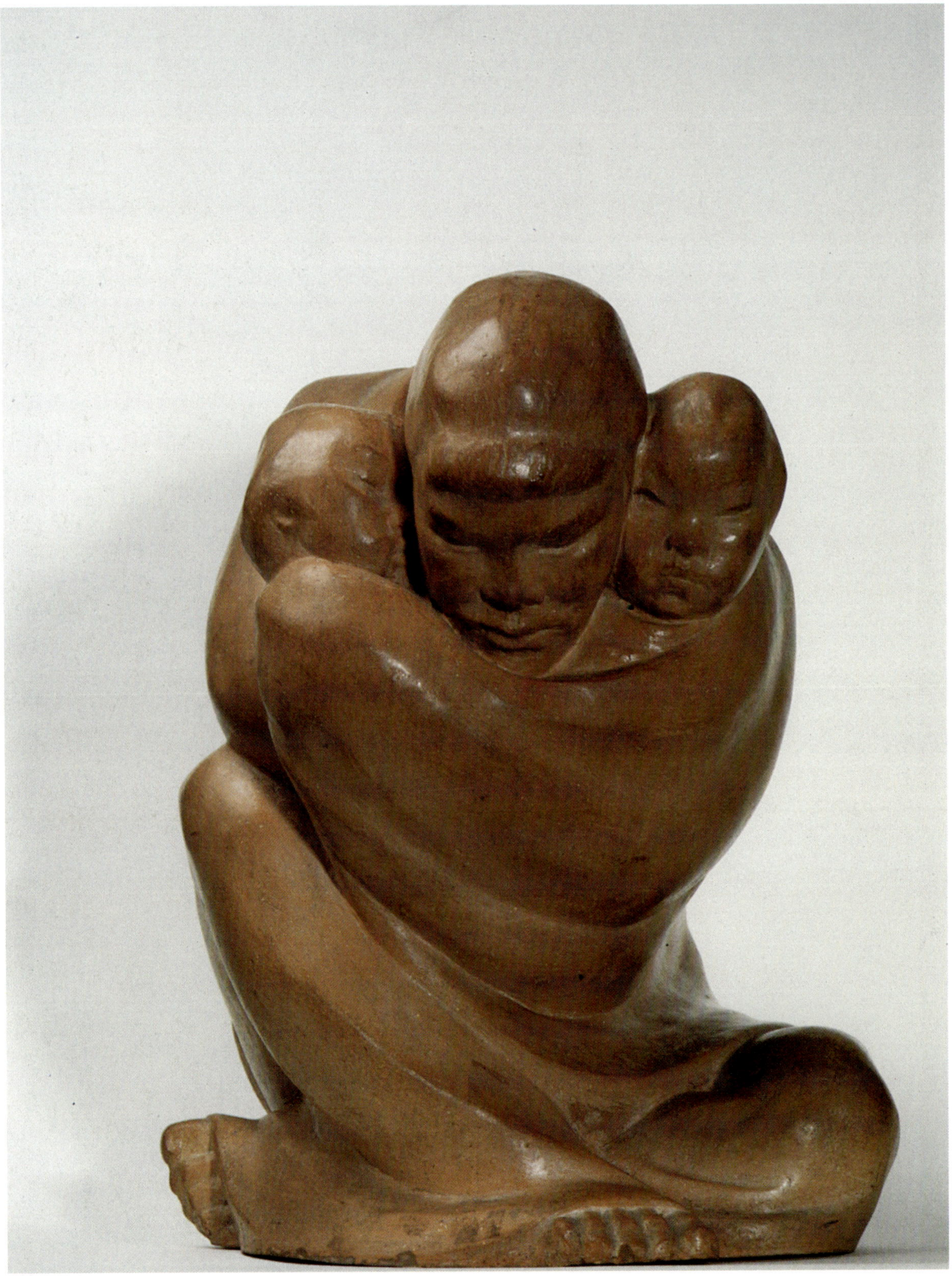

9 Bernhard Sopher, *Chinese Mother*, 1942 (Cat. 118)

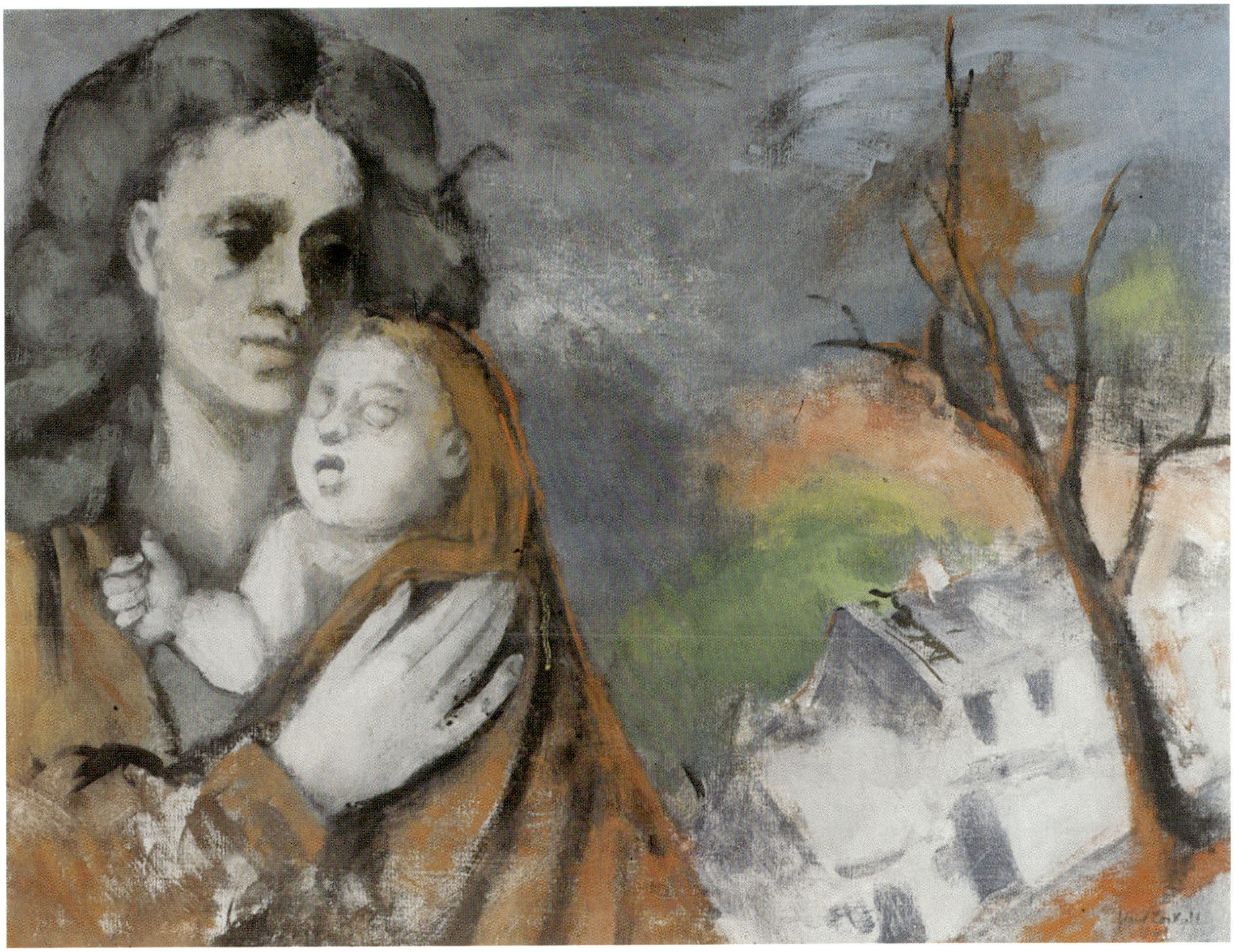

10 Paul Loskill, *Madonna of the Bombs*, 1943 (Cat. 119)

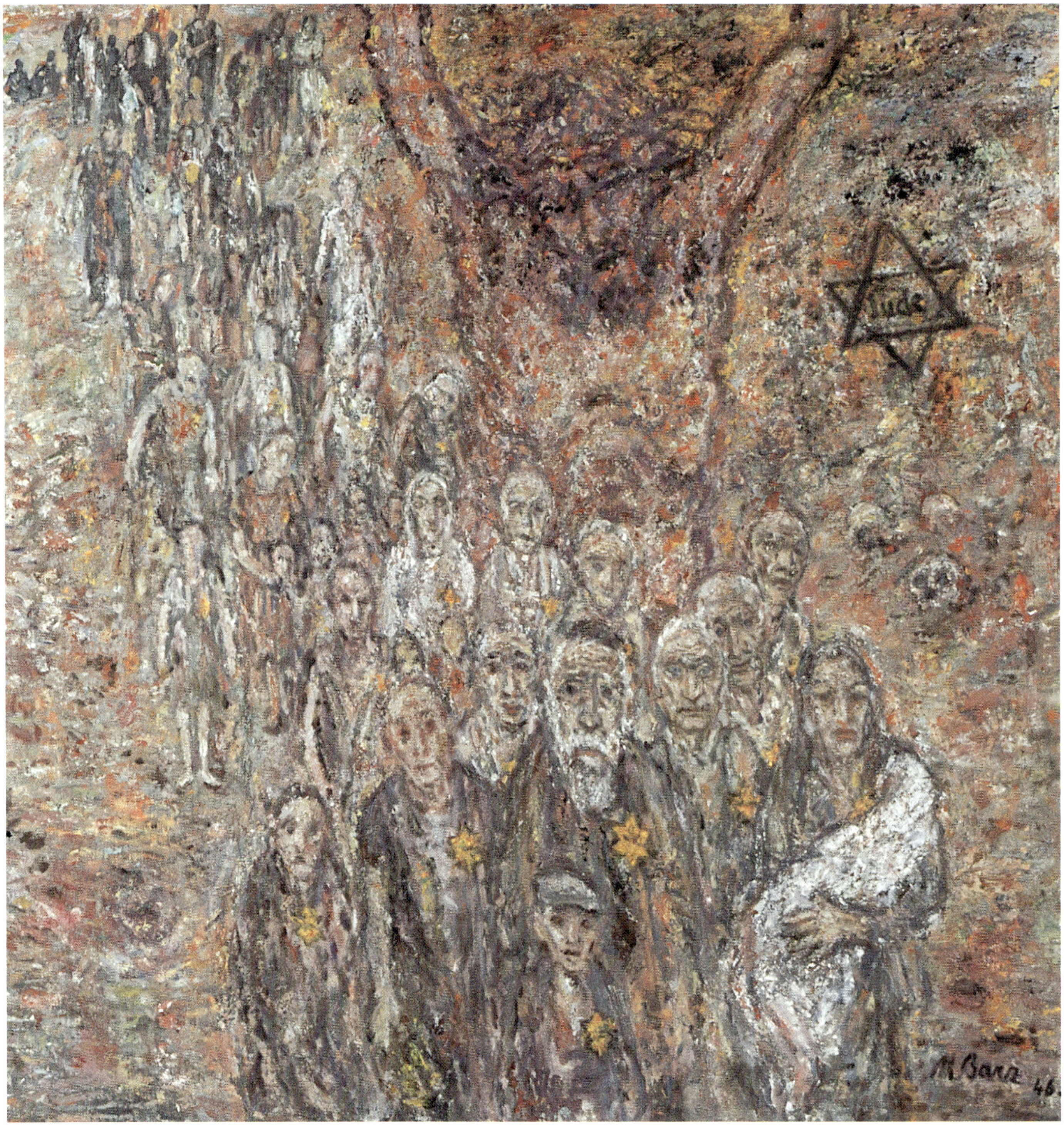

11 Mathias Barz, *Inferno*, begun 1945 (Cat. 122)

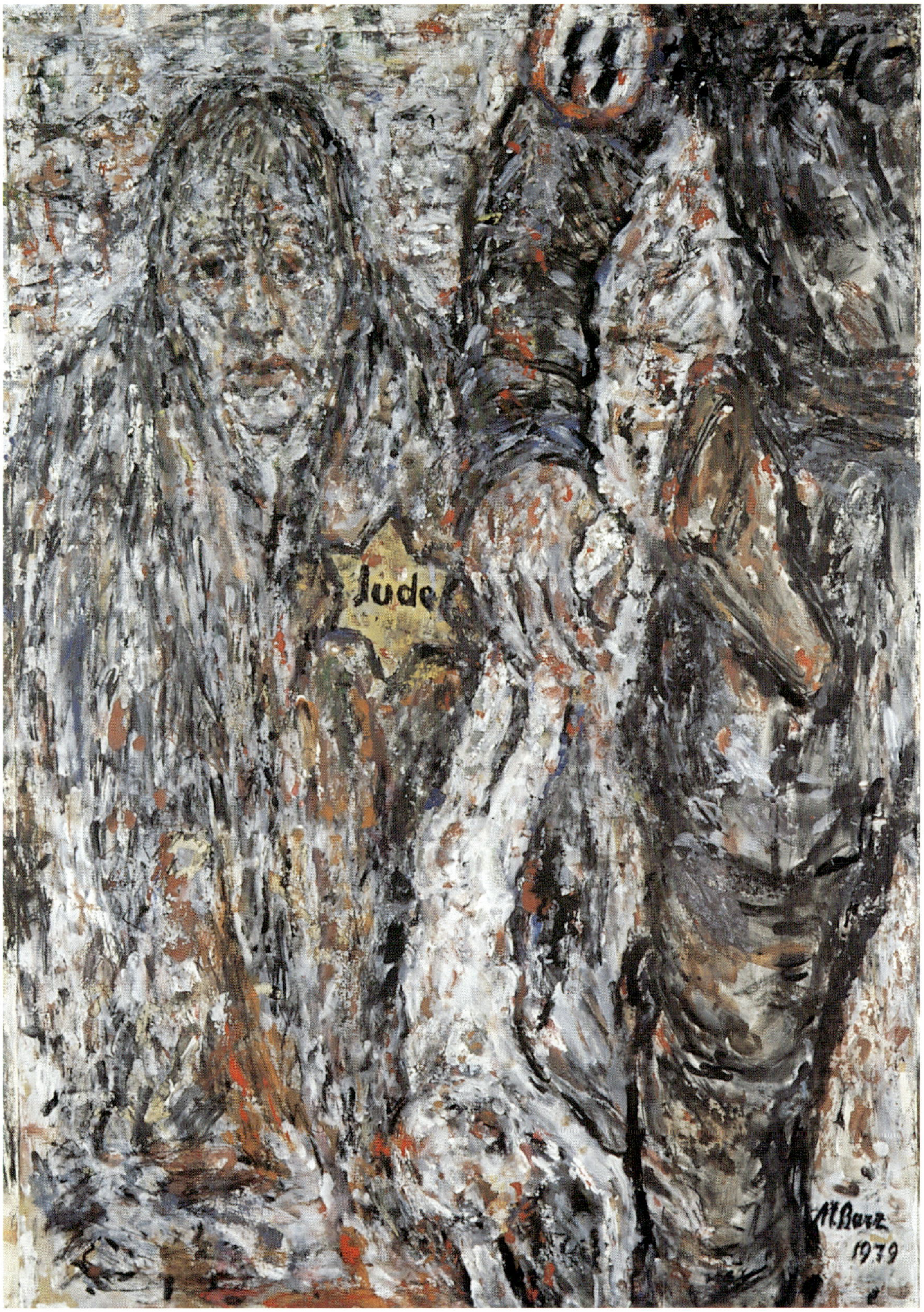

12 Mathias Barz, *SS Man*, 1979 (Cat. 123)

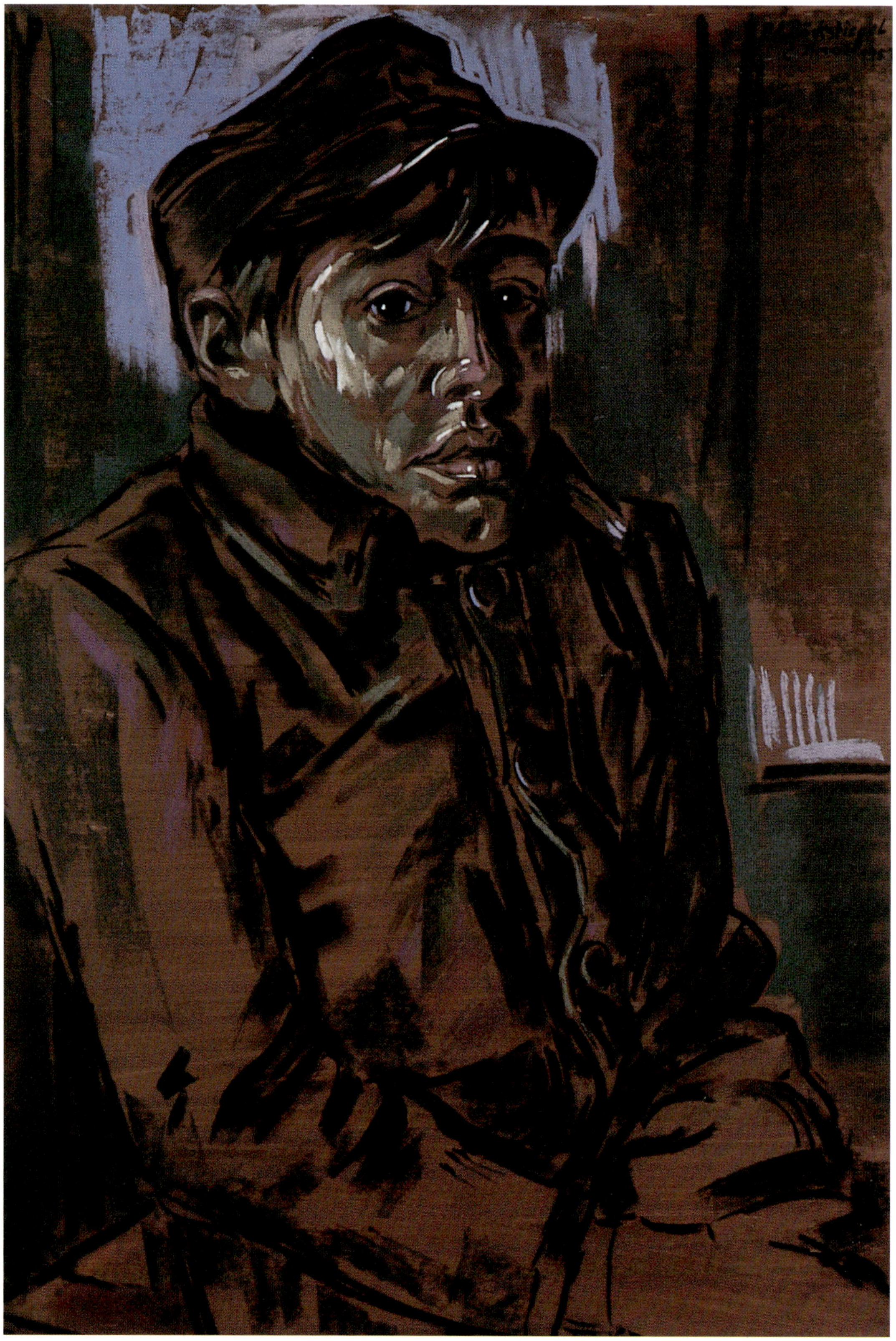

13 Peter August Böckstiegel, *Refugee Youth*, 1951 (Cat. 121)

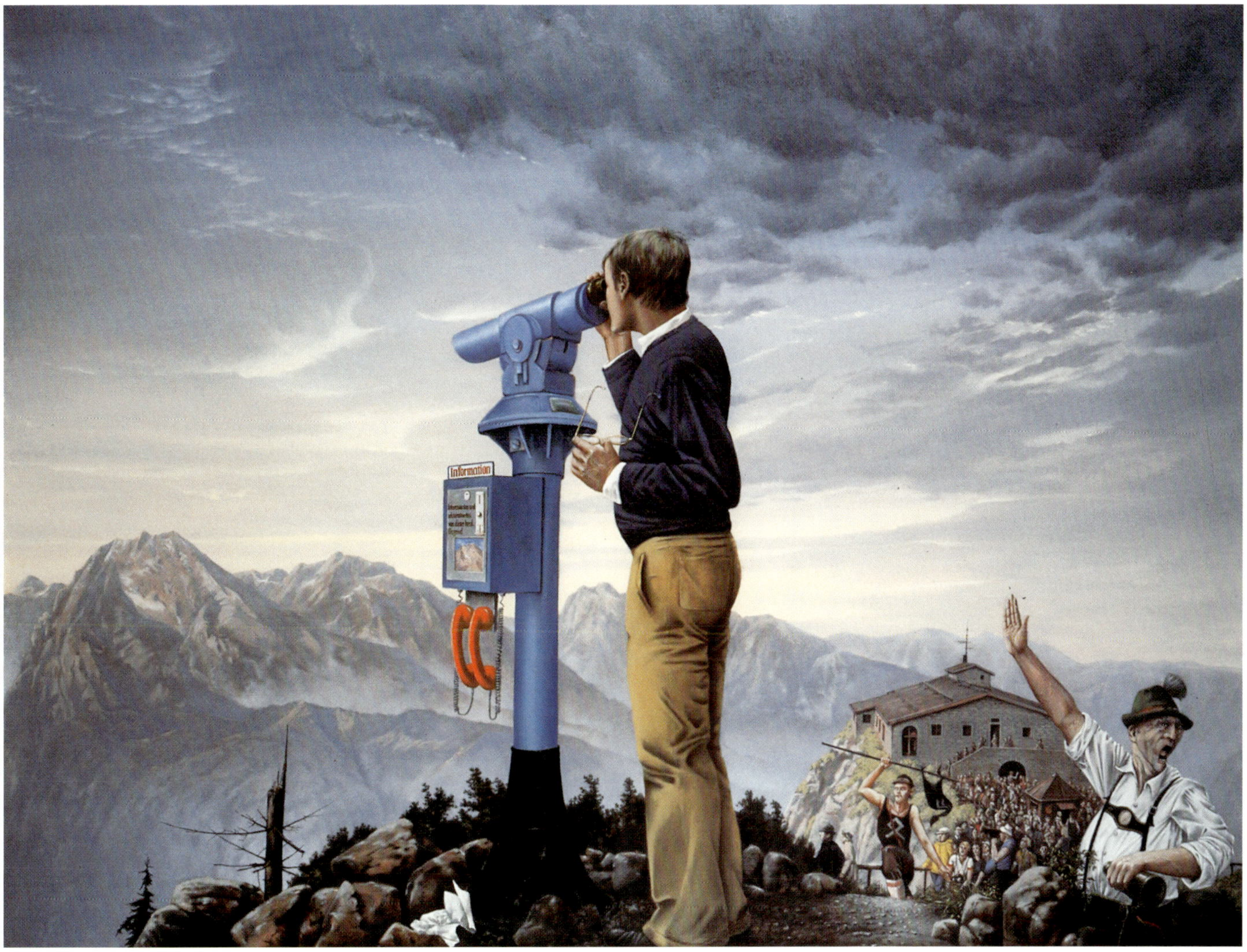

14 Matthias Koppel, *Looking Backward: The Führer's Tea House at Berchtesgaden*, 1985 (Cat. 126)

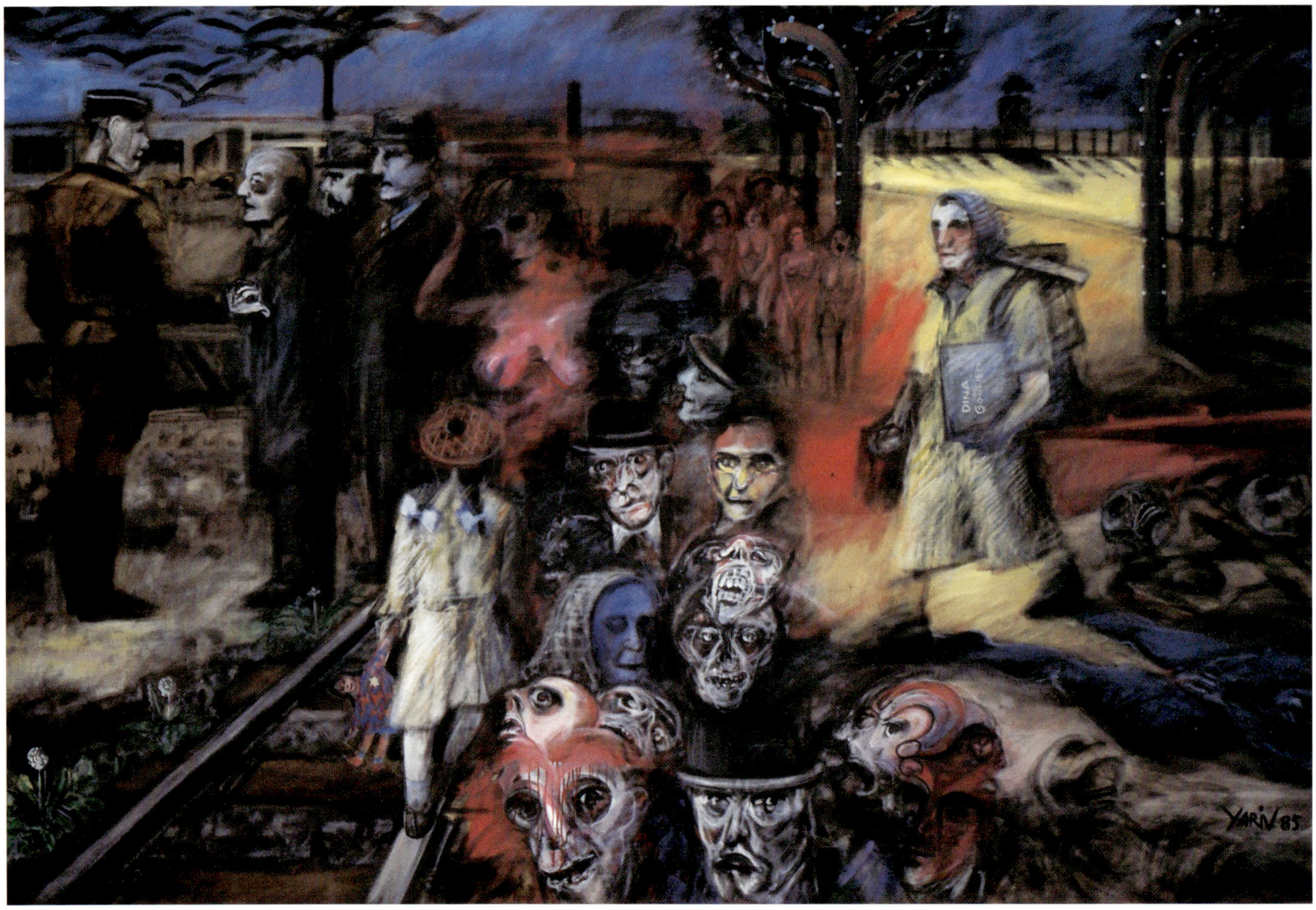

15 Youval Yariv, *The Artist on his Way to Work*, from the cycle »In Homage to Dinah Gottliebova, No. 1,« 1985 (Cat. 127)

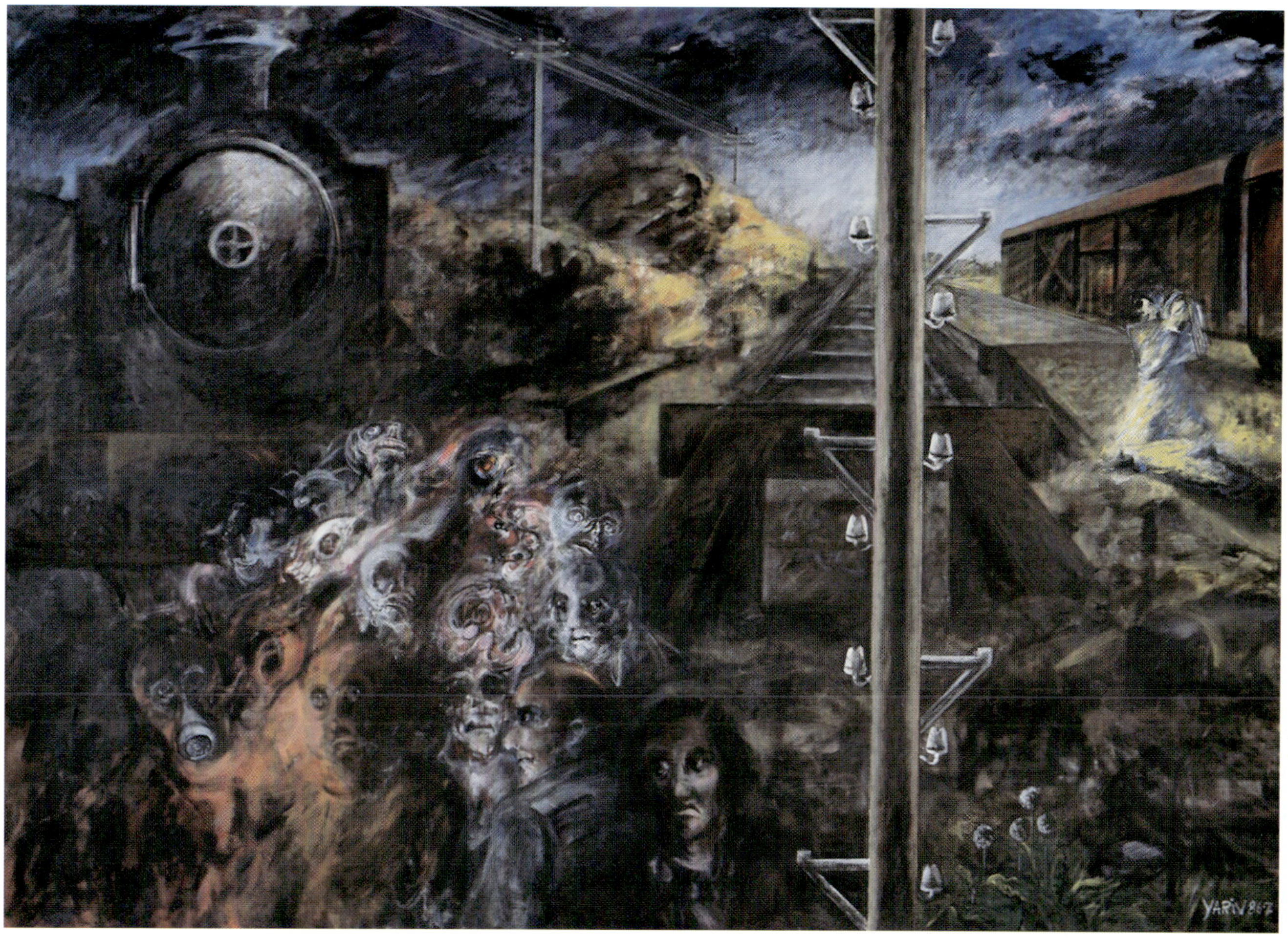

16 Youval Yariv, *The Artist on his Way to Work*, from the cycle »In Homage to Dinah Gottliebova, No. 4,« 1986–1987 (Cat. 128)

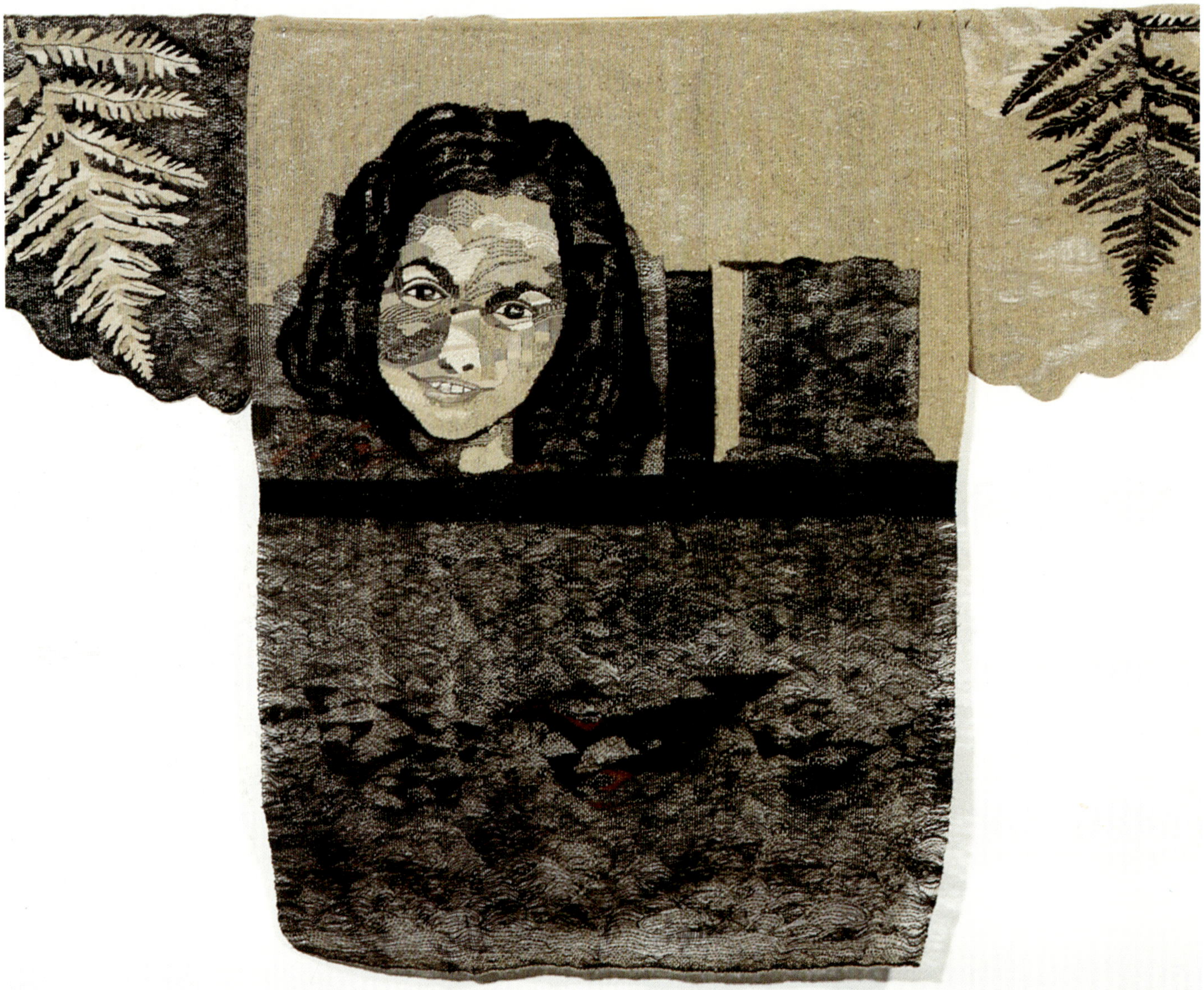

17 Sandra Ikse, *In Memory of Anne Frank*, 1985 (Cat. 129)

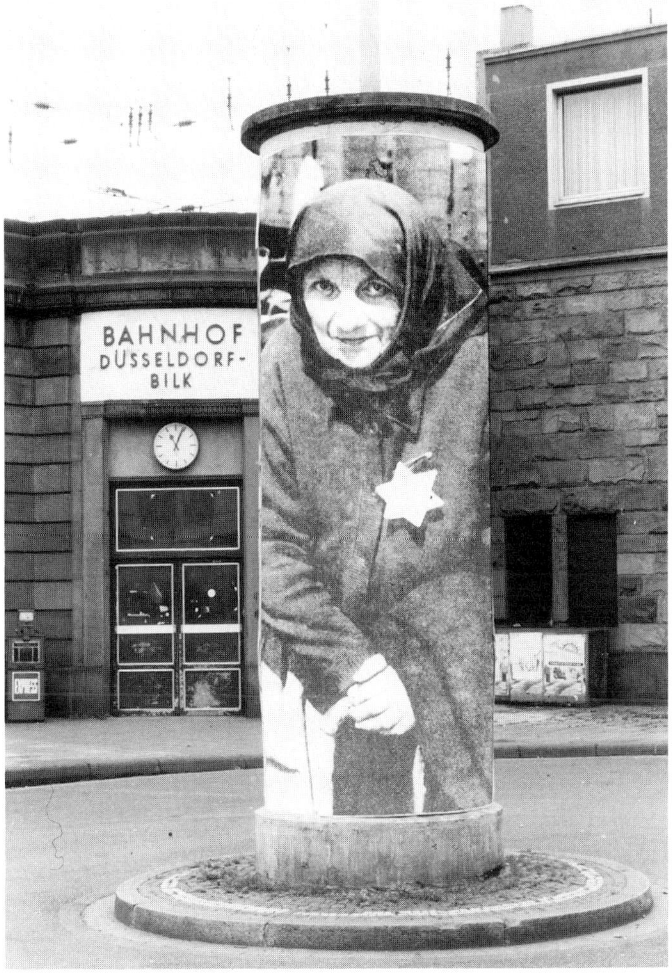

18 Lothar Spinn-Conradt, *City Scene: Deported from Here*, 1985 (Cat. 124)

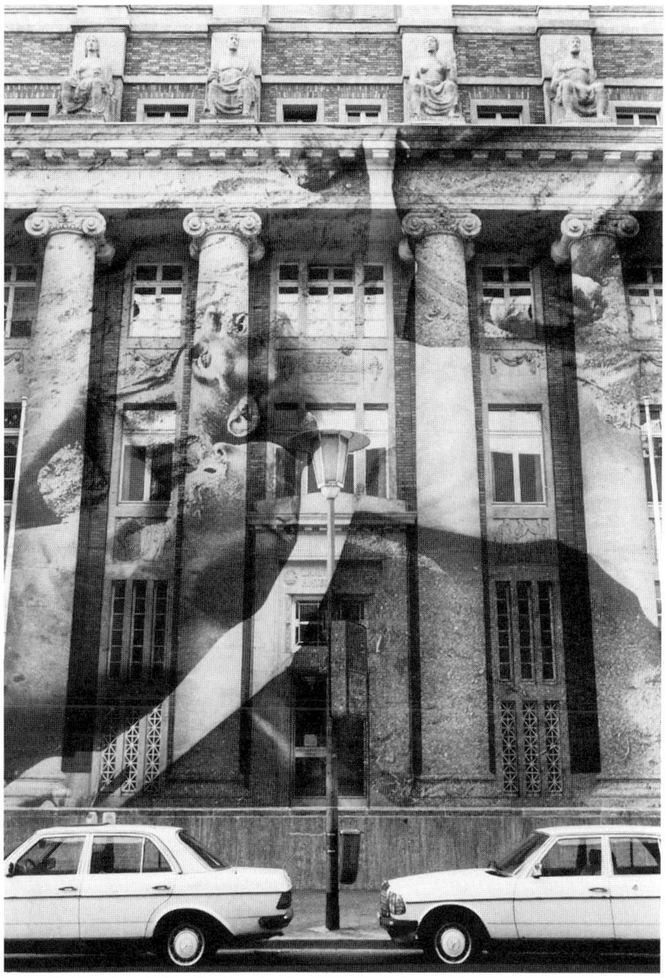

19 Lothar Spinn-Conradt, *City Scene: Mühlenstrasse, the Maidanek Trial*, 1985 (Cat. 125)

Memories of Julo Levin and Franz Monjau and the Story of the Students' Drawings

Mieke Monjau

I met Julo Levin for the first time in 1928 at a celebration of local Düsseldorf artists. During the so-called golden twenties, these Düsseldorf artists' festivities – especially during Carnival – were famous throughout Germany. It was obvious that we would go to these parties, since local artists and the students at the Art Academy had close relations with the female students of the Hilda Senff Eurythmics School in Düsseldorf, where I studied. I remember that the Carnival celebrations were at the zoo and had the theme "yes, we have no bananas," based on the lyrics of a hit song (which was more erotic in the German rendition). Julo Levin was my dance partner. He was then already working as an independent artist and was one of the creators of this celebration. It was typical that he selected me as his dance partner, since I was the only woman in the room without a costume. After this initial meeting, we did not immediately develop a closer acquaintance.

I again attended the Düsseldorf artists' Carnival celebration in 1929 at the Rhine Terrace, where I met Franz Monjau. Franz Monjau recorded this meeting in a 1929 painting (Fig. 4), that is today part of the permanent collection of the Düsseldorf City Museum. We were married on 10 May 1930.

Julo Levin and Franz Monjau had studied at the same time at the Düsseldorf Art Academy, where both were master students of Heinrich Nauen. Both had worked on the design of the 1926 Düsseldorf exhibition "Gesolei" (an acronym formed from the German words for health care, social welfare, and exercise). Both artists used their honoraria for separate individual study trips to Paris.

Both of them belonged to the artists' associations "The Young Rhineland" and the "Rhineland Secession" and were represented in exhibitions by these groups. Levin and Monjau were both also affiliated with the circle around the Düsseldorf art dealer Johanna Ey. At that time, they were only acquaintances and colleagues, without any closer relationship.

While Julo Levin worked as an independent artist until 1933, Franz Monjau had decided in 1928 to obtain a second degree. He had registered simultaneously at the Düsseldorf Art Academy and the University of Cologne for a program in art education; he passed his studio and teaching examinations by 1933, and completed most of the prescribed student teaching at two gymnasia.

Julo Levin meanwhile continued to be represented in nonjuried exhibitions in Berlin, Munich, Stettin, Hanover, and other cities. The Parisian magazine *La Revue Moderne* published an article about an exhibition in Hanover in 1928, that included the following remarks about the 27 year-old artist:

[Julo Levin] had not yet revealed his full powers. Hopefully soon, a time will come when Julo Levin will find occasion to express himself completely. At that time we will see several surprises, that he will have superseded both his teachers and predecessors and become a pioneer.

Who foresaw that he would have only a few years left? The high point of his life was the half year he spent in Marseilles in 1931. He worked there in an atmosphere of previously unknown freedom with utter intensity and the joy of discovery.

It was easy for him to become acquainted and to form friendships with Blacks, Javanese, Gypsies, Creoles, and Arabs and to reduce their mistrust of whites. When he drew their portraits, they opened their hearts to him, allowing him to share in their fate. He became their friend and recorded this in the painting *My Friend Ibrahim* (Fig. 7).

In his letters from Marseilles, he wrote:

15 July 1931 . . . I already have many good friends in the harbor, especially among Blacks. I have drawn portraits of some of them, but it is not easy to convince them. In the evenings, we took many long walks on the piers. I enjoy many undeserved good days here . . .

10 September 1931 . . . I am slowly reacquainting myself with German conditions in order to lessen the shock of awakening. How would it be in a city which had neither Blacks nor Turks, nor all the other riffraff, and not even a proper harbor? . . .

But the reawakening exceeded all expectations. It was the last year before Hitler's accession to power. We then met Julo Levin at anti-Hitler demonstrations and lectures; each found his own way to resistance. The slogan of the ASSO *(Association Revolutionärer Bildender Künstler Deutschlands*; the Association of Revolutionary Artists of Germany) was: "Whoever votes for Hitler votes for war"; it seemed so convincing to us that we could not imagine a Nazi victory.

But the political situation intensified until Hitler came to power. On 30 January 1933, the Führer became Chancellor and Franz Monjau celebrated his thirtieth birthday. A sad birthday. We were shocked, but by no means desperate, and not without hope. We could not imagine what lay ahead; but it now developed rapidly. All dissenters, including those artists who opposed Hitler, were persecuted and defamed, vulnerable to house searches, arrest, and concentration camps. The anxious wait for the sounds of heavy footsteps on the stairs at 5 A.M. and the furious pounding on house doors would last for twelve long years.

Each day brought new bad news. Julo Levin was suddenly a "Jew" and Franz Monjau a "*Mischling* of the first degree." Although Franz Monjau and his parents were Catholics, his maternal grandparents had been Jews and moreover, both artists were politically tainted.

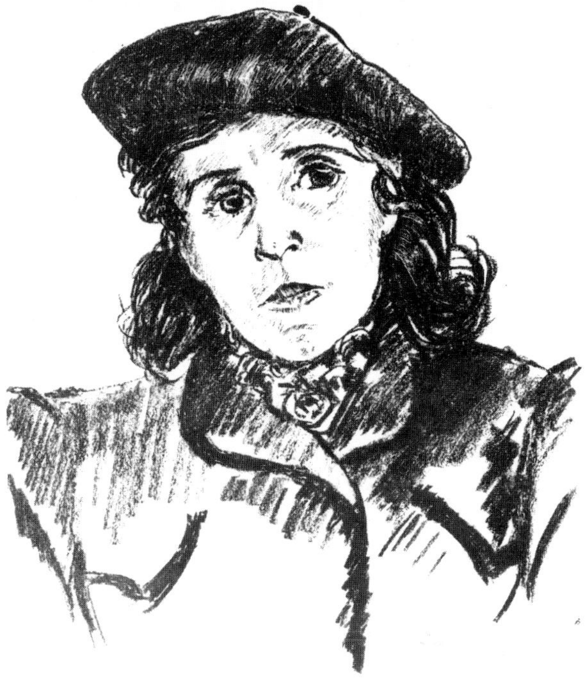

20 Hanna Fonk, *Mieke Monjau*, 1947 (Cat. 120)

Julo Levin had been denounced and arrested for giving shelter to a refugee. Franz Monjau and I were arrested in June 1933 for participating in an anti-Hitler New Year's Eve party in 1932. During a house search, an incriminating photograph had been found; it showed me wearing a hat decorated with an anti-Hitler slogan and a swastika. Although we were released, Franz Monjau was prohibited from completing his second year of teacher training at the Rethelstrasse Gymnasium in Düsseldorf. He was dismissed in the middle of his second state examinations, despite the recommendations by his professors of their most talented candidate.

Of course, neither Julo Levin nor Franz Monjau could be members of the Reich Chamber of Culture *(Reichskulturkammer)*, which meant that they were banned from exhibiting their works and even prohibited from painting in the privacy of their own studios. Furthermore, Franz Monjau was also blacklisted from teaching and my certificate as a gymnastics teacher was not renewed, because I was married to a non-Aryan.

This was a time of isolation, improvisation, and great poverty. Franz Monjau withdrew totally in order not to have to answer questions, especially avoiding former colleagues. With few exceptions, we had only Jewish friends.

Despite official prohibition, Franz Monjau privately coached several Jewish students in languages and mathematics. It turned out that the father of one of these students owned a large lumber company. He was busy exploring the possibilities for emigration and set up a small carpentry workshop in his garage for his older son, who was no longer permitted to study. Franz Monjau taught basic woodworking both to the boy and also to Julo Levin. Furthermore, Julo Levin, Franz Monjau, and I spent every Wednesday evening in this family's beautiful villa. This meant an interesting exchange of ideas; it also meant that we could really eat ourselves full and use the bathtub in succession.

Julo Levin had already recognized clearly that only Jewish laborers and artisans would have some chance of remaining unmolested. He decided to complete an apprenticeship on evenings and weekends with a friendly Aryan carpenter, alongside his compulsory labor assignment as a street cleaner and cemetery worker.

In 1936 there was an opportunity to teach art at the newly opened Düsseldorf Jewish school. Julo Levin had always had a very close rapport with children.

During the next two years, the friendship between Julo Levin and Franz Monjau deepened. They had long conversations about pedagogical methodology and the would-be teacher Franz Monjau was in his element. During his teacher training at the gymnasium, Monjau's art lectures had even attracted fellow teachers. He now helped Julo Levin prepare his class lectures and Monjau deeply regretted that he was unable to participate in the classes. Both artists came to life as they enjoyed the students' drawings, which were spread out all over our home. They discussed these works for hours. This all took place in the one room in which Franz Monjau and I lived.

In 1936, Levin had the opportunity to show several pictures in an exhibition organized by the Jewish Cultural Association *(Jüdischer Kulturbund)* in Berlin. The art critic Max Osborn wrote in a review:

Levin belongs to those passionate searchers and natural artists who use color courageously, because it is their natural means of expression. He is moreover a man of imagination, who can immediately render every aspect of reality into an artistic vision. One has the liberating feeling of meeting a forceful personality, whose innate talent and creative originality is able to take some chances . . .

This was the last public recognition Levin received, since he was considered a "degenerate" artist.

In the spring of 1938, through his sister Else, he was offered a position as art teacher at two Berlin schools (the Kaliski School and the Holdheim School), where he taught until they were closed. Hundreds of students' drawings have survived from these three years. They reveal Levin's enormous talent as an art teacher.

Levin's mother and his sister Else had left Stettin and moved in with relatives in Berlin. Berlin was then still viewed as a place of refuge. On 9 November 1938 synagogues were torched, Jewish businesses vandalized and looted, and Jews were beaten up and arrested. However, Levin was not molested. He had spent the evening with friends and despite their pleas to stay, he went home through the city around 11 P. M. He wanted to witness what was happening.

The morning after the pogrom, Else Levin had decided to emigrate. She left for England on 25 May

1939. She had requested from Julo a series of students' drawings in order to show them to British schools as proof of his successful work with children. She established contact with two schools that seemed interested, but it was too late; war had begun.

Levin's Berlin colleagues were deported gradually. Then his knowledge of carpentry stood him in good stead. The Berlin Jewish community urgently required skilled workers. Nazi officials had confiscated all property formerly owned by Jews and placed their own institutions, such as the SS or Gestapo, in buildings that had once served as hospitals, schools, or offices. When these buildings subsequently required repairs, the Jewish communtiy was again suddenly viewed as the owner and ordered to fix things. Levin was then sent with his tool box, perhaps to fix stuck doors, windows, and clogged plumbing. When it snowed, the Jewish community was required to clean the streets in front of their former properties. They also had to clean sewers and drains.

Jews were also often required to do white-collar jobs. For example, they had to sort and catalog stolen art treasures and organize political files from France. Levin often took some hastily snatched documents home in his jacket pockets. Undaunted by his own personal danger, he was happy to have perhaps saved the life of some Frenchman.

I experienced this last phase at first hand before Julo Levin's deportation to Auschwitz. At the end of 1941, I lived at a rest home in Birkenwerder near Berlin. I had been hospitalized for a nervous breakdown and had to recuperate in a peaceful place without constant air raids. Our room in Düsseldorf had become uninhabitable, having lost its outer wall. Our last friends, who had not fled, were required to wear the Star of David and were deported to the East, after assembling with their luggage at the Düsseldorf stockyards on 10 November 1941.

Even in Birkenwerder, the increasing persecution of the Jews and particularly the fate of Julo Levin and his family did not allow me to rest. Deportation orders also arrived at the Levin family home. His mother, whom I had meanwhile learned to respect and love, was the first to depart. Julo Levin and I spent that last night together at her bedside. When the trucks arrived outside the front door the next morning, we parted with heavy hearts. She was seventy-five years old. Two cousins, with whom she had lived, were even older. They were neither physically nor emotionally able to face deportation and opted for suicide by cyanide. We had discussed everything together and then parted sorrowfully.

I had promised Julo's mother to care for her son. For nine months, I visited his apartment at least three times a week and often daily, although there were no acceptable reasons for an "Aryan" woman to visit the home of a Jewish bachelor. I also shopped for him using his ration cards. Jews in Berlin were permitted to shop only from 4–5 P. M., when he was still at work. These purchases were only possible in those businesses where I could secretly give the salesperson his ration cards.

I always approached Levin's apartment with the greatest caution and in constant fear that I would bump into the superintendent. I frequently had to turn around at the last minute. Once in a while, I met this superintendent despite all my vigilance. For his silence, he demanded Levin's suits and pieces of furniture, one by one, commenting that "otherwise, the Gestapo would get everything."

Evenings when we were together, Levin told me what had occurred during the day. Freight trains with human cargo left without interruption from the Putlitzstrasse train station for the East. When the empty wagons returned, they had to be cleaned of blood and excrement – one of Julo Levin's last compulsory labor assignments. At the end of February 1943, trucks stood outside the factory gates and Jewish workers were deported straight from their workplaces. Levin nevertheless tried to bring the children waiting at home together with their parents. For one whole day, he ran alongside a train with two infants in his arms until he located their mother that evening. There were cattle cars packed tightly with small orphaned children from children's homes. Their nannies were locked up with them. A pail of water and an empty bucket were placed at their disposal. Despite the dreadful events, we didn't give up hope and clung to the possibility of survival.

When Jews were hunted in the streets at the end of February 1943, I waited fearfully in the dark hallway until late at night. The last local train had departed long ago, when Levin – beaten and bloody – finally arrived. I accompanied him to the apartment, washed his head wounds, and made bandages. It was the only time that I spent the night at his place. In the morning, we heard heavy boots on the stairs and, shortly thereafter, a wild pounding at the door. We didn't open up and, after a while, silence reigned again. When I later left, I expected to find a guard at the building entrance. But no one was there. Levin, who left the apartment after me, discovered that the apartment had been sealed and that we had damaged the seal. He pasted it together again and went to the Jewish communal offices. There he received an armband, which identified him as an employee of the Jewish community. This meant an additional brief respite.

On the evening of 7 May, heavy boots resounded on the stairs and again there was wild pounding at the apartment door. We were petrified and did not open the door. However, this time they went to the superintendent who had a key and the door opened. When I was discovered, blows rained down. Levin and I were brought to the assembly center at Grosse Hamburger Strasse. The large room was filled with people. I was the only person without a yellow star. Surprisingly, I was not separated from Julo, although we had previously been interrogated at a police station. When the Jews all received their transport numbers, I attempted to stake everything on one chance and demanded to talk to the senior SS officer on duty. I was brought forward. The man was drunk and cursed me in the conventional way as an "Aryan pig." A young woman was nagging him to leave with her. A younger SS man told him that he would attend to matters. I succeeded in convincing the young man that I had been accidentally in the apartment of my husband's friend. I explained that my husband was partly Jewish and thus I was "married to a non-Aryan." He checked my identity card by telephone and actually let me go. As I was being led out of the building, Julo Levin stood on the stairs, relieved and radiant. Levin had frequently tried to reject my help, because he felt he could not assume the responsibility for it. I had always told him that I was responsible for myself.

Franz Monjau arrived in Berlin with the next train in order to assist me. We couldn't believe that I had really escaped from the Gestapo. But nothing further happened. We also succeeded in receiving Julo's last secret letters via the Jewish community. These smuggled notes and two farewell letters were sent to us at cover addresses. Julo also sent me his fountain pen and a twenty-mark bill which he believed he would have no further use for.

The transport left for Auschwitz on 17 May, ten days after his arrest. It was possible to observe how people were driven into cattle cars on the train tracks between Putlitzstrasse and Wedding. I could still recognize Julo Levin in the distance; to the very end, he assisted the elderly, the ill, and mothers with children. The freight cars were bolted one by one; at the end, only the guards – their guns shouldered – stood on the platform. Only then did I stop going between the two train stations. After 1945, I learned from the Jewish community in Berlin that there had been no survivors from this transport.

After Levin's deportation, one day I discovered a normal train at the Stettiner station, whose stated destination was "Auschwitz." I found out that one could purchase a normal ticket to travel there! I reached a decision after consulting Franz Monjau. Through friends, I got the address of an SS man, who for cash had made contact possible between a prisoner and his sister in Düsseldorf. Our foolish hope was that we could thus perhaps learn something about Julo Levin. I wrote the SS man on the pretext of speaking to him about my friend's brother. A meeting was arranged and I traveled to Auschwitz. Even before the train reached the station, I saw columns of emaciated figures tilling the fields. In the town itself, I noticed prisoners, who – like horses – pulled heavily laden wagons, watched and driven by a big, strong SS man. I met my middleman as

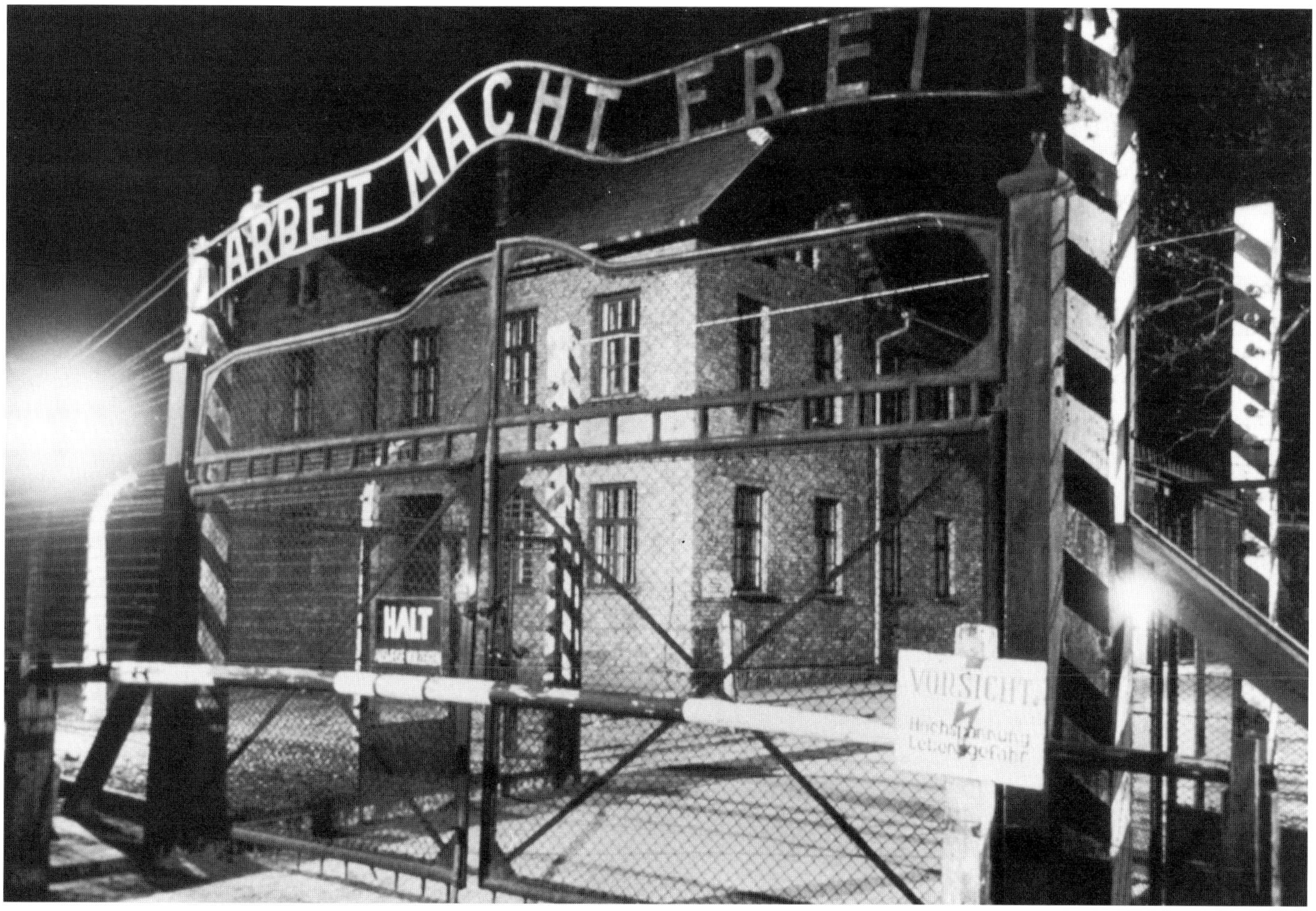

21 *Auschwitz Concentration Camp* (Bildarchiv Preussischer Kulturbesitz)

I entered the camp – obviously only the SS guards' building. He seemed affable, making excuses for the real situation of the prisoners, and regretted that it was Saturday, when the factories were not working. Otherwise he would have taken me there and I would have been able to speak directly to my friend's brother. I listened to his chatter, regretting my bad luck that I had unwisely arrived on a Saturday. For a long time we spoke in generalities. I fought with myself whether I dared mention Julo Levin's name at all. Would this harm Julo? Was he still alive at all? Finally, I asked about Julo. The SS man did not know him; why should he? He promised to make inquiries.

My train left only in the evening and so I walked around Auschwitz. I traveled around one of the subsidiary camps in a soldier's side-car. He poured out his troubles about what he was forced to watch.

That evening, I once again met my contact at the SS officers' mess. Our conversation, however, remained inconsequential. The mood there – with orchestral music and men drinking – was peculiar, eerie, and left me breathless. The walls were decorated with frescoes, with life-size figures from the "Minnesänger" era. I was informed that there were surely enough artists in the camp. I fled the room and hurried to the train station.

I thus became aware of the meaning of normal train service to Auschwitz. After all, the engineers, managers, foremen, and employees for all the firms whose name plaques were displayed for everyone to see at the administration building required transportation to and from Auschwitz. Do they also belong today to those who "knew nothing"?

Although we sensed that Auschwitz was the embodiment of hell, reality exceeded every imagination. On the return trip from Auschwitz, I heard the news about the Allied invasion at Normandy, renewing hope the Nazi nightmare would soon be over.

Meanwhile, Monjau's mother had already been in Theresienstadt for some time. She had scribbled a note on one of the form postcards acknowledging my letters and packages: "Your friend is together with my dear Max." Max had been my father-in-law and was already long deceased. We thus learned that Julo Levin's mother had already died.

After September 1944, couples in so-called privileged mixed marriages and *Mischlinge* were arrested and deported. Franz Monjau had gone underground, but was denounced. Arrested on 10 October 1944, he was taken to the Gestapo jail at Ratingen near Düsseldorf.

I left Berlin immediately and went directly to the Gestapo, to see Mr. Hamacher, a man feared throughout Düsseldorf. He received me abusively: "You came from Berlin for this Jew? You should be grateful to us, that we are freeing you from him."

I was allowed to speak with Franz and promised to do everything in my power. In Berlin, where meanwhile Franz's dossier had ostensibly been sent, I was given the run-around; one SS office referred me to the next higher SS or Gestapo office. Neither at Kurfürstenstrasse nor Prinz Albrecht Strasse – SS and Gestapo headquarters – was I able to achieve anything. In the end I was told that Monjau's papers were in Prague and that matters would be decided there. These officials told me with scorn: "The man doesn't want to hear from you at all, otherwise he would have written to you!" Sarcasm on top of everything!

I had already received letters from my husband that had been smuggled out of the Ratingen jail. During my last visit to Prinz Albrecht Strasse, I already knew that Franz was in Buchenwald, but I could not mention this. His last sign of life was a piece of paper postmarked in Weimar on 16 January 1945 with the words: "I am in Buchenwald-Weimar." As I later learned, he was dead five weeks later – five weeks before the Americans liberated the camp. His death was recorded in the Buchenwald death register on 28 February 1945.

I have been asked many times why Julo Levin never emigrated. All attempts to talk him into leaving had been in vain. He advised others to flee and even helped them with their preparations. He categorically rejected flight for himself, stating: "I am placed here and here I must work. I must follow my conscience."

After his mother's deportation in 1942, I tried once more to persuade him. His close friend, the artist Otto Pankok, offered to hide him in his house. With great effort, I had finally dispelled all of Julo's hesitations that he might endanger the Pankoks, their daughter Eva, and me, when a telegram arrived announcing that the Pankok house had been hit by bombs and the family were themselves seeking shelter. As though freed from a nightmare, Levin said: "You see that it was not meant to be."

An attempt to go into hiding in Bavaria also foundered: "I cannot endanger others to save myself." That time, the artist Peter Ludwigs and my husband Franz Monjau had traveled to Berlin to convince Levin. The result of these conversations was only that Levin produced illegal papers and false identity for others. Peter Ludwigs had established Levin's contact with a Berlin resistance group.

On 5 February 1943, 135 members of the Düsseldorf resistance group "Lower Rhine" were arrested, including Peter Ludwigs. Their connections with the Berlin resistance group were discovered. We were informed and expected Julo's arrest every day. But the Berlin comrades kep Julo's name secret. On 2 July 1943, Peter Ludwigs died in jail. Julo was meanwhile already in Auschwitz and our home in Düsseldorf, together with most of Franz Monjau's pictures, had burned at Whitsuntide.

Rescuing Julo Levin's Pictures

During the nine months that I cared for Levin, I tried to bring his pictures to safety. We looked at oil paintings, water colors, and prints piece by piece and Levin determined the sequence of their rescue. I learned how to remove oil paintings from frames and to roll and pack them professionally. This was my primary obligation during the last month, since Julo Levin had to work even on Sundays. I therefore got an apartment key and slipped into his rooms alone. I left the house again at night carrying rolls or portfolios, but also with large stiff cardboards that Levin often used for oils. Removing the paintings was dangerous because Jews were prohibited from selling or giving away their possessions. But if he survived, Levin would at least have found some of his pictures. I filled two large crates in his mother's home. I packed Levin's favorite pictures in mattresses and also added linen, underwear, clothing, shoes, even a spirit stove, and the necessary cutlery for him to make coffee or soup; there was also a tiny table and bench that Levin had made. He could begin a new life with these things. Even canvas, paper, and paints were packed in the crates. I had the mover pick them up in my name and store them. Everything burned in 1945.

I had brought other paintings to friends in Thuringia, to fishermen in the Baltic, and to other friends. Not all of these works survived the collapse of the Third Reich. The Baltic fishermen had hidden my things deep under the straw in their barn; they were terrified when the Russians searched the straw with bayonets for weapons. But everything went well; only the mice had eaten a hole in one case without, however, causing much damage. Elsewhere a portfolio containing the best watercolors had been destroyed during an air raid. But a great deal had been saved.

I realized that I had remained alone with these pictures and resolved to do everything to preserve the artistic heritage of these two friends, the artists Levin and Monjau. Their works have been shown in numerous exhibitions from 1946 to 1987. In 1964, watercolors by Julo Levin could be seen in four Israeli museums: the old Israel Museum in Jerusalem, Lohamei Haghetaot, and the two kibbutzim Hazorea and Dalia.

The rescue of the students' drawings was just as important to Julo Levin as his own paintings. He loved every sheet.

Although Levin had already taught at two Berlin schools since April, it was only during the 1938 summer vacation that he closed his Düsseldorf studio. Franz Monjau and I helped him. The carefully collected children's and students' drawings were packed with as much love as his own work. Once the movers had picked up the 56 packages, crates, and pieces of furniture, we stood in the empty atelier and were all very sad. Levin had also carefully preserved several hundred drawings by his Berlin students. These works – possibly the children's last statements prior to their flight, emigration, or deportation and death – survived.

Later, after the war was over, I was given special permission by the highest Soviet cultural authorities to cross the border between the Eastern and Western occupation powers with rolls, portfolios, and packages. The first official shipment was for the 1946 exhibition *Living Heritage* at the Düsseldorf Kunstmuseum. Fritz Figge reframed all of Julo Levin's and Franz Monjau's works shown and listed in that Düsseldorf catalog.

But the children's drawings were also to be seen in Düsseldorf and neighboring towns in a small exhibit under the auspices of the Kulturbund. Thereafter, no one was interested in them anymore until about 1980. Meanwhile Wieland Koenig had become Director of the Stadtmuseum Düsseldorf; he considered it his most important task to rescue from oblivion those artists who had been persecuted and banned for racial or political reasons between 1933 and 1945. One-man shows recalled the three artists – Peter Ludwigs, Franz Monjau, and Julo Levin – murdered during this period of terror. Other shows were dedicated to the survivors of this circle: Will

Küpper, Otto Pankok, Mathias Barz, Karl Schwesig, and Carl Lauterbach as well as Trude Brück, the only female member of the "Young Rhineland" and Mother Ey circles. Trude Brück had assisted Gert Wollheim during his flight to France when she had lived in Saarbrücken.

During preliminary discussions for the Julo Levin retrospective commemorating his eightieth birthday on 5 September 1981, I also mentioned the students' drawings from Jewish schools. Wieland Koenig was immediately interested and planned to exhibit them in the future. Koenig's engagement for persecuted artists and the Julo Levin retrospective received extensive coverage in the American newspaper, *The Herald Tribune*. Koenig also announced in this interview his plan to show the students' drawings.

On my eightieth birthday on 21 November 1983, I donated over 750 Jewish students' drawings from Düsseldorf, including some examples from Berlin Jewish schools, to the Stadtmuseum Düsseldorf.

The cities of Düsseldorf and Haifa are sister cities. A number of students' drawings were exhibited at the opening of the Heinrich Heine House, a gift built by the city of Düsseldorf in Haifa. I was present at the opening. Many former Düsseldorfers were startled to see the drawings made 50 years earlier. I was also overwhelmed with questions about the students' drawings and the fate of Julo Levin. The Israeli Dvora Diskin from Atlit, formerly Dora Moritz of Düsseldorf, discovered her sister's drawings on exhibit.

For some time, every year a group of Jewish former Düsseldorfers persecuted by the Nazis return as guests of the city. Thus, two years ago, I again met Mrs. Diskin from Haifa during her visit in Düsseldorf. She told me her recollections of Julo Levin, since she had close contact with him in the Jewish kindergarten on Grafenberger Allee. One of the teachers, Hilde Stiehl, had been Levin's close friend. He frequently visited Stiehl's classes and used these occasions to draw and paint with the children. This Israeli woman had delighted in his visits and painted pictures for him. When she later attended a gentile school, she had visited him in his studio to talk about her childhood problems. Levin gave her crayons and paper, and she drew her most beautiful dreams as well as her troubles. When she later transferred to the Jewish school because of the Nuremberg laws, she was happy to have Julo Levin as her art teacher. She also told me that she was not the only child who visited him in his studio. He was open to every child. She had worshipped Levin and had never forgotten him. This had already been my impression in Israel, when she spontaneously told me her experiences with Julo Levin in her joy at rediscovering these childhood drawings. She had gone to Palestine in 1938 and today lives on a kibbutz.

In 1986, I had a second surprising meeting with another Israeli in Düsseldorf. I could scarcely believe it when she introduced herself as Marianne Redlich from Bustan, née Marianne Löw. I owned a portrait photograph of Julo Levin signed by Marianne Löw and had used this photograph as an illustration in many exhibition catalogs. She had learned photography at the age of nineteen or twenty in preparation for emigration. Julo Levin had permitted her to photograph him in his studio and he had also invited friends who wanted to be photographed by her. She knew that he worked as an art teacher at the Jewish school and was very popular with the children. She felt that he had been a man of distinguished character, calm and well-balanced. She was very enthusiastic about his art works and spoke about their exciting conversations about art.

I learned from another Israeli that the schools had also built a small carpentry workshop, where Levin taught the basics of woodworking. This former student told me that he had many inhibitions about being able to draw or paint. Levin had encouraged him and even displayed several of his drawings, which had helped him to overcome these hesitations. There had been no distance in the relationship between student and teacher, and later they were even on first name terms.

Another former student, who lives in Los Angeles today, reported that Julo Levin had sent him to draw the Wilhelm Marx house. This was considered the first high-rise building in Düsseldorf. It was located close to Kasernenstrasse, and could be reached quickly from the school. It would be nice to be able to meet other former students and friends of Julo Levin through this exhibition.

I found great admiration and love for their former teacher and friend among those I have met. I have also met people who as children had met Julo Levin in their family circle. They told me how Levin had participated in their games and stories and won their hearts and trust. One of these children, today a professor at a music conservatory, had nicknamed him "venus tinctus." Her parents, both musicians, belonged to the circle of friends around Dr. Margarethe Brandenstein-Zaudy, a patron, sponsor, and friend of Julo Levin's mother. Dr. Brandenstein-Zaudy owned a respected interior design firm in Wesel and Bad Oeynhausen and had arranged many commissions for Levin to do decorative and stained-glass window designs. Thus Levin did a window for the home of the well-known Busch musical family, who, like Rudolf Serkin, belonged to the circle around Brandenstein. All attempts to discover whether the window and wall mural, both known through photographs, survived the Nazi era and air raids have heretofore failed.

Levin worked for the Brandensteins for almost a decade, drafting designs for windows, textiles, invitations, and printed matter. He was a close friend of the family, including the two young daughters.

His last visit with them was in late July or early August 1938. Franz Monjau and I also participated in these three days. We rowed our boat downstream along the Rhine and camped below the town of Wesel. Levin slept at the Brandenstein's. The next morning, Franz Monjau rowed upstream and picked Julo up at a prearranged location. They returned together and we spent the whole day until late afternoon together, also swimming and talking. I then accompanied Levin on foot until the outskirts of Wesel. Levin slept at the Brandenstein's. It would have been too dangerous for Levin to camp out overnight because of police patrols. We only had this one chance to spend three days together in the country.

Mrs. Brandenstein died sometime later and her two daughters emigrated abroad. Two letters that Levin had received from her in Marseilles have survived and provide us with a picture of this wonderful and committed woman.

Levin also had good friends in Mönchengladbach. The owner of a large bookstore exhibited works by Julo Levin in 1933–1934 – unsigned as a precaution – in order to assist him financially. By sheer accident I was able to purchase one of these works several years ago at an auction at Lempertz in Cologne. I learned from the seller that his mother had also been a friend of Levin's and that she had bought this picture from the display window of the Mönchengladbach bookstore.

Whenever I met Julo Levin's friends, I found great affection, admiration, and solidarity. Those artist colleagues who had supported the Nazis fell silent whenever Levin was mentioned and gave him a special place, with the phrase: "If only all Jews had been like him!"

Julo Levin had been an unusual person. Despite great modesty and shyness, he could win the hearts of others. It was probably the empathy and interest that he extended to others that made him so attractive. To the last, he was especially interested in political events, especially war news, such as the battle and retreat at Stalingrad. He looked for the truth between the lines of newspaper stories and also for a glimmer of hope, even if it were too late for him. For example, it was important for him to transmit verbally important radio news broadcast from London, that he wrote down anonymously on scraps of paper for others. I often threw such slips of paper in an envelope into various mailboxes. With the daily deportations of friends and acquaintances, it was important for him to offer some last assistance, to bring news to other family members, or simply to comfort them when necessary.

I could not hide him at my boarding house. The air raid warden, a hardcore Nazi, constantly searched the house from cellar to attic and had already denounced one couple among us. But Julo Levin would never have accepted an offer that would have provided him safety but would have endangered others.

Similarly, suicide was not a possibility for Levin. His mother had implored her two cousins not to carry out their plan before they were to be deported. Both of them were, however, absolutely resolute. It had cost me much argument and persuasion before Julo would accept their decision and bid them farewell.

The closing sentence in one of the last Levin letters smuggled out of Grosse Hamburger Strasse said: "I'll have a little drink to that." A short while ago, a journalist ignorant of the fact that Julo Levin never would have committed suicide, interpreted this as a covert reference that he would swallow poison. However, Julo had used this expression frequently as a toast and I understood this last greeting that way. Even at the end, he did not desert his fellow victims and went with them consciously to their deaths. I could never discover how or when he died.

A few years ago, art classes for children were scheduled coincidentally with a Julo Levin exhibition at the Rheinisches Landesmuseum in Bonn. To my astonishment, most of the students gathered in front of Levin's paintings although the entire museum was at their disposal. They copied Levin's self-portrait most of all and also his mother's portrait. His pictures still attracted these children fifty years after they were created and thirty-five years after his murder at Auschwitz.

But not only the children sensed the power of Levin's artistic legacy. This living heritage has been shown in nearly fifty exhibitions. On the occasion of Levin's 85th birthday, I entrusted most of his works to Wieland Koenig, donating them to the Stadtmuseum Düsseldorf. Levin's works now have a permanent abode there.

Levin's work will now become known outside the borders of Germany and Europe as a result of this traveling exhibition, for which I have written these reminiscences. I wish to thank Sybil Milton from the United States for this. We first became acquainted in 1975 through Walter Huder, who then wrote an introduction to an exhibition catalog about Julo Levin and Franz Monjau. At that time, Sybil Milton was researching her book *Art of the Holocaust*, for which I provided biographical information about both Julo Levin and Franz Monjau. The connection between us continued and, during a visit to Düsseldorf, I introduced her to Wieland Koenig's work and his engagement on behalf of those artists persecuted by the Nazis. I could not foresee that this meeting would eventually result in the idea for this exhibition. I am grateful on behalf of Julo Levin.

Artists have a special privilege: they live through their works. This was always Julo's wish:

"My works are my message: a silent solidarity with people, excluding anything divisive. This endures and will not diminish."

Julo Levin and his Düsseldorf Circle of Friends

Sybil Milton

The works of Julo Levin have been shown as a "living heritage" in more than fifty exhibitions in the Federal Republic of Germany.[1] This posthumous recognition is in part proof of the renewal of a democratic and multifaceted reception of art in postwar Germany, but it is even more an example of the growing understanding of the tragic fate of the German Jews and the loss of their cultural heritage. Levin is acknowledged today not only as a helpless victim of Nazi barbarity, but also as an artist and teacher. It is easy to overlook the important, but not obvious, fact that en route towards the abyss, he had retained his identity as an artist and had also transmitted this heritage as a teacher in German-Jewish schools.

Levin's conscious decision to stay in Germany after 1933 and to live as part of the ever-narrower Jewish world is clear in his work as an art teacher at the Jewish schools of Düsseldorf and Berlin, where he created an island of spiritual freedom and asylum for his students. Despite being banned from painting, he created a small but important body of work and also taught and collected more than 1,000 works made by his students. These were rescued for posterity by his friends Mieke Monjau and Carl Lauterbach.

Although there are still gaps in our knowledge of Levin's life and times, we have tried in this exhibition to reconstruct both his biography and his oeuvre through documentation and oral history by eyewitnesses. Several gaps still remain, such as the precise date of his death in Auschwitz; it is probable that this will never be conclusively established.

Levin's life can be subdivided into three main phases: (1) his childhood in a secure middle-class milieu; (2) his first professional successes as an artist and his entry into the "Young Rhineland" circle in Düsseldorf during the Weimar Republic; and (3) the last decade of his life under constantly increasing pressure, including his deportation and murder. His importance as an artist is secured through the surviving portraits of Blacks, Gypsies, and his family members as well as through his self-portraits and landscapes.

Levin declined to emigrate or to go into hiding during the Nazi period, although both options had been offered to him as possibilities for his rescue. After deciding to remain in Germany, he inevitably shared the fate of his German Jewish compatriots. He continued to work as long as possible as an art teacher in German Jewish schools.

Julo (Julius) Levin was born on 5 September 1901, the youngest of three children in Stettin, where he was raised by his mother and grandmother. He attended elementary and intermediate schools in his native town. His passion as a collector was revealed even in early childhood; at the age of six, he had already accumulated a collection of nearly 3,000 pictures enclosed in Stollwerck chocolate squares. Already as a child, he had sketched portraits of his friends, of animals, and also drawn landscapes. The family wanted him to become a businessman and to continue art only as a hobby.

The family council proposed that Julo embark on a business career . . . Mother comforted him, saying that he could paint as much as he wished in his free time. This was easier said than done. During his apprenticeship at a well-known Stettin company, Julo was to be found on Torweg opposite the Jacob church, which he was assiduously sketching. He had agreed to run an errand, had run in both directions, and thus freed some time for sketching. This happened with increasing frequency, e. g., he stared at customers with the intention of drawing them later in his sketch pad, which he kept hidden under the counter.[2]

In the evening after work, Levin attended the local commercial art school *(Kunstgewerbeschule)* in Stettin. In April 1919, he moved to Düsseldorf, living with his uncle, the merchant Max Arnfeld, at Brehmstrasse 26. He had matriculated at the commercial art academy in Essen. In order to live closer to the school, Levin moved in July 1919 to Mülheim an der Ruhr.[3] Levin studied with Jan Thorn-Prikker, the founder of modern glass painting. Essen at that time was a thriving modern art center in the Rhineland. In 1920, Levin followed his teacher Thorn-Prikker when the latter received an appointment at the art academy in Munich. In March 1923, Thorn-Prikker returned as a professor to the Düsseldorf art academy and Levin moved back to his uncle's home at Brehmstrasse, to study at the academy.[4]

Another of Levin's professors, Heinrich Campendonk, was a former student of Thorn-Prikker's and, in 1926, Thorn-Prikker's successor in mosaic, wall, and advertising art at the Düsseldorf academy. Levin also studied with Heinrich Nauen as did many other members of the "Young Rhineland" and "Rhineland Secession" groups.[5] It was here that the deep friendships between Levin and other artists, like Mathias Barz, Hanna Fonk, Carl Lauterbach, Peter Ludwigs, Franz Monjau, Otto Pankok, and Carl Moritz Schreiner originated.

After completing his studies in 1926, Levin received his first commissions. He designed the show windows of the furniture and interior-design firm of Brandenstein-Zaudy in Wesel and the interior of Brandenstein-Zaudy's branch in Bad Oeynhausen. He also prepared advertising brochures for Zaudy, did the painted-glass window at the Busch family home in Bochum (the Busches were famous classical musicians of that era), and designed two exhibition rooms for the "Gesolei," an international exhibition about health, welfare, and physical culture in Düsseldorf.[6] The strictly geometrical lines and planes of his interior wall designs for Zaudy and at the "Gesolei" revealed the influence of Rhineland expressionism.

In the summer of 1926, Levin and Pankok spent several weeks of their summer vacation in the Lower Rhine village of Crudenburg bei Xanten. This was their first attempt at teaching art to children. Else Levin, Julo's older sister, who lived in London until her death, has already told us about this adventure.[7]

Levin's brief pedagogical activity with the village schoolchildren in Crudenburg was his first attempt to research children's creativity, a subject that others, including Paul Klee, pursued at the Düsseldorf academy. This interest was part of the widespread movement for educational reform during the Weimar Republic. Two books were also published at that time about progressive art education: Philipp Franck's *The Creative Child*[8] and G. F. Hartlaub's *The Genius in Children*[9]. Levin, who was a close friend of the Francks, knew these books and discussed their contents with Carl Lauterbach and Franz Monjau in the mid-1930s, when he sought to apply that approach to the teaching of art at the Düsseldorf Jewish school.[10]

In 1926, Levin traveled to Paris for the first time; Paris was then the center of modern art. In the summer of 1931, he spent six months in southern France. His letters described the bustling world of the harbor in Marseilles, where he met and painted portraits of Blacks, Arabs, and Gypsies.[11]

It was there that Levin completed the oil portrait entitled *My Friend Ibrahim* (Fig. 7) as well as several watercolor portrait studies of Gypsies. Simultaneously, Levin's friend Otto Pankok had also discovered the life and culture of Gypsies in southern France.[12] These respective mutual experiences exerted a strong influence on both artists and contributed to Pankok's later close relationships with the Sinti in Düsseldorf. Levin had discovered a colorful

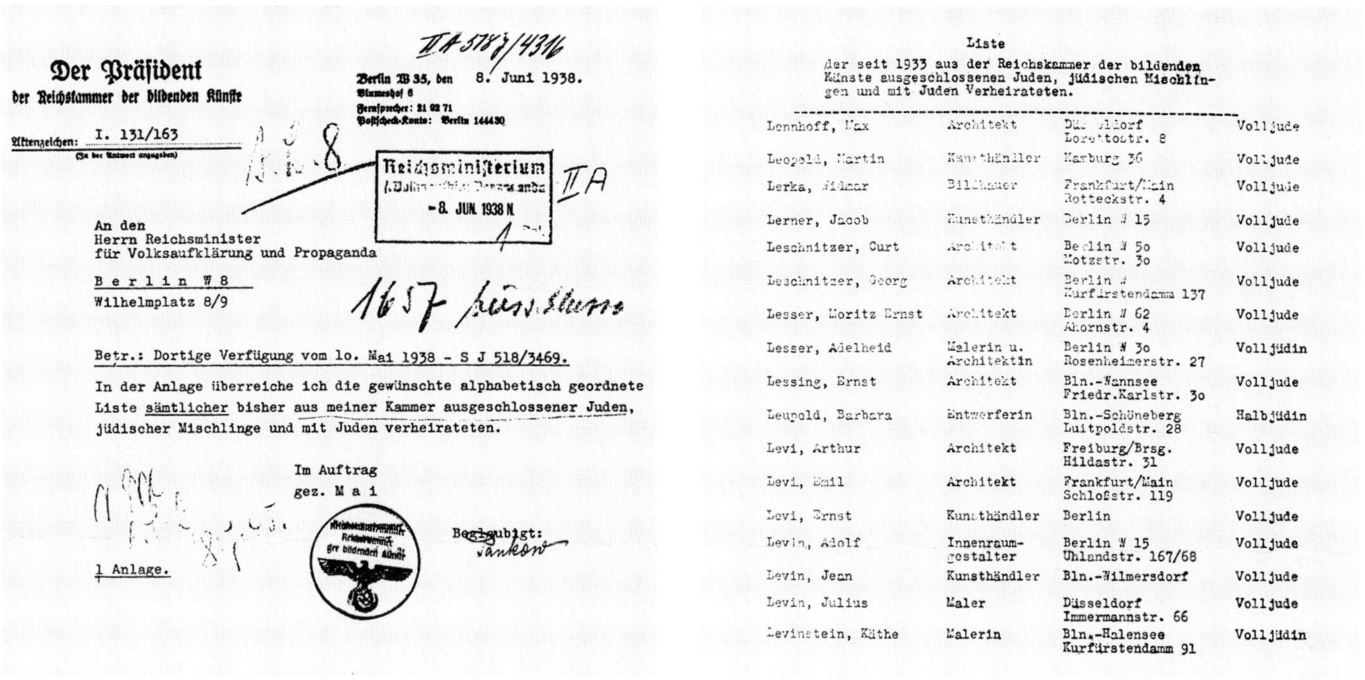

II A 5183/4316

Der Präsident
der Reichskammer der bildenden Künste

Berlin W 35, den 8. Juni 1938.
Blumeshof 6
Fernsprecher: 21 92 71
Postscheck-Konto: Berlin 144430

Aktenzeichen: I. 131/163
(In der Antwort angegeben)

Reichsministerium f. Volksaufkl. u. Propaganda
- 8. JUN. 1938 N.

II A

An den
Herrn Reichsminister
für Volksaufklärung und Propaganda

Berlin W 8
Wilhelmplatz 8/9

1657

Betr.: Dortige Verfügung vom 1o. Mai 1938 - S J 518/3469.

In der Anlage überreiche ich die gewünschte alphabetisch geordnete Liste sämtlicher bisher aus meiner Kammer ausgeschlossener Juden, jüdischer Mischlinge und mit Juden verheirateten.

Im Auftrag
gez. M a i

Beglaubigt:

1 Anlage.

Liste

der seit 1933 aus der Reichskammer der bildenden Künste ausgeschlossenen Juden, jüdischen Mischlingen und mit Juden Verheirateten.

Lennhoff, Max	Architekt	Düsseldorf Lorettostr. 8	Volljude
Leopold, Martin	Kunsthändler	Harburg 36	Volljude
Lerka, Widmar	Bildhauer	Frankfurt/Main Rotteckstr. 4	Volljude
Lerner, Jacob	Kunsthändler	Berlin W 15	Volljude
Leschnitzer, Curt	Architekt	Berlin W 5o Motzstr. 3o	Volljude
Leschnitzer, Georg	Architekt	Berlin W Kurfürstendamm 137	Volljude
Lesser, Moritz Ernst	Architekt	Berlin W 62 Ahornstr. 4	Volljude
Lesser, Adelheid	Malerin u. Architektin	Berlin W 3o Rosenheimerstr. 27	Volljüdin
Lessing, Ernst	Architekt	Bln.-Wannsee Friedr.Karlstr. 3o	Volljude
Leupold, Barbara	Entwerferin	Bln.-Schöneberg Luitpoldstr. 28	Halbjüdin
Levi, Arthur	Architekt	Freiburg/Brsg. Hildastr. 31	Volljude
Levi, Emil	Architekt	Frankfurt/Main Schloßstr. 119	Volljude
Levi, Ernst	Kunsthändler	Berlin	Volljude
Levin, Adolf	Innenraum-gestalter	Berlin W 15 Uhlandstr. 167/68	Volljude
Levin, Jean	Kunsthändler	Bln.-Wilmersdorf	Volljude
Levin, Julius	Maler	Düsseldorf Immermannstr. 66	Volljude
Levinstein, Käthe	Malerin	Bln.-Halensee Kurfürstendamm 91	Volljüdin

22 *Letter from the President of the Reich Chamber for Fine Arts dated 8 June 1938, containing a list of Jewish artists banned since 1933* (Berlin Document Center)

and powerful multiracial and multiethnic world in Marseilles, utterly unlike anything available in Germany, and he attempted to record these impressions on canvas.

After returning from France, Levin was represented in various exhibitions in Düsseldorf, Munich, and Berlin with watercolors of the harbor in Stettin and newer works about the Marseilles waterfront. The pictures of his home town, Stettin, expressed familiarity and security with his surroundings, whereas those from Marseilles were strong and vibrant. The legacy of Levin's Marseilles sojourn was a livelier brushwork with a new intensified sensitivity to bold color. Levin also at that time became a member of ASSO *(Association Revolutionärer Bildender Künstler*; Association of Revolutionary Artists) and was elected to their advisory board. Hitler's accession to power in January 1933 affected Levin almost instantaneously. He was arrested in "protective custody" *(Schutzhaft)* for the first time on 29 June 1933.[13]

Levin was detained in prison for three weeks, having been denounced as a communist sympathizer and a member of the Communist Party in Düsseldorf. He was also suspected of helping emigrants escape from Nazi Germany. During his interrogation, Levin declared that "he was not a member of any political party or political organization."[14] Surviving Gestapo and court records reveal that this initial wave of arrests had also involved many of Levin's colleagues and close friends, including Hanna Fonk,[15] Karl Schwesig,[16] and Micke and Franz Monjau.[17] Shortly after Levin's arrest, his atelier neighbor at Immermannstrasse 66 in downtown Düsseldorf, Karl Schwesig, was also arrested and severely beaten by SA thugs. Schwesig recorded those experiences several years later in his cycle and book *Schlegelkeller*, the cellar where he was initially incarcerated and tortured.[18] Levin articulated his experiences in prison in his self-portrait as *Job*, completed in 1933–1934 (Fig. 8), in which he portrayed himself as naked, exposed to the elements and

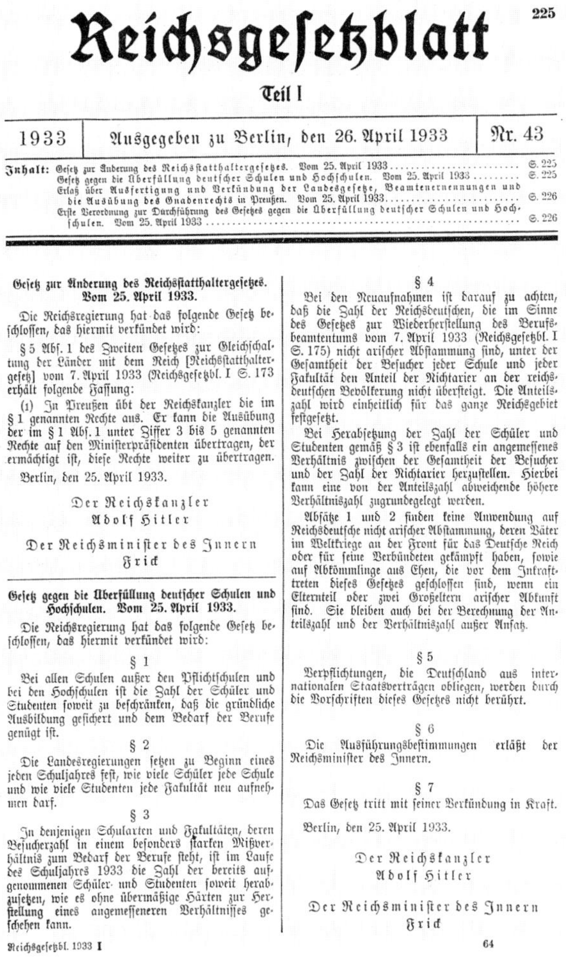

Reichsgesetzblatt

225

Teil I

1933	Ausgegeben zu Berlin, den 26. April 1933	Nr. 43

Gesetz zur Änderung des Reichsstatthaltergesetzes. Vom 25. April 1933.

Die Reichsregierung hat das folgende Gesetz beschlossen, das hiermit verkündet wird:

§ 5 Abs. 1 des Zweiten Gesetzes zur Gleichschaltung der Länder mit dem Reich [Reichsstatthaltergesetz] vom 7. April 1933 (Reichsgesetzbl. I S. 173 erhält folgende Fassung:

(1) In Preußen übt der Reichskanzler die im § 1 genannten Rechte aus. Er kann die Ausübung der im § 1 Abs. 1 unter Ziffer 3 bis 5 genannten Rechte auf den Ministerpräsidenten übertragen, der ermächtigt ist, diese Rechte weiter zu übertragen.

Berlin, den 25. April 1933.

Der Reichskanzler
Adolf Hitler

Der Reichsminister des Innern
Frick

Gesetz gegen die Überfüllung deutscher Schulen und Hochschulen. Vom 25. April 1933.

Die Reichsregierung hat das folgende Gesetz beschlossen, das hiermit verkündet wird:

§ 1

Bei allen Schulen außer den Pflichtschulen und bei den Hochschulen ist die Zahl der Schüler und Studenten soweit zu beschränken, daß die gründliche Ausbildung gesichert und dem Bedarf der Berufe genügt ist.

§ 2

Die Landesregierungen setzen zu Beginn eines jeden Schuljahres fest, wie viele Schüler jede Schule und wie viele Studenten jede Fakultät neu aufnehmen darf.

§ 3

In denjenigen Schularten und Fakultäten, deren Besucherzahl in einem besonders starken Mißverhältnis zum Bedarf der Berufe steht, ist im Laufe des Schuljahres 1933 die Zahl der bereits aufgenommenen Schüler und Studenten soweit herabzusetzen, wie es ohne übermäßige Härten zur Herstellung eines angemesseneren Verhältnisses geschehen kann.

§ 4

Bei den Neuaufnahmen ist darauf zu achten, daß die Zahl der Reichsdeutschen, die im Sinne des Gesetzes zur Wiederherstellung des Berufsbeamtentums vom 7. April 1933 (Reichsgesetzbl. I S. 175) nicht arischer Abstammung sind, unter der Gesamtheit der Besucher jeder Schule und jeder Fakultät den Anteil der Nichtarier an der reichsdeutschen Bevölkerung nicht übersteigt. Die Anteilszahl wird einheitlich für das ganze Reichsgebiet festgesetzt.

Bei Herabsetzung der Zahl der Schüler und Studenten gemäß § 3 ist ebenfalls ein angemessenes Verhältnis zwischen der Gesamtheit der Besucher und der Zahl der Nichtarier herzustellen. Hierbei kann eine von der Anteilszahl abweichende höhere Verhältniszahl zugrundegelegt werden.

Absätze 1 und 2 finden keine Anwendung auf Reichsdeutsche nicht arischer Abstammung, deren Väter im Weltkriege an der Front für das Deutsche Reich oder für seine Verbündeten gekämpft haben, sowie auf Abkömmlinge aus Ehen, die vor dem Inkrafttreten dieses Gesetzes geschlossen sind, wenn ein Elternteil oder zwei Großeltern arischer Abkunft sind. Sie bleiben auch bei der Berechnung der Anteilszahl und der Verhältniszahl außer Ansatz.

§ 5

Verpflichtungen, die Deutschland aus internationalen Staatsverträgen obliegen, werden durch die Vorschriften dieses Gesetzes nicht berührt.

§ 6

Die Ausführungsbestimmungen erläßt der Reichsminister des Innern.

§ 7

Das Gesetz tritt mit seiner Verkündung in Kraft.

Berlin, den 25. April 1933.

Der Reichskanzler
Adolf Hitler

Der Reichsminister des Innern
Frick

Reichsgesetzbl. 1933 I

64

23 *Law against the Overcrowding of German Schools and Universities, 25 April 1933* (Bundesarchiv Koblenz)

crawling on hands and knees. His vulnerability inside Nazi Germany as a Jew, a modernist artist, and a political dissident was unambiguous.

The initial wave of arrests intensified the personal and professional friendship between Levin and the Monjaus. Their unusual friendship and trust continued throughout the next decade, creating a bond that overrode mutual fears and despondency. Franz Monjau was considered politically suspect after his arrest and was excluded from teaching positions under paragraph 4 of the civil service code.[19] Both Levin and Monjau had also been banned from selling or exhibiting their works and even from painting in the privacy of their own studios. The Nazis also confiscated two of Levin's sketches as "degenerate" *(Entartete Kunst)* from the graphics collection of the Düsseldorf Kunstmuseum.[20]

After his release from prison, Levin was assigned to compulsory labor cleaning streets and cemeteries. The latter job provided the inspiration and setting for his oil painting *Farmers* in 1933.[21] He also decided that economic survival as a Jew in the progressively narrowing options available to Jews in Nazi Germany warranted learning a skilled trade; on evenings and weekends, he thus apprenticed himself to a carpenter and cabinetmaker. These skills later (between the autumn of 1941 and the summer of 1943) temporarily rescued him and others from deportation.

It must be noted that even the *Kulturbund deutscher Juden* (Cultural Association of German Jews) was unable to assist Jewish artists and sculptors between 1933 and 1938.[22] The art market, already limited in the inauspicious economic climate of the depression, was even more precarious for Jews, suddenly confronted by the expansion of Nazi professional restrictions and prohibitions. The absence of job possibilities was intensified by the curtailment of museum and gallery shows and commissions as well as by the reduced sales of art to a hostile German public and a progressively more impoverished potential Jewish audience. In January 1936, the *Reichsverband der jüdischen Kulturbünde* in Berlin opened a central "Secretariat for Fine Arts." Its task was to

> *solidify and improve the relationship between Jewish artists and the Jewish public by sponsoring exhibitions of various kinds . . . The secretariat would also promote and protect the interests of Jewish artists living in Germany within the Jewish community . . .*[23]

In the spring of 1936 (from 26 April to 7 June), the Secretariat for Fine Arts in conjunction with the Artists' Aid of the Berlin Jewish community, the *Reichsvertretung der Juden in Deutschland*, and the Jewish Museum in Berlin, sponsored a national exhibition of Jewish artists, containing works by 75 artists from ten cities, not including Jewish artists from Berlin. Düsseldorf was represented by four artists and nine works, of which three pieces were by Julo "Lewin" *(sic)*.[24] Levin's works were also exhibited in either the winter of 1936 or 1937 in the foyer of the Berlin Kulturbund theater and the exhibit was favorably reviewed by the art critic Max Osborn.[25]

By 1933, Levin's style had matured, although his productivity thereafter was minimal because of Nazi exclusionary measures. The color tonalities of his harbor scenes were neither garish nor too soft and his portraiture had acquired a new poignancy. His *Self-portrait with Hat* from 1932 and his portrait of the ship's cook Ibrahim were unequivocal statements against dehumanization. His gentleness in delineating individual features also characterized the style of "expressive realism of this lost generation."[26]

The economic battle for survival had intensified significantly by 1936 among Levin's colleagues and friends. Otto Pankok's Gypsy paintings and his cycle *The Passion* had been confiscated; moreover, both Otto and Hulda Pankok were prohibited from exhibiting or working and they were constantly threatened by Gestapo and police house searches.[27] Mieke Monjau had tried to obtain information about possibilities for emigration and traveled to Paris respectively in 1936 and 1937. The extremely precarious and marginal financial situation of the German refugee community was obvious and the Monjaus thus decided to remain in Düsseldorf.[28] Another friend, Peter Ludwigs, saw his works confiscated and defamed in the "Degenerate Art" campaign and he was arrested for attempted high treason in March 1937. Before Ludwigs was released from prison in June 1937, Julo Levin had been arrested and interrogated once again.[29]

Shortly before Easter 1936, Levin assumed a position as art teacher at the new Jewish school located in the Kasernenstrasse in Düsseldorf. As a direct result of the increasing legal exclusion of school-age Jewish children from German public schools after 1933, new Jewish elementary and intermediate schools were opened between 1933 and 1938 and existing Jewish schools expanded. A statistical survey by the *Reichsvertretung der Juden in Deutschland* from late December 1933 estimated that 15,000 of the 60,000 Jewish children of school age attended Jewish elementary schools; in other words, 75 percent of Jewish students in Nazi Germany still attended *German* schools.[30] A similar survey at the end of 1937 revealed that 23,670 of ca. 39,000 Jewish children of school age now attended *Jewish* schools; in other words, more than 60 percent of Jewish students now attended the separate *Jewish* school system.[31] The administrative report of the city of Düsseldorf covering the period from 1 April 1933 to 31 March 1936, revealed that the total number of Jewish students attending municipal elementary schools had decreased as follows: 323 at the beginning of May 1933, 274 at the beginning of June 1934, and 74 at the beginning of July 1935.[32] While the total number of Jewish students in public schools decreased steadily, the number of students attending the private Jewish elementary school in Düsseldorf increased from 210 at Easter 1935 to 365 in January 1937.[33] Foreign languages (Hebrew, English, and French) held a central place in the curriculum as did the study of Judaism (the Bible and Jewish history); central emphasis was also placed on training for agricultural, skilled labor, and household work. The school attempted to prepare students for emigration intellectually as well as practically, and created an explicit "emigration pedagogy."[34] "Art education was to help children understand who they were and crafts and sewing were designed to teach tidiness and manual technical skills."[35] The purpose of teaching art was discussed more fully in the guidelines published on 29 October 1937 by the *Reichsvertretung der Juden in Deutschland:*

Art lessons in all school years are to be based on material from the child's Jewish milieu. Images of family and communal religious life, religious objects, biblical and other Jewish themes are to be depicted through art.[36]

Levin, frequently a guest in the Monjau household, always discussed his lectures and class assignments with his friend Franz Monjau, who had been trained as an art educator. He also discussed curriculum subjects with Carl Lauterbach and gave him many students' drawings as a gift.[37] Levin's

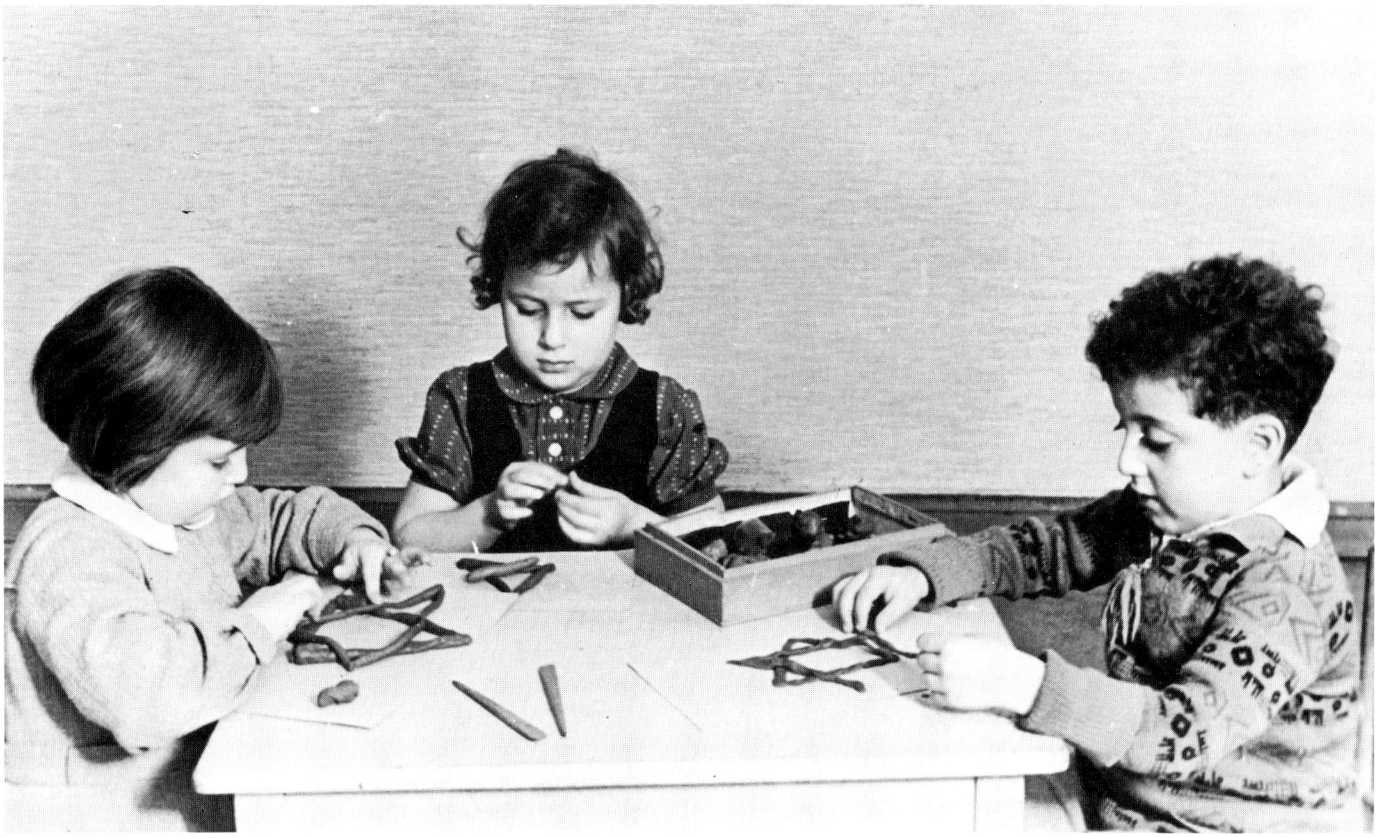

24 *The Kindergarten of the Berlin Jewish Community*, 1934 (Bildarchiv Preussischer Kulturbesitz)

affection for his students is evident from the scope of his collection.

Levin was the teacher, the inspiration, and the artist, who admired his small geniuses. The relationship between teacher and student was an exciting and ingenuous interplay. Julo Levin was an ideal teacher who knew how to inspire his students about everything; I could scarcely imagine a more devoted and amiable teacher. He was proud of the superb results produced by his students. Color was viewed as spiritual self-expression; the expressionists had created dramatic breakthroughs in their use of color. Color had also become a new and important element in the pedagogical discussion about self-fulfillment! Then and also again today . . . Our conversations in his studio about his students' art was filled with the spirit of universal humanism and despite the oppressive conditions, the fears and anxieties of those times, those discussions were a ray of light that stimulated our hopes.[38]

At the beginning of the new school year on 21 April 1938, Levin moved from Düsseldorf to Berlin.[39] He rented a small apartment (one and one-half rooms with foyer, kitchen, and bathroom) at Seydelstrasse 7 in what was then known as Berlin Southwest 68.[40] This city district, known as Friedrichswerder,[41] was a relatively poor section located near the Spittelmarkt, the well-known Red Town Hall, Jerusalemstrasse, and the adjacent *Scheunenviertel* district, where East European Jews were concentrated.[42]

With the help of his sister Else and an old Stettin friend, Dr. Richard Schäfer,[43] Levin obtained a position as an art teacher at the Private Jüdische Waldschule Kaliski in Dahlem until this school closed in 1939 and then at the Holdheim School for the ensuing years through 1941.[44] Levin's 75 year old mother had also moved from Stettin to relatives in Berlin-Halensee during 1938. After 1933, the Jewish population had left the villages and small towns in increasing numbers and moved into the larger cities. Between 1933 and 1939, the number of Jewish children residing in Germany was cut in half and the ratio of elderly Jewish women to men residing in Germany increased substantially. This relatively large increase in the number of Jewish women can be attributed to several factors: the excess number of German-Jewish women (including war widows) in the post-World War I population; the higher male mortality rate, since women usually outlived men and men were more vulnerable to confinement and maltreatment in Nazi concentration camps; and the substantial rise in international emigration by Jewish young and middle-aged single men after 1933. More than one-third of the subsequently deported Jews were above the age of sixty. The April 1939 census recorded respectively 123,104 female Jews and 90,826 male Jews in Germany. The comparatively large number of Jewish women meant that more German-Jewish women than men were deported and murdered after October 1941. The average age of the remaining Jews meant that a majority lived on pensions, savings, or welfare assistance.[45]

After the November 1938 pogrom, Else Levin decided to emigrate to England. She already left Berlin at the end of May 1939.[46] She took several works of student art from Julo's private collection from Jewish schools in Düsseldorf and Berlin, hoping that they would be of use to prepare her brother's eventual emigration. Levin categorically refused to leave, stating: "I was born and raised here and I will work here."[47] Shortly thereafter, Levin completed his last oil painting, a portrait, *My Mother* (Fig. 6). It portrayed an old lady seated in an armchair with a serious and melancholy expression. Her posture and her features convey disappointment, sadness, and isolation. The portrait is simultaneously a farewell and a lamentation; it reveals Levin's family bonds.[48]

We know very little about Levin's work as a teacher in Berlin, since most Jewish school records were destroyed during the November 1938 pogrom and the city school records were lost during the war. One of the immediate consequences of the November 1938 pogrom was the expulsion of all Jewish students from German schools, effective on 15 November 1938.[49] Jewish schools continued to exist under steadily deteriorating conditions and increasing pressure until they were closed entirely in June 1942.[50]

Every year Otto Pankok and Julo Levin exchanged Christmas gifts and hand-printed New Year's cards. Pankok's New Year's greeting in 1939 showed a monkey with the accompanying text: "Enter with caution."[51] The card for 1940 showed a creature like the Minotaur, half man and half bull. Levin's card for 1941 was a symbolic woodcut entitled: "Michael slays the dragon."[52] Despite the total domination of Nazi terror, Levin believed in the ultimate defeat of Nazi Germany with an almost boundless optimism.

With the closing of most Jewish schools at the end of 1941, Levin was conscripted for compulsory labor as a carpenter by the Berlin branch of the *Reichsvereinigung der Juden in Deutschland* (National Association of Jews in Germany).[53] Coincidentally the close friendship between Mieke Monjau and Julo Levin resumed when, at the end of 1941, Mieke Monjau rented a room in a rest home located in the Berlin suburb of Birkenwerder. The first deportations of German Jews occurred at the same time between October and December 1941. Mieke had already shown remarkable courage one month before, when in November 1941 she had spent the last night with her Düsseldorf Jewish friends Martha Oppenheim-Cohn-Schweriner before the latter's deportation to Minsk. Martha had been a member of the Monjau-Levin circle.[54]

From the beginning of 1942, Levin was assigned to work as a handyman for the Berlin Jewish community and thus became an eyewitness to the deportations. "Levin performed many small services, including delivering coded clandestine letters, for the doomed. He was also assigned to clean the cattle cars on the train tracks between Wedding and Putlitzstrasse (in Berlin)."[55] Levin's New Year's card for 1942 was a symbolic woodcut: "Cart rolling downhill,"[56] an objective artistic reflection of the deteriorating conditions and attendant difficulties.

In the spring of 1942, ninety so-called "Transports of the Elderly" *(Alterstransporte)* began from Germany and Austria (Vienna) to Theresienstadt, which had served as a transit camp for Czech Jews since late November 1941.[57]

Emma Levin, née Arnfeld, was deported to Theresienstadt with the 56th "Transport of the Elderly" that departed from Berlin on 23 September 1942.[58] Her two cousins, both somewhat older than she, decided to commit suicide prior to deportation.[59] Mieke Monjau and Julo Levin spent the last night before the deportation convoy at the bedside of his 75-year-old mother and Mieke promised her to care for Julo.[60]

Julo Levin (in Berlin) still maintained sporadic contact with his sister Else (in London) through telegrams exchanged by the German and British Red Cross during 1942 and 1943. This contact also included several messages from Hedwig Köpke, her mother's neighbor in Berlin-Halensee. The death of his two aunts was reported by Julo on 22 October 1942 and also by Hedwig Köpke on 1 December 1942. Julo's last communication to his sister was dated 28 April 1943 and reached her in London on 1 July.[61]

Peter Ludwigs visited Julo in Berlin in the autumn of 1942 and tried to convince him to go into hiding. Levin refused: "I cannot endanger others in order to save myself."[62] At the beginning of 1943, Peter Ludwigs and 135 other members of the Düsseldorf communist underground group "Lower Rhine" were arrested and Ludwigs died in prison of diabetes on 2 July 1943.

Levin's last letters to the circle around Peter Ludwigs, written between the fall of 1942 and May 1943, revealed his growing fears about the hopelessness of his situation. In coded language, he described the deportations he had witnessed: "Journeys are continued; one must adjust to winter; it has grown very quiet here; and most of my friends departed after the vacation was over." He also spoke of "a sudden illness" as a metaphor for deportation. He protected himself from identification with a simple precaution: the letters were always addressed to a third party without any direct connections to Peter Ludwigs; moreover, Levin changed his first name on each letter he signed.[63]

His friend, the artist Otto Pankok, offered to hide Levin in his home. When Julo finally agreed after a long period of vacillation, Pankok's house had meanwhile been destroyed by an air raid on Düsseldorf.[64] Levin's last art work was the small woodcut "Prometheus," sent to Pankok as his 1943 New Year's greeting.[65]

Levin was arrested without warning during the so-called Factory Operation at the end of February 1943, when Berlin Jews and Jews in privileged mixed marriages had been rounded up at their workplaces. As an employee of the Berlin Jewish community, Levin had been issued a "yellow certificate" and consequently he was finally released, though only after being badly beaten.[66] On 7 May 1943 Levin was rearrested, together with hundreds of employees of the Jewish community of Berlin and many members of the Reichsvereinigung. Mieke Monjau, who was then managing his household, was arrested with him. Both were taken to the assembly center at Grosse Hamburger Strasse 26–28, where Mieke succeeded in talking her way out of arrest and securing her freedom.[67]

The Grosse Hamburger Strasse assembly center existed from the middle of 1942 until the spring of 1944. Originally a Jewish old age home, it was used for its new purpose after the residents had been deported to Theresienstadt. An indictment by the public prosecutor at the Berlin district court *(Landgericht Berlin)* described this facility:

The camp could accommodate an average of 100–150 Jews based on its size. They were usually held upstairs where one large room 3 x 6 meters [ca. 10 x 20 ft.) had adequate space, although they were forced to sleep on the floor. During unusual occurrences, such as the so-called Factory Operation during the spring of

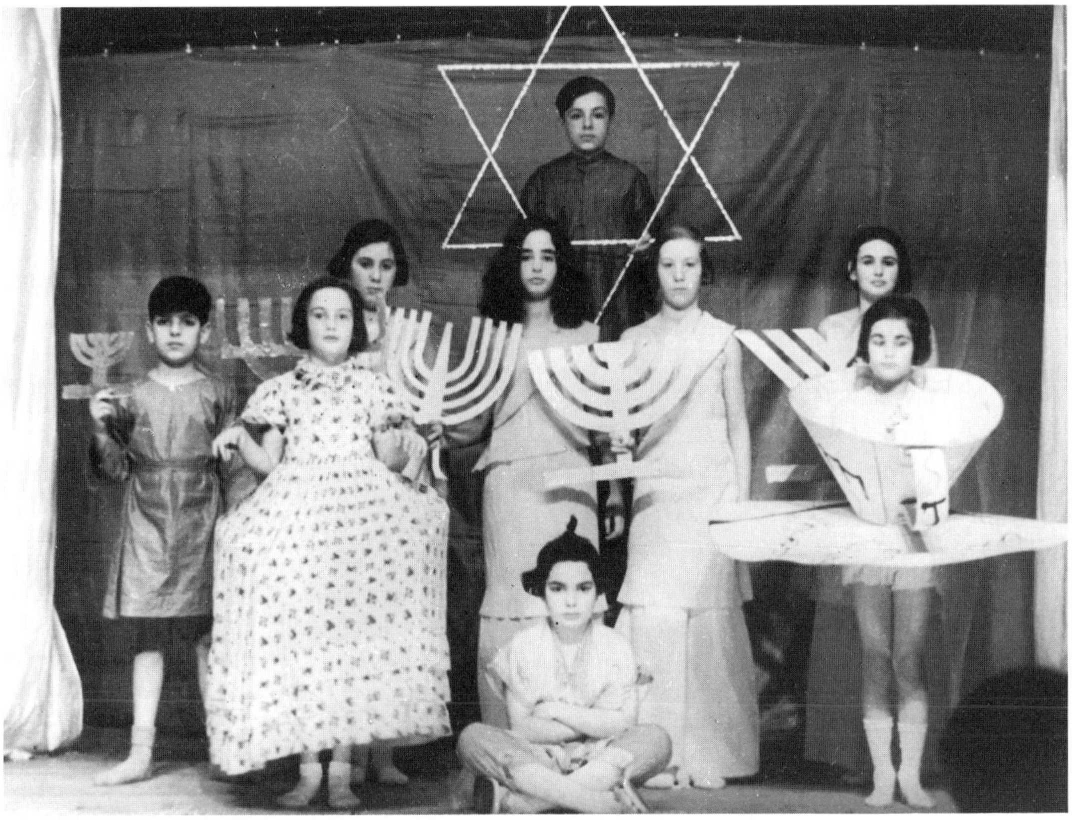

25 *Hanukkah Play at the Kaliski School in Berlin*, 1936 (Bildarchiv Preussischer Kulturbesitz)

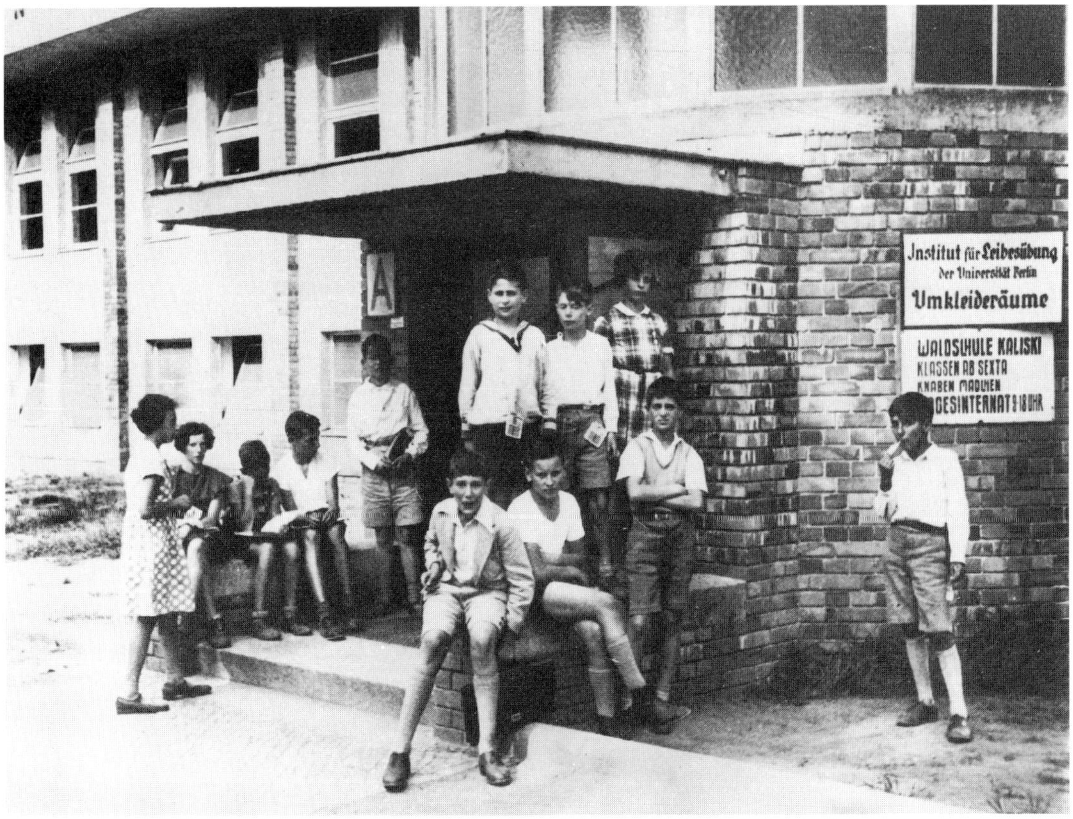

26 *The Kaliski School in Berlin*, 1936 (Bildarchiv Preussischer Kulturbesitz)

Erziehung

a) Für das Reich

558. Schulunterricht an Juden.

Nach der ruchlosen Mordtat von Paris kann es keinem deutschen Lehrer und keiner deutschen Lehrerin mehr zugemutet werden, an jüdische Schulkinder Unterricht zu erteilen. Auch versteht es sich von selbst, daß es für deutsche Schüler und Schülerinnen unerträglich ist, mit Juden in einem Klassenraum zu sitzen. Die Rassentrennung im Schulwesen ist zwar in den letzten Jahren im allgemeinen bereits durchgeführt, doch ist ein Restbestand jüdischer Schüler auf den deutschen Schulen übriggeblieben, dem der gemeinsame Schulbesuch mit deutschen Jungen und Mädeln nunmehr nicht weiter gestattet werden kann.

Vorbehaltlich weiterer gesetzlicher Regelung ordne ich daher mit sofortiger Wirkung an:

1. Juden ist der Besuch deutscher Schulen nicht gestattet. Sie dürfen nur jüdische Schulen besuchen. Soweit es noch nicht geschehen sein sollte, sind alle zur Zeit eine deutsche Schule besuchenden jüdischen Schüler und Schülerinnen sofort zu entlassen.
2. Wer jüdisch ist, bestimmt § 5 der Ersten Verordnung vom 14. November 1935 zum Reichsbürgergesetz (RGBl. I S. 1333).
3. Diese Regelung erstreckt sich auf alle mir unterstellten Schulen einschließlich der Pflichtschulen.

Berlin, den 15. November 1938.

Der Reichsminister
für Wissenschaft, Erziehung und Volksbildung.
In Vertretung: Zschintzsch.

An die Unterrichtsverwaltungen der Länder (außer Preußen), den Herrn Reichskommissar für das Saarland in Saarbrücken, die Herren Oberpräsidenten (Abteilung für höheres Schulwesen), den Herrn Stadtpräsidenten der Reichshauptstadt Berlin (Abteilung für höheres Schulwesen, Abteilung für Volks- und Mittelschulen und Abteilung für Berufs- und Fachschulen), die Herren Regierungspräsidenten (Schulabteilung). — Abschrift zur gefälligen Kenntnisnahme an den Herrn Preußischen Ministerpräsidenten, den Herrn Reichsminister des Innern, den Herrn Reichsminister für Volksaufklärung und Propaganda und den Stellvertreter des Führers. — E I b 745 (b).

(RMinAmtsblDtschWiss. 1938 S. 520.)

27 *Decree Prohibiting Jews from Attending German Schools, 15 November 1938* (Bundesarchiv Koblenz)

57

Der Reichsminister
für Wissenschaft, Erziehung
und Volksbildung

Berlin W 8., den 7.Juli 1942.
- Postfach -

E II e Nr. 1598

Schließung jüdischer Schulen.

- - - - -

Im Hinblick auf die Entwicklung der Aussiedlung der Juden in der letzten Zeit hat der Reichsminister des Innern (Reichssicherheitshauptamt) im Einvernehmen mit mir die Reichsvereinigung der Juden in Deutschland angewiesen, sämtliche jüdischen Schulen bis zum 30.Juni 1942 zu schließen und ihren Mitgliedern bekannt zu geben, daß ab 1.Juli 1942 jegliche Beschulung jüdischer Kinder durch besoldete und unbesoldete Lehrkräfte untersagt ist.

Ich gebe Ihnen hiervon Kenntnis. Von einer Veröffentlichung dieses Erlasses ist abzusehen.

Im Auftrage
gez. Holfelder.

Beglaubigt:
[signature]
Angestellte.

An die
Unterrichtsverwaltungen der Länder
(außer Preußen),
Herren Reichsstatthalter in den
Reichsgauen.

Herren

28 *Decree Closing Jewish Schools, 7 July 1942* (Yad Vashem, Israel)

1943, the rooms were overcrowded. Then 30–40 people were packed together like sardines in one room.[68]

The cellars of this collecting center contained

air raid shelters, several punishment solitary confinement cells where prisoners were locked up in total darkness. Maltreatment was a common occurrence.[69]

Between the 7 and 16 May 1943, Levin smuggled two encoded letters out of the Grosse Hamburger Strasse assembly center. In the first letter, he thanked Mieke Monjau

for everything, especially for the last parcel, that I still received. We are still well cared for here. I know that, since mother's departure, I never lacked anything and was cared for, as always. It would have been impossible for me to attend to food purchases, laundry, sewing, and other essentials, which are very difficult to accomplish today. I now know for the first time how vital this is with such a sudden illness, and how much courage it required because of the dangers of infection, and I do not know how I can repay this. I know that meanwhile everything has been stored safely and confirm your power of attorney to dispose of things, which mother had already given verbally . . .[70]

The letter empowered Mieke Monjau to serve as Levin's executrix.

Mieke Monjau received the second farewell letter

together with Levin's fountain pen and some cash. His last words were:

Everything until now has gone well and will probably not be all that bad. We are able to keep everything here and lugging everything will be heavy. We leave Monday. Otherwise I have not been bothered and hope that this is also true for you. I couldn't return home again and this is very painful, because I really did want to see you again and to have shaken your hand. I do so in my thoughts. May you be well and enjoy the beautiful vacation days, if possible. A healthy reunion as soon as possible . . .[71]

On 10 May 1943, Levin had itemized the contents of his apartment: "one wardrobe, three chairs, two chests of drawers, one couch, two arm chairs, and diverse pots and pans."[72] These details were registered on the mandatory inventory of property and household possessions, filled out by all Jews prior to their deportation.

On 17 May 1943, Eastern transport number 38 including Levin and 395 others left from the Putlitzstrasse train station in Berlin for Auschwitz. Hermann Langbein, Secretary of the International Camp Committee, informed us that:

That specific deportation of Berlin Jews arrived at Auschwitz on 19 May 1943. The following data are known:
'Eighty men survived the selection on arrival and received numbers 122,476 to 122,555; 115 women received the numbers 45,169 to 45,282. The others were gassed.'
The names are unknown. I couldn't locate the name Julo Levin in other records.[73]

Levin's death date is not known. His mother, Emma Levin, died in Theresienstadt in 1944.

After Levin's deportation, Franz Monjau traveled to Berlin where, together with his wife, they arranged the safekeeping of Levin's artistic estate. The pictures were hidden with acquaintances and friends in several localities and thus rescued for posterity.

In October 1944, Franz Monjau was also arrested. After several months' imprisonment at the Ratingen Gestapo prison, he was sent to Buchenwald on

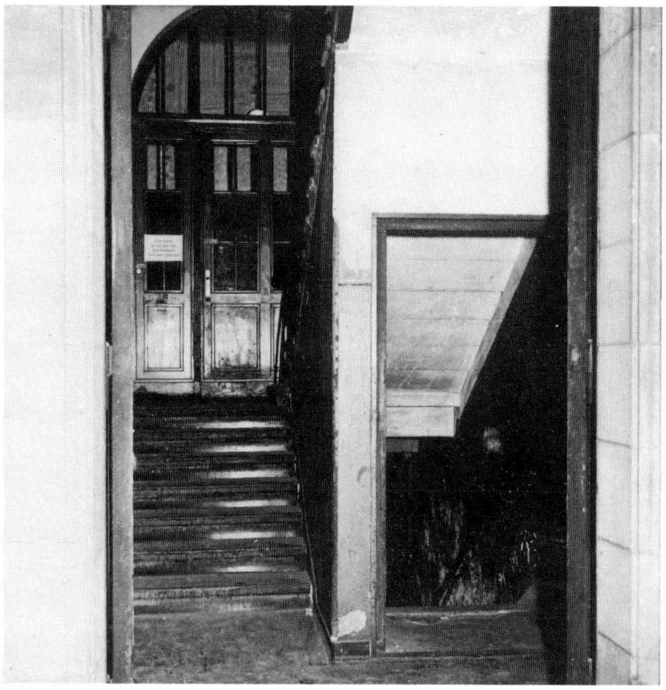

29 *Assembly Center at Grosse Hamburger Strasse 26, Berlin: Basement Staircase* (Bildarchiv Preussischer Kulturbesitz)

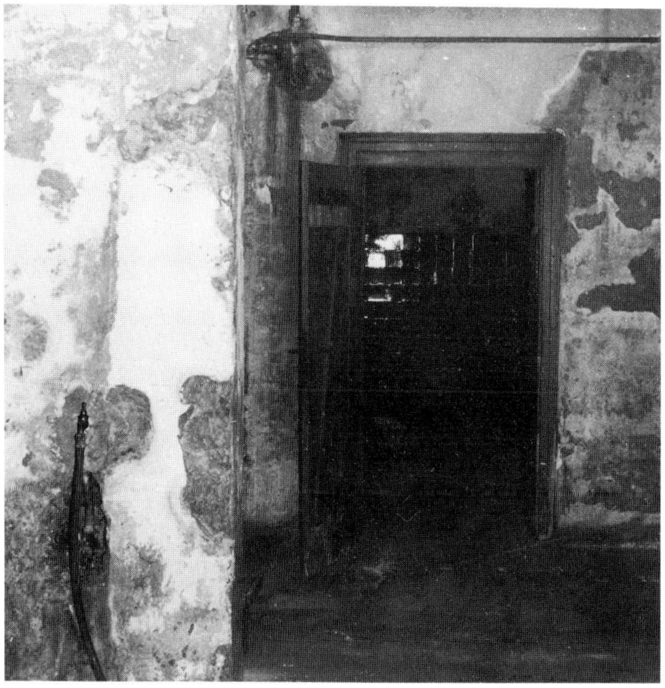

30 *Basement Cells in the Assembly Center at Grosse Hamburger Strasse 26, Berlin* (Bildarchiv Preussischer Kulturbesitz)

16 January 1945, where he was murdered on 28 February 1945. Since 1946, Mieke Monjau has exhibited works by both her husband and Julo Levin that she had rescued. Levin had once said: "Only my paintings are my testimony, a silent bond with people, that excludes everything divisive."[74] The last fifty years have made the paintings of Julo Levin and his circle a symbol for understanding and humanity. The works of both the teachers and their Jewish students survive as their living memorial.

Notes

1 Unpublished manuscript of the opening remarks of Else Levin and Mieke Monjau at the exhibition *Lebendiges Erbe*, Hetjens Museum, Düsseldorf, 1946.

2 Else Levin, "Erinnerungen" (London, Jan. 1981), in: Stadtmuseum Düsseldorf and Volkshochschule Papenburg, ed., *Julo Levin: Gemälde, Graphiken, Dokumente* (Düsseldorf, 1981), p. 10.

3 Stadtarchiv Düsseldorf: Einwohnermeldeamt microfiche.

4 Ibid. For Thorn-Prikker, see Paul Vogt, *Geschichte der deutschen Malerei im 20. Jahrhundert* (Cologne, 1976), pp. 79 f. and Ulrich Krempel, ed., *Am Anfang: Das Junge Rheinland; Zur Kunst- und Zeitgeschichte einer Region 1918–1945* (Düsseldorf, 1985), pp. 64–72, 341.

5 For Campendonk and Nauen, see Krempel, *Das Junge Rheinland*, pp. 68–69, 316–17, 355.

6 Levin, *Erinnerungen*, p. 13. The Julo Levin collection at the Stadtmuseum Düsseldorf includes photographs of his advertising brochures, glass painting, and interior decorations for Brandenstein-Zaudy.

7 Letter from Else Levin to Stadtmuseum Düsseldorf, 29 August 1987. See Annette Baumeister essay, pp. 74–75.

8 Berlin, Otto Stollberg Verlag, 1928.

9 Breslau, Verlag von Ferdinand Hirt, 1922.

10 Letter from Carl Lauterbach to Stadtmuseum Düsseldorf, 16 August 1987.

11 Mieke Monjau, "Am 17. Mai ging der Transport nach Auschwitz – niemand kehrt zurück: Über den Maler Julo Levin," *Tendenzen* v. 20, no. 128 (Nov.–Dec. 1979), p. 46.

12 Otto Pankok, *Zigeuner* (Düsseldorf, 1985).

13 Nordrhein-Westfälisches Staatsarchiv Münster, Bestand Prozessakte Gesch. Nr. 779/33: Oberlandesgericht Hamm, v. 1, pp. 125, 248 from 29 June 1933 and 6 Nov. 1934.

14 Ibid.

15 Stadtmuseum Düsseldorf, *Hanna Fonk: Gemälde, Graphik, Dokumente* (Düsseldorf, 1984), pp. 7–8.

16 Herbert Remmert and Karl Barth, ed., *Karl Schwesig: Leben und Werk* (Berlin, 1984), pp. 57–80.

17 Stadtmuseum Düsseldorf, *Franz Monjau: Gemälde, Aquarelle, Dokumente* (Düsseldorf, 1983), p. 4.

18 Karl Schwesig, *Schlegelkeller*, ed. Galerie Remmert and Barth (Berlin and Düsseldorf, 1983).

19 Badischer Kunstverein and Elefanten Press, *Widerstand statt Anpassung: Deutsche Kunst im Widerstand gegen den Faschismus 1933–1945* (Berlin, 1980), pp. 64–5.

20 Berlin Document Center (BDC), File of the Reichskammer der bildenden Künste, Berlin, List of 8 June 1938 containing the names of Jews, Jewish *Mischlinge*, and those married to Jews excluded since 1933. This list included Levin's name with the notation *"Volljude."* Material courtesy Mr. Daniel P. Simon, Director, BDC. See also Franz Roh, *'Entartete' Kunst: Kunstbarbarei im Dritten Reich* (Hannover, 1962), p. 154.

21 Monjau, "Am 17. Mai ging der Transport," p. 46. See note 11.

22 Kurt Düwell, "Jewish Cultural Centers in Nazi Germany: Expectations and Accomplishments," in: Jehuda Reinharz and Walter Schatzberg, ed., *The Jewish Response to German Culture: From the Enlightenment to the Second World War* (Hanover, NH and London, 1985), pp. 294–316 and Herbert Freeden, *Jüdisches Theater in Nazideutschland* (Frankfurt, Berlin, and Vienna, 1985), pp. 127 f.

23 *Informationsblätter der Reichsvertretung*, Jan.–Feb. 1936.

24 The Julo Levin Collection of the Stadtmuseum Düsseldorf includes a photocopy of the 16 page catalog, in which Levin's name is spelled "Lewin" *(sic)*, p. 6. The other three Düsseldorf artists included in this exhibition were Max Stern, Max Westfeld, and the sculptor Leopold Fleischhacker. See also Hermann Simon, *Das Berliner Jüdische Museum in der Oranienburger Strasse* (Berlin, 1983), p. 54.

25 Joachim Hemmerle, "Der Maler Julo Levin," in: *Julo Levin*, p. 18, reprinted from *Israel Forum* v. 10, no. 6 (June 1968).

26 Rainer Zimmermann, *Die Kunst der verschollenen Generation: Deutsche Malerei des Expressiven Realismus von 1925 bis 1975* (Düsseldorf and Vienna, 1980).

27 Karl Ludwig Hofmann, Christmut Präger, and Barbara Bessel, ed., *Otto Pankok* (Berlin, 1982), pp. 14–21.

28 Bernd Stappert, "'Zu denen halten, die verfolgt sind!': Zeitgeschichtliches in der Lebensgeschichte der Mieke Monjau," 28 pp. manuscript, copy provided by Südwestfunk, Stuttgart, p. 9. See also Ruth Fabian and Corinna Coulmas, *Die deutsche Emigration in Frankreich nach 1933* (Munich, New York, London, and Paris, 1978).

29 Stadtmuseum Düsseldorf, *Peter Ludwigs: Malerei, Grafik, Dokumente* (Düsseldorf, 1983), p. 15. For Levin, see Hauptstaatsarchiv Düsseldorf, Record Group RW 58, Gestapo File Peter Ludwigs 27912.

30 *Arbeitsbericht des Zentralausschusses der deutschen Juden für Hilfe und Aufbau*, ed. Reichsvertretung der Juden in Deutschland (Berlin, 1935), p. 26.

31 Ibid. (1937), pp. 54–55. See also Joseph Walk, "Jüdische Schüler an deutschen Schulen in Nazideutschland," *Bulletin des Leo Baeck Instituts* v. 19, no. 56/57 (1980), pp. 101–109

and Werner T. Angress, "Jüdische Jugend zwischen nationalsozialistischer Verfolgung und jüdischer Wiedergeburt," in: Arnold Paucker, Sylvia Gilchrist, and Barbara Suchy, ed., *Die Juden im Nationalsozialistischen Deutschland 1933–1943* (Tübingen, 1986), pp. 211–21.

32 Angelika Voigt and Falk Wiesemann, *Geschichte original – am Beispiel der Stadt Düsseldorf* (Münster, 1983), p. 7.

33 Kurt Herz, "Die private jüdische Volksschule Düsseldorf, 25. Januar 1937," 4 pp. typescript, courtesy Bernd Dieckmann, Cultural Affairs officer of the City of Düsseldorf.

34 Hermann Weil, "Nach fünf Jahren, Zum Arbeitsbericht der Reichsvertretung: Das jüdische Schulwerk," *C. V. Zeitung* no. 21, 1. Beiblatt (26 May 1948), pp. 3–4.

35 Kurt Herz, "Die private jüdische Volksschule in Düsseldorf," p. 3.

36 Landesarchiv Berlin, Pr. Br. Rep. 57, No. 374, v. 1, 1936–1937.

37 Stadtmuseum Düsseldorf: Archiv Lauterbach.

38 See pp. 85–86.

39 Stadtarchiv Düsseldorf: Einwohnermeldeamt microfiche.

40 Oberfinanzdirektion Berlin: Akten des ehemaligen Oberfinanzpräsidenten Berlin-Brandenburg, Vermögenserklärung einschliesslich des Wohnungsinventarverzeichnisses Julius ("Julo") Levin, 10 May 1943, courtesy Mr. Herda.

41 Karl Baedeker, *Berlin und Potsdam* (Leipzig, 1936), pp. 52–3.

42 Eike Geisel, ed., *Im Scheunenviertel: Bilder, Texte, Dokumente* (Berlin, 1981); see also Carola Hilker-Siebenhaar, ed., *Wegweiser durch das jüdische Berlin* (Berlin, 1987).

43 Further data about Dr. Richard Schäfer could not be located.

44 Pädagogisches Zentrum, Berlin: Fragebögen für höhere Schulen, 25 May 1938 for the Waldschule Kaliski and the Holdheim Schule. See Michael Daxner, "Die private jüdische Waldschule Kaliski in Berlin, 1932–1939," in: Paucker, ed., *Die Juden im nationalsozialistischen Deutschland*, pp. 249–57; idem, "Dokumente: Der Erfolg der Überlebenden: Die private jüdische Waldschule Kaliski in Berlin, 1932–1939," *Neue Sammlung* v. 26, no. 1, pp. 68–78; and Hilker-Siebenhaar, *Wegweiser durch das jüdische Berlin*, p. 106.

45 Leo Baeck Institute Archive, New York: Bruno Blau, "Die Entwicklung der jüdischen Bevölkerung in Deutschland," manuscript, New York, 1950.

46 *Julo Levin*, pp. 14–15. See note 2.

47 Monjau, "Am 17. Mai ging der Transport," p. 47. See note 11.

48 Annette Baumeister, "Mit Bildern widerstehen," in: Krempel, ed., *Das Junge Rheinland*, p. 111.

49 Runderlass des Reichsministers für Wissenschaft, Erziehung und Volksbildung, 15. Nov. 1938, in: Joseph Walk, ed. *Das Sonderrecht für die Juden im NS-Staat; Eine Sammlung der gesetzlichen Massnahmen und Richtlinien, Inhalt und Bedeutung* (Heidelberg and Karlsruhe, 1981), p. 256 (No. III 17).

50 Ibid., p. 377 (No. IV 376): Unpublished decree by the Reichsministerium für Wissenschaft, Erziehung und Volksbildung together with the RSHA, 20 June 1942.

51 *Otto Pankok*, p. 106. See Otto Pankok Archive, Haus Esselt, Hünxe-Trevenack, correspondence between Otto Pankok and Julo Levin at year's end 1939–1940.

52 Monjau, "Am 17. Mai ging der Transport," p. 49. See note 11.

53 Oberfinanzdirektion Berlin, Vermögenserklärung Julius ("Julo") Levin, p. 1.

54 *Franz Monjau*, pp. 41–42. See note 48.

55 Ibid., p. 43.

56 Stadtmuseum Düsseldorf: Loan Mieke Monjau.

57 Henry Friedlander, "The Deportation of German Jews: Postwar German Trials of Nazi Criminials," *Leo Baeck Institute Yearbook* 29 (1984), pp. 216–17.

58 Oberfinanzdirektion Berlin, Vermögenserklärung Emma Levin from 18 Sept. 1942 and the List of Deportees for the 65th Transport of the Elderly to Theresienstadt on 23 Sept. 1942.

59 Stappert, "Zu denen halten, die verfolgt sind," p. 13. See also Konrad Kwiet, "The Ultimate Refuge: Suicide in the Jewish Community under the Nazis," *Leo Baeck Institute Yearbook* 29 (1984), pp. 135–67.

60 *Franz Monjau*, p. 42. See note 48.

61 Photocopies courtesy Else Levin, London.

62 *Franz Monjau*, p. 42 and *Peter Ludwigs*, pp. 16–21. See note 48.

63 Photocopies courtesy Mieke Monjau, Düsseldorf.

64 *Franz Monjau*, p. 42. See note 48.

65 Janet Blatter and Sybil Milton, *Art of the Holocaust* (New York, 1981), p. 183 (Fig. 177).

66 See Hildegard Henschel, "Aus der Arbeit der Jüdischen Gemeinde Berlin während der Jahre 1941–1945," *Zeitschrift für die Geschichte der Juden* (Tel Aviv), v. 9 (1972), pp. 33–52.

67 *Franz Monjau*, p. 43. See note 48. See also Kurt Jakob Ball-Kaduri, "Berlin wird Judenfrei: Die Juden in Berlin in den Jahren 1942–43," *Jahrbuch für die Geschichte Mittel- und Ostdeutschlands*, v. 22 (1973), pp. 196–241.

68 StA Berlin, 1 Js 9/65, Anklageschrift Bovensiepen, pp. 192–2.

69 Ibid., p. 193.

70 Photocopies courtesy Mieke Monjau, Düsseldorf.

71 Ibid.

72 Oberfinanzdirektion Berlin, Vermögenserklärung Julius ("Julo") Levin, p. 8.

73 Letter from Hermann Langbein, Vienna, to the author, 16 July 1987.

74 *Julo Levin*, p. 15. See note 2.

"There is no school anymore!" The History of the Private Jewish Elementary School in Düsseldorf, 1933–1942

Barbara Suchy

In March 1877, it was said for the first time in the history of Düsseldorf Jews: "There is no Jewish school anymore." After 41 hard and troublesome years of service, the teacher N. Frank ended his work at the one-class "mixed Jewish primary school" on the Marienstrasse. At the end he had taught 42 children between the ages of five and fourteen.[1]

At that time, a total of approximately 950 Jews resided in Düsseldorf, of whom 134 were children of school age; seven attended other non-Jewish primary schools and 83 went to non-Jewish private and secondary schools. The small Jewish school was dissolved and the students as well as the bust of "His Majesty, the Emperor" were distributed among other schools.[2] This corresponded to the general process of assimilation typical of that era. The majority of non-orthodox middle-class Jews in medium and large-size cities viewed the education of their children in public schools (whether Protestant or Catholic) or in private gentile schools as a prerequisite for social advancement, economic success, and much sought for recognition as equal German citizens of the Jewish faith, thereby showing emphatic Jewish support for acculturation in nineteenth century Germany.

In 1941, two generations later, Siegfried Falk, head of the Düsseldorf Jewish community, wrote in a short letter to a friend in Switzerland: "There is no school anymore." In retrospect this letter seems the barely perceptible cry of despair of someone already bound and gagged.[3]

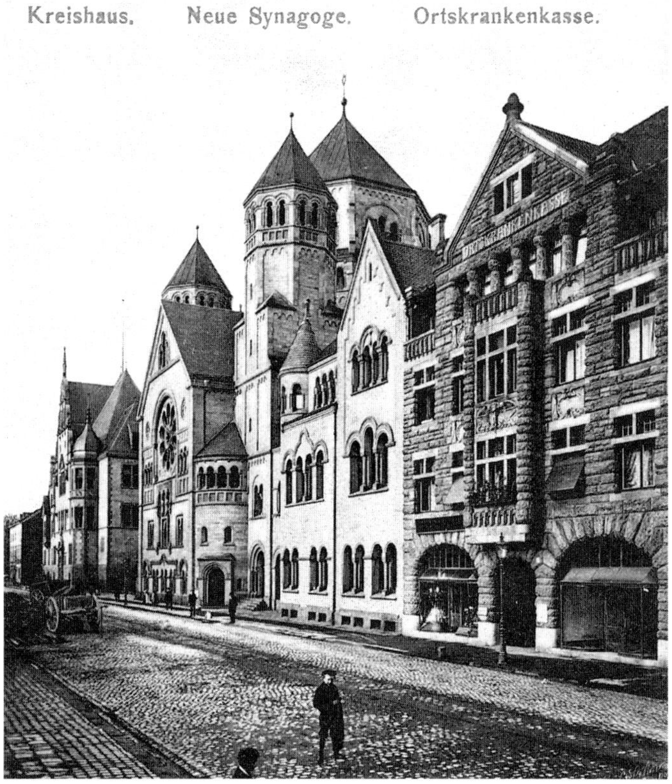

31 *The Synagogue and the Adjacent Rabbi's House at Kasernenstrasse in Düsseldorf* (Postcard)

The drawings surviving from the Düsseldorf Jewish school during the Nazi era are both the reason as well as an important component for reconstructing this almost forgotten chapter of German-Jewish local history after 1933. Only fragments of this story can be established. The archives of the Jewish community were destroyed and the records of the school authorities burned. It would therefore be desirable if this exhibition served to bring to light additional fragments of this history, thus adding to our knowledge about this school.[4]

Official statistics in 1925 reveal that 5,130 Jews lived in Düsseldorf.[5] This represented 1.19 percent of the total city population of 432,633. The 1933 census showed that 5,053 Jews lived in Düsseldorf,[6] thereby reducing them to 1.01 percent of the population. It is also known that 570 Jewish children attended primary, middle, and secondary schools. In 1932, the total number of Jewish students had been higher; many families had already fled or emigrated before the census took place.

What were the statistics in 1935, the year the Jewish school opened? There were 63 students in primary schools, 25 in middle schools, and 143 in upper secondary schools. Before the end of 1938, when Jews were prohibited from attending public schools, there was still one student at a middle school and thirteen at upper secondary schools.[7]

In 1928, five years before Hitler became Chancellor, representatives of the orthodox community had already attempted to create a new Jewish primary school.[8] Their spokesman, S. Gottdiener, also served on the executive board of the Jewish community. His proposal, again presented in 1930, found little support with the liberal majority of Jewish communal representatives. It was felt that this project would founder solely because of the heavy financial burden. Nevertheless, it was resolved to hire a new full-time teacher of religion to relieve the two rabbis, Dr. Eschelbacher and Dr. Klein. Until then, they had held religious classes in the afternoon after school.[9] Several weeks later, Gottdiener again tried to present his request: "It must be the task of the Jewish communities in our time – a period characterized by the loss of Jewish values – to establish Jewish schools, which can bring youth closer to Judaism."[10] A scant three years later, this became the demand of the day, although in 1930 it had caused vehement discussions. It was above all feared that the negative repercussions of creating such a school could be seen as "isolation" and "ghettoization." Meanwhile almost all the communal representatives also saw the advantages: "A rapprochement betweeen Eastern and Western Jews and above all, the more effective transmission of Jewish knowledge."[11]

At that time, orthodox Jews already had their own religious school, Machsike Hatorah, founded in 1920 by East European Jews, where three teachers taught Hebrew and Judaism every afternoon. It was attended by more than 100 children at the beginning of 1931.[12]

It was in January 1931 when, for the first time, stones were thrown through the large synagogue window.[13]

In December 1932, when the Hebrew Language Association was formed, 80 students assembled to the surprise of its founders.[14] A possible explanation might be the increased activity of the Zionists inside the community. Already during these months, the Kasernenstrasse synagogue was smeared with graffiti for the first time, including swastikas and the slogan "Jews die" *("Juda verrecke")*.

Six weeks after Hitler's appointment as Chancellor, seventeen window panes of the Jewish communal welfare offices, located adjacent to the synagogue, were smashed. The Reichstag elections of 5 March 1933 were followed in Düsseldorf (as

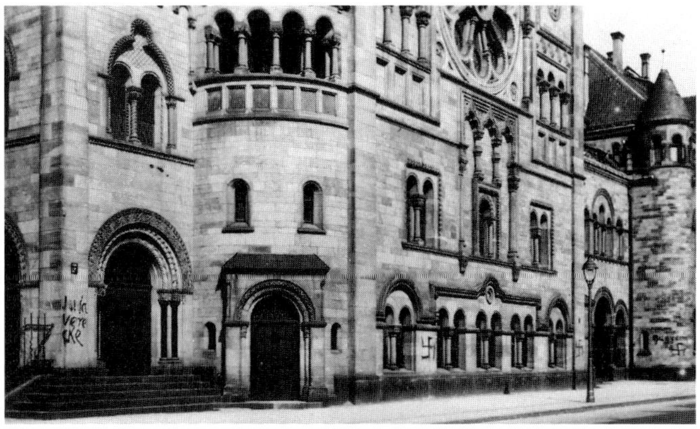

32 *The Düsseldorf Synagogue with Graffiti: A Swastika and the Slogan "Juda verrecke" ("Jews Die")*, 1932 (Private Collection)

elsewhere in Germany) by the state-organized anti-Jewish boycott of 1 April and also by the first far-reaching antisemitic legislation. German Jews were made strangers in their own land, people of inferior legal status. As the historian Reinhard Rürup has correctly pointed out: long before the deportations, these measures completely shattered the prerequisites for the continuation of Jewish life in Germany.[15] This was at that time also clearly recognized expressed by Rabbi Leo Baeck: "The thousand years of history of German Jews have now ended."[16]

What did it mean for Jewish children growing up in this atmosphere? They were especially hard hit. One of the first antisemitic laws affected Jewish students. The "Law against overcrowding in German schools and universities" of 25 April 1933 restricted the number of Jewish children, not to exceed 1.5 percent of the total number of students. Children of war veterans and those with a non-Jewish parent were initially exempted. This by no means mitigated the injustice of these and other similar pieces of legislation. Rather it emphasized this restriction in a shameless way and, moreover, left the shocked and utterly shaken German Jews with a demoralizing and debasing subdivision into two groups with different "rights."

The world of Jewish children was rapidly restricted. Traumatic experiences are hidden behind the catch words: isolation, defamation, and alienation from a familiar daily environment. In June 1933, the *Gemeindezeitung* published the concern of an unidentified father: "It is, above all, essential that our children be spared feelings of inferiority."[17]

Many schools had placed Jewish students on vacation in April 1933, a temporary expedient while awaiting legislative developments. A still somewhat open article entitled "School Questions" was published in the *Gemeindezeitung*, which soon thereafter was decisively affected by censorship requirements. The article reported that children were generally satisfied. "They praised their teachers and mostly lived in peace with their fellow students." However, in several schools, the students felt utterly "isolated," probably a euphemism. Jewish students had been forced to sing insulting and offensive songs, and race science had been introduced into the curriculum. "One teacher of race science informed his student that the lecture was not directed personally against him, but against Judaism in general; whereupon the student replied that he would prefer it attacked him personally rather than Judaism."[18]

Those in positions of authority had meanwhile recognized that it had become absolutely essential to establish their own Jewish school. Education had previously prepared Jewish students for careers and life; it now "sent them into a void without prospects."[19] This was also supported in September 1933 by the newly created *Reichsvertretung der deutschen Juden*. This first central organization for all German Jews recognized from the start that the support and care of Jewish education was one of their most important tasks.

A school association was organized in Düsseldorf in October 1933 to prepare the financing of a school. It was reported in the *Gemeindezeitung* on 14 October that Düsseldorf was at the time the only Rhineland community without a Jewish elementary school. The communal newspaper also encouraged youngsters to record their thoughts and feelings about "current events." This was intended to foster feelings of comfort and solidarity. One youth stated his observations and anxieties as follows:

The Synagogue

It is somehow different –
More serious, more ceremonial.
I don't know how this happened.
I have this feeling.

Here they are: Men and women.
All Jews. All Jews?
Do not many feel for the first time
that they are Jews?

Previously – one didn't know the other.
Each person was better.
The others only: "Just somebody!"
One attended synagogue on Yom Kippur.

This is different today. Completely different.
It was overdue!
You know: even he suffers as I do.
We understand one another.

The synagogue?
It is somehow different.
We know that we are Jews.
Does this time after all have a positive side?[20]

At the beginning of 1935, the Jewish community executive board hired Dr. Kurt Herz as the prospective director of the new school. Born in Offenbach in 1903, Kurt Herz had already worked as a young teacher at high schools in both Giessen and Mainz. He was active in the Jewish youth movement in the *Bund Kameraden* and the *Jüdischer Jugendverein*. From 1929 until his dismissal in 1933, he had taught at the Kaiser Friedrich *Realgymnasium* in Berlin-Neukölln. This school, known as the Karl Marx *Realgymnasium* for several years, had been a progressive school dedicated to educational reform. Until he assumed the post as director of the Düsseldorf school, Herz had also worked at the progressive Theodore Herzl school in Berlin. Kurt Herz had never dreamed that he would one day become director of a Jewish school. This had originally been outside his career expectations. Herz arrived in Düsseldorf accompanied by his young wife and small son. Mrs. Herz taught home economics and needlework at the school. She commuted between the two Jewish schools in Essen and Düsseldorf.[21]

Dr. Herz outlined his program in the *Gemeindezeitung*.[22] The preceding two year process of deprivation of rights and segregation had caused a deep insecurity among German Jews, often a loss of identity. German Jews had been made into Jews in Germany – outsiders and aliens. Herz was compelled to describe this state of affairs in veiled terms: "The new situation for Jews in Germany has led to a new and deep consciousness of the value of Jewish learning." This had consequences for Jewish schools. It was essential to provide a new identity and stability for the Jewish child through the "educational community" of teachers, students, and parents as well as through Jewish youth organizations. "Jewish youth in Germany can only find security, pride, happiness, and knowledge, where the values of Jewishness are consciously emphasized." Moreover, the "German cultural heritage" should also be transmitted to the children. Although this may sound a bit vague, it clearly indicates that, despite being forced into a segregated existence, German Jews could and would not permit themselves to be expelled from the German cultural community.

Furthermore, the Jewish school would also apply the methodology of progressive education. "Children will gladly attend school, which should be a happy place of assembly and work. Teachers should be friends and advisers and should empathize with their students, but also show them the path to life." It was already clear to Herz, that for many this "path to life" would mean emigration abroad. Herz also assumed, since it was impossible to foresee later developments, that some children would remain in Germany without being able to follow traditional educational or career patterns. Schools must take this into consideration by preparing youth for practical careers, i. e. "job retraining." Herz concluded with an appeal to parents to let their children be educated in a Jewish school, "because here they will be in a congenial circle of individuals with similar goals; here they will be shaped into happy and conscious Jewish individuals, able to overcome all difficulties and dangers with pride and knowledge."

On Sunday, 28 April 1935, the Düsseldorf Private Jewish School *(Jüdische Privatschule Düsseldorf)* was ceremonially opened. Classrooms were located in the building adjacent to the synagogue, the remodeled conference rooms and offices of the Welfare Office. The rabbi's residence on the first floor was, however, still occupied by Dr. Max Eschelbacher. The ceremony concluded with a mixed chorus accompanied by an organ performing Heinrich Schalit's "Thank the Lord."

The school was coeducational, something relatively uncommon at that time. Classes were held five days a week from Monday to Friday, also during the afternoon. A small school playground located behind the synagogue was available for recess. "We have only a small schoolyard for our children, but the most beautiful school playground could not be more cheerful, happier, or higher spirited. May our school be granted a happy life."[23]

In November 1935, Kurt Herz published an article in which he tried to confront "the apathy of a broad spectrum of Jewish public opinion towards the pressing problems of Jewish education." This allows us to conclude that Jewish schools in Düsseldorf and elsewhere had not yet found adequate spiritual or financial support in the Jewish community and that many parents continued to hold illusions about the Nazi policy of exclusion. This article, published in the *Jüdische Rundschau*, was not only a sober and realistic assessment of the situation, but also an impressive document of Jewish self-assertion in the face of a depressing present and a gloomy future; the Nuremberg Laws had been promulgated a short time before. Let us quote a few sentences from this article:

The Jewish bourgeoisie represents only in some of its individual representatives, but not in its totality, the middle class that once existed. Today it is in a state of dissolution, in a present without a future. The middle class ideal of individual education no longer has any possibility of realization, because the economic foundation is missing. Schools cannot transmit education in a vacuum; there is no such thing as education untested by life. Life requires engagement in a specific and determinable community. Therefore Jewish schools must have a definite and distinctive educational goal: the integration of our youth into a new Jewish community . . . The time of the fathers has passed. The time of the sons has not yet arrived. We are intermediaries between these times. This position challenges us as individuals. Let us not wait any longer; rather, we must take up the task. It is futile just to see the signs of the present or to perceive all the distress and misery; it is essential that we begin the work of the future.[24]

Dr. Herz succeeded in bringing an excellent small team of teachers to Düsseldorf, a fact unanimously confirmed by all living eyewitnesses. There were orthodox educators like Julius Kleinmann and Grete Eichelberg, who had been trained at the *Israelitische Lehrerbildungsanstalt* (the Jewish Teachers' Training Institute) in Würzburg. Others at first had not been close to Jewish life, traditions, and religion. They nevertheless supplemented each other in the collegial school atmosphere. The different social and religious backgrounds of the teachers corresponded to a similar diversity among the students.

The change to a Jewish school was a relief for many Jewish children; some, however, could not cope with the new situation. For a few, the change had been more of a shock. Hannelore Zürndorfer, for example, describes her two years at the Jewish school somewhat skeptically in her book about her Düsseldorf and British childhood. The ten year old girl mastered the problems of the long school trip of more than one hour rather well.

I found the school a big change from Gerresheim. For one thing the children seemed different. They were Jewish children. They were bright-eyed and volatile; discipline was not strict and regimented. Some children were pushy and cheeky and the competitive spirit was strong. The atmosphere was far less formal than in German state schools and the convention of modest self-effacement was forgotten. Children called out their answers eagerly and knew how to assert themselves. They were intelligent and ambitious and since the older ones realized that this was their last chance of preparing for a very hostile world, they were eager to absorb as much as they could. Instead of the larking and time-wasting that one finds in most schools, there was a great sense of urgency . . .

I don't remember my years at this school. I never really felt that I belonged. There was an air of unease and impermanence. I couldn't settle down to the new studies and I don't think I did very well. Although there were lessons in English and maths [sic] *on the syllabus, when I later came to these subjects in England, they seemed new to me, as though everything I had learnt during those two years had been obliterated from my mind. Perhaps I had wiped them out along with other memories.*[25]

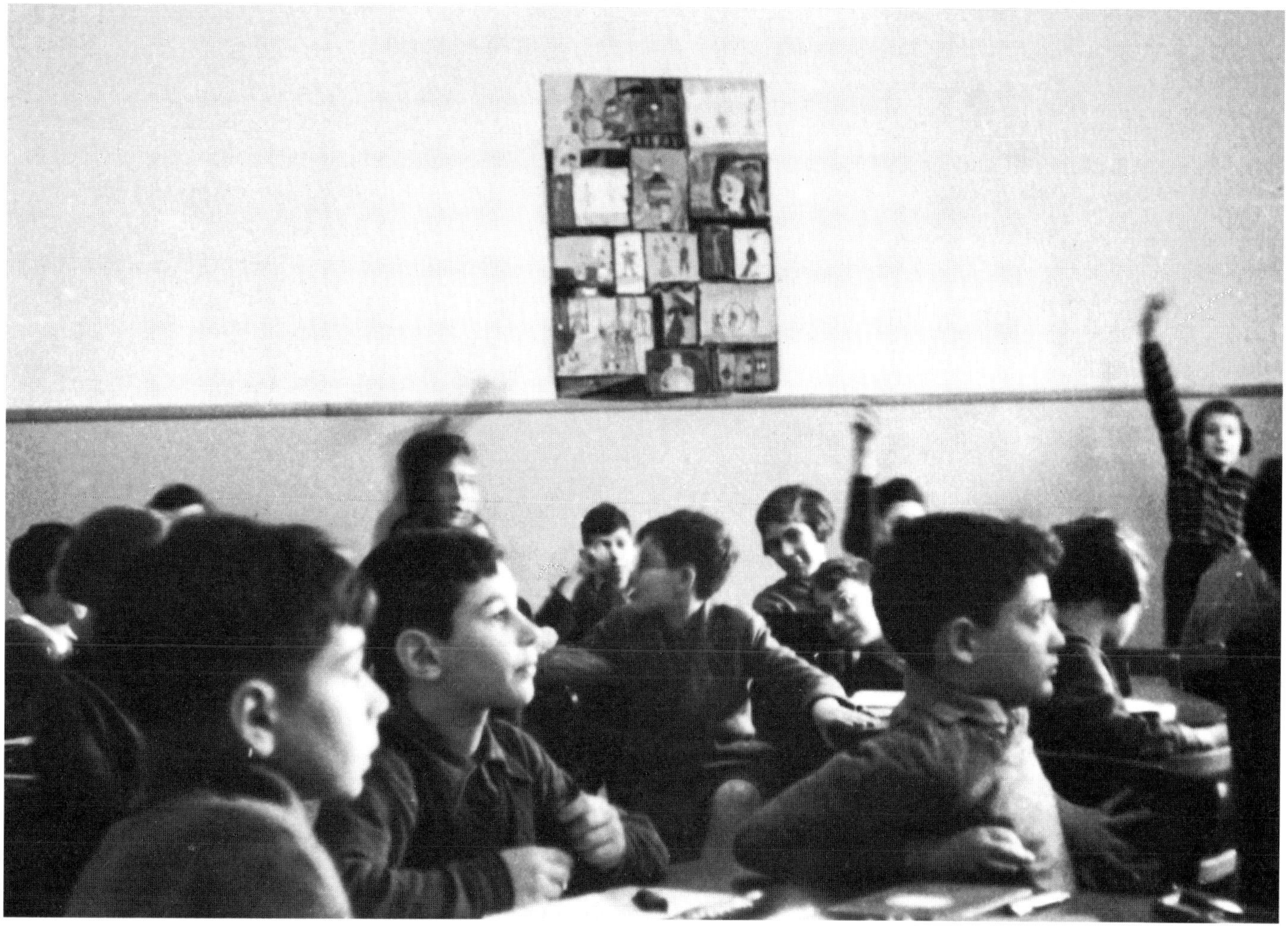

33 *Classroom at the Private Jewish Elementary School in Düsseldorf, students' drawings on the wall* (Kurt Bergel)

It is of course indisputable that many children suffered a great deal in non-Jewish schools and that this was detrimental to their development.[26] It was frequently the children who especially insisted on leaving their old schools, whereas their parents were still convinced of the sense of a "regular" and "normal" education. But adults – to a greater extent fathers than mothers – were not exposed to the ideological distortions of daily life as were their children, who usually were not yet equipped with the ability to repress unpleasant occurrences to the same extent as their parents. On the streets and in schools, the children were more immediately exposed to humiliation, chicanery, and rebuffs. Hannele Zürndorfer reported about those experiences:

At first I only sensed that I was less welcome in the street games; then some of the other children became actively hostile, teasing and baiting me and pushing me about when I was on roller-skates, so that I no longer liked going out to play . . .

I also remember an occasion when I had been out on my roller-skates and wanted to go back indoors. A bunch of boys and girls, some of whom had been my playmates and others who were complete strangers, sat on our doorstep barring my way. They didn't say anything at all, but sat there looking at me mockingly, waiting. I felt completely helpless, but did not want them to see me cry or shout for Mummy [sic]. *It was only when the occupant from the flat upstairs came home and wanted to get past, that I managed to slip in with him. I was very upset and frightened.*

This sort of thing went on more and more. Parents who were not active Nazis and disapproved secretly, no doubt told their children not to take part, but not to interfere either. 'Just keep out of it.' It was not wise to show sympathy to Jews. Some people came and told my parents privately how terrible they felt about it all, but explained that in public they had to be 'discreet.'[27]

There was such a rush to attend the Jewish school that the estimated number of 160 students was exceeded by 90. The prepared budget was totally overturned. There were neither enough classrooms nor teachers. To help out, Dr. Max Eschelbacher moved out of the familiar and spacious apartment in which he had lived, together with his wife and four children, since he had first arrived in Düsseldorf as Leo Baeck's successor in 1911. The rooms were converted into classrooms. Rabbi Eschelbacher moved into an apartment at Haroldstrasse 1; that street had been renamed Adolf Hitler Strasse. It must have cost the head of the Düsseldorf Jewish community a great deal of effort to constantly have to use this address!

Meanwhile the school filled almost the entire building. Arts and crafts were taught in the cellar, during the last year by the teacher Werner Weiss, who was one of the Düsseldorf leaders of the Zionist-oriented youth association *Habonim noar haluzi*, and is today a resident of Hazorea, Israel. Dr. Herz wrote in Weiss's school certificate after the November 1938 pogrom: "Because of the sudden reduction in the size of the school, we can regrettably no longer employ Mr. Weiss."[28]

Cooking lessons were also given in the cellar by Gony Katzenstein. They were available not only for young girls, but also for those women who because of impoverishment and prohibitions about employing non-Jewish domestic help under the age of 45, now had to get along without servants.[29]

In the autumn of 1935, Kurt Bergel arrived as a young teacher at the Düsseldorf Jewish school; he rapidly won the hearts and affections of his students. Born in 1911 in Frankfurt am Main, he had studied in both Frankfurt and Berlin. He brought rich experiences acquired at the Jewish country school in Herrlingen and at the *Jüdisches Lehrhaus* in Frankfurt, where he had worked together with Martin Buber during 1934 and 1935. Like Dr. Herz, Bergel had already published in Jewish periodicals about the problems of Judaism and Jewish education. Challenged by the Nazi seizure of power, Kurt Bergel was concerned about formulating a Jewish position beyond reform and orthodoxy and to develop the educational consequences.

Nothing could better convey the teaching methods and curriculum content as well as the atmosphere of the Düsseldorf Jewish school than Professor Bergel's memoirs, which are reprinted below slightly abridged.[30]

Jewish children suffered increasingly under officially sponsored antisemitism during the years of consolidation of Nazi power. Parents who had identified themselves culturally as Germans and who therefore had never before sent their children to a Jewish school, now sought physical and emotional protection for these children in a Jewish school . . .

The responsible heads of the community, men like Felsenthal and Franken, showed excellent judgment when they appointed Dr. Kurt Herz as director of their new school. Herz had previously taught in Berlin. He proved to be an excellent school director in Düsseldorf, who rapidly assembled a group of young, educationally progressive teachers, who served the school with devotion. Virtually all the teachers hired in 1935 were still teaching in November 1938, when the Nazis burned down both synagogue and school. These included: Messrs. Bergel, Kleinmann, and Schnook; Mesdames Eichelberg, Friedländer, Herz, Nussbaum, and Strauss; and for special subjects the artist Julo Levin, the musician Erwin Palm, and Ms. Katzenstein for home economics.[31]

Dr. Herz was a democratic person, who received the loyalty of his teachers; he gave them his trust and granted them a large degree of freedom. This alone was already an act of silent defiance in a country where the Führer principle was accepted everywhere. The same spirit also prevailed in the classroom; it was the spirit of the work school as it had developed during the Weimar Republic. Irrespective of what occurred around us, our school did not resemble a barracks square. Respect for its own sake did not exist in our school.

Teachers and students often laughed together, since humor was an especially necessary medicine for the endangered emotional health of our children. During my study trip to Palestine in March and April 1936, my class wrote me a letter stating: 'We don't want to pounce on you with our burning curiosity, since you will certainly not be able to describe everything, since the many impressions have assuredly overwhelmed you. Thus we, your problem children, will tell you about us.' There then followed an extensive description of a colorful Purim masquerade: 'The first number made fun of the teachers. And with you, dear Mr. Bergel, we dealt mildly, since one should not speak ill of someone behind his back. Despite this, your much praised Martin Buber has had it. We are looking forward happily to bad marks and the short vacation. P. S.: We await you anxiously.'

Whoever knows the authoritarian German schools of those times might easily recognize the very different tone of this letter . . .

A Jewish school in those days naturally had to prepare the children for emigration. This goal influenced the curriculum in many directions. English and Hebrew were mandatory subjects. Geography became more historical, paying special attention to potential countries of emigration: Mandate Palestine, the countries of North and South America, Australia, and New Zealand. There were also practical courses like home economics.

As a reply to antisemitism, which threatened the children on all sides, the teachers at the new Jewish school felt it their mission to uphold Jewish values. This was done neither from blind chauvinist self-assertiveness nor from fanaticism. There was a consensus that the school should not only be a school for Jewish children, but a Jewish school.

The teachers agreed that Jewish history, Judaism, the history of Palestine, and Hebrew belonged in the curriculum, but they had many different ideas about what Judaism was. They came from a variety of religious backgrounds ranging from orthodoxy to agnosticism; moreover, there were various types of Zionists and non-Zionists. Neither were the students homogeneous; different ideologies usually reflected different backgrounds. The typical German-Jewish middle class was religiously liberal and accepted Zionism slowly, if at all, whereas the East European lower middle classes and the workers usually were orthodox and Zionist.

Teachers from 'un-Jewish' homes, former civil servants who after many years of public service had lost their positions, were generally less rooted in Jewish traditions than those teachers who had been educated in Jewish teacher-training seminars. Several Düsseldorf teachers attempted to close the gaps in their Jewish education and many began to study modern Hebrew. For several years, their Hebrew teacher commuted once a week between Essen and Düsseldorf to assist them in learning this language. Several teachers had connections with the Zionist youth movement, which helped them in teaching about Palestine and in their personal contact with the children.

The solidarity among the students as well as with their teachers was extraordinarily strong. I still have letters expressing these feelings. For example, the student Margot Cohn who had moved to Berlin wrote to me on 19 July 1938: 'Do the boys and girls from my class revisit the school? I would be very happy to see all of them once again. When I look at our class photograph, I'd love to breathe life into each of them and speak with them for five minutes.' She also compared the Düsseldorf and Berlin schools in her letter: 'In my opinion, it is not easy to leave our Düsseldorf school, since it was something special.' She also spoke about one teacher at the Berlin school, the only one of her teachers whom she liked, reminding her of the Düsseldorf teaching staff. She wrote in a letter to her classmates: 'Who knows, if such a close-knit class could occur a second time?'

The feeling of community was strengthened by

occasional class outings to Bröhltalhaus, where the children could spend a few days in nature, since the Kasernenstrasse didn't even have a small patch of grass. For some, this was their only experience of nature in their childhood.

When in the beginning of November 1938, a 17 year old shot a German diplomat in Paris, the Jews expected revenge by the Nazis. Despite this, we were totally unprepared for the pogrom of 10 November which showed us as did no other operation after 1933 that the extermination of our people in Germany had begun. On that morning, I went as I did every day from my home to the school and saw to my horror that both the synagogue and school were in flames. The firemen protected the neighboring buildings, but did not extinguish the flames in the Jewish buildings. Thousands of people stood in the streets, but I saw no one grinning maliciously or expressing satisfaction through either words or gestures.

I went into the school director's office; the rooms were utterly vandalized: shards of glass, broken objects, books, and overturned shelves chaotically covered the floor – a picture of senseless and brutal destructiveness. A trembling Mrs. Herz said that uniformed Nazis had done this shortly before and that her husband had been arrested and taken away. She also knew that other Jewish men had been taken away in a truck. Together with my wife (whom I had married two and one half months before), I resolved to go into hiding in Cologne . . .

The school, as I knew and loved it, ended on 'Crystal Night.' Chaos followed in Jewish life, with more intensive emigration by some and despair for those unable to leave because the doors to other countries were increasingly closed. Kurt Schnook became the director of a substantially smaller school. An atmosphere of depression was apparent in the several letters he wrote to me in England and the United States. According to his description, in March 1941, there were still 52 students, of whom 11 (the entire eighth and ninth school years) departed at Easter. This school had almost 400 students several years earlier.

When I once again look at the letters from my students, probably the most moving one reached me indirectly via Palestine during the war, when we were already professors at American colleges. Melanie Lesekewitz was an especially sensitive and intelligent girl. She wrote on 5 September 1941: 'I am in Neumarkt in Dunajec, Cracow District. I have not been able to learn anything until now. I give German lessons, thus helping my parents and easing their fight for daily bread. My father works; my mother is ill. My sister also lacks much.' In another section of this letter, she said: 'The greater the distance and the longer the time from my sunny beautiful childhood, the more I long for my teachers and classmates, who were then

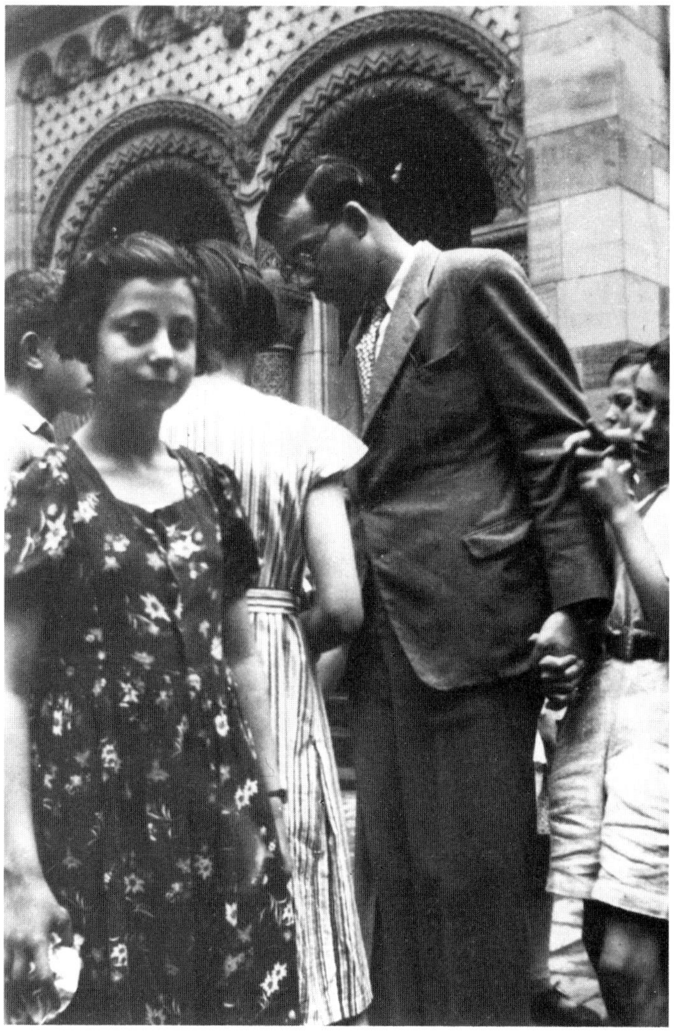

34 *Students and Teachers at the Private Jewish Elementary School in Düsseldorf* (Kurt Bergel)

close to me and understood me . . . I think often of you as the only person who knew my soul, heart, and mind and who could empathize with me as well as others in our close school community.'

When I read these words by a strong and sensitive girl, I ask myself how Melanie's life had ended.[32] *It can only have been a variation of the collective horror. Poor Melanie did not know how close Neumarkt was located to Auschwitz and Birkenau, nor what those places would mean shortly after she had written that letter. Melanie, like Anne Frank, remembered with youthful optimism the beautiful things she had experienced, while people – not only Jews – were degraded into objects and children cheated of their unlived lives.*

In January 1982, my wife and I visited Israel. Among the many friends we saw again, we met two of my former Düsseldorf students. I am quoting from my diary: 'David Ariel (formerly Kurt Lion) and Schmuel Tamir (formerly Günther Heymann) . . . visited us in Tel Aviv. David made a comment that meant more than he could know. Spontaneously he said that the Düsseldorf school in general and I in particular had then created for him and the other children an atmosphere of relative security amidst a world crumbling for their families and thus had given them direction and hope for a very uncertain future . . . Schmuel agreed with him.'

In this school, teachers and students had made a virtue of surviving the daily peril. We teachers responded to dangers of emotional illness, common to every ghetto existence, by trying to rescue our children unharmed for a future life in freedom. Under the pressure of circumstances, the pedagogical enterprise had to become a therapeutic one.

Schools like Düsseldorf were islands of temporary Jewish cultural autonomy. Although objectively questionable, these schools subjectively created for the individual student an important sense of security in a world threatened by Nazi inundation. These rapidly improvised and briefly flourishing institutions built with so much devotion were quickly destroyed. Together with the Jüdischer Kulturbund, *they were the cultural swan song of German Judaism.*

The Jewish school stood unter the administrative supervision of the municipal school authorities. The city also paid the teachers' salaries.[33] Dr. Herz recalled that the school board supervisor was an "extraordinarily decent" person, who apparently did not create additional difficulties to those already overwhelming the teachers.[34] Often, during inspections, the supervisor sat quietly in the back of the classroom. Dr. Herz could no longer remember that official's name, but it must have been the city school supervisor Dr. Johannes Schmitz, who died in February 1939. When visiting the Jewish school, Schmitz followed the maxim: "I have always found it painful that the teacher paled at my presence when I walked into a classroom. The soulless grandeur of an unapproachable superior never appealed to me."[35]

The following observation can be made about Dr. Herz's memories of the behavior of the school supervisor Dr. Schmitz: in a process of reversal, the "normal" became the extraordinary. Decency and correctness was – in the context of the Nazi system of injustice – reversed into something special and unexpected in the memories of Jews. Nevertheless, such decency or propriety should not be equated with an act of resistance.

At Easter 1936, the number of students grew to 400 and the enlargement of the attic floor was attempted. At the beginning of 1937, ninth and tenth grades were established. Kurt Herz explained the rationale for the addition of these classes in an article published on 2 January 1937 in the *Gemeindezeitung*.[36] To be sure, it is essential to read between the lines in order to judge how difficult it was to offer a meaningful school and career education for Jewish youth trapped in a no man's land between the alternatives of an increasingly hostile German milieu and the insecure and often unreachable world of the potential countries of refuge.

The question of a career choice is more difficult than ever before for Jewish youth, because a large number of careers are today closed to them or no longer have any meaning for the structure of their lives. It is now the task of the school to support parents and children with their decisions.

The number of apprentice positions is not large;

other training positions require longer school preparation than eight years of primary school. Thus, many female careers (as for example, kindergarten or technical teacher) require ten years of schooling. The Hachshara *usually presupposes a minimum age of fifteen.*

It is therefore essential to expand the Jewish school today in order to prepare the students for careers as part of their classroom instruction.

This is the purpose for establishing the ninth and tenth school years. The variety of subjects taught during the ninth school year should facilitate the career choice of our youth, since here they can determine whether and for which practical careers they are suited. It imparts to them practical skills as well as the advanced training which every Jewish youth today requires for life.

The tenth school year is especially for those students who are capable of receiving further theoretical education. Language instruction is especially important. In general, practical instruction will be given to the usual extent.

Classes are organized in our school by these criteria and include:

Ninth School Year

I. Theoretical Classes:

1. Judaism *(Hebrew and Bible Studies, General and Jewish History, History of Palestine and Contemporary Judaism).*
2. General Cultural Subjects *(German Literature, Composition, Art, Music, Geography, and Economics).*
3. Foreign Languages *(English and French).*
4. Mathematics and Natural Science *(Accounting and Mathematics, Biology and Hygiene).*
5. Stenography and Typing *(optional).*

II. Practical Courses:

1. Crafts *for boys (Wood and Metal Work).*
2. Needlework *for girls (Introductory Sewing, Cardboard and Light Woodwork).*
3. Home Economics *for Boys and Girls (Cooking, Materials, and Housework).*
4. Horticulture *for Boys and Girls.*

III. Physical Education

Tenth School Year

1. Judaism *(Hebrew, Bible Studies, General and Jewish History, Palestine Studies, and Contemporary Judaism).*
2. Cultural Subjects *(German Literature, Composition, Geography, and Economics).*
3. Foreign Languages *(English and Business English, French and Business French, and Spanish and Business Spanish [optional]).*
4. Mathematics and Natural Sciences *(Mathematics: Algebra and Geometry, Nature Study, and Biology).*
5. Practical Subjects *(Drawing and Art, Crafts, and Needlework).*
6. Music *(Voice, Theory, and Music History).*
7. Physical Education.

Two months later an article once again discussed these almost insoluble problems. One thing is very clear: it was the voice of responsible, deeply distressed individuals forced to serve as liquidators of the Jewish community:

To prepare our 14 to 18 year olds for emigration is increasingly and emphatically the goal for all job-training measures. Planning must be directed accordingly. We know that our young do not have the slightest possibility of finding their place professionally inside Germany. Therefore, while on the one hand we wish to shorten the duration of education for financial reasons, we realize on the other hand the necessity of making the most of these four years. At the same time, we recognize the tragic contradiction that the increasing impoverishment and shrinking mobility of the Jewish community in Germany are juxtaposed with the growing expenses necessary to care for youth between the ages of fourteen and eighteen.

Simultaneously, the desperate question emerges: how long will it be possible for the Jewish community in Germany, including help from our friends abroad, to fulfill the fundamental right of the young: to provide proper vocational training for them? . . .[57]

Furthermore, a special psychological and organizational problem lay in the strong numerical fluctuations of students as well as of teachers. Scarcely had one become familiar with the others, then one lost friends, companions, and also teachers who moved away, emigrated, or transferred into the *Hachshara*, the Jewish collective job training centers located in Germany and abroad.[38] Moreover, the number of students increased constantly; they came especially from smaller towns that had no Jewish school. There was also a steady increase of children with one non-Jewish parent, creating additional problems for the children themselves as well as for family members and teachers.[39] Consequently, the teachers tried to intensify a close working relationship between teachers, parents, and students.

Under the pressure of circumstance, the leitmotif of emigration recurred throughout the lives of these prematurely grown-up students. One student at a Hamburg Jewish school wrote in an essay about the theme "Your destiny is within yourself [Schiller]": "The main thing is to get out of this country."[40] Thus the children continuously discussed with utter seriousness the possibilities of Youth Aliyah, *Hachshara*, children's transports, and above all, immigration goals, quotas, and affidavit procedures.[41]

Youngsters were almost constantly confronted with the perplexity, helplessness, despair, and resignation of their families. Moreover, there was often the impending separation from their parents.

In school, one could escape this oppressive atmosphere for a while.

Wherever these children met and became a group, there was noise, feverish movement, and often hectic agitation. This exaggerated liveliness, approximating a constant state of excitement, corresponded to the unconscious wish to sublimate the shock they had experienced, to forget their parents' depression, and not to regain consciousness.[42]

In October 1937, one of the many continuing education conferences for teachers took place in Düsseldorf. The seriousness and commitment of the teachers is revealed in a short report published in the *Gemeindeblatt* of 23 October 1937, in which only very little could be explicitly stated:

Arrivals and departures inevitably caused strong disturbances. The difficulty of our fate was felt by children especially at home. A number of factors complicated school work considerably: the enormous differences of social background, of education, the differing talents of students, and also, the often outdated parental attitudes.

There was also an exhibition of works by students in the Düsseldorf Jewish school on the occasion of this conference. It included crafts, needlework, the results of cooking lessons, and also drawings. The following was reported in the *Gemeindeblatt* of 23 October 1937:

The drawings met with less approval; drawing from nature was totally absent (e. g. flowers, birds, fruits, etc.). There were also no recognizable drawings showing 'perspective,' although much was certainly not exhibited.

This relatively harsh criticism may have moved Julo Levin to present his ideas about what he tried to transmit to children in his art classes to a wider audience.[43] The following notice was published in the *Gemeindezeitung*:

Private Jewish elementary school exhibits students' works, accompanied by an introductory lecture, on Sunday, 21 November, from 11 A. M to 1 P. M. and 3 P. M. to 5:30 P. M. The Jewish school will exhibit art, crafts, needlework, and the products of cooking classes in the school building at Kasernenstrasse 67. Julo Levin will present an introductory lecture, 'Art Instruction in the School,' at 11 A. M. Parents and friends of the school are cordially invited to this event.

Did he succeed? Was this criticism part of the reason why he left Düsseldorf and moved to Berlin? Was it his position as an outsider, which he apparently held at the school? Julo Levin had virtually no personal connections to the other teachers according to Prof. Kurt Bergel's reminiscences:

I had the feeling that he didn't really feel well in a Jewish school, because Judaism was probably distant to him. I could be wrong. But since Levin was only *the art teacher, he stood a bit on the periphery of the school. School was not the center of his life (as it was for the majority of teachers). Probably his art was central to him. I believe that he was not primarily a teacher but an artist, which does not mean that he wasn't a good teacher.*[44]

The very last teachers' continuing education conference took place in Düsseldorf one year later in August 1938. At that time, a book edited by the teacher Heinemann Stern, *Didactics in Jewish Schools, (Didaktik der jüdischen Schule)*, was published in Berlin. It summarized both theoretical considerations and practical work. It included a contribution by Dr. Beatrice Strauss about the ninth school year for girls. Dr. Strauss, certified as a business teacher, had taught at the Düsseldorf Jewish school until she moved to the Jewish school in Essen. She was later deported from Essen and murdered. Her energetic appeal for female education as a prerequisite for emigration will be quoted below and can be considered as her intellectual legacy. It stated:[45]

The difficulties of male children are today recognized and acknowledged by parents as well as by all other organizations interested in their education. This has proved more difficult for girls, in part because of social factors that must be stated explicitly, i. e.: the contradictory interests of the older generation living in Germany and the younger generation trying to reach Palestine and other countries. The prohibition against employing Aryan female servants under the age of 45 has resulted in an acute absence of Jewish domestics. In some instances, this has been compensated by taking girls who have left school into household work. Employers are happy to have even the most minimal help. In other cases, fourteen year old daughters are taken out of school to assist their mothers, who are not used to coping with housekeeping by themselves. We must make it clear that we must also educate our girls for emigration. Female youngsters must also be accorded the same opportunities as males. We may not hold them here for selfish reasons and they also cannot be held back here . . .

As future wives of emigrants, our girls often have double duties. They will not only become housewives and mothers in utterly different economic and social conditions, but will often also be breadwinners for their families, since in several countries there are more job opportunities for women than for men. The personal and social behavior of the emigrant woman is a significant factor against spiritual and social decline into economic indigence in foreign countries.

If women are to be strong enough to maintain their own position as well as their family, they must have spiritual and intellectual reserves on which they can draw. The most important educational task for our girls, besides actual vocational training, is to create these resources.

In the same book, there is a section called "local history" *(Heimatkundliche Anschauung)* in the longer chapter about German language instruction *(Deutschunterricht)*, written by Heinemann Stern. One reads it with some uneasiness. It is not an accident that the old familiar word *Heimat* is absent. What in fact was *Heimat* or "home" for these children?

A sample lesson for the second school year suggests a walk through Jewish homes to point out everything one could see there . . . At no point in that volume, which in itself represents a memorial of enormous courage, a memorial to "spiritual resistance," is it more evident how confined and narrow the concept of *Heimat* (literally meaning both home and Fatherland) had become. Actually such a *Heimat* no longer existed for Jews, since the Nazis had already robbed both parents and children of their "homes," while they were still in Germany. All that had remained were their dwellings and synagogues. A sample lesson for the first school year suggested a visit to a synagogue:

Our class visits a nearby synagogue. The room is empty. An unusual silence. The teacher speaks; the words sound different than usual in the empty temple. We sit quietly and sing the Sch'ma. Even today, God listens to our voices. God knows we want to be good Jews and observe the commandments. But we still must learn a great deal; we want to learn to read Hebrew soon. There is a slate with Hebrew script. And high above there is a tablet with the ten commandments. How beautiful it is here. There is a large candelabrum, fine covers, and curtains . . .[46]

Two months after the publication of Stern's volume, even these remaining parts of their "home" *(Heimat)* were destroyed and lost.

In May 1938, there were still sixteen public Jewish elementary school with 2,250 Jewish students in the Rhineland. Further, there were an additional 732 students with one non-Jewish parent ("Jews of mixed blood"). In Germany, ca. 14,000 children of Jewish religion and 7,000 children with one non-Jewish parent attended Jewish elementary schools.[47]

What child had not at some time during his or her school days longingly wished not to have to go to school – perhaps because of a bad conscience or fear of classroom assignments? The following report by Dvora Diskin of Atlit, Israel, is printed below in slightly abridged form. It reveals her unusually precise and lively childhood reminiscences. As a small child, she had attended the Düsseldorf Jewish school.[48]

I am writing this to honor the memory of my teachers. It is interesting how the impressions of my suddenly interrupted childhood remain sharply etched in memory. Today, I am almost 62 years old. I can recall my Jewish kindergarten in Grafenberger Allee. I adored my kindergarten teachers: Rosa Tawrogi, Hilde Stiel, and Aunt Thea, the cook . . . Thanks to this education (based on the Montessori system), I could already mix colors and draw at the age of five; I could bind books, listen to classical music, learn by heart and recite, sew and mend, and much more. No child was ever hit or punished. This marvelous kindergarten provided a broad basis for my subsequent education. Although I remember the names of all my Jewish teachers, I cannot recall other teachers' names either from Düsseldorf or in Belgium, where I attended school after the November 1938 pogrom. After kindergarten, I attended the Protestant school in Helmholtzstrasse. I can only remember one thing about it: I was often hit on the hand with a ruler, because I didn't read or write correctly. This was also true for the other children; that school was hell for me.

At the end of 1935, Dvora Diskin had transferred to the Jewish elementary school.

This was a relief for me. Children were never beaten there . . . My teacher was Dr. Nussbaum; she also taught English, mathematics, and German literature. Mr. Bergel taught history and geography. Assistant Rabbi Dr. Klein instructed us in religion.[49] *(The Chief Rabbi Dr. Eschelbacher did not teach at the school.) Mr. Vogel was our voice and music teacher. He also conducted the synagogue choir as well as many other musical performances. Julo Levin taught art. I remember all of my revered teachers; almost all of these teachers were murdered by the Nazis.*

The teachers were the best . . . I especially remember Miss Nussbaum, who trained us with a smile in mental arithmetic. This included problems such as $2 + 2 + 4 \times 5 + 6.2$ equals what? She only smiled if I didn't know an answer and then asked the other children. She would interrupt other lessons to suddenly give us such a problem. We all excelled in arithmetic until we left school, a skill that is still with me. This thoroughness was also true for all other subjects we studied. The only subject we didn't like was religion.

All the children had agreed that each time during religion classes, a different child would play a prank. It was my turn. I had brought ground pepper with me from home. When Dr. Klein had turned his back to the class to write a sentence on the blackboard, I blew a handful of pepper into the air. We all began to sneeze, laugh, and cough. Dr. Klein quickly opened a window. As soon as we had settled down again, we said we were cold and Dr. Klein closed the window. I asked Dr. Klein very innocently if he would again write the sentence on the blackboard. I again blew a handful of pepper into the air and Dr. Klein got pepper dust in his face when he turned around. Like all of us, he began to sneeze and cough. The class went wild. He ordered me to get out; and while sneezing and laughing, I left the classroom. I felt cold in the hallway and knocked on the classroom door, saying 'I'll be good again,' and burst out laughing with my classmates. Dr. Klein again told me to get out. The school director, Dr. Herz, suddenly appeared and asked me why I was in the corridor. 'Dr. Klein kicked me out.' Dr. Herz knocked on the door, which opened suddenly and he was pushed away, since Dr. Klein had assumed that I had again knocked on the door. I started laughing once again. Dr. Herz, whom I greatly respected, told me: 'Dora, go home; you won't be readmitted without your father!' My father was away on a business trip and would only return home the day after tomorrow. I was deeply worried and that evening begged God to help me. The next morning our doorbell rang fiercely. It was our neighbor's son: 'Mrs. Moritz, the children can't go to school, because the synagogue is burning.' I couldn't believe my ears. Mother allowed me to run to school, where I saw the horrible fire. I saw my school burn! Dear God, I hadn't wanted this to happen.

This is the first time I have written about these memories. For many years, I felt the pangs of my conscience and repeatedly dreamed about the school and the burning synagogue and the horrible Crystal Night.

More than 400 synagogues were burned and destroyed between 9 and 11 November 1938; more than 90 Jews were murdered, thousands beaten up, and nearly 30,000 Jewish men were deported to the concentration camps of Dachau, Buchenwald, and Sachsenhausen. Innumerable prayer rooms, businesses, and homes were also vandalized. Mass flight began from Germany. During the last few months prior to the beginning of the war, as many people fled or emigrated from Germany as during the previous five and a half years.

In Düsseldorf, where the vom Rath family resided, "spontaneous popular rage" – in reality, organized by the government – was particularly brutal and frenzied. At least three people were murdered and more than seventy injured had to be sent to hospitals.[50]

Only one sentence, containing veiled reference to these terrible events, could appear in the *Arbeitsbericht des Zentralausschusses für Hilfe und Aufbau:* ". . . Nineteen thirty-eight represented an historic turning point in Jewish fate."[51] German Jews, long since forced to become Jews in Germany, were condemned to almost complete silence. The sole Jewish newspaper, the *Jüdisches Nachrichtenblatt,* scarcely deserving this name, was published under strict censorship and official control in Berlin. It included scanty notices about the subsequent fate of the Düsseldorf Jewish community and the Jewish school.

The Düsseldorf synagogue community was compelled to pay for the demolition of the synagogue and school buildings and to sell this property to the city. The *Rheinische Landeszeitung* reported on 2 December 1938:

The Kasernenstrasse synagogue, offensive to all German Volksgenossen *(racial comrades) for many years, will now disappear shortly. Popular outrage about the cowardly and foul Jewish assassination of the Embassy Councillor Ernst vom Rath was, as is well known, directed primarily against the Jewish temple during the night of 9–10 November . . . Demolition work already began yesterday. We hope that the Jewish school will be removed at the same time . . . The citizens of Düsseldorf no longer wish to be reminded of those former times when the Jew* (Juda) *brazenly raised his head in Germany . . .*

In March 1939, under massive pressure the synagogue site was sold for the ludicrous price of 191,870 Reich Marks. The city subtracted the enormous sum of 75,000 Marks for demolition costs. Siegfried Falk, then chairman of the Jewish community, attempted to obtain concessions by negotiations and numerous letters:

We request a substantial reduction of the assessed demolition costs for the sake of fairness, since effective 1 January 1939 all indemnification by the city of Düsseldorf for Jewish welfare recipients has ceased. Apart from our expenses for emigration assistance, the removal of former municipal subsidies to Jewish schools, and the cessation of rental tax abatements, we must moreover carry additional costs for all sanatoria and hospitals, including long-term patients. We are not even granted reduced welfare rates, but must on the contrary pay the full costs. All reductions have also ceased for the various homes for the aged and similar institutions.

Consequently our monthly expenditures for these purposes have escalated to such heights, that despite a sharp reduction in the number of residents, we must

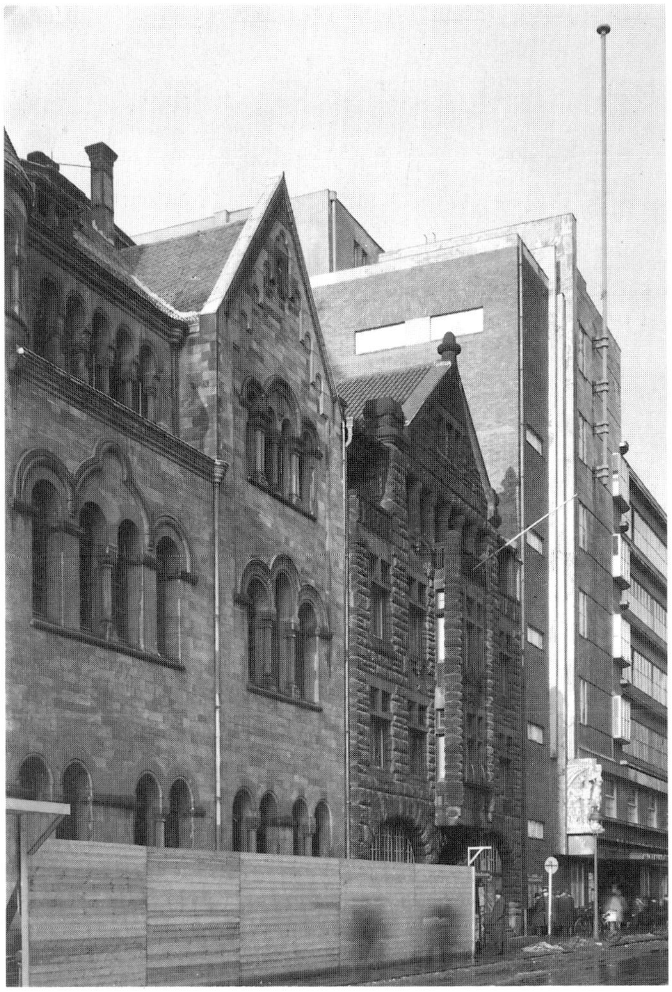

35 *The Rabbi's House on Kasernenstrasse in Düsseldorf before Demolition*, 1939 (Stadtmuseum Düsseldorf)

now pay monthly approximately what we formerly paid for an entire year . . . We therefore entreat you to understand our situation and in this connection request that you waive a significant portion of the demolition costs initially mentioned . . .[52]

In response to Siegfried Falk's description of the financial emergency and his request that the city be conciliatory about the arbitrarily high demolition assessment, the official in charge noted in the margin: "Has nothing to do with the matter."

In November 1939, the municipal surveyor's office complained that remnants of wallpaper were still attached to remains of the gabled roof at the site of the Jewish school that meanwhile had been torn down. "In the interest of the appearance of the street, it is requested that these remains be removed." The marginalia this time stated: "Won't work!"[53]

The last traces of the beautiful synagogue and school were removed at the latest in 1941, when the city – with the help of Jewish forced labor – built an air raid shelter on this site.[54]

What had meanwhile happened to the school and its students? In November and December 1938, new legislative regulations mandated that Jewish students could no longer attend German public schools. Furthermore, the provisions of the Tenth Decree Implementing the Reich Citizenship Law of 4 July 1939 transferred Jewish schools to the exclusive responsibility of the *Reichsvereinigung der Juden* (the successor organization of the *Reichsvertretung*). The Jewish communities now had to carry all costs for schools, just as Siegfried Falk had written. Jewish schools thus attained virtually complete autonomy in educational matters, although parents' evenings and similar meetings required Gestapo permission.

The school found a new home at Grafenberger Allee 78. Since 1923, this villa had belonged to the Düsseldorf Lodge of the Independent Order of B'nai B'rith. After 1926, the upper floors of this building contained the day-care-center and kindergarten of which Dvora Diskin had so many happy memories. After the destruction of the synagogue, religious services were also held at this address. The community administrative offices were located at Bilker Strasse 25. It required at least a thirty minute walk to go between these two islands of remaining Jewish communal life in Düsseldorf.

The communal welfare office looked in despair for families who could house non-resident students. In October 1939, 66 children still attended school.[55] It was reported in the *Jüdisches Nachrichtenblatt* that all candidates for Youth Aliyah as well as for domestic and foreign *Hachshara* had to pass Hebrew courses.

There were also still Bar Mitzvah celebrations in the community. On 19 August 1939, Isi Magier celebrated his Bar Mitzvah.[56] The only reference to him is a small notice in the *Nachrichtenblatt* and one of the drawings; he was deported and murdered together with his parents two years later. Two weeks after his thirteenth birthday, the war began. This meant the demise of all emigration efforts for most Jews still living in Germany. It also meant that they were no longer only objects for persecution and robbery, but that during the war they would also become vulnerable to extermination. The Jewish New Year, Rosh Hashanah, fell during the first week of September. The year 5700 had begun. In the 5 September 1939 issue of the *Nachrichtenblatt*, as in all subsequent issues, it was forbidden to mention the war, the anguish and despair, with even a single word. Above all, one could not in any way hint at the anxious hope for the defeat of Hitler's dictatorship. This is all hidden behind the laconic reference that Jews now stood at the "turning point to a new Jewish century."

In October 1939, the *Reichsvertretung* requested that the communities complete questionnaires for all Jews between the ages of 16 and 55. These documents are no longer to be found. Nevertheless, the City Archives *(Stadtarchiv)* has a document indicating that 1,400 Jews still lived in Düsseldorf in December 1940.[57] In the spring of 1940, the children had organized a small celebration at the conclusion of the school year with recitations, small performances, dialogues, and choral music. In retrospect, one reads with uneasiness the remark that "everything offered revealed the best school spirit and preparation for life."[58]

Shortly thereafter in May 1940, the first large air raid on Düsseldorf occurred. Where did the children, the teachers, and the many other people who were in the old villa or who resided in the adjacent garden house on Grafenberger Allee find shelter? Siegfried Falk, the chairman of the Jewish community, was also responsible for air raid shelters. On 26 June 1940, he wrote to the Police President, who was responsible for local air raid protection. His letter concerned the breach in a fire safety wall in the basement of Grafenberger Allee 78, where obviously the air raid shelter for students and other residents was located. For today's readers, that inconspicuous document is instructive in a frightening way. The letterhead used by Siegfried Falk read "Executive of the Jewish Religious Association of the Düsseldorf Synagogue Community, Bilker Strasse 25." The responsible city official had crossed through these words with a thick colored pencil and written, either in outrage or amazement: "This sort of thing still exists?!"[59]

The Jewish community executive could barely cope with the ever-increasing administrative work; it had already been transformed into a virtually powerless instrument of the Gestapo. Every day there were new regulations, edicts, and orders.[60] Destitution also increased steadily. There were no adequate means to support all those in need. Volunteer collectors went twice a month to all Jewish households in Düsseldorf. Despite everything, the former banker Siegfried Falk nevertheless bravely learned English and how to type. Other members of the community tried to acquire practical skills that would serve better as prerequisites for the emigration they so fervently desired.

The conveyance of mail abroad became more and more difficult due to ever stricter controls and restrictions. Many letters written during those months never reached their intended recipients or did so only after a delay of many months. On 9 December 1940, Siegfried Falk typed a letter to his son that "more than four pages will not be forwarded." The women had set up dressmaking, millinery, and hairdressing courses. The availability of Spanish classes also reveals the hope for emigration, although after the beginning of war and until the general emigration prohibition of 25 October 1941 only a few privileged individuals could still achieve this.

Edith Falk wrote in a letter on 18 January 1941:

All my dear ones! . . . My classes and work help me very much, even if one asks once again: For what? . . . And where will we finally be driven? Siegfried learns English and typing very diligently, but here too, I have to ask: For what? . . . It is a completely futile life and existence without any perspective and one doesn't want to know anything about the future. Never again to see my dear children, grandchildren, siblings, and friends and to die miserably! This *will assuredly be the outcome!*[60]

One learns something about the Jewish students from one of Edith Falk's last letters to "all her dear ones." The letter is undated, but must have been written at the end of 1940, around the time of Hanukkah. The Falks visited various old-age homes and school celebrations for lighting the Hanukkah candles. "There are still 55 students here."

Moreover, it is clear from Professor Bergel's essay that, in March 1941, 42 children still attended the Jewish school. At that time there were still 1,406 Jews "registered on lists"; 49 of them with one non-Jewish spouse. It is possible that this figure would have been higher, since no data was given about the deceased spouses of the widows and widowers listed. Of those 1,406 Jews, there were still 108 children and adolescents born in 1920 or thereafter.[61]

The Ministry for Science and Education *(Reichsministerium für Wissenschaft, Erziehung und Volksbildung)* ordered the closing of all Jewish schools as of 30 June 1942. The schooling of Jewish children through paid or voluntary teachers was thereafter prohibited. "This finally ended the macabre juxtaposition of the beginnings of mass murder alongside legally mandated and state-controlled compulsory school education as preparation for life."[62] For the Düsseldorf Jewish school children and their teacher Kurt Schnook, the journey into destruction had already begun when compulsory schooling for Jewish children had still been required. Six months before schooling for Jewish children was prohibited in Düsseldorf, there was – as stated at the beginning of this essay – no school anymore. When Siegfried Falk wrote that letter in which he stated: "There is no school anymore," two large Jewish transports had already left on 27 October and 10 November 1941, deporting Düsseldorf Jews to Lodź (then called Litzmannstadt) and Minsk. A third transport was in preparation. In December 1941, Edith and Siegfried Falk committed suicide with an overdose of veronal. Their secretary, Hildegard Eltzbacher, wrote in a letter to Switzerland: "We want to grant them rest." Shortly thereafter, she too was deported and murdered.

Nothing is known about the last days of the students and of their teachers, or of the couple Kurt and Thea Schnook. He was "a very quiet person, who found it somewhat difficult to control us, being such lively children, but he never lost his composure . . . I still remember his pale face very clearly."[63] The Schnooks' desperate efforts to emigrate were condemned to failure as was the case with so many others.

"Education as spiritual resistance" is the heading that Joseph Walk has given to this chapter of Jewish history, that ended with the violent death of both teachers and students:

Completely conscious of their responsibility, the teachers saw no other possibility than following their theory as if, which also stood behind the pedagogical program of the great Polish Jewish educator Janusz Korczak. Or ought the teachers have prepared their students for death and bloodshed in the face of the approaching destruction? . . .[64]

All that remains are a few memories, a picture, the words that Kurt and Thea Schnook wrote into the *Poesiealbum* [similar to an autograph album, but containing lines or verses of an original or copied poem, Ed.] of one of their young students, Gisela Wolf.[65]

Who were the children who attended the Jewish school and what was their fate? It is only because most of the drawings were signed that we could identify or reconstruct the names of 290 students. Nothing is known about 123 of them at this time. Some of the names are illegible. Other names were probably those of Berlin students, although this frequently cannot be determined. Obviously, many of those youngsters had been commuters, residing outside Düsseldorf. Others were children with one non-Jewish parent, about whom scarcely anything can be discovered in the documentary project "Biographical Data of Düsseldorf Jews."

We have established more information about 166 Düsseldorf students. One hundred and fifty parents and siblings of these students were murdered by the Nazis; 43 of those 166 students were also killed.

The fate of these children surpasses our imagination. Their drawings are the only tangible link to their remembrance.

Notes

The author would like to express her gratitude to the following individuals for their generosity and trust and for sharing information, documents, and photographs with her: Prof. Dr. Kurt Bergel, Orange, CA; Dvora Diskin, Atlit, Israel; Ilse Eton, St. Leonards-on-Sea, England; Dr. Frank Falk, London; Dr. Salo Gottdiener, Haifa; Mira Guttmann, Kiryat Bialik, Israel; Dr. Kurt Herz and Ellen Herz, New York; Gloria N. Lachmann, Houston; Ms. K. H. Regent, Newport-on-Tay, Scotland; and Seev Weiss, Hazorea, Israel. I also want to thank Prof. Dr. Hugo Wiedenhaupt and his colleagues at the Stadtarchiv Düsseldorf; Roth Roecher, Siegen; Dr. Annette Baumeister of the Stadtmuseum Düsseldorf; and Dr. Sybil Milton, Chevy Chase, MD, for their fruitful and collegial collaboration.

Abbreviations:

StA Düss	Stadtarchiv Düsseldorf
Gemeindezeitung	*Gemeindezeitung für den Synagogenbezirk Düsseldorf*
Gemeindeblatt	*Jüdisches Gemeindeblatt für den Synagogenbezirk* (after August 1937)

1 StA Düss: V 2763.
2 Ibid.: V 2763; II 727.
3 Copies of these letters courtesy Dr. Frank Falk, London.
4 Questions and correspondence may be sent to the author, c/o Kulturamt Düsseldorf, Ehrenhof 3 or at the Stadtmuseum Düsseldorf, Bäckerstrasse 7–9.
5 *Jahresberichte des Statistischen Amtes der Stadt Düsseldorf*, 1939.
6 According to statistics published in the *Gemeindezeitung*, 5 Aug. 1933, the number of community members was 5,624. The reason for this somewhat larger figure is that it probably includes community members who resided outside the city limits.
7 *Jahresberichte* 1935. These statistics are based on the racial definition of "Jews."
8 Information provided by Dr. Salo Gottdiener, Haifa.
9 *Gemeindezeitung* no. 5 (15 Nov. 1930).
10 Ibid., no. 12 (21 Feb. 1931).
11 Ibid.
12 Ibid., no. 9 (10 Jan. 1930).
13 Ibid., no. 10 (24 Jan. 1931).
14 Ibid., no. 5 (10 Dec. 1932).
15 Reinhard Rürup, "Das Ende der Emanzipation: Die antijüdische Politik in Deutschland vor der 'Machtergreifung' bis zum zweiten Weltkrieg," in: Arnold Paucker, ed., *Die Juden im nationalsozialistischen Deutschland: The Jews in Nazi Germany, 1933–1943* (Tübingen, 1986) p. 99.
16 Fred Grubel, "Geleitwort," idem, p. viii.
17 *Gemeindezeitung* no. 19 (24 June 1933).
18 Ibid.
19 Ibid.
20 Ibid., no. 8 (6 Jan. 1934).
21 Information communicated to the author, Sept. 1987; see also *Biographisches Handbuch der deutschsprachigen Emigration nach 1933*, vol. 1, p. 289.
22 *Gemeindezeitung* no. 13 (16 March 1935).
23 Ibid., no. 17 (11 May 1935).
24 *Jüdische Rundschau* no. 94 (22 Nov. 1935), p. 4.
25 Hannele Zürndorfer, *The Ninth of November* (London, Melbourne, and New York, 1983), pp. 48–49; the German edition is entitled *Verlorene Welt: Eine Kindheit im Dritten Reich* (Pfaffenweiler, 1988). Zürndorfer's extensive erasure of childhood memories in Nazi Germany could be confirmed by numerous conversations with her contemporaries, who also had to survive very bad times as children. Her parents, Adolf and Else Zürndorfer, were deported and murdered. Her father, Adolf Zürndorfer, after losing his job, began to organize the archives of the Düsseldorf Schauspielhaus for Gustav Lindemann, known today as the Dumont Lindemann Archive. He also built the community library under the most difficult conditions and had amassed 2,000 books by 1937; see *Gemeindezeitung* no. 6 (20 Nov. 1937). It is astonishing to what extent Hannele's childhood impressions of the Düsseldorf Jewish school corresponded to similar experiences of Hans Gärtner, a teacher and deputy director of the Theodor Herzl School in Berlin until 1939. See Hans Gärtner, "Probleme der jüdischen Schule während der Hitlerjahre," in: Robert Weltsch, ed., *Deutsches Judentum: Aufstieg und Krise* (Stuttgart, 1963); translated and published in English in *Leo Baeck Institute Yearbook* 1 (1956): pp. 123–41.
26 Werner T. Angress, *Generation zwischen Furcht und Hoffnung: Jüdische Jugend im Dritten Reich* (Hamburg, 1985), p. 17; idem, "Jüdische Jugend zwischen nationalsozialistischer Verfolgung und jüdischer Wiedergeburt," in: Paucker, ed., *The Jews in Nazi Germany*, p. 214.
27 Zürndorfer, *The Ninth of November*, p. 47.
28 The completion certificate *(Abgangszeugnis)* is the only school document located until now and was sent to me by Seev Weiss, Hazorea, Israel.
29 This was part of the 15 Sept. 1935 Law for the Protection of German Blood and Honor. Together with the Reich Citizenship Law, these formed the so-called Nuremberg Laws.
30 This essay will be published in unabridged form in: Barbara Suchy, *Die Geschichte der Düsseldorfer Juden von den*

Anfängen bis zur Gegenwart, working title of a book in preparation.

31 The names of the teachers and their fates are found on p. 104

32 Melanie, her sister Lydia, and her parents, Viktor Lezerkewitz and Betty, née Haupt, held Polish citizenship and were probably expelled from Germany on 27–28 Oct. 1938. A total of ca. 18,000 people with Polish passports were expelled from Germany, 361 of them from Düsseldorf. Melanie's mother had been born in Oświęcim (Auschwitz), and it is probable that her family returned there after their expulsion from the Reich. Much however remains unclear. The last meager entry in Düsseldorf read: "Moved on 8 May 1941; address unknown." The names of all four family members are found in the Bundesarchiv (Koblenz) *Gedenkbuch*. The parents were murdered in Auschwitz; the places and dates of death for both daughters are unknown. For the expulsion of Polish Jews, see: StA Düss. XXIII, Report by Rabbi Dr. Eschelbacher and Sybil Milton, "The Expulsion of Polish Jews from Germany, October 1938 to July 1939: A Documentation," in: *Leo Baeck Institute Yearbook* 29 (1984): pp. 169–200.

33 Mandatory school attendance for Jewish students existed even after many Jews, including children, had already been deported. Jewish schools received a broad degree of autonomy only in March 1939. See Joseph Walk, *The Education of the Jewish Child in Nazi Germany: The Law and its Execution* (Jerusalem, 1975), in Hebrew; Germania Judaica, Cologne, has an English manuscript summary of this monograph. A good survey of the legal and organizational development is found in: Ruthy Roecher, "Die Entwicklung eines jüdischen Schulwesens im Dritten Reich," Diplomarbeit, Universität und Gesamthochschule Siegen, 1983; Ms. Roecher is currently completing her dissertation on this subject.

34 Letter from Dr. Kurt Herz to the author, Sept. 1987.

35 *Düsseldorfer Tageblatt* no. 45 (14 Febr. 1939).

36 *Gemeindezeitung* no. 8 (2 Jan. 1937).

37 Ibid. no. 13 (13 March 1937).

38 *Hachshara* (pl. *Hachsharot*) literally means "to make useful," or training. In 1936, there were more than 40 of these training centers in Germany, where agriculture, gardening, crafts, and homemaking were taught. The best known were the Gartenbauschule Ahlem near Hanover, Gross-Breesen in Silesia, Winkel near Spreenhagen, Schniebinchen in Brandenburg, and Neuendorf near Fürstenwalde. They were attended by Düsseldorf adolescents between the ages of 14 and 18. A survey of these training centers, that also includes foreign centers, is found in: *Arbeitsbericht des Zentralausschusses für Hilfe und Aufbau bei der Reichsvertretung der Juden in Deutschland* (1939), pp. 152–59.

39 Walk, *The Education of the Jewish Child*, p. x.

40 Idem, "Jüdische Kinderaufsätze und Kinderbriefe im Nazi-Deutschland," *Bildung und Erziehung* 33 (1980): p. 348.

41 Youth Aliyah: *Aliyah* means "going upward." It is the Zionist designation for immigration to Palestine or Israel. Children's transports were organized by Jewish welfare organizations in Germany and abroad, and permitted Jewish children without parents to emigrate to Palestine, England, the United States, the Netherlands, etc. It increased dramatically after the November 1938 pogrom. Affidavits were maintenance guarantees provided by sufficiently wealthy citizens in the country where the immigrants landed.

42 Hans Gärtner, "Probleme der jüdischen Schule während der Hitlerjahre," p. 335.

43 *Gemeindeblatt* no. 6 (20 Nov. 1937); according to this announcement a second exhibition of students' drawings took place in November. Many of the children's drawings from the Stadtmuseum collection were already displayed in both 1937 exhibitions. This is revealed by residual strips of paper pasted on the backs of many drawings.

44 Letter from Prof. Dr. Bergel to the author, 22 Sept. 1987. It must be noted as both an addendum and correction that Julo Levin had a close personal relationship with Dr. Beatrice Strauss and Dr. Thea Nussbaum, both teachers at the Düsseldorf Jewish school; information courtesy Mieke Monjau.

45 Heinemann Stern, *Didaktik der jüdischen Schule* (Berlin, n. d. [1938]), pp. 52–3.

46 Ibid., pp. 168–74.

47 *Arbeitsbericht* (1938), p. 74.

48 Letter to the author, 2 Sept. 1987.

49 The deputy rabbi, Dr. Siegfried Klein, was the real "pastor" of the community; this was repeatedly mentioned in conversations by many former community members. Apart from his many other duties, he also edited the *Gemeindezeitung* between 1930 and Nov. 1938 and probably wrote the majority of articles himself. Both he and his wife were deported and murdered.

50 Angelika Voigt and Falk Wiesemann, *Juden in Düsseldorf: Die Zerstörung der jüdischen Gemeinde während der nationalsozialistischen Herrschaft* (Münster, 1983), part of the series "Geschichte original 1," p. 9.

51 *Arbeitsbericht* (1938), p. 104.

52 StA Düss: III 20785, pp. 43–45.

53 Ibid.: VI 17289.

54 After the war began, Jewish men and later also women were assigned to Jewish labor groups compelled to perform various jobs, especially very difficult physical labor. They participated in building the air-raid bunker in Kasernenstrasse according to Günter Katzenstein, who was assigned to this job. Mr. Katzenstein, Stockholm, is one of the very few survivors of the deportations to Minsk.

55 *Jüdisches Nachrichtenblatt*, 14 April 1939; *Arbeitsbericht* (1939), p. 53.

56 *Bar Mitzvah* literally means "child of the commandment." Jewish males undergo this ceremony on their thirteenth birthday, thereby becoming mature members of the community.

57 StA Düss: IV 12317.

58 *Jüdisches Nachrichtenblatt* no. 28 (5 April 1940).
59 Bauamt der Stadt Düsseldorf: Hausakten, Grafenberger Allee 78.
60 Joseph Walk and Dan Brecher, ed., *Das Sonderrecht für die Juden im NS-Staat: Eine Sammlung der gesetzlichen Massnahmen und Richtlinien, Inhalt und Bedeutung* (Heidelberg and Karlsruhe, 1981).
61 StA Düss: IV 12315.
62 Roecher, "Die Entwicklung eines jüdischen Schulwesens im Dritten Reich," p. 61.
63 Letter from K. H. Regent (Hannele Zürndorfer) to the author, 10 Sept. 1987.
64 Walk, "Erziehung als geistiger Widerstand," p. 245.
65 Mr. and Mrs. Norbert Lachmann (née Gisela Wolf from Gerresheim) donated her two poetry albums to the Stadtmuseum Düsseldorf; they are moving documents from her simultaneously protected and endangered childhood. Schnook had written in Gisela's Album in February 1937: "One requires three things above all: power, understanding, and will."

Dreams, Hopes, and Realities

Annette Baumeister

The Stadtmuseum Düsseldorf (the Düsseldorf City Museum) has for several years held a collection of more than 1,200 drawings by German-Jewish school children. These pages had formerly belonged to the artist Julo Levin. In the mid-1930s, he had already given more than 450 pictures as a gift to his friend, the artist Carl Lauterbach (Figs. 43, 45), who was also interested in children's art. Levin kept the remaining works for himself.

Mieke Monjau has previously described in her reminiscences the dramatic rescue operation that saved the students' drawings once owned by Julo Levin. Carl Lauterbach had stored his share of the collection in Burscheid, along with his own extensive collection of art and documents hidden from seizure by the Gestapo.[1] The children's and students' drawings from Lauterbach's collection were acquired by the Stadtmuseum after the city of Düsseldorf received the Lauterbach Archive in 1982. Mieke Monjau donated 750 works from her collection to the Stadtmuseum in 1983.

The largest part of these works was made in the art classes that Julo Levin had taught at the Düsseldorf Jewish School (1936–1938) and at the Kaliski and Holdheim Schools in Berlin (1938–1941). Since Levin had reported a change of address to Berlin to the police on 21 April 1938, we must assume that all pictures dated after April 1938 were made in Berlin.

The surviving drawings reveal the variety of materials and techniques used in teaching art to children. For children younger than ten years old, there are pencil, crayon, and pastel chalk drawings; for older students, there are also watercolors, collages, and transparencies. Although younger children worked with various types of paper, the most common material was regular reinforced art paper. Occasionally the cardboard covers of a sketch pad were used, although they were less suitable because of their rough surfaces. That these works were genuinely made by schoolchildren is in part clear from the many notations on the backs of the drawings, including class, date, and mark received.

Many drawings also carry the names of the students, but some of these names were written in adult handwritings. These clues enable us to investigate the fate of these individuals. Many were murdered in concentration camps and killing centers; others left Germany together with their parents or alone on "children's transports," expelled from their homes and compelled to begin anew in foreign countries. Several of the surviving students of the Düsseldorf Jewish elementary school have corresponded with Dr. Barbara Suchy, whose essay in this volume describes the fate of the Düsseldorf school and its students.

When Julo Levin began to teach art at the private Jewish elementary school in Düsseldorf in 1936, he had already survived three years of persecution and constant danger, since the Nazis suspected that he was a supporter of the Communist Party. He kept silent about this personal danger with his students.

The full gravity of the psychological situation of German Jewish children in 1936 can today only be partly known or reconstructed. Parents were concerned and depressed, often without giving their children the details or reasons. Close friends suddenly avoided their company, sometimes becoming hostile, unfriendly, and even spiteful. German Jewish students, often without fully understanding the reasons, were forced to leave their familiar schools to attend a new all Jewish school located on the Kasernenstrasse in Düsseldorf. For many, this change of schools meant long commutes, which in turn caused constant fear for their parents. The former Düsseldorfer Hannele Zürndorfer movingly described the oppressive atmosphere in her memoirs, *The Ninth of November,*[2] when terror lurked just below the surface but could not be openly expressed because of the Olympics. Hostility was still limited to slogans like "Jews not wanted here" and antisemitic agitation was left to extremist tabloids like the *Stürmer* and the *Volksparole.*

But even Düsseldorf contributed to discrimination against its Jewish citizens. The Düsseldorf art publisher J. Knippenberg published in 1933 a new edition of the 1895 antisemitic tract *The Song of Levi,* with text by Eduard Schwechten and illustrations by Siegfried Horn (Fig. 36). The preface to this new edition by Hermann Bartmann opened with the sentence: "Dr. Eduard Schwechten is one of those men who in the 1890s introduced antisemitism to the German people," a comment that is as historically inaccurate as it is repugnant. According to Bartmann, Schwechten had published before 1893 a booklet *To the Gypsies,* which "wittily attacked the student liberal democratic slogan that there should be equality for all." *The Song of Levi* was ostensibly witty. It was modelled on Schiller's poem *The Bell* and contained the entire litany of antisemitic agitation. We must assume that the book reached wide circles in Düsseldorf, the city where it was published. Such publications were the direct precursors for such scurrilous concoctions as Elwira Bauer's infamous picture book *Trust No Fox in the Green Meadow and No Jew Taking an Oath (Trau keinem Fuchs auf grüner Heid und keinem Jud bei seinem Eid),* published in 1936 by Stürmer Verlag. Bauer is a typical example of the impact of anti-Jewish propaganda, especially by the *Stürmer,* on impressionable youngsters. Letters from children to the editors of *Stürmer*[3] reveal a shameful potpourri of stupidity, fanaticism, and egotism; the editors of *Stürmer* did not hesitate to ingratiate themselves with offers of help to their correspondents. The eighteen year old Elwira Bauer had also requested their assistance. In order to earn money to study art, she had written and illustrated a book, that she assumed any Nazi publisher would

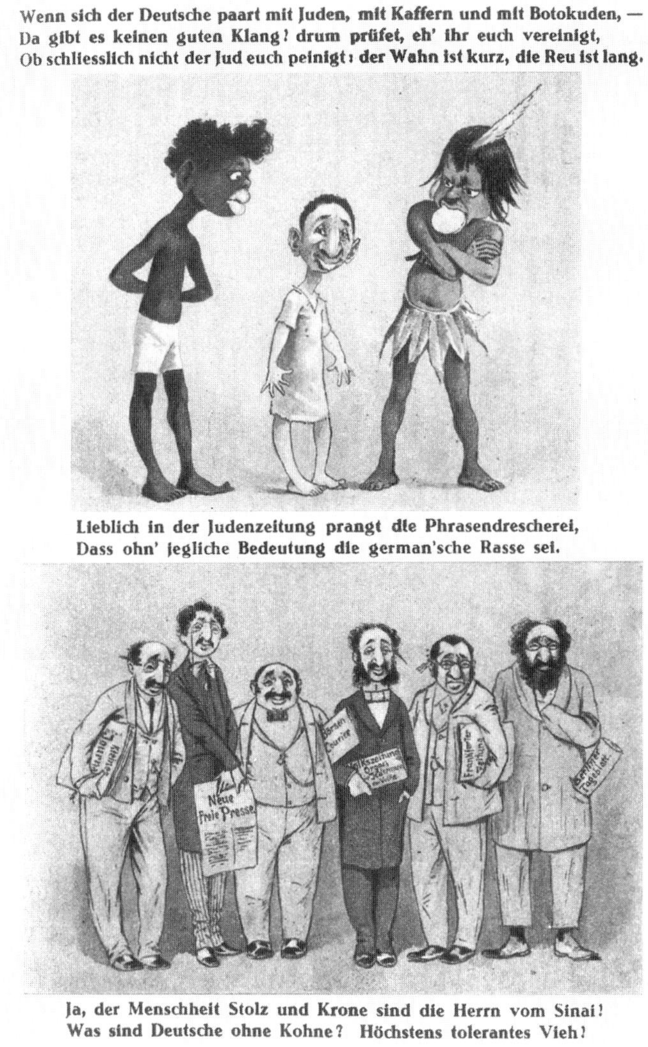

36 Eduard Schwechten, *Das Lied vom Levi,* illustrated by Siegfried Horn, published Düsseldorf 1933, reprinting an 1895 pamphlet of J. Knippenberg Kunstverlag (Stadtarchiv Nuremberg)

want. However, it was rejected by many publishers, not because of the contents but because of the absence of artistic quality. However, Stürmer Verlag accepted this crude concoction (Figs. 120–125).

As with Eduard Schwechten, Elwira Bauer had also written a previous racist work prior to her anti-semitic book. Her *Ten Little Negroes* had been purchased by a publisher, although it has not been possible to locate a copy or to establish further information about it. The book *Trau keinem Fuchs* was published for a mass market; the Stadtmuseum's copy is from the fifth edition that included copies 61,000–70,000. It was advertised in the *Stürmer* no. 48 (1936):[4]

Such knowledge about the dangers Jews pose to non-Jewish nations cannot be lost, if the hearts and minds of impressionable youngsters are engaged. The impressions already received in earliest childhood remain undiminished throughout life. If the essence of the new Germany is to be transmitted and preserved for posterity, then we must already win the hearts of this youth, in their earliest years, for what they must later preserve and develop.

The picture book Trust No Fox in the Green Meadow and No Jew Taking an Oath *has just been released in German-language countries; through bright colors and understandable verses, this book will transmit serious knowledge to German youth. But Elwira Bauer has created a unique picture book not only for young children; it is also intended for adults.*

For as long as there are still people who believe that conversion can transform a Jew into a non-Jew; as long as people do not recognize that a "decent Jew" is a devil in disguise; as long as people still see Jews as compatriots, this unique illustrated book can also serve these 'grown-up children.'

Whoever wishes to communicate with younger or with more mature children must know the language and receptivity of children. Elwira Bauer knows how to communicate with children of all age groups. Both the young and the mature will thank her for creating this first and best illustrated book that can be included on every Christmas gift list for the new Volk *in this new Reich.*

One can scarcely imagine that parents actually bought this book for their children at Christmas. It is probable that it had wide distribution among adults, who were already mentioned in the advertisements as a precaution with the phrase "grown-up children" *(grosse Kinder)*. There was also an uncontrolled and probably clandestine distribution network among fanatic juveniles who sought to "enlighten" their peers. Characteristically, this book is not included among the lists of selections prepared by the National Socialist Teachers' Association *(Nationalsozialistischer Lehrerbund)*.[5]

Another way of influencing children was through toys and games. Artifacts such as the Hitler Youth doll (Fig. 119) are very rare today, since such toys were mostly destroyed after 1945. The "idealized" image of the Hitler Youth is found in Elwira Bauer's book: columns of blond young men with utterly identical features. They could have emerged directly from the laboratory of Aldous Huxley's 1932 novel *Brave New World*, which included this terrifying vision of conformity.

Although the preceding examples were not necessarily seen by all German and German Jewish children and adolescents, all children were affected by classes on "race science" taught in the schools (Figs. 37, 38). To meet such indoctrination with mental reservations was probably possible for only a few. The consequences of racist teachings are still visible today and many are not even conscious of this.

All German Jewish children were affected by the curriculum at school. Every drawing in this exhibition reflects not only their fate as a group, but simultaneously confronts us with individual experiences. Nevertheless, we will analyze these works collectively.

In order to correctly understand the genesis of these pictures, we must again remember that the teacher Julo Levin had already experienced Nazi terror. Levin already knew the attitudes of the rulers and hoped that they were not shared by all Germans. In 1933, Levin had been arrested during mass roundups of communists and he had experienced the

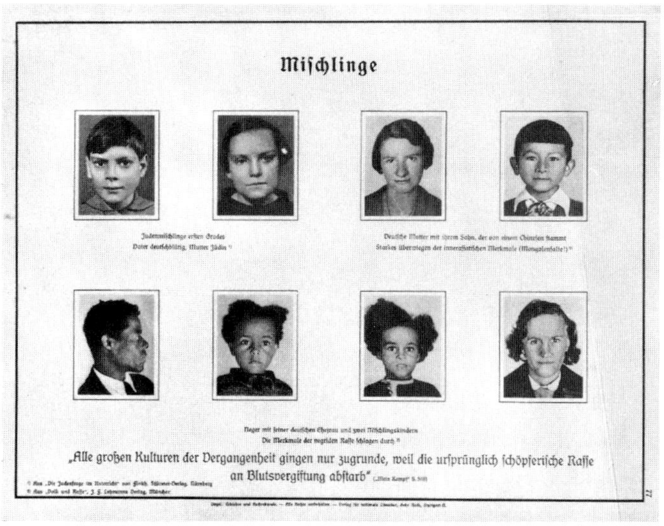

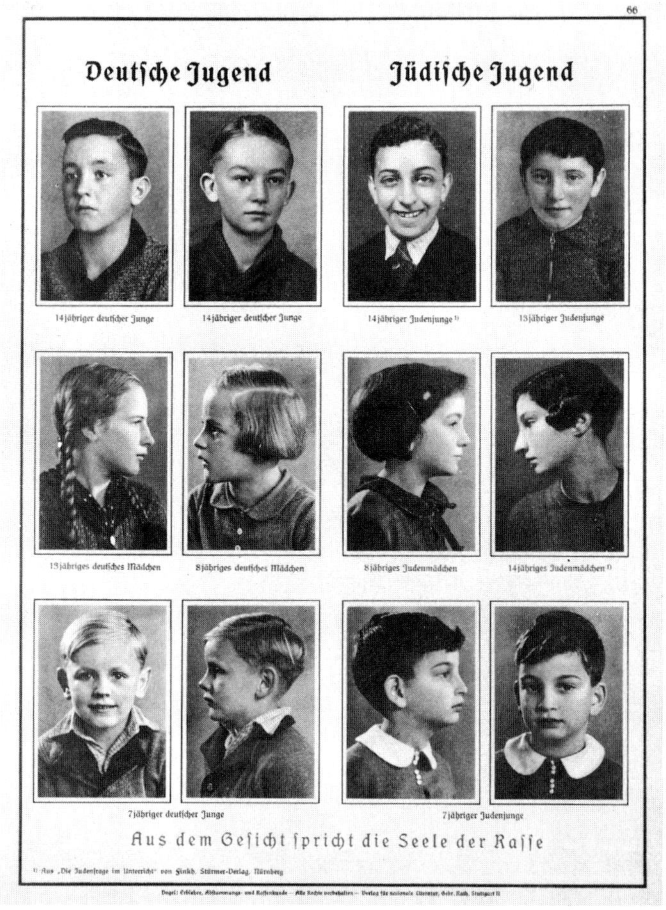

37 Classroom chart about *Mischlinge*

38 Classroom chart entitled "German Youth–Jewish Youth"

These charts were published in Alfred Vogel, *Erblehre, Abstammungs- und Rassenkunde in der bildlichen Darstellung* [Trans.: Illustrated Heredity, Genealogy, and Racial Studies], 2d edition; Stuttgart, 1938 (Stadtmuseum Düsseldorf).

confinement of his friends. Several of his friends had also fled abroad. Levin reacted to these persecutions with poignant paintings, such as *Job* (1933–1934), showing a tortured naked male exposed to a cold and hostile world (Fig. 8).

With his knowledge Levin could not give art lessons that would minimize the situation. Nevertheless it was clear that Levin would not ask his students to depict subjects that would endanger them. Despite this, many of the students' pictures express critical views, reflecting the spontaneity of the children and their reflections of a hostile world – perhaps also one reason why Levin saved certain selected works.

Julo Levin had no formal training as an art educator, although his interest in the creativity and talents of children dated back ten years. His sister, Else Levin, recalled:

In 1926, Julo Levin and his friend Otto Pankok spent several weeks in Crudenburg bei Xanten. The village school teacher, an acquaintance of Otto Pankok's who taught all subjects, offered the artists the possibility of teaching drawing to the children for two weeks, since the subject was previously unknown to the children. Both artists found in this rural environment children utterly uninfluenced by art, who would therefore apply only their inborn creativity. As they did not want to influence the students, they sought only to awaken the children's interest. The children should express their ideas and imagination in pencil and colored crayons on a sketch pad.

Both artists wandered through the Lower Rhineland countryside around Crudenburg with the children. Frequently, Julo Levin went out alone in the early morning with easel and painting materials to sketch and paint the landscape. A girl in the class discovered this and informed the other children: 'I found him!'

The children assembled around him in the morning and soon it grew too noisy for Julo Levin. He left his quarters at 6 A.M. in order to work undisturbed. For several days, the children asked Levin's landlady in vain: 'Where is the painter?'

I also took part in one art lesson. The initial question was: 'What should we paint?' One student had the idea: 'May I paint you, Mr. Artist?' The proposal found unanimous approval. My portrait was also made. The results were exciting. Julo kept the best portraits for his collection. Where might they be now?

Julo convinced the children to use large sketch blocks. The larger format was liberating, whereas smaller-size pads would be restricting.

Otto Pankok provided a special surprise. In a small forest, where a number of trees had recently been cut, Pankok had carved heads out of roots and placed them in the notches. Each face was different. Pankok painted them and inserted glowing coals as eyes, which shined eerily in the evenings.

Among the students, one boy was deeply attached to his horse. Julo encouraged him to draw his friend. The youth set to work with enthusiasm. Julo considered this spontaneous drawing one of the best in his collection. He later showed this picture to a friend, noting: 'Before we professional artists could again express ourselves so originally and animatedly, another ten years would pass by.'

When Levin began his job as an art teacher in 1936, his friend Franz Monjau – who was not allowed to teach for political reasons – assisted him in planning the lessons. Moreover, Levin also used art pedagogical literature, which he had discussed many years previously with Carl Lauterbach.[6]

The broad curriculum guidelines for teaching art are known, although the syllabus and lesson plans can only be reconstructed in part from the students' surviving drawings. In 1934, the *Reichsvertretung der deutschen Juden* issued "Guidelines for writing syllabi for Jewish elementary schools," which stipulated that "the necessary career retraining can be prepared through the cultivation of manual skills (drawings, needlework, crafts)." In the January 1937 report submitted by the school director Dr. Kurt Herz, entitled "The Düsseldorf Private Jewish Elementary School," the purpose of teaching drawing was "to bring the children to a realization of themselves . . ." In a new version of the *Reichsvertretung* "Guidelines" issued in 1937, it was stated that:

Art lessons in all grades should take their subjects from the Jewish life of the children. Pictures from family or communal religious life, religious objects, biblical scenes, and other Jewish materials should be depicted in art.

How these guidelines would look in a classroom setting was described in detail in an essay by Otto Geismar entitled "Jewish Themes in Art Lessons," written as part of the volume *Didaktik der jüdischen Schule* (1938).[7] Geismar divided the eight mandatory years of school into three broad groups: the first and second school years focus on individual objects and people; the third and fourth years include pictures based on experiences; and the fifth through eighth grades expand to drawing from nature. These broad themes were also repeated and applied in the individual classes.

Despite the large collection of works that have survived, these children's drawings represent only a fraction of the works that had been completed. We do not know Levin's criteria for selecting works for his collection. A small group of works, not included in the drawings selected for this exhibition, were done by younger children at the Düsseldorf Jewish kindergarten and also by Levin's young friends from Düsseldorf, Stettin, and possibly other cities as well. The students' works – usually definitely identifiable – came from the fourth through the tenth school years. Levin did not save only those works with the best marks; he also included pictures that impressed him because of their quality and originality, despite their inadequate technique or which students gave to him as gifts, when they could part with them.

Very few of the surviving student works are dated from 1936, the first year that he taught. Nevertheless, the single most moving work of the entire collection, Ilse Marx's *Job* was made in October 1936 (ninth school year; Fig. 55). We have already mentioned Levin's oil painting *Job* from 1933–1934 (Fig. 8). This painting could have been known to the student and served as her inspiration. Levin's Job was a figure laboriously crawling on the ground, whereas Ilse Marx's Job, is tensely erect, with head thrown back and mouth opened wide in a scream. The latter Job rebels against his fate, an interpretation that corresponds better to the views of a youngster.

The ninth grade, in which Ilse Marx's picture was created, focused on preparation for future careers and life abroad. We know about Ilse Marx's class, the ninth grade in Düsseldorf during 1936–1937, from the former Düsseldorf teacher Beatrice Strauss, who wrote about her experiences for the previously mentioned volume *Didaktik der jüdischen Schule.*[8] Strauss stated that spiritual self-reliance and independent work were the educational goals of the ninth grade. The storm signals of the time required a different kind of woman than what the more traditionally inclined parents expected from their daughters. Strauss's report enables us to see that the psychological situation was especially difficult for female students. This may help explain how Marx's unique representation of Job was made, since this subject is not present among the other surviving student art works.

The picture *Art Class* (Fig. 56) made in December 1936 contains a conversation between teacher and student in a balloon with the following dialogue: "Teacher: 'Now stop talking.' Student: 'I didn't say anything.'" The teacher was probably Julo Levin. A drawing by Gerd Westfeld from the same date is entitled *Roosevelt's Victory* and depicts a history class. It is possible that it also shows the history teacher.

An exception among the surviving works is an India ink drawing from October 1937 containing a life-like portrait of Rabbi Dr. Siegfried Klein, who conducted religious instruction at the Düsseldorf school (Fig. 47). Although the portrait does not contain the name of the student artist, the grade marked on the back places the portrait clearly among the students' drawings. There is also a careful pencil sketch by Dora Moritz, sixth grade, from the same date, showing a shoulder-level portrait of a man in vestments. This work could also possibly be a portrait of the rabbi (Fig. 46).

In October and November 1937, the seventh grade in the Düsseldorf Jewish school was assigned the theme "school concerts." One work by Marianne Seligmann (Fig. 74) shows an orchestra with six musicians and a singer. It is possible that these included portraits of her fellow students performing serious music. In contrast, Kurt Mayer drew a student jazz concert (Fig. 75). In Düsseldorf during 1938, there was not only the official exhibition *Entartete Kunst* (Degenerate Art), but also an exhibition entitled *Entartete Musik* (Degenerate Music).[9] The brochure published for the latter event had a caricature of a black jazz musician with a Star of David on his lapel as the frontispiece (Fig. 118). Kurt Mayer's drawing was in conscious opposition to the official Nazi denunciation of jazz as "degenerate" and "unnatural." To be sure, such prohibitions were without influence on what German Jewish students drew, since their works were by their very nature and authorship considered as "degenerate."

One of the drawings from Berlin must be considered together with the category teachers' portraits. It is a humorous work in a mature style and is entitled *The Teachers' Track Race* (Fig. 99).

A considerable number of the students' works deal with the themes: the city, city life, and transportation. These drawings reflect the immediate surroundings and usually show the undisturbed daily routines, although in retrospect we know that these peaceful scenes were sometimes interrupted. One drawing by a relatively young child shows airplanes flying above a city (Fig. 89). Planes and dirigibles were especially fascinating to children and a favorite subject of their drawings. However, not only harmless planes flew in the skies above Düsseldorf; there was also the plane advertising the *Stürmer.*

Alongside events like the circus or annual city fair *(Kirmes)*, several pictures refer to typical aspects of the physical geography or folklore of the city of

Düsseldorf. There are thus several scenes from the *Hofgarten*, an old inner city park. The work selected as exemplary in this exhibition was made in November 1937 and shows *The Gröne Jong* (Fig. 80), a moss covered figure of a triton that served as a fountain. The student had transformed a triton frightened by a hippopotamus into a green devil, an image he could more readily imagine.

There are also two depictions of street scenes in the market square of the old city in Düsseldorf, where the equestrian statue of Jan Wellem is located. (Jan Wellem is the historic figure the Elector Johann Wilhelm of the Palatinate, 1658–1716, referred to in popular folklore.) In November 1937, the seventh grade student Gerhard Wahrenberg rendered the colorful bustle of this outdoor market square (Fig. 69). The picture also includes a youth doing cartwheels. Local Düsseldorf tradition links this custom of doing cartwheels with an episode from the wedding of the Elector Jan Wellem. Even today, contemporary Düsseldorf idioms refer nostalgically to "the good old days" of Jan Wellem. This is also touched upon in the drawing of the market square by the ten-year-old student H(einz) Leopold in October 1937. One of the pedestrians in his picture is given the words: "Times were better when he (Jan Wellem) lived" (Fig. 68). Drawings by other students show more contemporary street scenes. One picture shows three housewives meeting in a large square, their heads held together to exchange gossip and rumors (Fig. 116).

The contemporary political scene is reflected directly in two drawings by younger children. One work shows a man in a brownshirt SA uniform (Fig. 91); the second scene shows a truck standing in front of a house with a swastika flag. The artist of the latter work was five years old (Fig. 90). These obvious leitmotifs of daily life in Nazi Germany were among the visual impressions of even the youngest Jewish students.

Other themes were drawn from the immediate and more distant environs of Düsseldorf, such as a romantic landscape entitled *Wine Harvest on the Rhine*. The technical skill of this picture reflects the knowledge of students in either the eighth or ninth year of school. A somewhat younger student made a painstaking colored-crayon drawing of the Herman Memorial in Teutoburg Forest (Fig. 83). This patriotic and nationalist monument honors the Germanic tribal leader Arminius, also known as Herman – who, according to Tacitus, defeated the Roman Legions in 9 A. D. – and this monument was and still is a favorite destination for class excursions. It was possible to combine sightseeing with hiking there.

Walking tours and hikes were frequently assigned as themes for art lessons, since they could include aspects of sports, comradeship, the changing seasons, and even organized youth activities. It is possible that some drawings even contain oblique references to day trips by the Jewish youth movement, that had been rigidly restricted by Nazi legislation. However, we should not overinterpret the children's drawings. Some of these themes are reflected in the picture *The Hikers*, which shows two young men in *lederhosen* carrying back-packs against a black but sunny sky (Fig. 82).

Explicit drawings from nature and rural settings appeared frequently in the students' art. Typical examples include *The Woodcutter* (Figs. 89, 93) and *The Sower* (Fig. 94), and *The Milker* or *The Peasant*, drawn both in male and female versions. The drawing of a peasant woman is particularly interesting because of the details of her traditional folk costume. These themes depicting idealized or generic types intersected with assignments to draw various occupations. A whole series of colorful studies depict *The Tailor, The Hairdresser, The Road Repairman, The Miner*, and other jobs. It is not known whether the subject *The Carpenter* was explicitly assigned or whether other drawings have been lost, since Julo Levin had himself learned carpentry skills as part of his strategy for survival and he had moreover set up a small carpentry workshop for students at the school.

A special place must be assigned to several pictures that depict criminals, as, for example, burglars. This subject is exemplified by Leo-Wolf Klarmann's, drawing *The Thief*, completed in October 1937. Totally absorbed in picking a lock, the thief is portrayed sympathetically in this study by a sixth-grade student (Fig. 72).

Several works in the collection also focus on the subject of the family. It is possible that this category is larger in size than it seems, since several unidentified works may include figures that were parents or grandparents. Within this thematic category, there is one unusual picture showing a poor family assembled around a kitchen table (Fig. 115). Direct references to poverty and need were unusual in children's art. The norm was to show good middle-class milieus, although such images may well have been more imagined than real at that time. A typical bourgeoisie setting is found in the watercolor showing an elegant woman seated at a dresser, while putting on a hat in the mirror (Fig. 114). It is clear that the shared German Jewish communal experiences of persecution and pauperization had obvious repercussions on the home life of German Jewish children, although most of the drawings reflect normality and warmth – whether actual or remembered.

The world of childhood and adolescence, usually a time of testing and experimentation, became inverted into a world of shrinking horizons and vulnerabilities after 1933. The relatively mundane drawings concerned with home life, neighborhoods, and native towns acquired a tragic meaning in the context of Nazi Germany. German Jewish children were systematically driven from the wider German milieu, creating a community under beleaguered isolation.

One goal of education was spiritual preparation for emigration that provided students with realizable prospects for the future and a way of alleviating the abruptness of the rupture with familiar things and surroundings. Thus, even art classes included assignments that reflected a preoccupation with foreign countries and cities. Nevertheless, it is evident that students were more engrossed with the exotic than the mundane. Rather than drawing typical American scenes, they drew an American cowboy (Fig. 60), a veiled Indian woman dancing gracefully in front of a prince (Fig. 61), and other similar images. A rare sense of self-criticism is found in one work depicting a Chinese coolie pulling an arrogant European riding in a rickshaw (Fig. 62). Levin also frequently assigned Africa and the Orient as subjects for his various classes. Drawings of water carriers, Bedouin, camels, and assorted but not fully identifiable Oriental scenes were in all likelihood suggested by the mandatory subject of Palestine studies.

It is noticeable that Levin also frequently assigned the broad subject of Africa. This was, in part, probably determined by Levin's friendship with the Black ship's cook in Marseilles in 1931; the theme Africa may also have been related to the required subject of geography. It is perhaps in this context that one drawing from the thematic complex "Faces, Masks" can be explained. The picture carries no indication of the student's name, class year, or date of completion. It is not a realistic portrait of a Black man, but is drawn from imagination (Fig. 58). Levin had himself drawn many portraits of his Black friend Ibrahim, and it is possible that a student had seen one of these pictures. Although the unknown student's technique is not especially skillful, the portrait is neither clichéed nor derogatory. Another drawing with the unambiguous title *Africa* shows a peaceful meeting between two African archers, without focusing on racial characteristics (Fig. 59). Two colorful drawings depicting masked tribal dancers are indicative of the quality of the students' works on this subject (Figs. 97, 98).

Although the theme of Black Africans could be rationalized and explained under the pretext of teaching "racial science," there was no possible rationalization for focusing on Gypsies. Blacks, Roma, Sinti, and Jews had all been classified by Nazi theorists as racially inferior and juxtaposed to Aryan racial types. The illustrations reproduced above (Figs. 37, 38) were used as mandatory classroom materials in German schools, where students were indoctrinated in a bizarre mélange of racial biology that excluded all outsiders and minorities.

During his trip to Marseilles, Levin had become

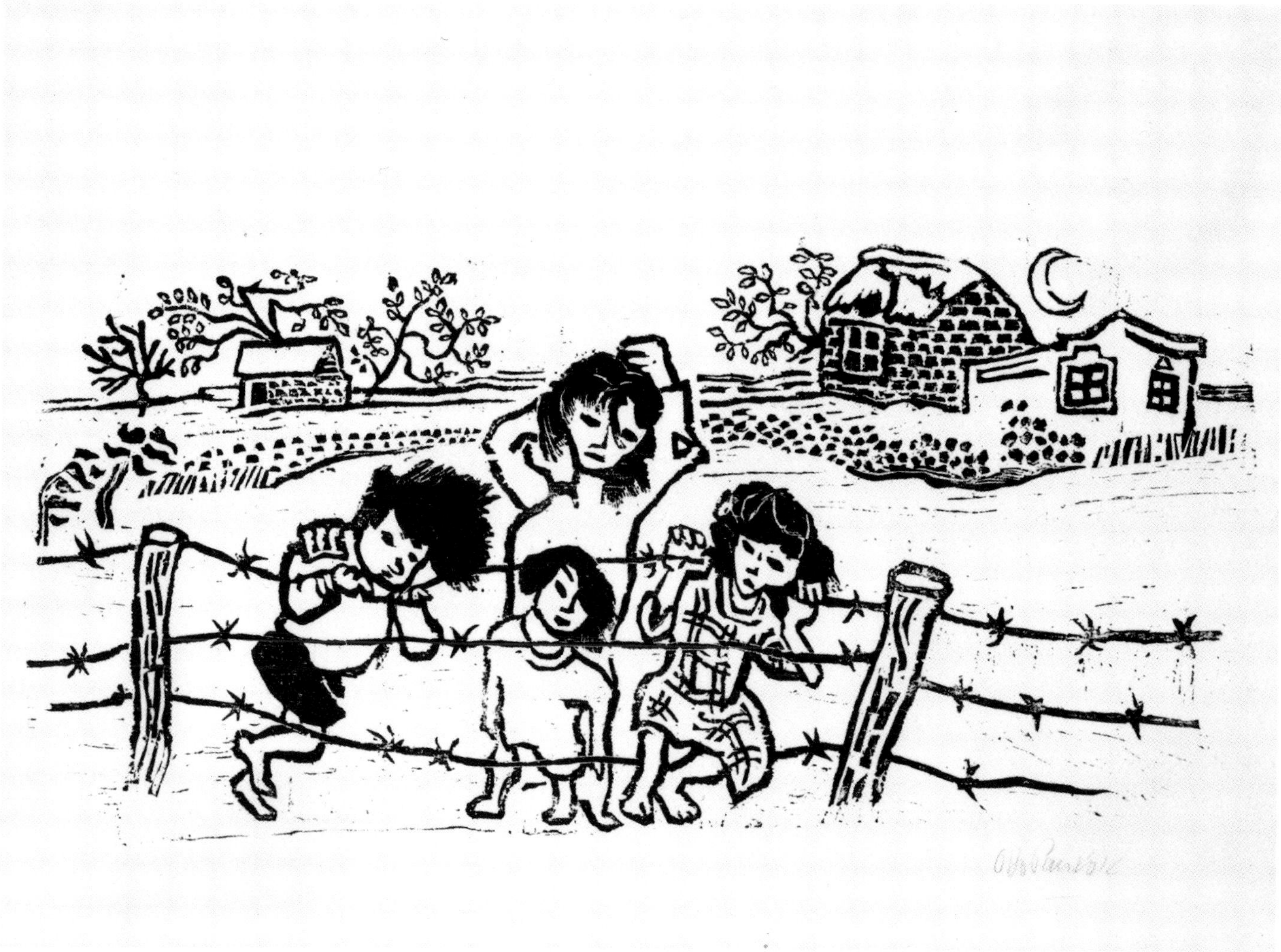

39 Otto Pankok, *Gypsy Children behind Barbed Wire*, 1937 (Cat. 112)

friends with several Gypsies, who had allowed him to draw their portraits. Levin had also learned about the merciless Nazi persecution of Gypsies from his friend Otto Pankok (Figs. 39–41). Pankok had erected his atelier in a Gypsy camp at Heinefeld in Düsseldorf at the beginning of the 1930s and had thus witnessed the Nazi destruction of these Gypsy homes and the deportation of the Sinti inhabitants.

Levin's students were probably not fully conscious of the tragedy of Gypsies trapped in Nazi Germany. The surviving student drawings focus on aspects of an ostensibly "free" Gypsy life. Nevertheless, it is interesting to note that Julo Levin had assigned the theme of Gypsies to both his Düsseldorf class in October 1937 and also to his Berlin students in November 1939 (Fig. 70).

It is clear from the surviving collection of student works that literary themes drawn from German language and literature assignments were also given as subjects for artistic interpretation. These included Friedrich von Schiller's ballads *The Glove* and *The Guarantee* as well as Ludwig Uhland's *The Blind King*. Schiller's *The Glove* is about the testing of love and valor, involving a knight who must retrieve a glove dropped deliberately into a cage with wild animals. It concludes with the words: "'Dear Lady,

40 *Gypsy Camp in Düsseldorf,* his daughter Eva Pankok in the middle, 1930–1933; photograph by Otto Pankok (Otto Pankok Archive)

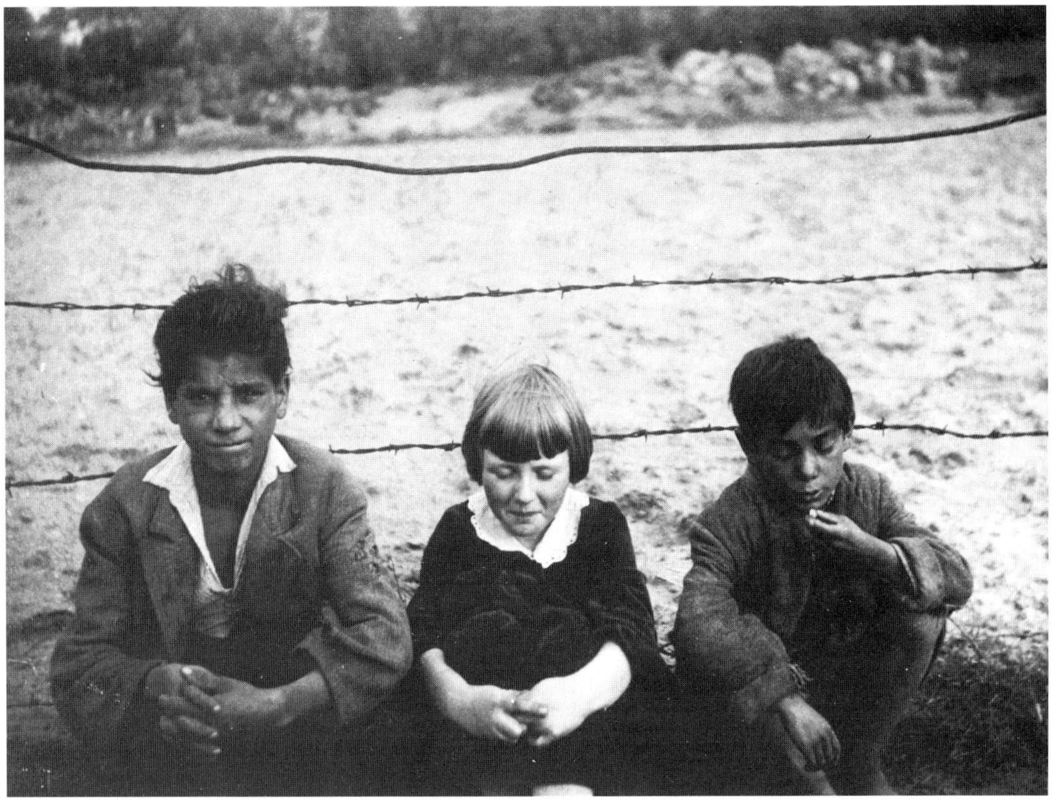

41 *Gypsy Camp in Düsseldorf,* 1930–1933; photograph by Otto Pankok (Otto Pankok Archive)

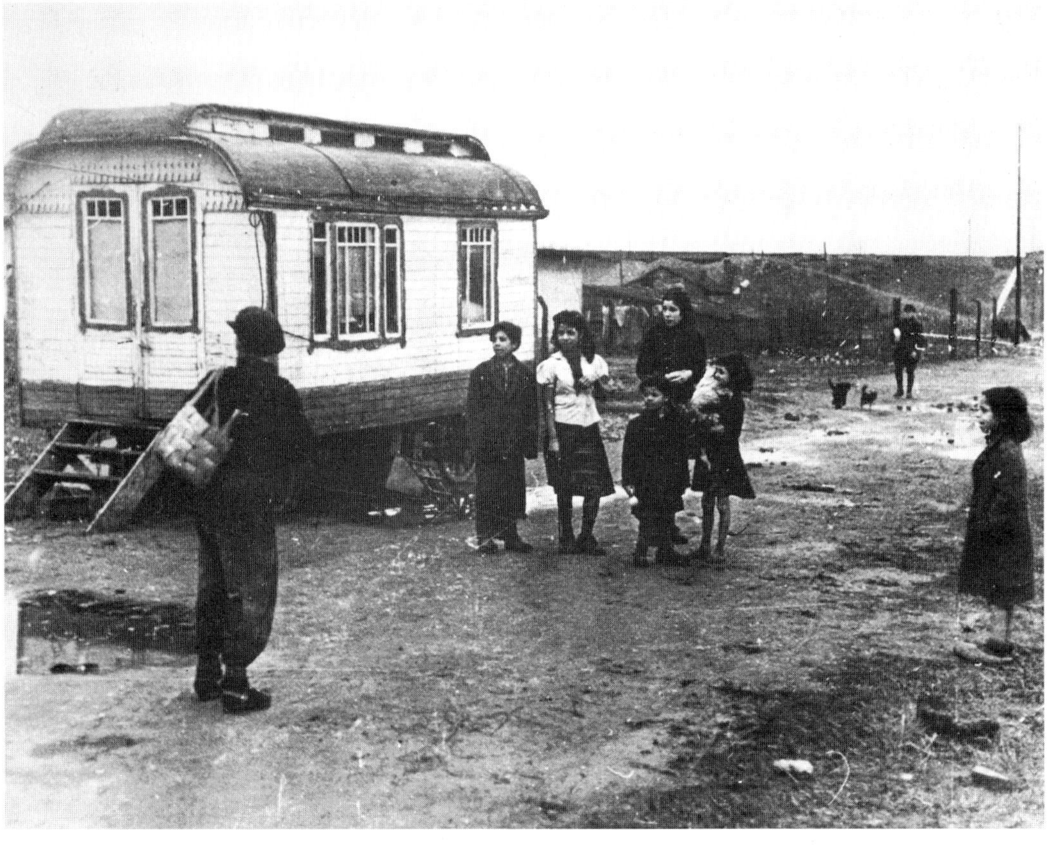

I do not wish your thanks!' and he left her." The ending had a special appeal to children.

Schiller's *The Guarantee*, whose main theme is true friendship despite mortal danger, has frequently been parodied by school classes and is reflected in ironic and comical drawings. In December 1937, Levin assigned his art class to illustrate Uhland's *The Blind King*. The story is about a blind king whose daughter has been abducted. Only his son is prepared to fight for her release. The pathos of the story lies in the king's blindness, since he must depend on others to fight and also to tell him the outcome of the battle between his son and the bandit. This scene is the subject of one student's drawing (Fig. 79).

Other literary works used as a basis for art were two plays: Schiller's *William Tell* and Shakespeare's *A Midsummer Night's Dream*. The latter is represented by a humorous version of the craftsmen's scene (Fig. 100) and the former play is depicted through the Rütli oath, thereby emphasizing the solidarity of Swiss freedom fighters (Fig. 78). The motif of individual heroism – when Tell must shoot an arrow through an apple balanced atop his son's head – is virtually ignored in the class drawings.

Apart from themes derived from German literature, other assignments drew substance from fairy tales and Greco-Roman mythology, such as the legends of Hercules, Prometheus, and Atlas. One drawing completed in January 1940 is especially moving because of its date. It shows an imaginary land of plenty, where all inhabitants had enough to eat and were free from anxieties (Fig. 113). Powerless to change their everyday lives, the student artists either remembered a normal past or projected their dreams of a life without indignities and shortages.

It is possible that several pictures whose contents cannot be explained or correlated with potential class themes might derive from as yet unidentified literary works. These works include one battle scene drawn in prehistoric perspective by Albert Tell (Fig. 101). It also includes two drawings of disabled World War I veterans respectively completed in June and September 1939 by two female eighth grade students. The first shows two medics carrying a wounded man on a stretcher in front of a house flying a French flag (Fig. 108). The second drawing shows a group of disabled veterans in front of ruins and rubble (Fig. 109). Between the dates of these two drawings, World War II had begun. These students' works were potentially dangerous, since fear of war, sympathy for the (French) enemy, and disabled soldiers were openly depicted in contravention of the official vision of radiant images of Aryan heros. Works with similar content, such as Otto Dix's *War Cripples* (Fig. 42), had already been confiscated and destroyed as politically subversive and degenerate by the Nazis.

It is self-evident that Jewish subjects were heavily represented in the students' drawings, conforming to the curricular guidelines for Jewish schools. One undated picture showed two bearded Jews; however, this type of generalized statement was rare among the drawings about Jewish subjects (Fig. 84).

It seems clear from the surviving drawings that Levin never assigned his class to draw individual religious or ritual objects either from actual artifacts or from memory. When such objects appear, they are invariably placed in a wider context. One colored-pencil drawing by the fourth-year student Ellen Wallach from September 1937 shows a man wearing a prayer shawl and blowing the Shofar. This work depicted the celebration of the Jewish New Year and is the only work on this subject in the collection.

In both Düsseldorf and Berlin, Levin assigned the Temple in Jerusalem and synagogue buildings in general as class themes. The picture by Max Rosner, a fourth-year student, in December 1937 belongs to the drawings grouped around Hanukkah (Fig. 85). It shows the Temple in Jerusalem with a high gate and dome-shaped roofs on the side towers. Atop the building is a seven-branch candelabrum. Three men are approaching the building from the right. Both the temple and the candelabrum have explicit Stars of David. The artist intended to show the purification of the Temple by Judah Maccabee, annually commemorated on Hanukkah. Another colorful synagogue interior was painted by Gisela Blau in November 1939 (Fig. 111), exactly one year after the destruction of most German synagogues in the November 1938 pogrom.

Several biblical themes are represented only by single works in Julo Levin's collection. Apart from the aforementioned painting *Job*, other subjects include: *Elijah's Ascent to Heaven, Scouts (or Spies) from Canaan* (October 1938), *Lot's Flight from Burning Sodom* (August 1939, Fig. 110), and *Noah Releases the Dove* (August 1940, Fig. 117). The last picture embodies that courage born of desperation, the hope that the flood of horrors threatening to swallow Jews still living within the Nazi orbit might, like the flood, recede.

In January and February 1937, Levin's seventh grade class in Düsseldorf illustrated scenes from the life of Moses, a theme linked to the annual celebration of Passover. Two different versions of the discovery of the infant Moses show varied styles of student artistic vision. One student limited the scene to a close-up of Pharaoh's daughter with the basket (made of rushes) containing Moses (Fig. 48). The second work focused on the personalities and geographical elements of the story (Fig. 50). Other themes evident in art works linked to Moses and Passover include: slave labor in Egypt, Moses killing the overseer, and the parting of the Red Sea (Figs. 49, 51, 52).

Every February, Levin also assigned another subject to his classes: *Faces and Masks* (Fig. 57). The works ranged from portraiture to caricature. Rarely were actual masks depicted, since the students usually interpreted the assignments to mean faces without make-up. These heads were not connected with carnival in Düsseldorf, but were instead related to cheerful customs of the Purim holiday. These included masks, costumes, and music as well as dance performances in school. It is possible that Rolf Cohn's undated drawing *Cossack's Dance* (Fig. 77) was painted in this connection.

Levin assigned not only joyous themes at Purim, but also focused on serious topics connected with the biblical story of Queen Esther, her uncle Mordecai, and the wicked adviser Haman, the prototypical enemy of the Jewish people. Mordecai overheard the conspiracy of two officials, Bigthan and Teresh, against King Ahasuerus. He informed his niece, the Jewish Queen Esther, who in turn reported it to the king (Fig. 107). Shortly thereafter Haman, the king's most powerful adviser, planned the destruction of all Jews on Persian soil as well as the seizure of their property, because Mordecai had refused to obey a royal decree that he bow before Haman. Esther was able to change the king's decision and thus avert the killing of her people, the Jews. Mordecai was rewarded by the king and Haman ended up on the gallows he had built for Mordecai. Purim is a story about the rescue of the Jews from extermination, relevant in the context of Nazi Germany.

The surviving students' works focused on certain scenes from the Book of Esther: the conspiracy, the triumphal march which Haman had to organize for Mordecai, and Esther's intercession with the king.

An unusual colored pencil drawing was made about the Purim story in March 1937 by a fourth year student. It showed a tall man dressed in a stormtrooper's uniform with brown cap and jacket (Fig. 86). Bowing to him from the left, the right, and in front, are men and women in long garments. Their clothing indicates that despite the central brown uniformed figure, the scene was in fact historical. The back of the drawing provides the title: *Forced to Pay Homage*. It is likely that the uniformed man is Haman, who is being honored by his Persian subjects. Clearly for the unknown ten year old student, SA men were as dangerous as the historical Haman. The student artist had a frightening understanding of the political forces of his time.

Two further drawings from fourth grade students show a man hanging on a gallows (Figs. 87, 88). The people in both pictures are dressed in modern clothing. Heinz Marcus placed the gallows at the center of his drawing, to the left are two hangmen holding the noose and two witnesses stand on the right. Eugen Wallach, the second student, drew a house on the left side of the paper, placing the gallows on the right. One figure is sandwiched in between the house and the gallows. In German script, the word "Hanan" can be read above the door,

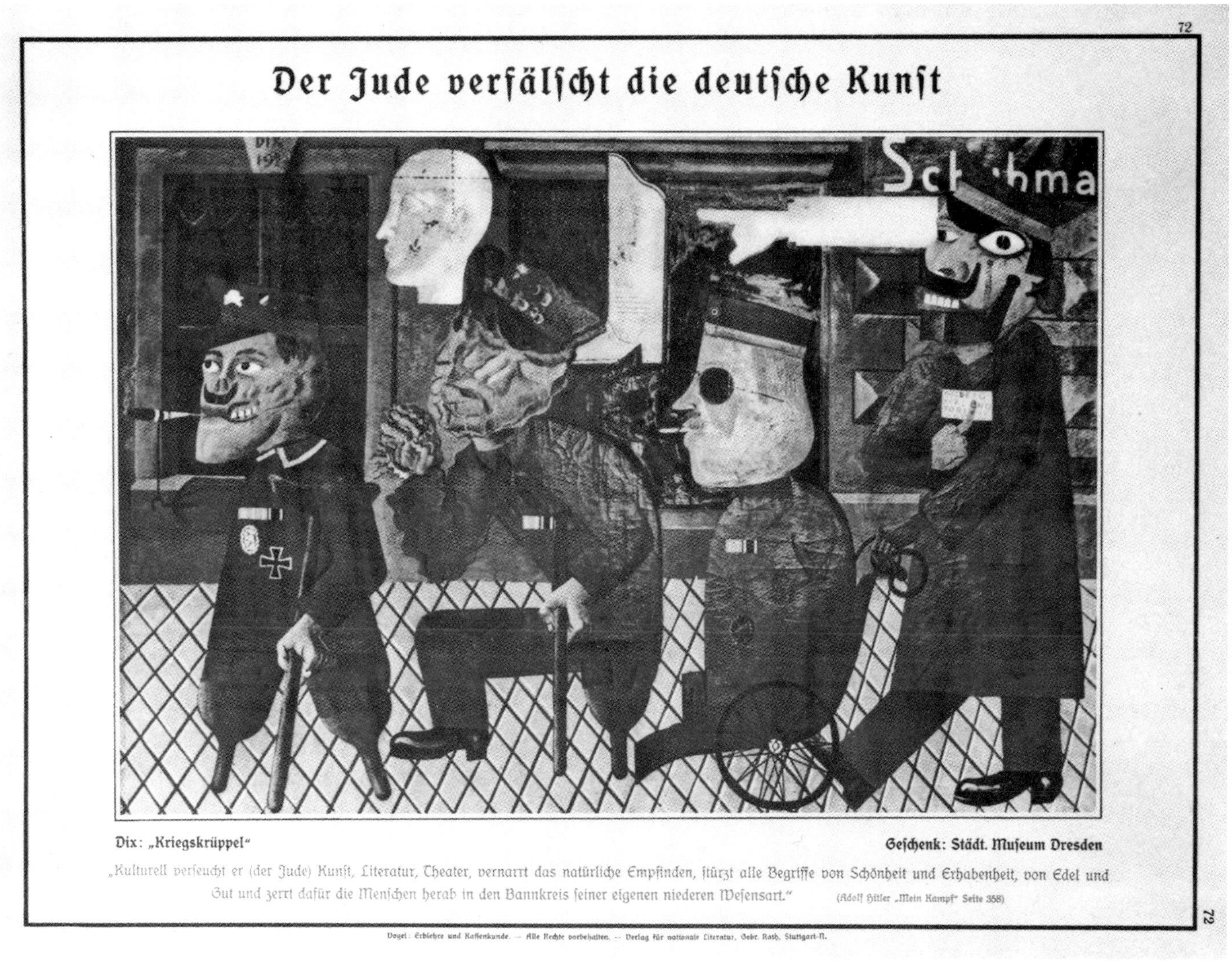

42 “The Jew Forges German Art,” illustration from Alfred Vogel, *Erblehre, Abstammungs- und Rassenkunde in der bildlichen Darstellung*, 2d edition (Stuttgart, 1938) (Stadtmuseum Düsseldorf)

possibly a child’s misspelling of the name Haman. Haman had historically built the gallows, on which he was later hung, adjacent to his own house. It is probable that both drawings depict Haman. Both pictures are also undated and without grades, possibly because Levin had retained these very dangerous works of art for himself and requested that the students submit new drawings for this assignment. A second picture by Eugen Wallach is in fact found in the collection, depicting the scene with Esther pleading in front of Ahasuerus.

Apart from Passover and Purim, the Hanukkah festival was also extremely important for art lessons. The biblical story of the Maccabees and their revolt against Greco-Syrian rule also provided numerous motifs and themes for art instruction. In December 1938, Werner Lier painted a duel between an archer (the Maccabee) and a policeman, wearing the *Schako*, the typical and distinctive headpiece worn by German police (Fig. 103). Entitled *The Maccabean* on the reverse side, it is a condensed version of one of the many battle scenes of Judah Maccabee and his brothers, in order to protect Israel from surrendering. The picture was completed shortly after the pogrom of 9–10 November 1938 and it seems inconceivable that the student would depict a Jewish soldier in the uniform of a German policeman. In all likelihood, the policeman represented the Greco-Syrian forces. The drawing reveals the Jewish student's skeptical opinion of the police as protectors of law and order inside Nazi Germany.

Another picture about the subject of the Maccabees was completed in December 1938 and is entitled *Idolatry* (Fig. 104). It portrays uniformed men, forcing the Jewish populace to kneel before a huge antique statue inside a house of worship (the Temple in Jerusalem); the uniforms resemble the SA brownshirts. One of the villains is swinging his whip, a reminder of the beatings in SA torture cellars and the bastinado in concentration camps.

The last drawings from Düsseldorf that I will mention concern the theme of emigration. Hermann Feldmann drew a Rhine steamer flying a Zionist flag with the Star of David. In front of the ship is a sailboat with the name *Müllmer Bötchen* (Müllmer's Small Boat), which was also the title of a German popular song (Fig. 66). Eugen Wallach also depicted a refugee reaching his destination in October 1937. The immigrant is standing alone with his luggage in between two skyscrapers; an American flag flies from each building (Fig. 65).

The students' works in Julo Levin's art classes conformed to contemporary curriculum guidelines for art instruction. They also reflect the environment from the perspective of German-Jewish children. The art reveals the attempt to interpret knowledge and milieu through the language of art as well as the belief and hope in a better future both as dream and as reality. The inescapable tragedy of many of these children is clear in their surviving drawings.

Notes

1 Carl Lauterbach, *Gemälde, Grafik, Dokumente: Katalog Stadtmuseum Düsseldorf* (Düsseldorf, 1981), p. 29.

2 Hannele Zürndorfer, *The Ninth of November* (London, Melbourne, and New York, 1983), pp. 45–49.

3 Fred Hahn, *Lieber Stürmer: Leserbriefe an das NS-Kampfblatt 1924 bis 1945; Eine Dokumentation aus dem Leo Baeck Institut* (Stuttgart, 1978), pp. 165–77.

4 Ibid., p. 158.

5 Reichsvertretung des Nationalsozialistischen Lehrerbundes, ed., *Das deutsche Bilderbuch. Ein Auswahlverzeichnis*, compiled by R. Kressner (Bayreuth, n. d. [ca. 1940]).

6 Julo Levin was inspired by the book by Philipp Franck, *Das schaffende Kind* (Berlin, 1928). Levin's class assignments closely resemble many of Franck's suggestions and examples of children's art.

7 Otto Geismar, "Das jüdische Motiv im Kunstunterricht," in: Heinemann Stern, ed., *Didaktik der jüdischen Schule* (Berlin, 1938).

8 Beatrice Strauss, "Das neunte Schuljahr der Mädchen," idem, pp. 51–61.

9 See the exhibition catalog: Albrecht Dümling and Peter Girth, ed., *Entartete Musik: Eine kommentierte Rekonstruktion zur Düsseldorfer Ausstellung von 1938* (Düsseldorf, 1988) and Peter-Klaus Schuster, ed., *Nationalsozialismus und 'Entartete Kunst'* (Munich, 1987).

Julo Levin and his Children's Art Collection

Carl Lauterbach

When we met at Julo Levin's studio, the childrens' drawings provided us with one of our most treasured and liveliest subjects of conversation, since as artists we were fascinated by the psychology of creativity. A whole new world had opened up with Sigmund Freud's discovery of scientific psychology, focusing on uniqueness and individuality.

At the end of the 1920s, two seminal pedagogical works about art were published: *The Creative Child* and *The Genius in Children.* These books provided new materials for the training of future art teachers enrolled at the Düsseldorf Academy of Art. A remnant of the spirit of the "golden twenties" was found in this progressive child-oriented approach to childhood development, learning, and personality.

The lively and often provocative results of even the youngest child's artistic expression fascinated us. In this earliest phase up to the age of twelve, children tried to draw what they saw and observed, although their technical skills were often inadequate to their intentions. After the age of twelve, this spontaneity was usually suppressed by the inevitable desire to achieve a more advanced and precise level of skill. It is very rare that a youthful childhood talent developed fully after the age of twelve. Practical concerns and career choices emerged, leaving little time or room for artistic development.

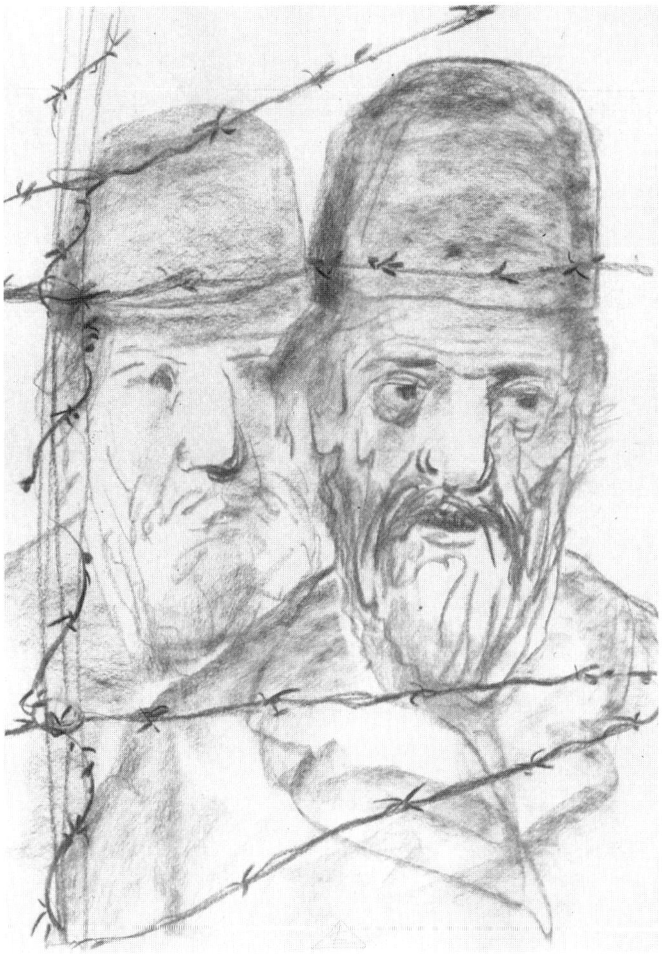

43 Carl Lauterbach, *Behind Barbed Wire*, 1942 (Cat. 117)

Julo Levin was the teacher and these drawings were part of his collection. He was the initiator who admired his young geniuses. The interactive relationship between teacher and students involved a creative tension. Levin was an ideal teacher,

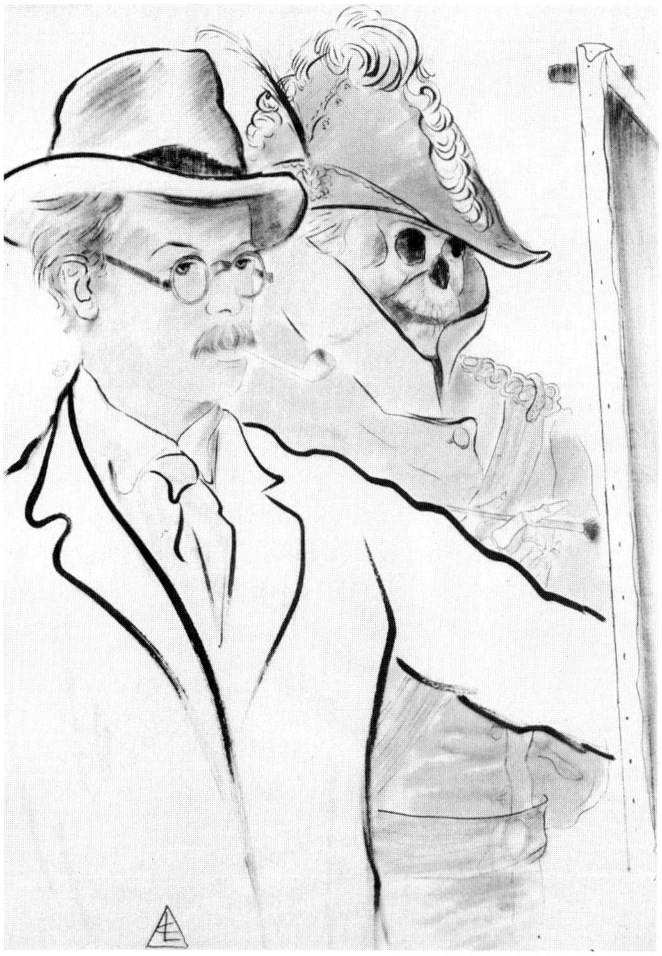

44 Carl Lauterbach, *Self-Portrait with Death*, 1939 (Cat. 116)

enthusiastic and supportive; a more devoted and open mentor could scarcely be imagined. He was proud of his students' excellent results. Color was viewed as an expression of emotions, a dramatic breakthrough that had occurred in expressionism. Color became a major new subject of discussion, and, then as now, was part of self-realization and self-expression. Naturally, the great names of Kandinsky and Klee were associated with this new pedagogical breakthrough at the beginning of the twentieth century. The decisive role of both these trailblazing personalities cannot be overlooked. This is almost forgotten today, since this now seems obvious to us, although at the beginning of the 1930s it was the hallmark of a progressive outlook. The so-called golden twenties had opened new possibilities for our understanding of creativity and integrating it with thought and feelings.

Our conversations in Levin's atelier as we looked at his students' works were invariably filled with the spirit of universal humanism that we shared. This was a beacon of light invigorating our hopes despite the depressing circumstances, threats, and fears.

Children's Art during the Holocaust

Sybil Milton

Children who drew and painted in ghettos and concentration camps during the Holocaust faced radically different conditions than those confronting Jewish students in Düsseldorf and Berlin after 1933. Nevertheless, their surviving works of art prior to 1941 have much in common with works completed in various settings during the Holocaust. More than 4,000 drawings by children have survived in Theresienstadt alone, where 15,000 (mostly Czech) children were incarcerated among the 140,000 prisoners between November 1941 and May 1945.[1] Children's art is also closely related to the work of amateur artists during the Holocaust. The small number of especially talented and artistically mature children, some of whom later became professional artists, must be treated apart from children artists as a whole.[2]

The differences between the conditions of daily life for Jewish students in Nazi Germany after 1933 and children in the camps and ghettos are relatively obvious. The former children still lived at home in deceptively normal circumstances and still had access to a variety of reasonably good-quality art supplies, whereas children in ghettos and camps suffered the horrors common to all Nazi places of incarceration. In the camps, the children had virtually no privacy. Upon arrival they were separated from parents and siblings; moreover, they rarely had more than the most primitive art materials at their disposal. Despite these differences, there are a substantial number of parallels between the artistic development of children in German-Jewish schools after 1933 and those in ghettos and camps after 1940, irrespective of locality.

In the clandestine schools created in most ghettos and concentration camps, there was a relatively large degree of pedagogical freedom, despite – and paradoxically perhaps because of – the conditions. Teachers could usually establish their curricula without outside interference. Art was considered to be especially important as a form of psychological therapy, as the transmission of a cultural and religious heritage, and as a means of spiritual resistance and thereby survival. Art served to express emotions, memories, and experiences that had to be shaped into a symbolic language, irrespective of the age or degree of skill of the child artists. Teachers held special places as role models and surrogate parents; they understood how to forge a bond with the children and how to motivate them to give meaning to their experiences through the symbolic language of art. Teachers like Friedel Dicker-Brandejsova[3] and Fredy Hirsch in Theresienstadt played roles similar to that of Julo Levin in the Jewish schools of Düsseldorf and Berlin. Secret schools existed not only in Theresienstadt, but also in Auschwitz, Buchenwald, Westerbork, and Gurs. Thus, in the Theresienstadt Family Camp at Auschwitz, Fredy Hirsch continued the job he had previously assumed at Theresienstadt.[4]

Other teachers served as adoptive parents, educators, and resisters. In late 1939, Robert Siewert founded a stonemasons' school in Block 49 at Buchenwald. He thereby saved the lives of many

Jewish adolescents, who were retained at Buchenwald because they qualified as specially skilled labor.[5] Similarly, the Block Elder Wilhelm Hammann in children's barracks 8 at Buchenwald founded a secret school at the beginning of 1945. He thus saved the lives of at least 150 Jewish children and adolescents.[6] In the Dutch transit camp at Westerbork, Gerhard Frank organized school classes and Hanna Schramm founded a school in the French transit and internment camp at Gurs.[7] The spiritual and intellectual life of the incarcerated children was protected and also encouraged by these progressive teachers; inside the ghetto walls and the barbed wire of concentration camps, children were being "educated for life." The children painted and drew freely, using art as an outlet for their imagination as well as an escape that enabled them to gain control of their own personal space and time. The pattern and results were similar to art classes at the Jewish schools in Düsseldorf and Berlin in the late 1930s.

Of course, it is probably impossible to conceptualize the persecuted children as a single or unified group, because of the enormous and complex variations in their backgrounds and the distinct needs of the three different age groups between infants and adolescents. Even the word "children" is an umbrella concept that includes three distinct subgroups: (1) infants and toddlers up to age 6; (2) young children ages 7 to 12; and (3) adolescents from 13 to 18. Their respective chances for survival and their ability to perform physical labor varied enormously by age. Chances of survival were somewhat higher for older children, since they could potentially be assigned to forced labor.

It must be stated explicitly that children as such were seldom the targets or victims of Nazi violence simply because they were children. They were persecuted along with their families for racial, religious, or political reasons. Nazi persecution, arrests, and deportations were directed against all members of Jewish families, without concern for age; this was also often the case with Gypsy families. Inevitably the children were among the prisoners at highest risk. Homeless, often orphaned, they had witnessed the murder of parents, siblings, and relatives. They faced starvation, illness, brutal labor, and other indignities until they were consigned to the gas chambers. In relationship to adult prisoners, their chances for survival were usually smaller although their flexibility and adaptability to radically changed circumstances could sometimes increase the odds in their favor. That they survived at all and also created works of art in virtually all ghettos and concentration camps is truly remarkable.

Art was one means that adults used to help children who had lost the safety and security of their families and homes; it served as a bridge between memories of the past and hopes for the future. Thus, teachers in Düsseldorf and Berlin selected themes from Jewish history, such as the Exodus and Purim, to awaken consciousness of emigration to Palestine and to strengthen the will to live and to resist. In Theresienstadt and other Holocaust settings, teachers used images remembered from the past to encourage spiritual resistance. Children were assigned to draw the lost worlds of remembered fairy tales and games, memories of family and home, and pictures of life outside the concentration camps. These themes were also reflected in the surviving art, poetry, and diaries by adults and children alike. Conditions in the ghettos and camps were, however, so extreme that therapeutic pedagogy sometimes failed. At least 40 percent of the surviving children's art from Theresienstadt reflected the realities and routines of daily life: barracks, stone walls, barbed wire, roll call, camp infirmaries, and transports to the East. These same themes were also a major component of the surviving works of adult and professional artists from Theresienstadt.[8]

Alongside drawings and paintings, there were also musical and theater performances, that attempted to transmit national, ethnic, and religious traditions to the young. In Theresienstadt, the Czech children's theater repertoire included Hans Krasa's opera for children *Brundibar* and Karafiat's classic fairy tale *Glow Worm*, performed with a children's chorus. Children also performed in concerts and also wrote, edited, published, and read the magazine *Vedem*.

The vast majority of surviving children's art from Theresienstadt was from 1943 and 1944; only scattered works remain for the periods before and after these dates.

Most of the surviving art works carry the date of origin, the student's name, birth date, and often the barracks name or number. These details assist us in reconstructing the fate of these children as well as the circumstances of their lives.

For those camps where few works of children's art survived, the memoirs of adult artists and social workers who often served as teachers provide glimpses of certain aspects of camp life. Thus, the German communist artist Max Lingner reported in his memoirs that *Schweizer Hilfe* set up classes for Jewish and Spanish Republican children interned in Gurs.[9] In Auschwitz, the young artists Halina Olomucki and Yehuda Bacon depicted their surroundings with realism; they were assisted by fellow prisoners in scrounging the necessary supplies to complete these works. After the war, Olomucki and Bacon developed some of these themes as professional artists.[10] One of the most astonishing facts was the maturity of the nine-year-old artist Samuel Bak, whose first exhibition was held in Vilna in March 1943.[11]

One can also learn about the children by studying the works of their teachers, whose art often depicted conditions and scenes from the children's barracks. In Theresienstadt, the Czech artist Bedrich Fritta made an illustrated children's book for the third birthday of his son Tommy in January 1944. The work, still reprinted today, has become a posthumous classic.[12] Although Fritta was subsequently murdered in Auschwitz, Tommy survived through the assistance of the artist Leo Haas.[13] Haas also taught art to Yehuda Bacon in both Theresienstadt and Auschwitz. Among Haas's surviving works are numerous pictures of children in groups at Theresienstadt.[14] Other artists, as for example Anna Kyndinis in Athens and Gele Seksztein in Warsaw did portraits of local children.[15] These portraits by professional artists embodied their hopes that the younger generation would survive for a better future.

The surviving works from the Jewish schools of Düsseldorf and Berlin and the surviving children's art of the Holocaust form a tragic continuum. This is described in one stanza of a poem written in Theresienstadt by 15-year-old Hanus Hachenburg:

How tragic, then, is youth which lives
With enemies, with gallows ropes,
How tragic, then, for children on your lap
To say: this for the good, that for the bad.[16]

Notes

1 Janet Blatter and Sybil Milton, *Art of the Holocaust* (New York, 1981).
2 The children artists who became professionals include: Yehuda Bacon, Helga Weissova-Hoskova, Avigdor Arikha, Samuel Bak, and Halina Olomucki.
3 Österreichische Galerie im Oberen Belvedere in Wien, ed., *Die uns verließen: Österreichische Maler und Bildhauer der Emigration und Verfolgung* (Vienna, 1980), pp. 62–3.
4 Ruth K. Angress, "Lanzmann's *Shoah*," in: *Simon Wiesenthal Center Annual* 3 (1986), pp. 251–2; and Dorothea Stanic, *Kinder im KZ* Berlin, 1979), pp. 50–53.
5 Hermann Langbein, ... *Nicht wie die Schafe zur Schlachtbank: Widerstand in den nationalsozialistischen Konzentrationslagern* (Frankfurt, 1980), pp. 198–99, 205–6. See also Geert Platner (and Schüler der Gerhart-Hauptmann-Schule in Kassel), ed., *Schule im Dritten Reich: Erziehung zum Tod? Eine Dokumentation* (Munich, 1983), pp. 184–6.
6 Platner, *Schule im Dritten Reich*, pp. 188–94. See also Heinz Albertus, *Kinder in Buchenwald* (Weimar, 1981), pp. 21 ff. and Klaus Drobisch, "Wilhelm Hammann," in: *Antifaschistische Lehrer im Widerstandskampf* (Berlin, 1967), pp. 141 ff.
7 For Westerbork, see Jacob Boas, *Boulevard des Miseres: The Story of Transit Camp Westerbork* (Hamden, CT, 1985) and for Gurs, Hanna Schramm, *Menschen in Gurs* (Worms, 1977).
8 Hana Volavkova, ed., *I Never Saw Another Butterfly ...: Children's Drawings and Poems from Terezin Concentration Camp* (New York, 1962); Frantisek Ehrmann, Otto Heitlinger, and Rudolf Iltis, ed., *Terezin* (Prague, 1965).

9 Max Lingner, *Mein Leben und meine Arbeit* (Dresden, 1955).
10 Blatter and Milton, *Art of the Holocaust*, pp. 64–5, 190, 199, 232.
11 Avram Kampf, *Jewish Experience in the Art of the Twentieth Century* (South Hadley, MA, 1984), pp. 125–28.
12 Bedrich Fritta, *Tomickovi* (the Hague, 1980).
13 Stanic, *Kinder im KZ*, pp. 128–30.
14 Pamatnik Terezin, ed., *Leo Haas* (Terezin, 1969).
15 Blatter and Milton, *Art of the Holocaust*, pp. 254, 263.
16 Volavkova, *I Never Saw Another Butterfly*, p. 22.

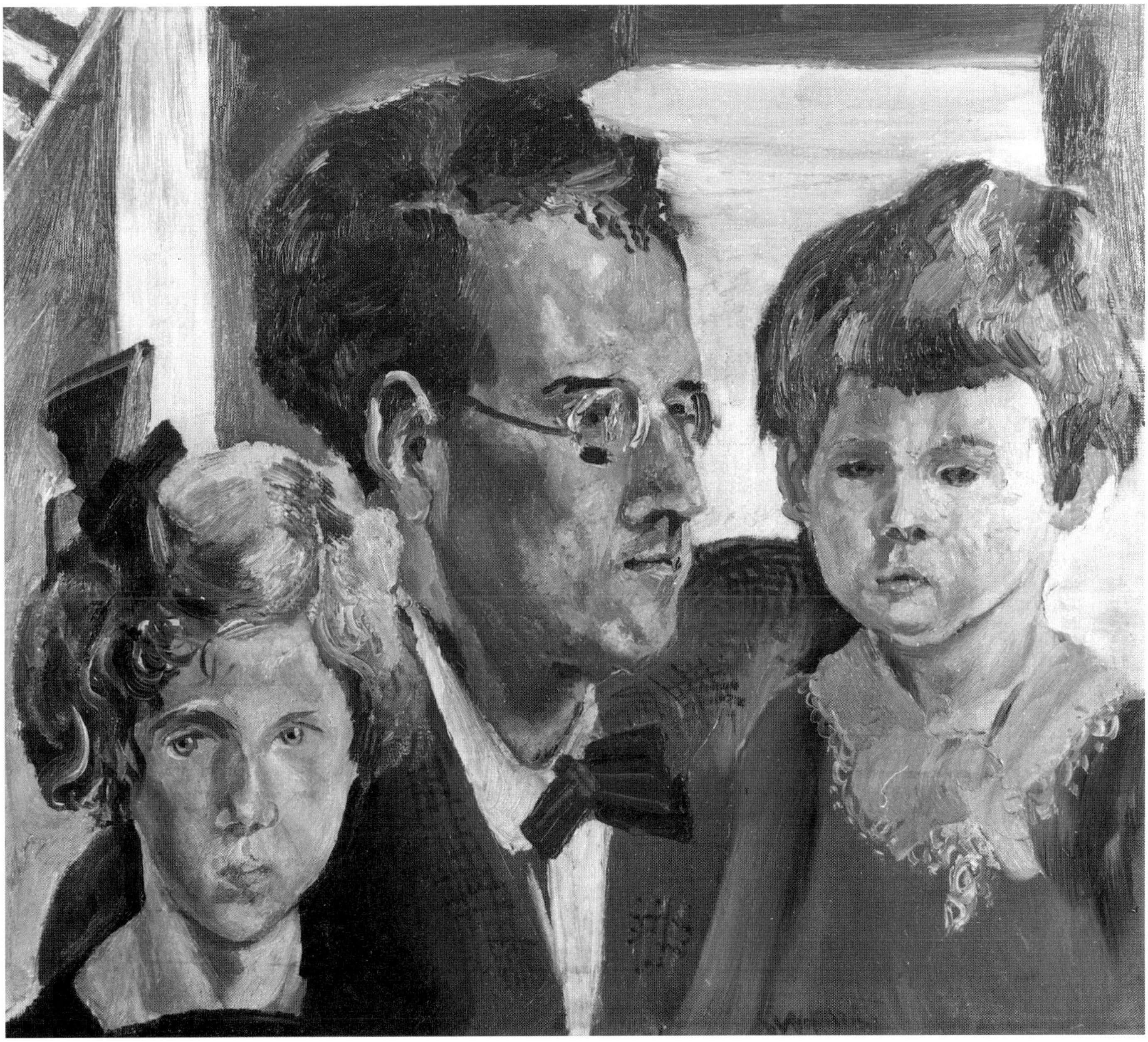

45 Gert Wollheim, *Arthur Kaufmann with his Children, Miriam and Hans,* ca. 1925 (Cat. 107)

The Fate of the Students at the Düsseldorf Private Jewish Elementary School

The names listed below are found on the students' drawings in either German or Latin script. Not all names could be completely deciphered; moreover, some works were not signed. The names were checked against archival and biographical sources as well as personal correspondence and discussions with former Jewish students of the Düsseldorf school. The last entry is often the phrase: "moved, address unknown," since this was frequently the last official entry on registration records at the Düsseldorf *Einwohnermeldeamt* (registry office). It was unfortunately not always possible to trace the actual fate of all former students from Düsseldorf.

We know that the names belong to former Düsseldorf students because of the date on which the drawing was created, the student's school year or class, from which we could in turn estimate the year of birth, and also in part, because of the subjects and themes depicted in the drawings. In several instances, we are not positive that the names belong to former Düsseldorf Jewish students. We have included all names found in Carl Lauterbach's collection, since it is overwhelmingly – albeit not exclusively – the work of Düsseldorf Jewish students.

Abraham, Günter
Born 23 Feb. 1928 Düsseldorf
6 Nov. 1941 deported to Minsk
Murdered

Ackerfeld, Heinrich
Born 13 June 1923 Düsseldorf
6 July 1939 deported to
Cracow
Murdered

Adler, Karl-Heinz
Born 3 July 1926 Frankfurt
20 Feb. 1939 United States

Adler, Karl-Heinz
Born 17 May 1927 Düsseldorf
8 June 1939 moved,
address unknown

Alexander, Eva
Born 14 July 1924 Cologne

Alexander, Margot
Born 15 March 1926 Mannheim
6 Sept. 1940 moved,
address unknown

Altmann, Alfred
Born 18 Dec. 1921 Düsseldorf
6 Feb. 1939 England

Appel, Berta
Born 24 April 1925 Bonn
11 Aug. 1939 England

Appel, Ellen
Born 11 Sept. 1926 Düsseldorf
13 July 1939 moved,
address unknown, Belgium (?)

Arom, Eduard
Born 30 March 1927 Düsseldorf
7 Feb. 1939 moved,
address unknown

Asch, Eva
Born 5 Nov. 1924 Allenstein,
East Prussia
15 July 1939 England

Bahn, Karl

Balsam, Helene
Born 5 April 1922 Duisburg
21 Sept. 1937 Australia

Barsch, Ruth

Berger, Traute

Biesdorf, Adele

Birnbach, Isaak
Born 24 Oct. 1927 Düsseldorf
Brother of Mechthild and Rosa
Birnbach
30 Jan. 1939 Cracow

Birnbach, Mechthild
Born 22 July 1925 Düsseldorf
Sister of Isaak and Rosa, Birnbach
30 Jan. 1939 Cracow

Birnbach, Pescha
Born 1927 (?)

Birnbach, Rosa
Born 24 Aug. 1926 Düsseldorf
Sister of Isaak and Mechthild
Birnbach
30 Jan. 1939 Cracow
Murdered

Blankenstein, Rolf
Born 12 Sept. 1924 Düsseldorf
Deported to Sobibor
Murdered

Blitzer, Madi (Martha)
Born 3 Jan. 1926 Düsseldorf
2 June 1939 Ecuador

Blumenthal, Lore
Born 5 Dec. 1922 Geldern
8 Nov. 1941 deported to Minsk
Murdered

Borg, Hans

Boveland, Gustav

Brasch, Ludwig
Born 3 March 1926 Düsseldorf
8 Nov. 1941 deported to Minsk
Murdered

Breslauer, Hanni
Born 1927 (?)

Brinks, Hans

Brünell, Herbert
Born 8 June 1926 Goch
4 Nov. 1941 deported to Lodź
Murdered

Buckow, Christel

Burzlaff, Herta

Cahn, Günther
Born 17 Aug. 1925 Düsseldorf
Brother of Helmut Cahn
27 March 1939 England

Cahn, Helmut
Born 25 Aug. 1923 Düsseldorf
Brother of Günther Cahn
26 June 1939 England

Cahn, Rolf
Born 11 May 1924 Düsseldorf
8 Nov. 1941 deported to Minsk
Murdered

Cappel, Margot
Born 8 July 1928 Düsseldorf
23 Aug. 1937 United States

Caro, Lore
Born 19 Jan. 1926 Düsseldorf
5 Aug. 1938
Berlin-Charlottenburg

Cleffmann, Margot
Born 28 June 1922 Düsseldorf
3 Oct. 1938 United States

Cohn, Margot
Born 10 Dec. 1922 Düsseldorf
17 March 1937 Berlin
Deported to Auschwitz
Murdered

Cohn, Willi

Dehen, Arthur

Deilmann, Elisabeth

Drillmann, Susanne
Born 5 Dec. 1923 Düsseldorf
19 Jan. 1939 moved, address unknown
Deported to Auschwitz
Murdered

Drönbach, E.
Born 1924 (?)

Eckstein, Kurt
Born 2 July 1923 Düsseldorf
7 Nov. 1941 deported to Minsk
Murdered

Eckstein, M(arianne)
Born 12 Dec. 1924 Düsseldorf
23 Sept. 1937 United States

Elias, K(urt)-H(einz)
Born 31 Dec. 1924 Dresden
27 Dec. 1938 Netherlands

Emmerich, Fritz
Born 30 Oct. 1927 Düsseldorf
24 Nov. 1938 United States

Ephraim, Liesel
Born 31 May 1924 Wuppertal-Elberfeld
24 Nov. 1938 United States

Fahr, R.

Faust, Moses
Born 16 Jan. 1922 Düsseldorf
28 July 1939 Zbaszyn, Poland

Fehlings, Adolf

Feigenbaum, Hella
Born 27 Dec. 1921 Düsseldorf

Feldberg, Frieda
Born 24 Feb. 1926 Düsseldorf
14 Aug. 1939 Poland

Feldberg, Frieda
(Friedel Louise)
Born 8 June 1926 Düsseldorf
Deported to Auschwitz
Murdered

Feldmann, Hermann
Born 1926 (?)

Franck, E(dith)
Born 23 May 1928 Düsseldorf
Deported to Sobibor
Murdered

Frank, Kurt
Born 7 Dec. 1927 Witten
2 Jan. 1939 Netherlands

Frank, R(einhard)

Frank(en), Hilde
Born 1926 (?)

Frankenberg, Werner
Born 6 Oct. 1927 Bigge
2 May 1939 Bigge

Frankfurter, S(alli)
Born 1924 (?)

Freimark, Alfred
Born 28 July 1923 Sontra
Deported to Lodź
27 May 1942 Murdered

Freimark, Alfred
Born 29 June 1924 Düsseldorf
8 June 1939 Haiti

Ganz, Ernst Rainer

Ganz, Herbert

Gärtner, Lore
Born 1 May 1924 Düsseldorf
26 Aug. 1939
Wuppertal-Elberfeld

Gatz, Karl

Geldern, Karla von
Born 30 Nov. 1924 Düsseldorf
Sister of Marianne von Geldern
14 Jan. 1939 Chile

Geldern, Marianne von
Born 13 March 1928
Düsseldorf
Sister of Karla von Geldern
14 Jan. 1939 Chile

Geldern, R. von

Geldern, I.

Gellert, Cilli
Born 8 Jan. 1925 Düsseldorf
Feb. 1938 Netherlands

Gerstenberg, Fritz

Ge...mann, Grete
Born 1922 (?)

Goldberg, Harald
Born 1926 (?)

Goldberg, Simon
Born 26 Feb. 1923 Düsseldorf
10 Sept. 1936 Palestine

Goldmann, Fel(l)a
Born 14 Dec. 1925 Leżajsk, Galicia
9 Jan. 1939 moved,
address unknown

Gröschler, Hans

Grossmann, Werner
Born 21 Dec. 1927 Düsseldorf
19 May 1939 England

Grünewald, Margot

Gumprich, Günter
Born 1924 (?)

Guttmann, H(ans)
Born 18 April 1925 Düsseldorf
4 Oct. 1937 New Zealand

Handgriff, Mira
Born 23 April 1927 Düsseldorf
12 April 1939 England

Harmann, Herbert
Born 1926 (?)

Hartmann, M(argit)
Born 27 May 1927 Kassel
12 May 1938 United States

Heimann, Hanns
Born 4 May 1926
Deported to Minsk
Murdered

Heinemann, Lotti
Born 1926 (?)

Heptner, Willi

Herz, Leo
Born 3 Aug. 1923 Hamborn
20 April 1937 moved, address unknown

Herzog, M(anfred)
Born 15 July 1926 Krefeld
6 July 1939 England

Heumann, Grete
Born 23 June 1923 Neviges
20 Nov. 1938 Netherlands

Heymann, Ellen
Born 1925 (?)

Hirsch, Rudi
Born 18 Nov. 1925 Düsseldorf
20 June 1939 Denmark

Hirschland, Thea
Born 29 Dec. 1927 Düsseldorf
Sept. 1938 Belgium

Hoffmann, Bubi

Hohewald, Inge

Holländer, Tilly
Born 3 Feb. 1923
July 1939 Belgium

Horowitz, Max
Born 27 June 1926
Wallenscheid
Palestine

Imhof, Karl Heinz

Imhof, Siegfried

Jacobsen, Ruth
Born 1 Dec. 1924 Düsseldorf

Jalowitz, Heinz
Born 16 May 1924 Düsseldorf
Brother of Karola Jalowitz
30 May 1939 moved,
address unknown
Deported to Bergen-Belsen
Murdered

Jalowitz, Karola
Born 7 Sept. 1927
Sister of Heinz Jalowitz
30 May 1939 moved,
address unknown
Deported to Auschwitz
Murdered

Jonas, E(rich)
Born 6 Feb. 1925 Düsseldorf
Brother of Ursula Jonas
4 Aug. 1936 Netherlands
Deported to Auschwitz
Murdered

Jonas, Ursula
Born 6 Feb. 1925 Düsseldorf
Sister of Erich Jonas
4 Aug. 1936 Netherlands

Jordan, Inge
Born 15 July 1926 Düsseldorf
3 March 1939 England

Kadisch, Pauline
Born 7 Aug. 1928 Düsseldorf
30 May 1938 United States

Kanarek, Rosa
Born 9 March 1923 Düsseldorf
31 July 1939 moved,
address unknown

Kann, Helga
Born 1927 (?)

Kaufmann, Liselotte

Kaufmann, Manfred
Born 5 Jan. 1926 Hilden
10 Oct. 1938 United States

Klaeme (?), H.
Born 1926 (?)

Klarmann, Herbert
Born 8 April 1926 Düsseldorf
Brother of Leo Wolf Klarmann
22 Aug. 1939 moved,
address unknown

Klarmann, Leo Wolf
Born 21 July 1924 Düsseldorf
Brother of Herbert Klarmann
22 Aug. 1939 moved,
address unknown

Klever, H.
Born 1926 (?)

Koch, Brigitte

Koch, Marlise

Kokotek, Gertrud
Born 1924 (?)

Kokotek, Moritz
Born 6 Dec. 1923 Düsseldorf

Koswicht (?), Anne

Kramer, St.

Krohn, Ruth

Krüger, Irma

Kruppe, E.

Kurzke, Heinz

Landmann, I.
Born 1924 (?)

Lau (?), Kurt
Born 1924 (?)

Laus, Adolf
Born 23 Jan. 1923 Nuremberg
31 Oct. 1938 moved,
address unknown

Leidenstreich, Robert

Leisser, H.
Born 1925 (?)

Lender, Luise

Lenneberg, Ursula
Born 24 April 1926
16 July 1942 deported to
Theresienstadt

Leopold, Heinz
Born 4 April 1924 Frankfurt
30 June 1938 United States

Lesekewitz, Lydia
Born 31 Aug. 1927 Düsseldorf
Sister of Melanie Lesekewitz
8 May 1941 moved,
address unknown
(Neumarkt, Cracow District)
Murdered

Lesekewitz, Melanie
Born 4 March 1924 Düsseldorf
Sister of Lydia Lesekewitz
8 May 1941 moved,
address unknown
(Neumarkt, Cracow District)
Murdered

L(esser), Tamara
Born 7 Nov. 1925 Berlin
25 March 1937 England

Lesser, I.

Levy, E.
Born 1926 (?)

Levy, M(ax)
Born 22 July 1923 Düsseldorf
Deported to Minsk
Murdered

Lewin, Inge(borg)
Born 9 Oct. 1925 Düsseldorf
15 Dec. 1938 Netherlands

Lewin, Mirjam
Born 1927 (?)

Lewy, A.

Lewy, Erich

Lion, Kurt
Born 26 May 1924
Oberhausen
9 Dec. 1938 Aachen
Palestine (Israel)

Loeb, Ruth
Born 1925 (?)

Löwenstein, Ernst
Born 1926 (?)

Löwenstein, Kurt

Lorch, R(olf)
Born 22 Nov. 1924
Deported to Minsk
Murdered

Lubascher, Kurt
Born 31 Dec. 1926 Solingen
26 Oct. 1941 deported to Lodź
Murdered

Mageno (?), Ita
Born 1926 (?)

Magier, Isi
Born 13 Aug. 1926
8 Nov. 1941 deported to Minsk
Murdered

Maier, Willi

Mallong, Eugen
Born 1927 (?)

Mansbach, Ernst
Born 2 Dec. 1927 Duisburg
Brother of Fritz Mansbach
Deported to Riga
Murdered in Stutthof

Mansbach, Fritz
Born 5 Oct. 1926 Osnabrück
Deported to Riga
5 Jan. 1945 Murdered in
Buchenwald

Marcus, Heinz

Margel, T(oni)
Born 18 Jan. 1927 Cologne
28 April 1943 (?) moved,
address unknown

Marx, Eva

Marx, Ilse
Born 1921 (?)

Mayer, Kurt
Born 7 Feb. 1924 Cologne

Maysner, H.

Mehr, Samuel
Born 2 Sept. 1923 Düsseldorf
31 March 1939 United States

Mendel, Dorrit
Born 27 June 1924 Düsseldorf
11 Feb. 1939 England

Mendel, Mira
Born 19 Aug. 1926 Düsseldorf
5 Nov. 1941 deported to Lodź
Murdered

Mendel, R(uth)
Born 28 Dec. 1921 Düsseldorf
5 Nov. 1941 deported to Lodź
Murdered

Meyer, Eva
Born 11 Jan. 1924 Düsseldorf
11 Oct. 1939 Hanover

Mezer, G.
Born 1924 (?)

Michels, Ursula
Born 10 Nov. 1925 Düsseldorf
6 Nov. 1941 deported to Minsk
Murdered

Milchtajch, H(elmut)
Born 15 Dec. 1923 Rheydt
Palestine

Monger, Kurt
Born 1924 (?)

Moritz, Dora
Born 17 Dec. 1926 Glogow,
Galicia
Sister of Isaak and Rosa Moritz
6 March 1939 moved,
address unknown
Palestine (Israel)

Moritz, Isaak
Born 11 Aug. 1924 Glogow,
Galicia
Brother of Dora and Rosa
Moritz
6 March 1939 moved,
address unknown

Moritz, K.
Born 1923 (?)

Moritz, Rosa
Born 6 Feb. 1925 Glogow,
Galicia
Sister of Dora and Isaak Moritz
10 Sept. 1938 Jessen, Lausitz

Mosebach, Lore

Motzler (?), Gertrud

Mundt, Hilde

Nathan, Paul M(artin)
Born 10 Nov. 1921 Düsseldorf
England

Nechemie, Rudi
Born 27 Feb. 1927 Düsseldorf
2 Jan. 1940 moved,
address unknown

Nickel, Christel

Niklaus (?), Hilde

Orbach, Günther
Born 27 Feb. 1927 Düsseldorf
10 Aug. 1939 England

Ortmann, Mali
Born 9 Dec. 1921 Düsseldorf
9 Sept. 1938 Jessen, Lausitz

Ott, Anneliese

Ott, Ingeborg

Papendorf, Gerda

Paradies, Sella Helga
Born 8 April 1924 Düsseldorf
8 Nov. 1941 deported to Minsk
Murdered

Philipp, H(annelore)
Born 26 Jan. 1925 Düsseldorf
Deported to Minsk
Murdered

Pluntke, Alfred

Przepiorka, Esther Ruth
Born 6 Jan. 1924 Düsseldorf
13 Dec. 1939 England

Pschednowek, Ruth
Born 14 Jan. 1924 Cologne

Ran, Lotti (Charlotte)
Born 19 Jan. 1925 Düsseldorf

Rechtmann, S(elma)
Born 26 Nov. 1924 Hamburg
20 July 1939 England

Rechtmann, S(onja)

Reich, Kurt

Reich, Leo
Born 21 July 1924 Düsseldorf

Reuter, Lotte
Born 28 May 1925 Wuppertal-Elberfeld
11 Oct. 1938 Belgium

Robert, Marga (Margit)
Born 8 May 1927 Düsseldorf
25 Jan. 1937 Italy

Röhl, Anke
Born 1921 (?)

Rokotter, G.

Rosenbaum, Herta
Born 12 Dec. 1927 Düsseldorf

Rosenblatt, Hilde

Rosenstock, M.

Rosenstock, Werner
Born 22 Feb. 1927 Frankfurt am Main
Deported to Minsk
Murdered

Rosenthal, B(ernhard?)
Born 19 Oct. 1922 Düsseldorf
16 Feb. 1938 moved

Rosenthal, Friedel
Born 1925 (?)

Rosenthal, Gerd
Born 24 June 1926
Oberhausen

Rosenthal, Ruth
Born 13 July 1925 Diez/Lahn

Rosner, Max
Born 2 July 1928 Düsseldorf
3 March 1939 moved,
address unknown

Rothbein, Edith
Born 21 July 1922 Düsseldorf
22 Sept. 1938 Berlin
11 March 1939 Palestine

Rothbein, Friedel (Fritz)
Born 8 May 1925 Düsseldorf
Murdered

Rothschild, Georges
Born 1924 (?)

Rüssler, Esther
Born 14 Oct. 1927 Düsseldorf

Rustmann, Sonja

Säbel, Lotte
Born 1922 (?)

Säbel, Reni
Born 7 Oct. 1922 Solokow,
Galicia

Salomon, Margot
Born 14 April 1924 Laub
11 Dec. 1941 deported to Riga
Murdered

Salpeter, Doris (Dorothea?)
Born 24 Feb. 1928 Düsseldorf
23 May 1939 moved,
address unknown

Salpeter, Kläre
Born 30 May 1923 Düsseldorf
23 May 1939 moved,
address unknown

Sauerhaft, Sofie
Born 25 Sept. 1922 Düsseldorf

Schade, E.

Scheidemann, Helmut
Born 14 Sept. 1924 Berlin

Schiff, Ilse

Schindelheim, Leontine

Schlön, Grete

Schmidheim, L.

Schmidt, Elisabeth

Schnick (?), Heinz

Schönbach, Ellen V.
Born 2 April 1924 Cologne
Sister of Helga Schönbach
19 Aug. 1942 murdered at
Auschwitz

Schönbach, Helga
Born 4 Aug. 1921 Cologne
Sister of Ellen V. Schönbach
31 Jan. 1939 Cologne
Deported to Lodź
Murdered

Schuster, Vera
Born 6 Nov. 1925 Düsseldorf
19 Jan. 1939 Belgium
Deported to Auschwitz
Murdered

Schwarz, H(einz)
Born 27 June 1926 Eschweiler
Brother of Henni Schwarz
27 April 1938 Netherlands

Schwarz, H(enni)
Born 29 Nov. 1923 Düsseldorf
Sister of Heinz Schwarz
27 April 1938 Netherlands

Seelig, Gerda
Born 1923 (?)

Seligmann, Heleni (Leni)
Born 7 June 1926 Düsseldorf
9 June 1939 Belgium
8 Nov. 1941 deported to Minsk
Murdered

Seligmann, M(arianne)
Born 26 Nov. 1924 Düsseldorf
2 Sept. 1939 England

Sichel, Ellionor

Sichel, Stefan

Sondermann, Kurt
Born 6 May 1924 Düsseldorf
Brother of Stella Sondermann

Sondermann, Stella
Born 10 April 1928 Düsseldorf
Sister of Kurt Sondermann

Sonnenberg, Klaus
Born 1926 (?)

Sostheim, G.

Spiess, Ruth

Steggel, Paul

Steinfeld, Gerda
Born 18 Dec. 1926 Düsseldorf
8 Nov. 1941 deported to Minsk

Steppel, Henni
Born 23 Sept. 1925 Lancut, Galicia
6 June 1939 moved, address unknown

Stern, Fritz
Born 1922 (?)

Sternlicht, Leo
Born 1926 (?)

Stock, W(alter)
Born 21 July 1925 Düsseldorf

Straus, Gisela
Born 24 Sept. 1923 Krefeld
Sister of Inge and Rudi Straus
21 June 1938 United States

Straus, Inge
Born 24 Sept. 1923 Krefeld
Sister of Gisela and Rudi Straus
21 June 1938 United States

Straus, Rudi
Born 19 Feb. 1927 Krefeld
Brother of Gisela and Inge Straus
21 June 1938 United States

Strauss, Hans
Born 1926 (?)

Skodig..., Olga

Tändel, Vera
Born 1922 (?)

Taufer, Erich

Testiler, Helene
Born 2 March 1926 Düsseldorf
31 July 1939 Lodź

Tugendhaft, Emanuel
Born 10 March 1922 Sokolow, Galicia

Udenwald, Ruth
Born 19 July 1925 Wuppertal-Elberfeld
23 Dec. 1938 United States

Vogel, Inge
Born 1924 (?)

Wahrenberg, Gerhard
Born 13 Nov. 1924 Sieniawa
15 March 1939 Poland

Wahrenberg, I.
Born 1925 (?)

Wallach, Ellen
Born 8 May 1928 Düsseldorf
August 1938 Cologne

Wallach, Eugen
Born 10 March 1937 Düsseldorf
8 Aug. 1939 England

Walter, Helga

Weissmüller, Edith

Westfeld, Gerd
Born 22 Dec. 1925 Düsseldorf
15 March 1939 England

Wilk, Lena
Born 5 Sept. 1923 Düsseldorf
22 July 1939 moved, address unknown

Winter, Adolf
Born 27 May 1923 Düsseldorf

Winter, Vera
Born 28 Dec. 1924 Krefeld

Wolf, Berthold
Born 23 March 1925 Hülchrath
11 Dec. 1941 deported to Riga
Murdered

Wolf, Ernst
Born 28 March 1927 Düsseldorf
Brother of Hella Wolf
26 Aug. 1937 United States

Wolf, Gisela
Born 21 July 1925 Gerresheim
2 Sept. 1938 United States

Wolf, Hella
Born 8 May 1924 Düsseldorf
Sister of Ernst Wolf
26 Aug. 1938 United States

Wollschläger, Waltraud

Zander, Otto
Born 11 Aug. 1925 Düsseldorf
8 Nov. 1941 deported to Lodź
Murdered

Zelmann, Ephraim
Born 18 Sept. 1927 Düsseldorf
16 Dec. 1938 Netherlands

Zuckermann, Leo
Born 25 Feb. 1929 Düsseldorf
15 Feb. 1939 moved, address unknown

Zuckermann, Norbert
Born 2 July 1926
15 Febr. 1939 moved, address unknown

Zürndorfer, Hanna
Born 5 Dec. 1925 Düsseldorf
19 May 1939 England

The Fate of the Teachers at the Düsseldorf Private Jewish Elementary School

A report by Dr. Kurt Herz from January 1937 revealed that the Düsseldorf school had eighteen teachers, of whom ten were employed full time. The following names could be identified:

Bergel, Kurt
Feb. 1939 England, later United States

Eichelberg, Grete
Feb. 1939 Palestine

Friedländer, Erma
Jan. 1939 England

Gerszonowicz, Luser Mendel
1939 left Essen for Belgium
Murdered

Herz, Ellen
1939 England,
later United States

Herz, Dr. Kurt
1939 England,
later United States

Klein, Dr. Siegfried
1941 deported to Lodź
Murdered

Kleinmann, Julius
March 1939 Belgium, later United States

Levin, Julo
1943 deported to Auschwitz
Murdered

Nussbaum, Dr. Ruth
April 1938 Berlin, later Palestine

Palm, Erwin
1941 deported to Minsk
Murdered

Ms. Schmidt

Schnook, Kurt
1941 deported to Minsk
Murdered

Schnook, Thea
1941 deported to Minsk
Murdered

Strauss, Dr. Beatrice
1937 Essen
1941 deported to Minsk
Murdered

Vogel, Leopold
1941 deported to Minsk
Murdered

Ms. Weinberg

Weiss, Werner
1939 Palestine

The Students' Art and Other Illustrations

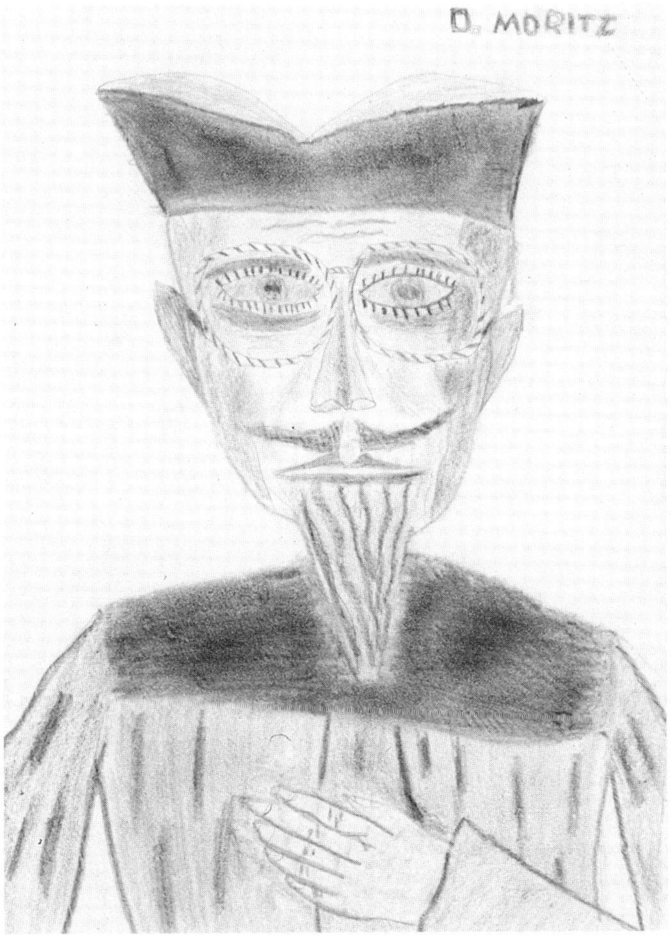

46 Dora Moritz, *Rabbi*, Oct. 1937 (Cat. 24)

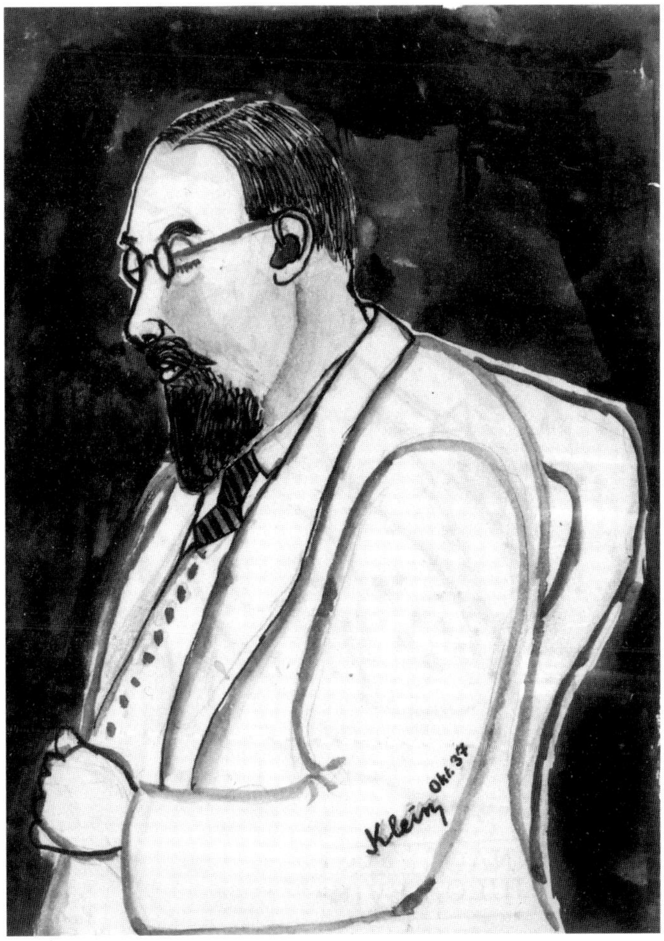

47 Name unknown, *Dr. Siegfried Klein*, Oct. 1937 (Cat. 23)

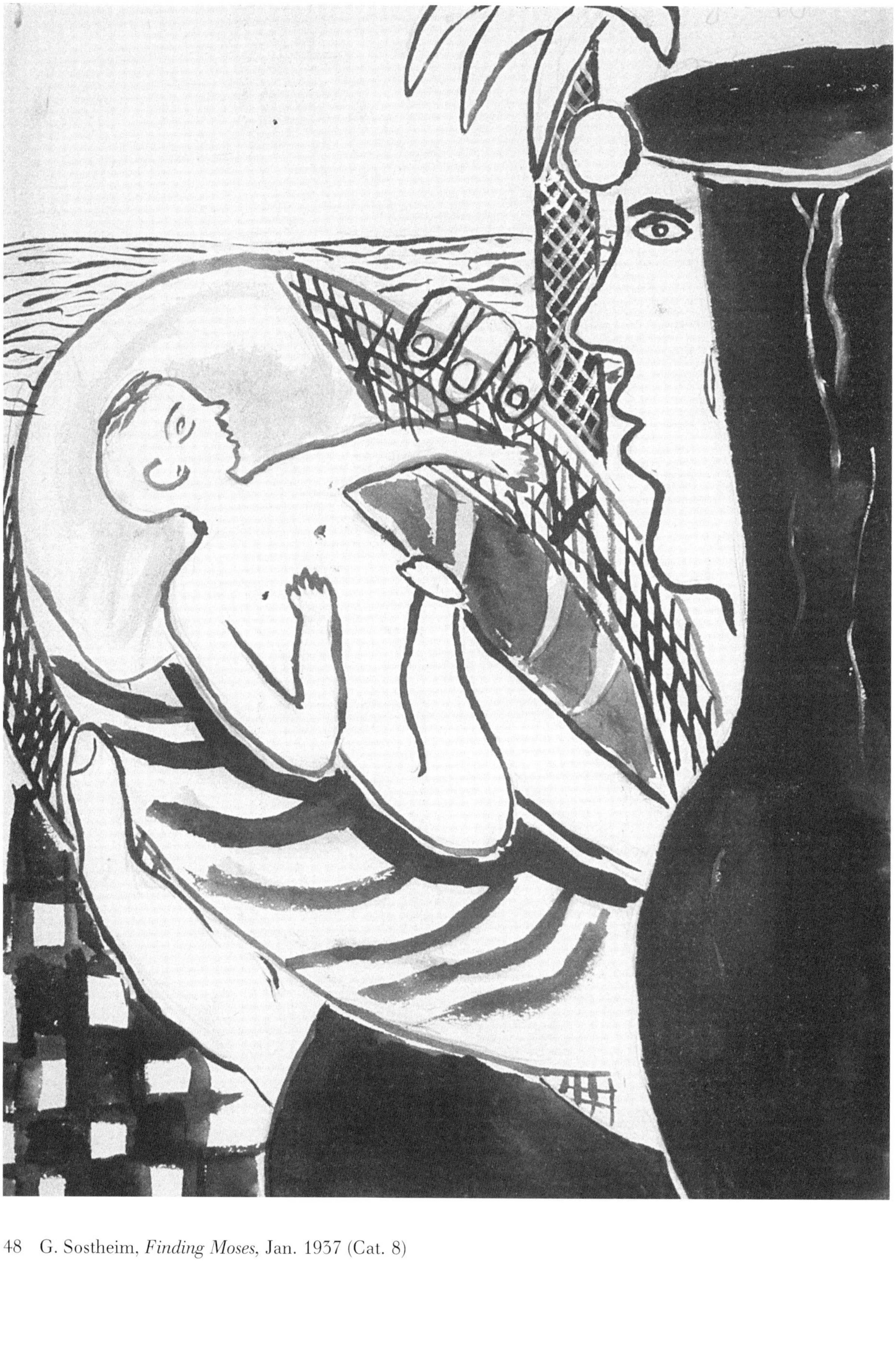

48 G. Sostheim, *Finding Moses*, Jan. 1937 (Cat. 8)

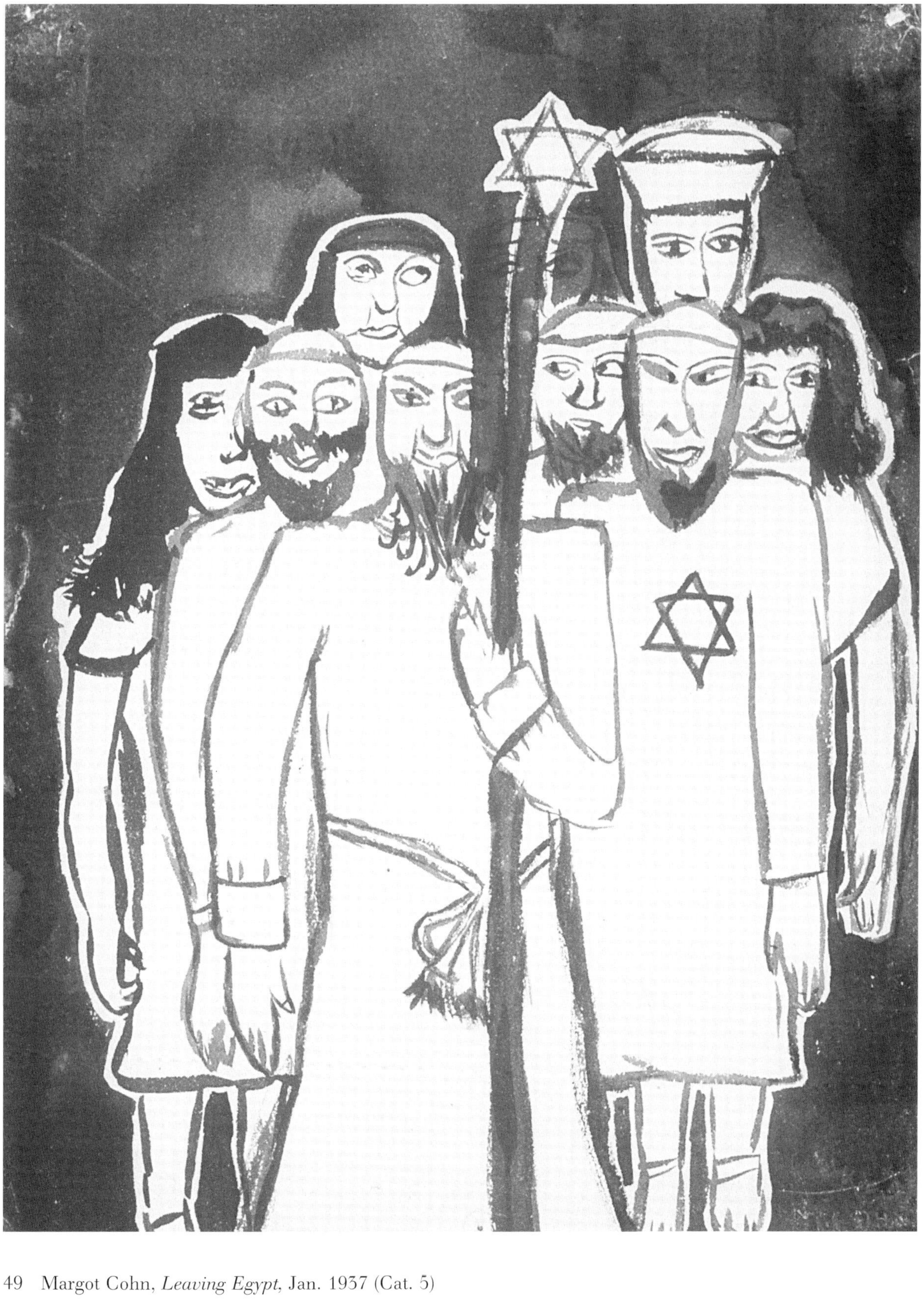

49 Margot Cohn, *Leaving Egypt,* Jan. 1937 (Cat. 5)

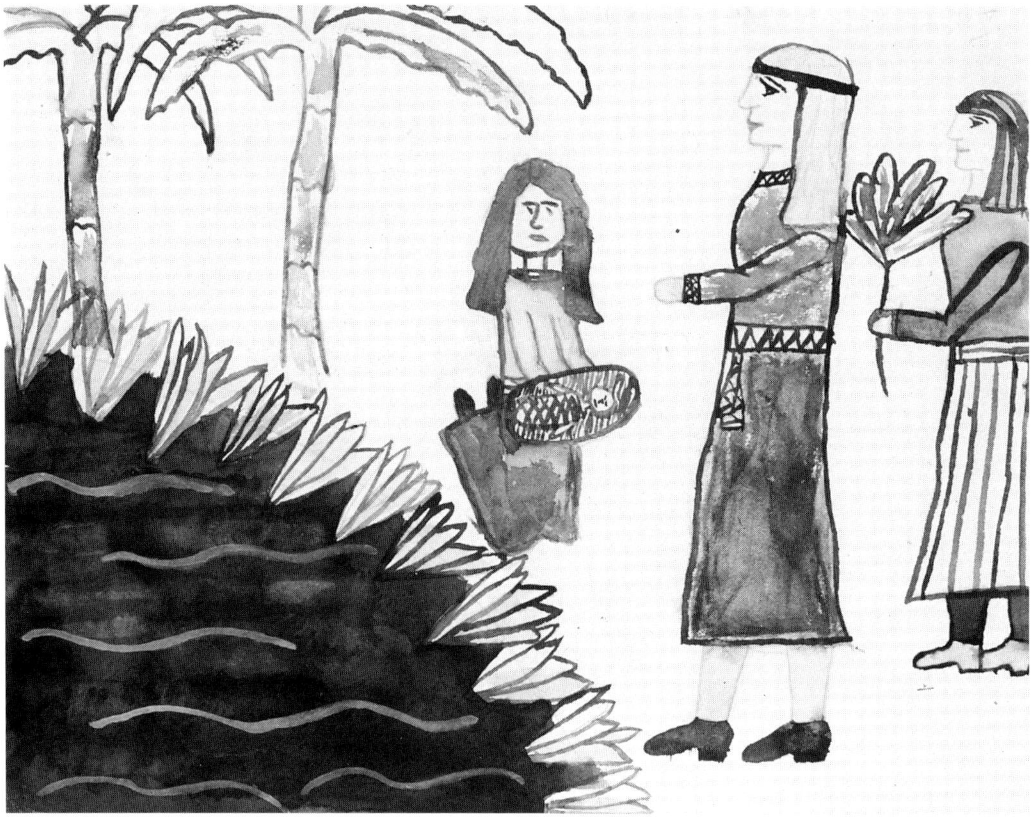

50 Name unknown,
Finding Moses,
Feb. 1937
(Cat. 9)

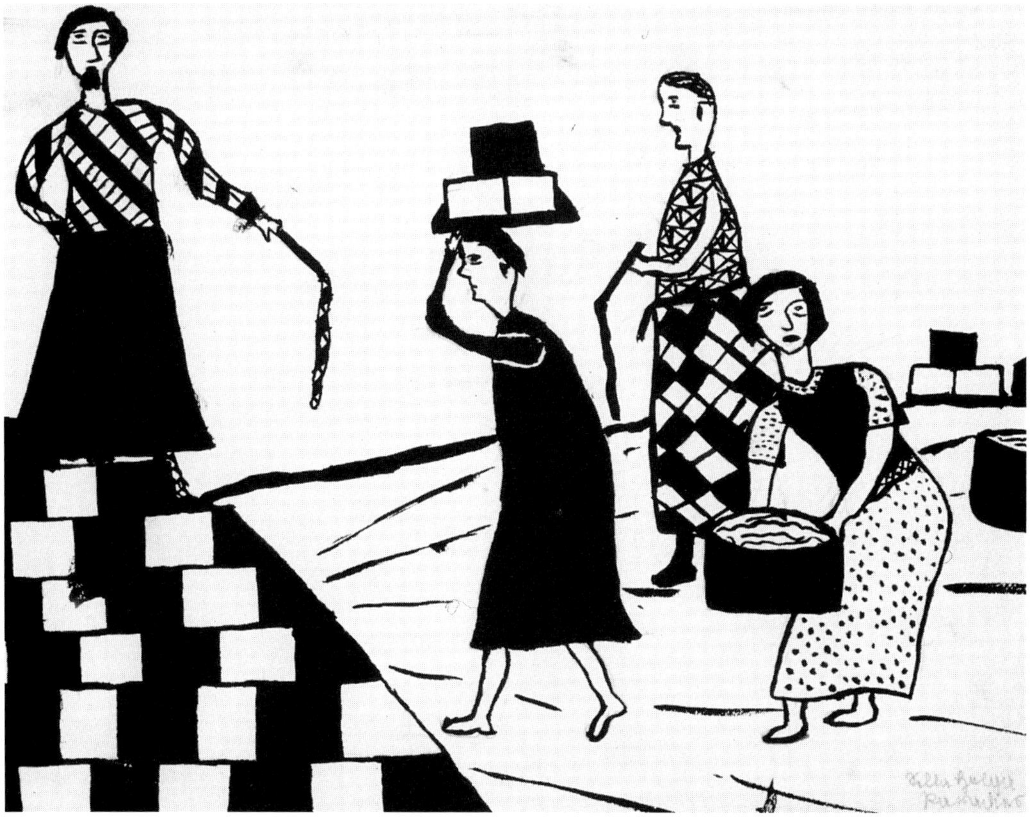

51 Sella Helga Paradies,
Slave Labor in Egypt,
Jan. 1937
(Cat. 7)

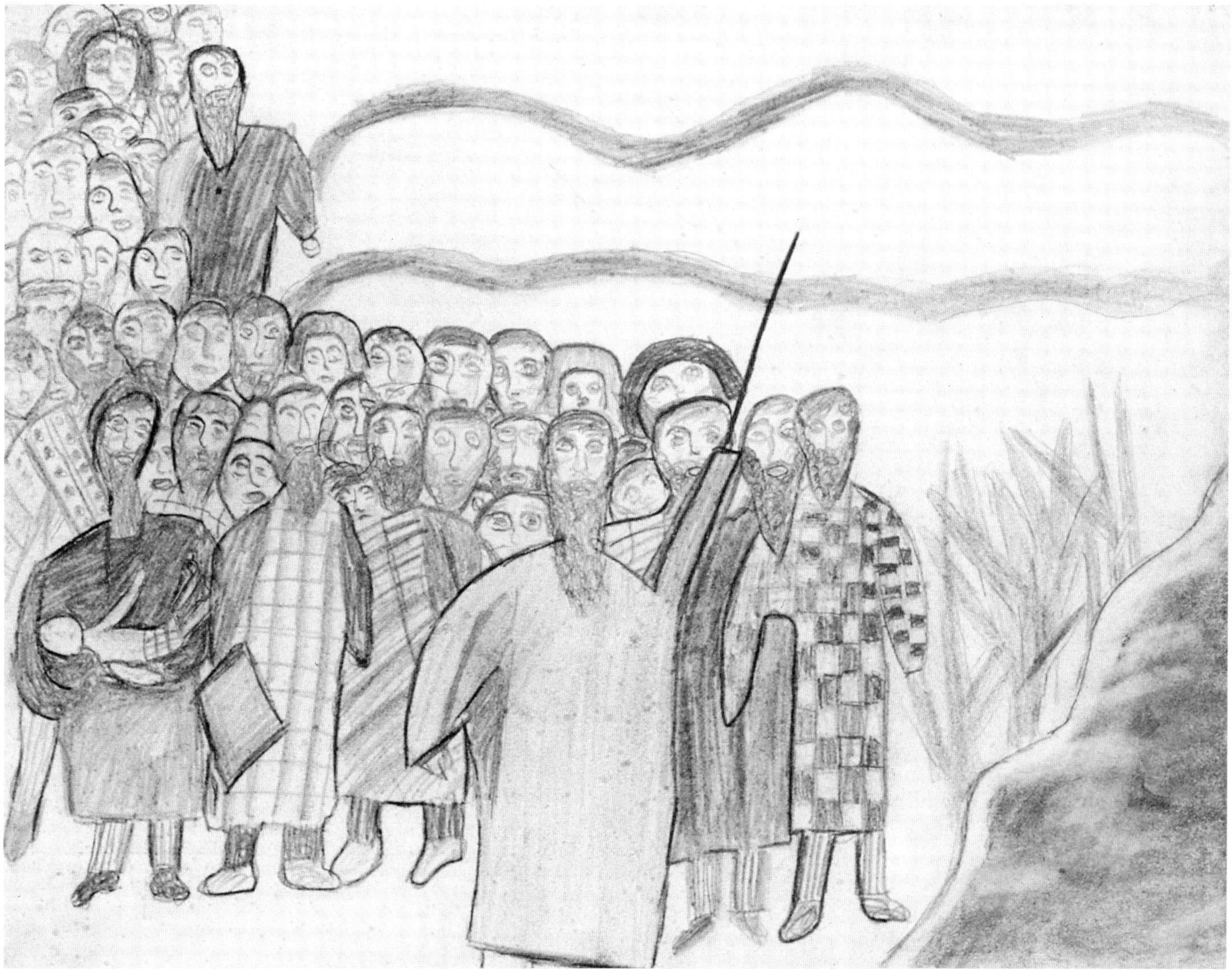

52 Name unknown, *Moses Parts the Red Sea*, undated (Cat. 6)

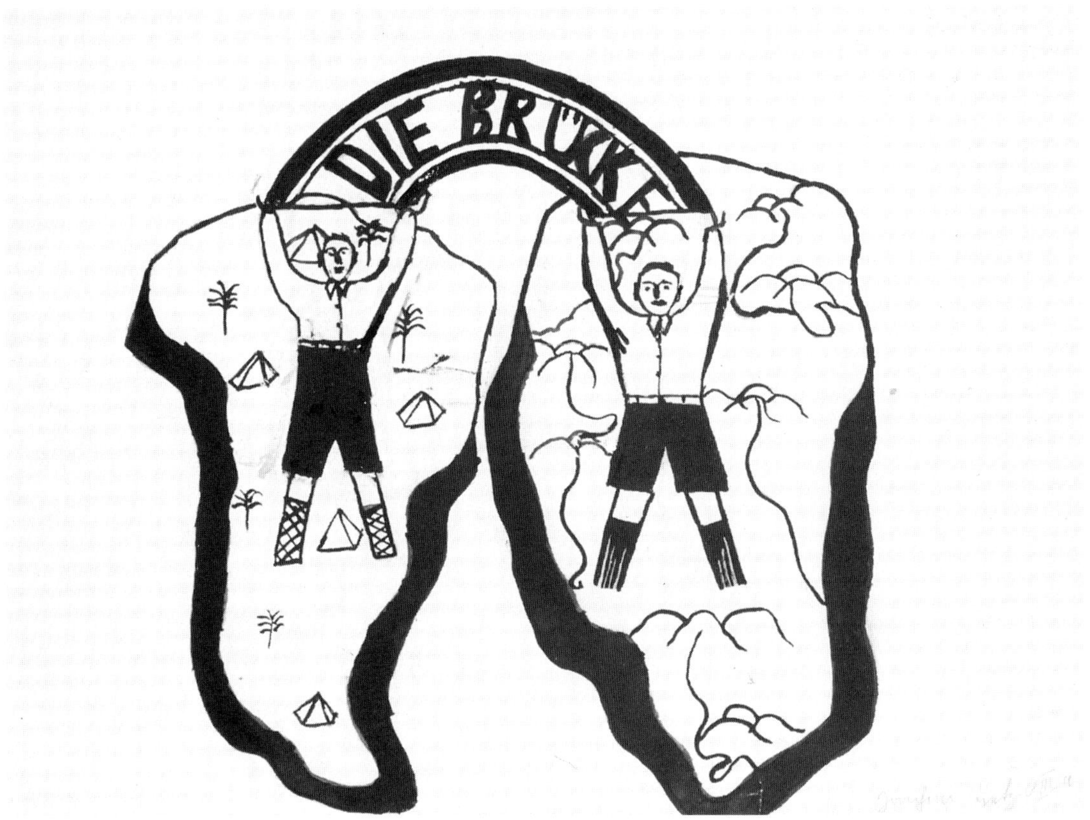

53 Joachim Tietz, *"Die Brücke" [The Bridge]*, competition for frontispiece design of student magazine in the Kaliski School, Berlin, Nov. 1938 (Cat. 56)

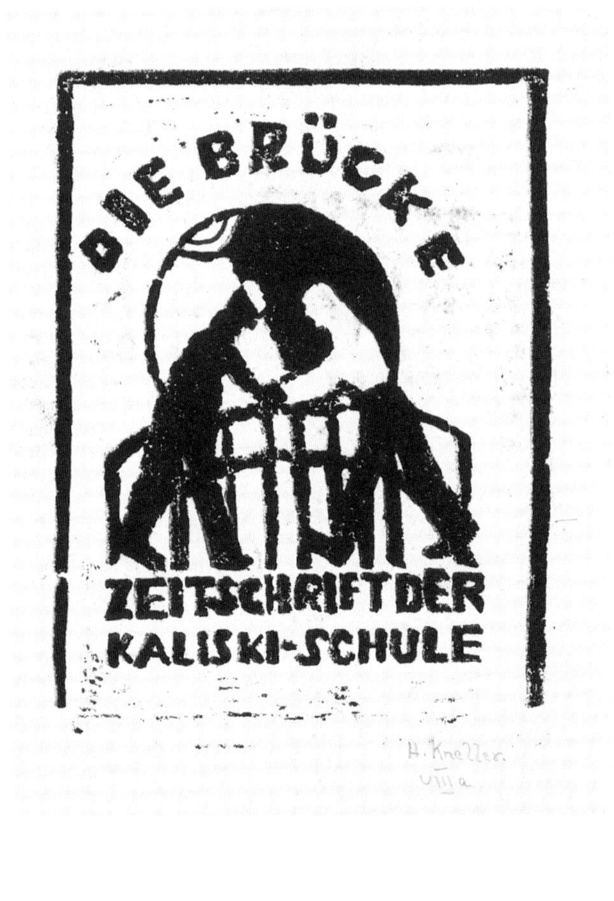

54 H. Kneller, *"Die Brücke" [The Bridge]*, Nov. 1938 (Cat. 57)

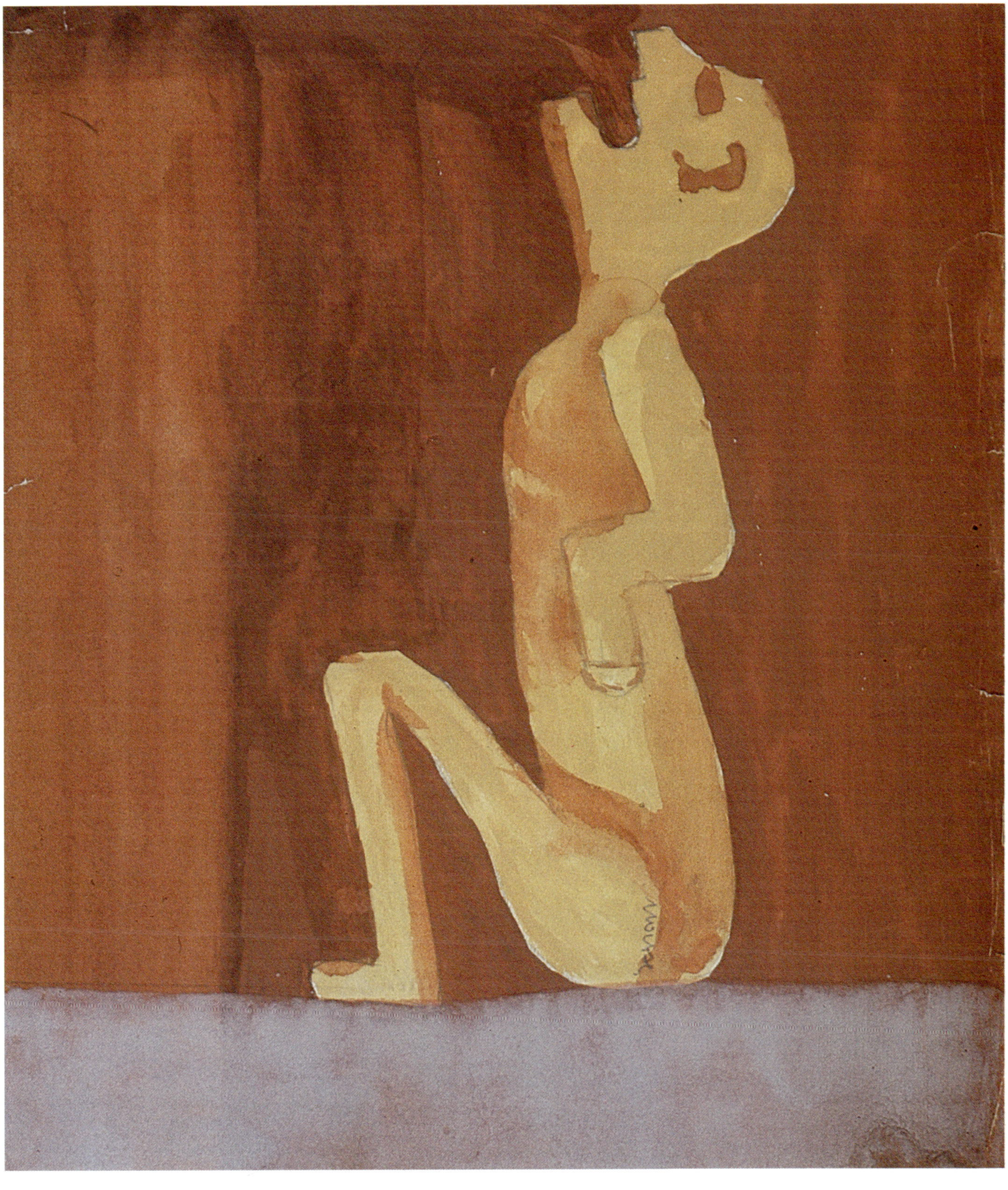

55 Ilse Marx, *Job*, 1936 (Cat. 1; front cover)

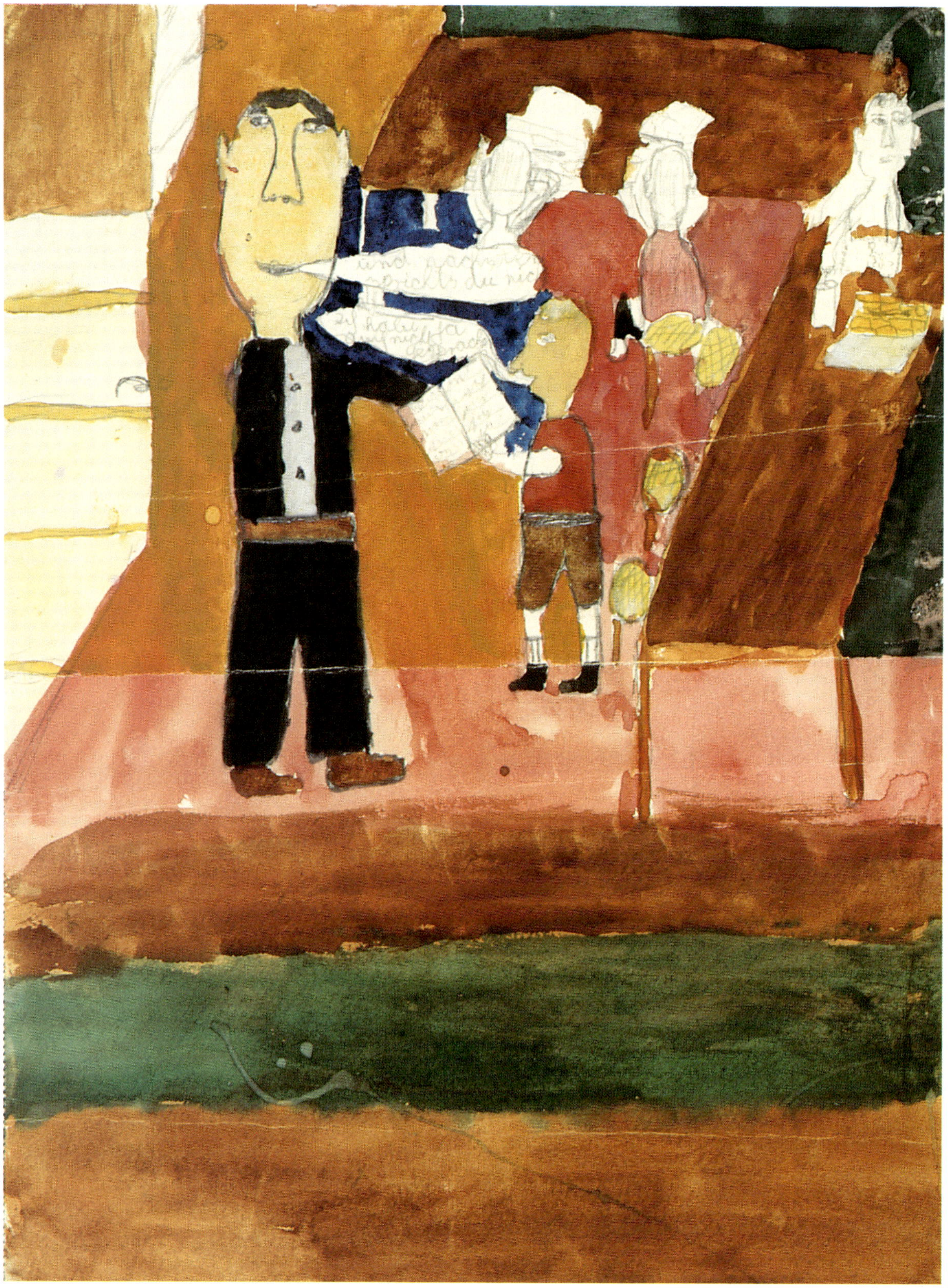

56 Name unknown, *The Art Class*, Dec. 1936 (Cat. 2)

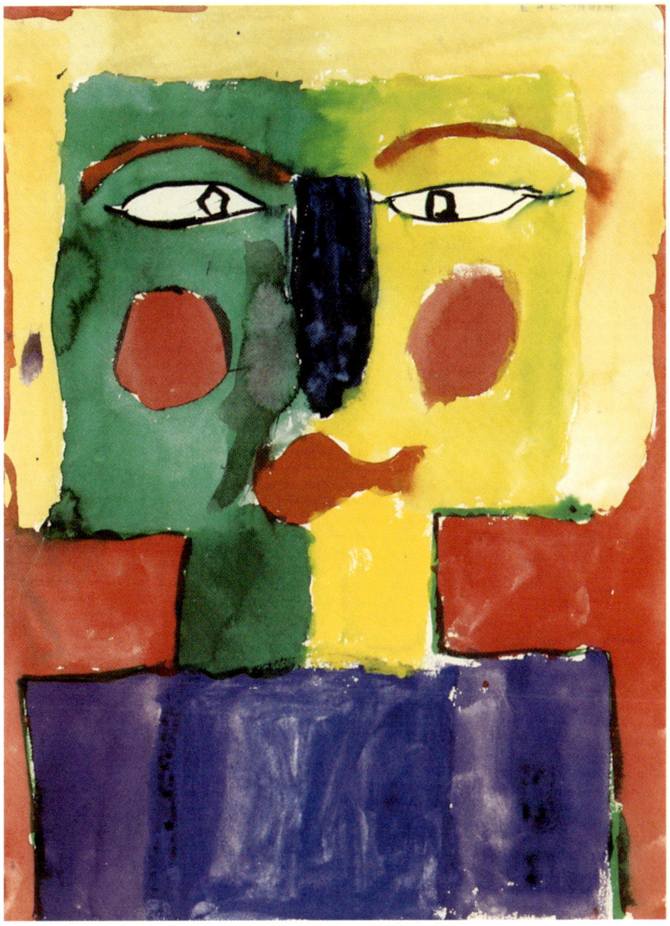

57 Eva Alexander, *Faces, Masks*, Feb. 1937 (Cat. 10)

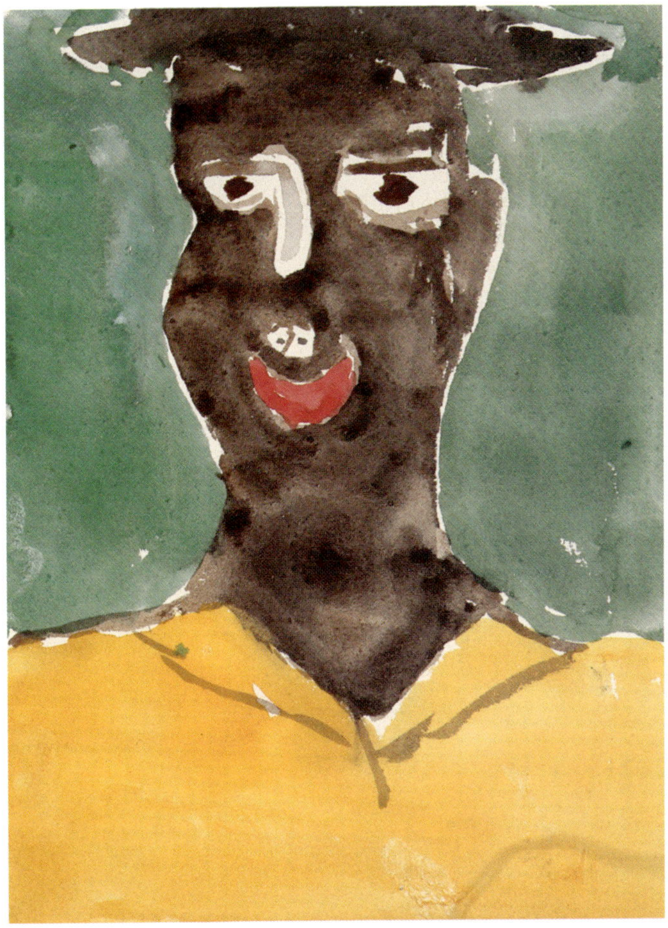

58 Name unknown, *Black Man*, undated (Cat. 14)

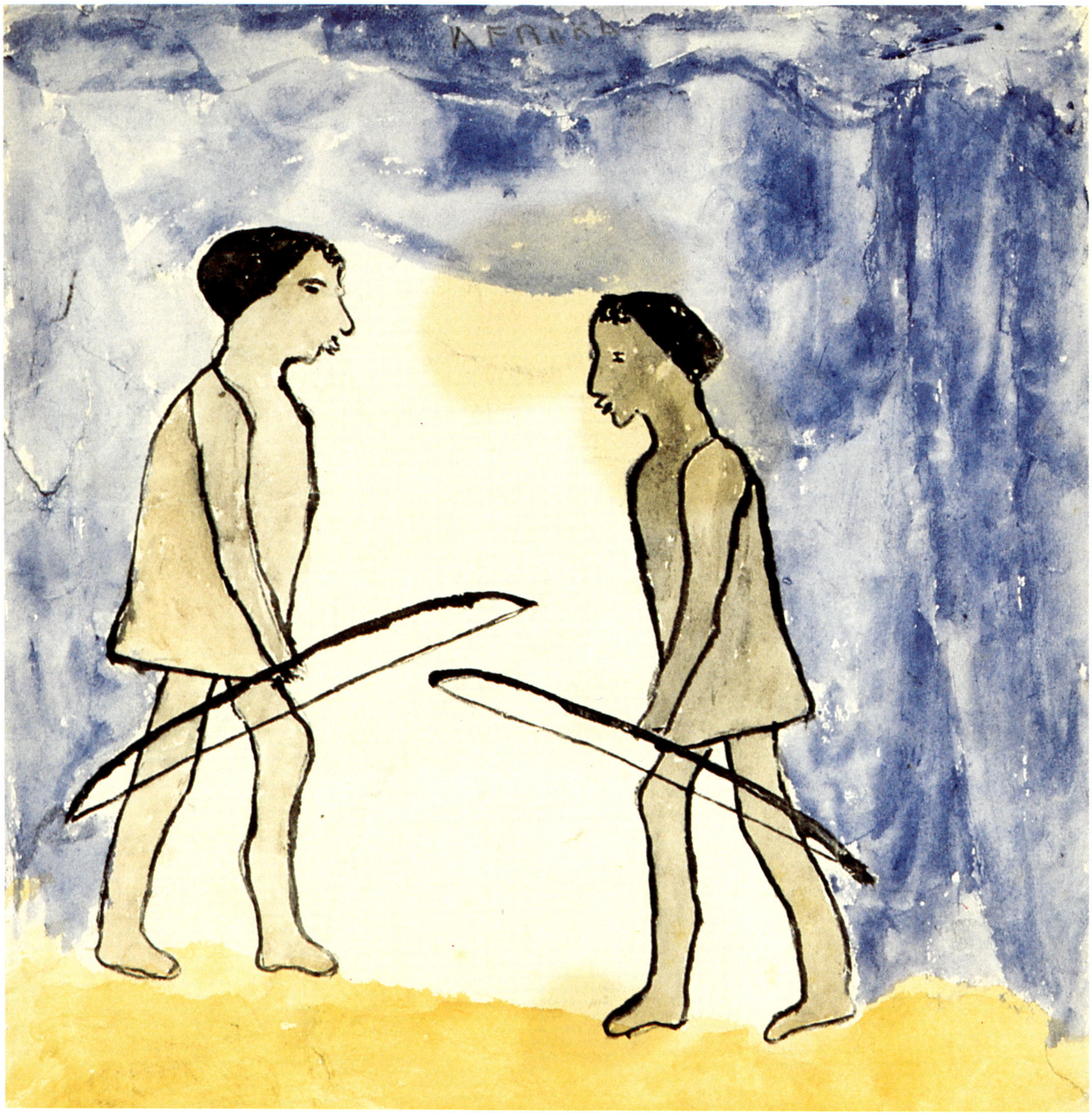

59 Margot Salomon, *Africa*, March 1937 (Cat. 12)

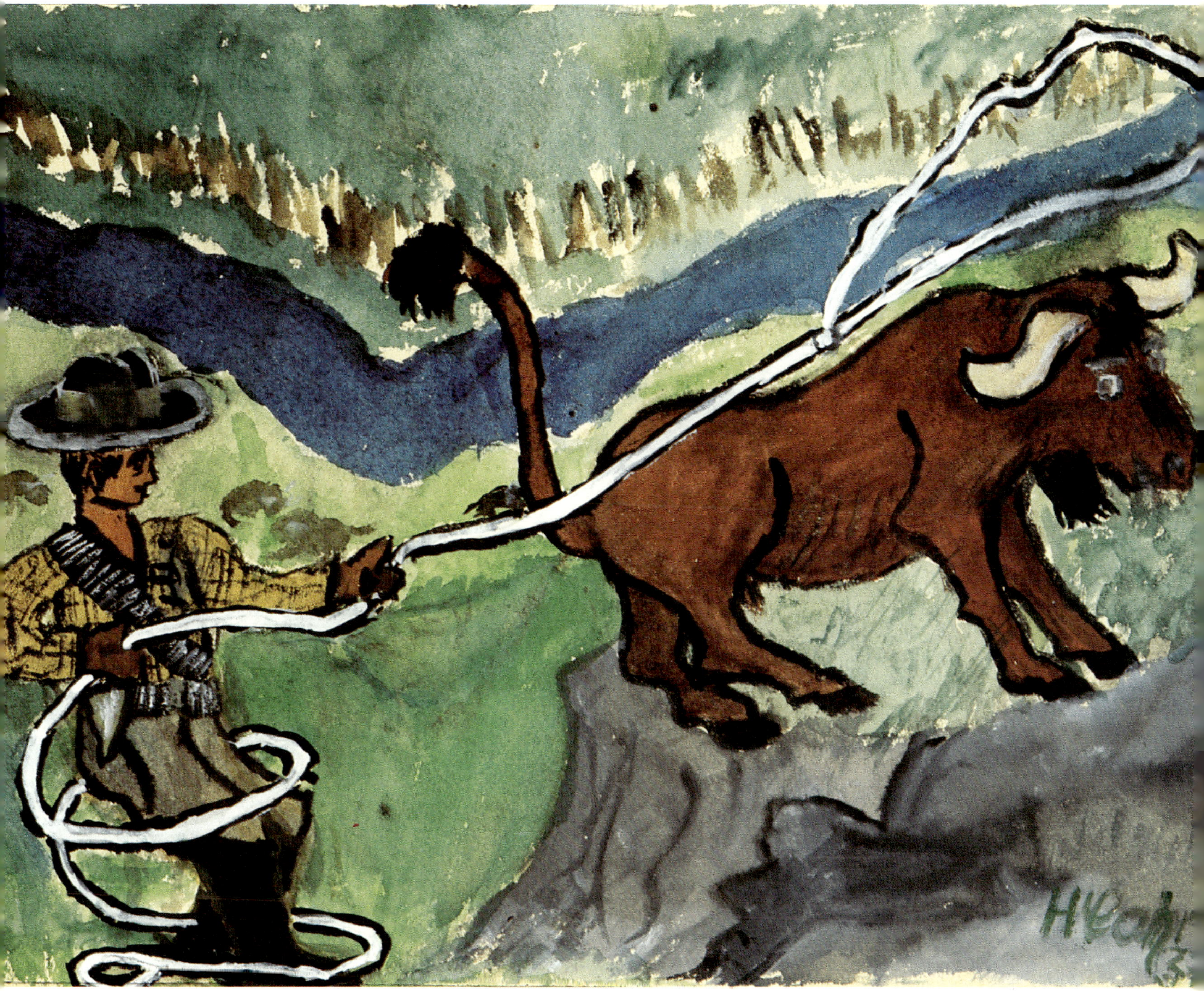
60 Helmut Cahn, *Cowboy*, 1937 (Cat. 4)

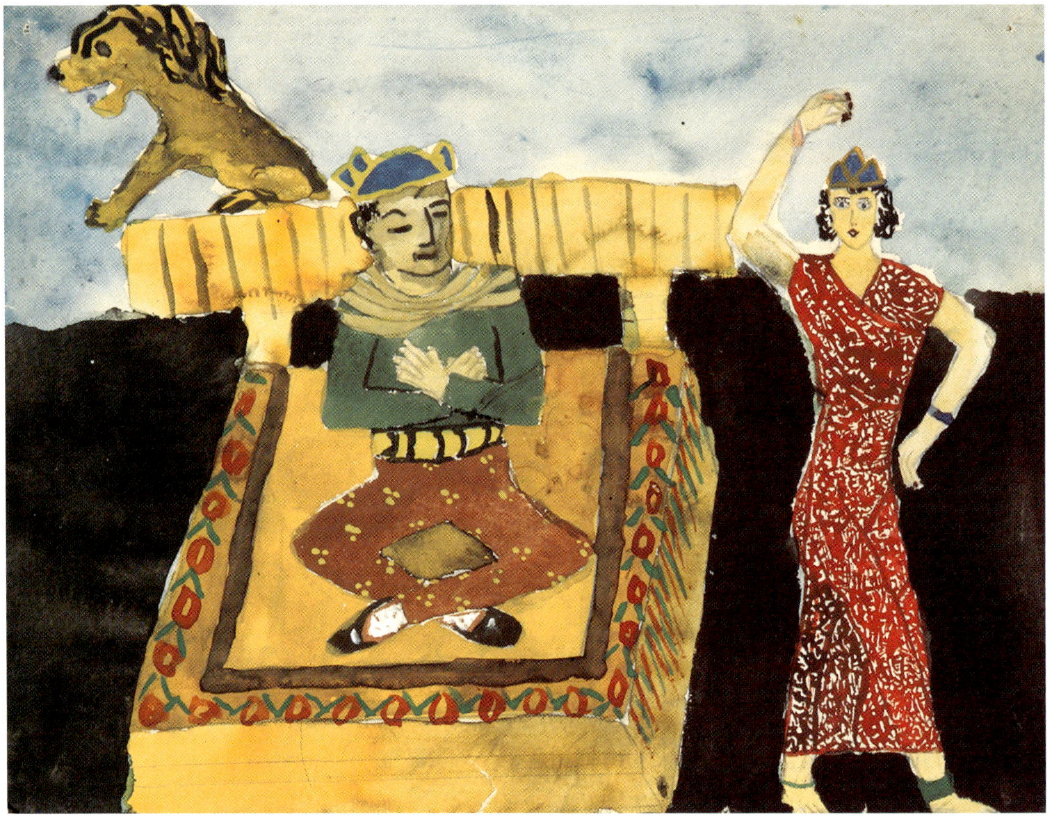

61 Henni Schwarz,
India,
May 1937
(Cat. 16)

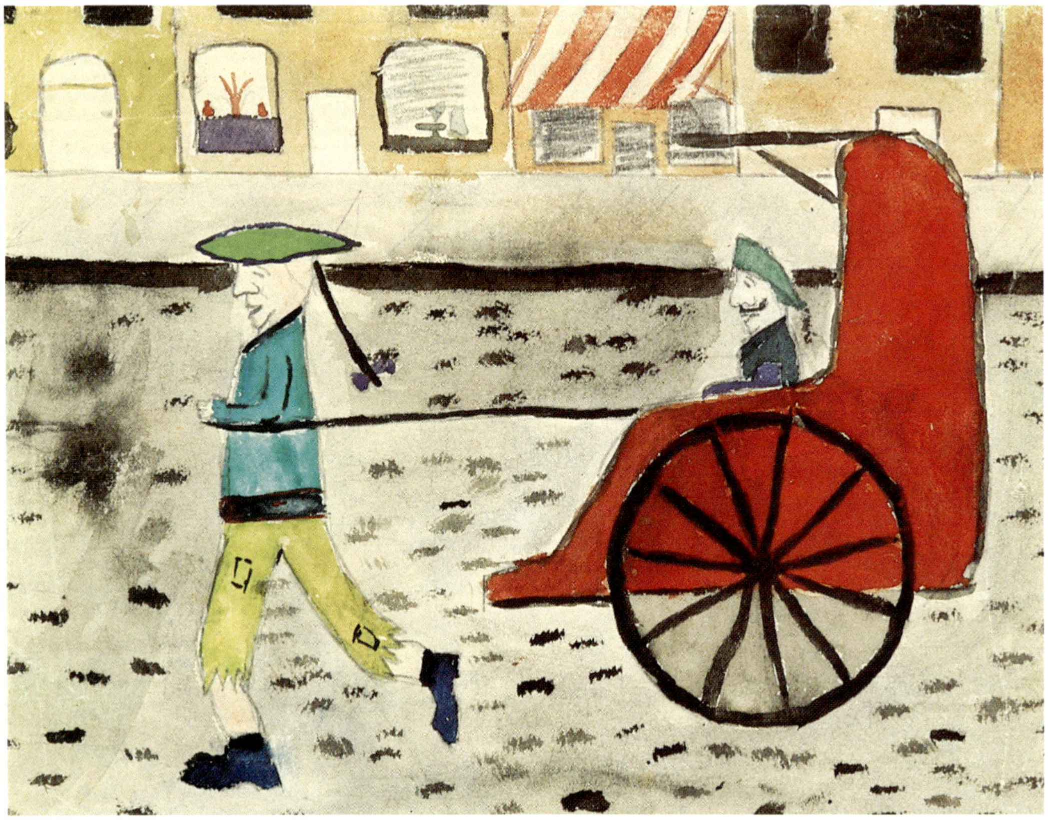

62 Name unknown,
China,
May 1937
(Cat. 17)

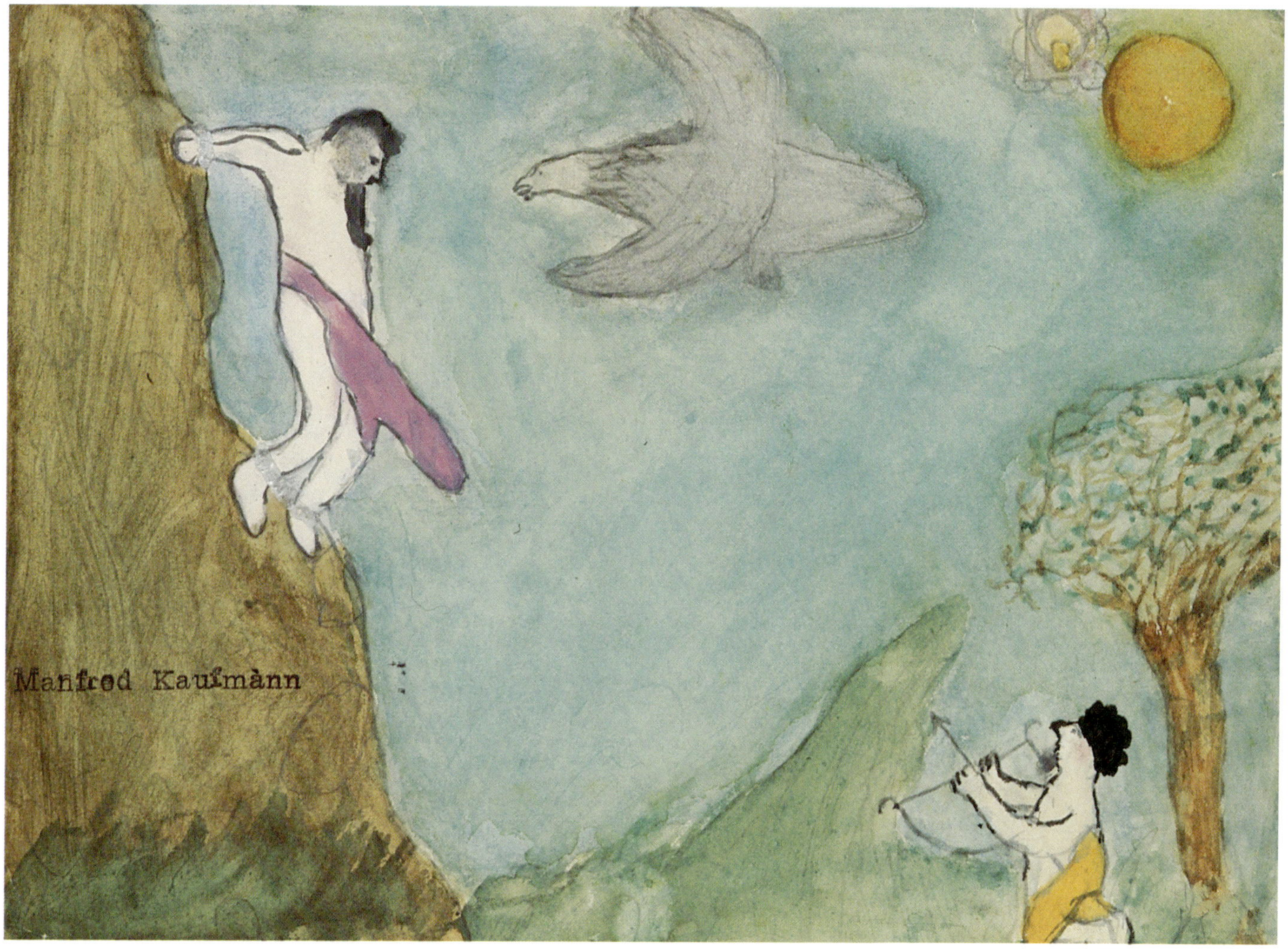

63 Manfred Kaufmann, *Prometheus*, May 1937 (Cat. 15)

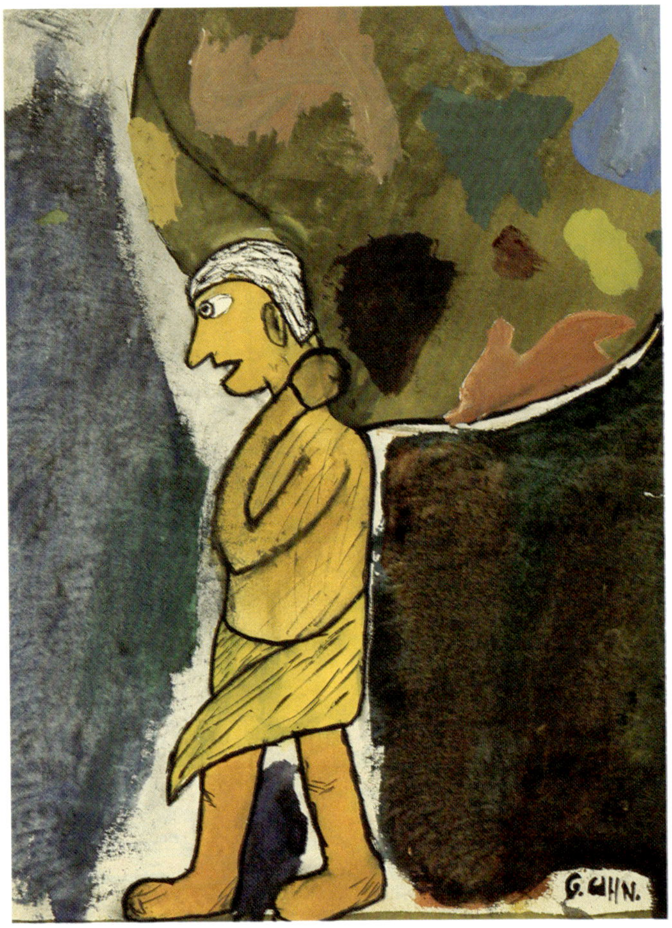

64 Günther Cahn, *Atlas*, June 1937 (Cat. 19)

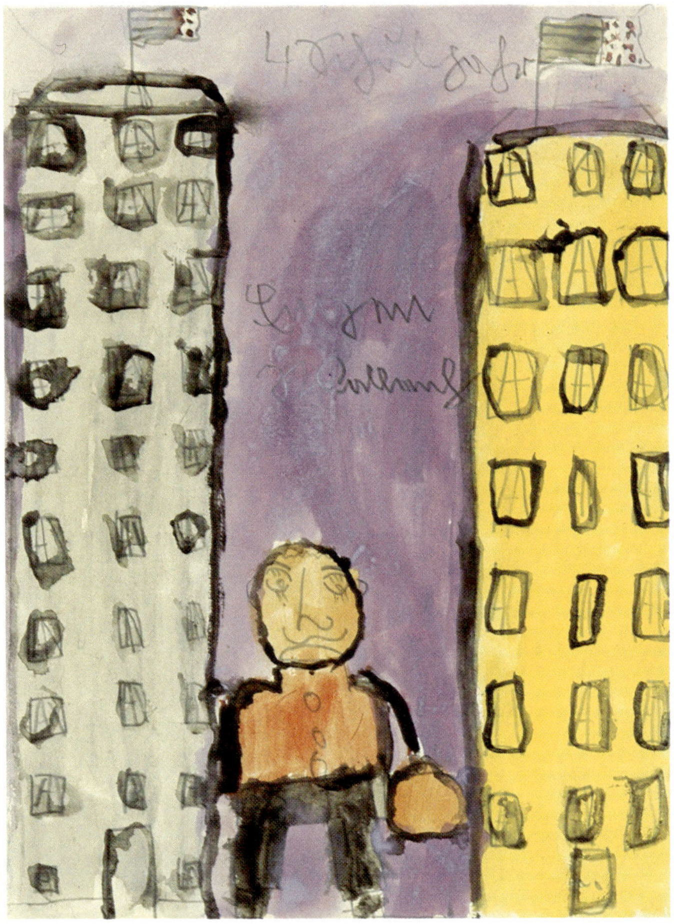

65 Eugen Wallach, *The Emigrant*, Oct. 1937 (Cat. 25)

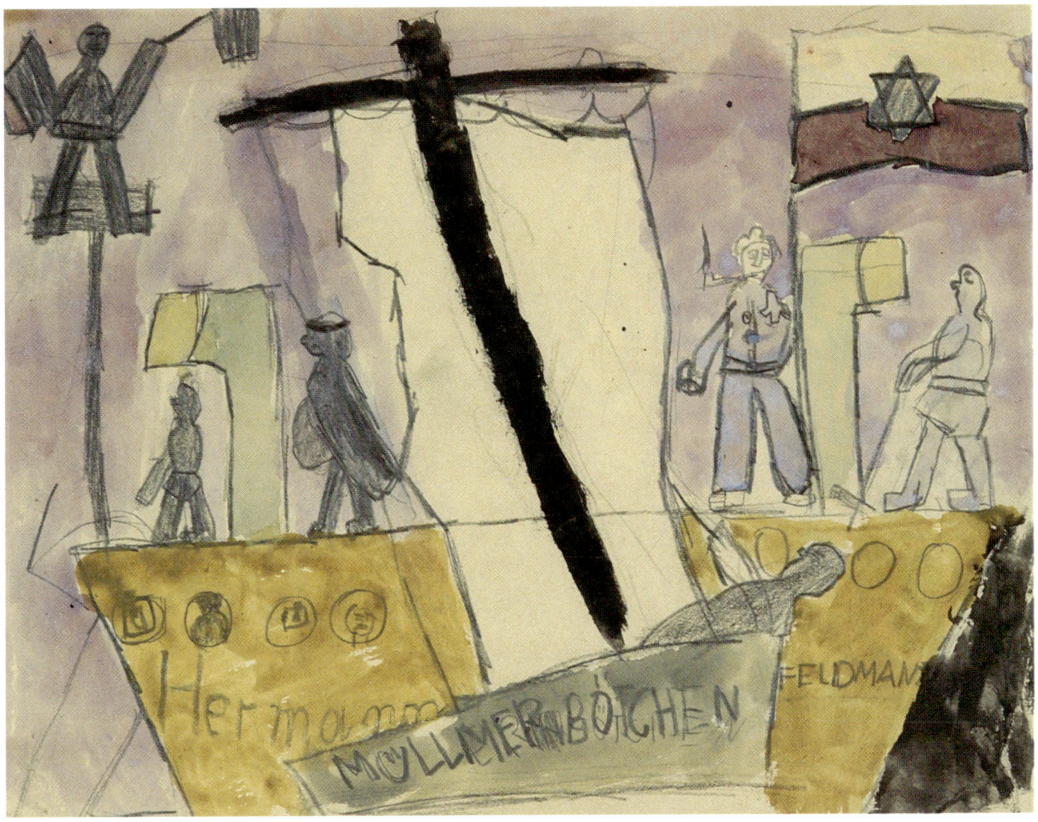

66 Hermann Feldmann,
Müllmer's Small Boat,
undated
(Cat. 26)

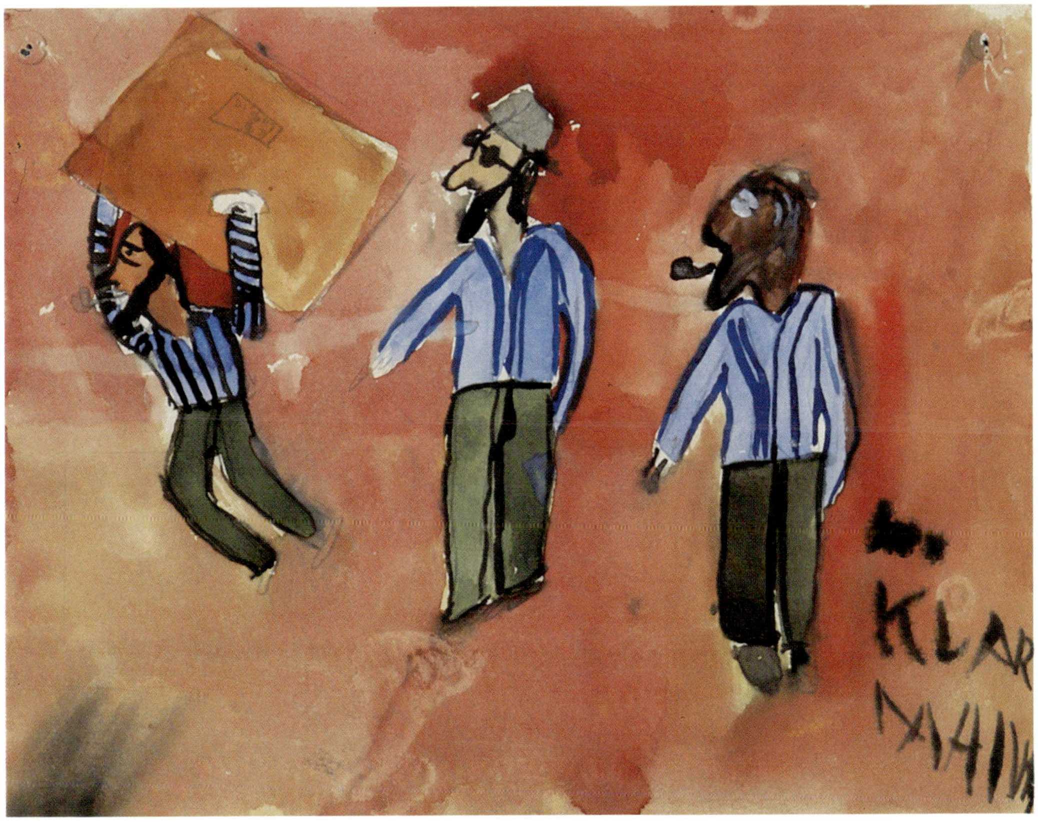

67 Leo-Wolf Klarmann,
The Mover,
Oct. 1937
(Cat. 31)

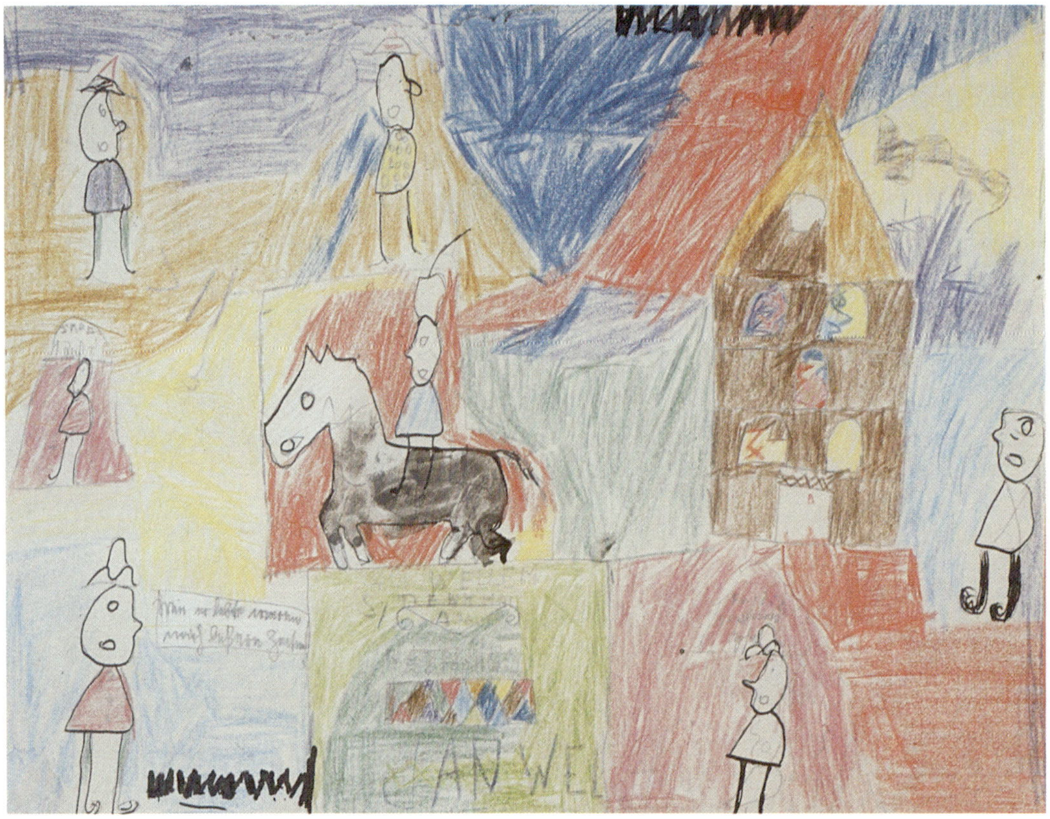

68 Heinz Leopold,
Düsseldorf: The Old City,
Oct. 1937
(Cat. 29)

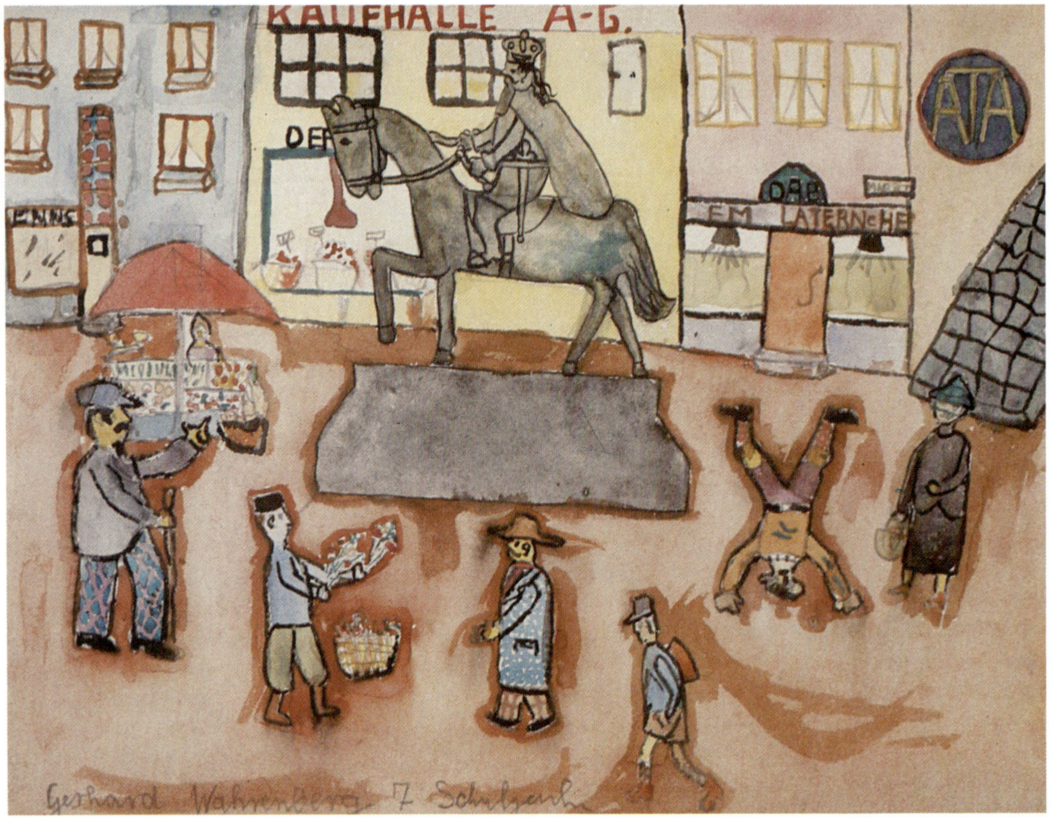

69 Gerhard Wahrenberg,
Düsseldorf: The Old City,
Nov. 1937
(Cat. 40)

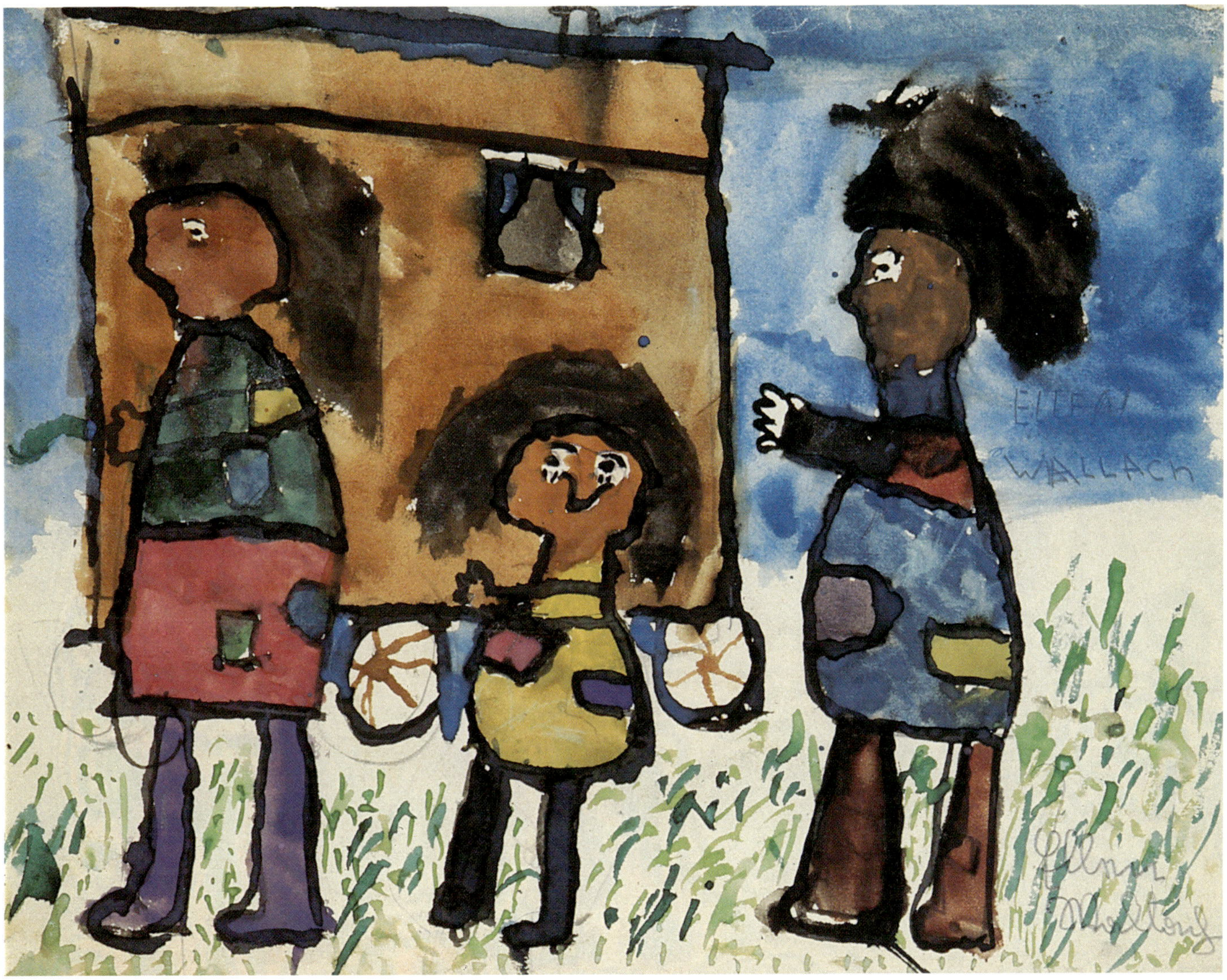

70 Ellen Wallach, *Gypsies*, Oct. 1937 (Cat. 27)

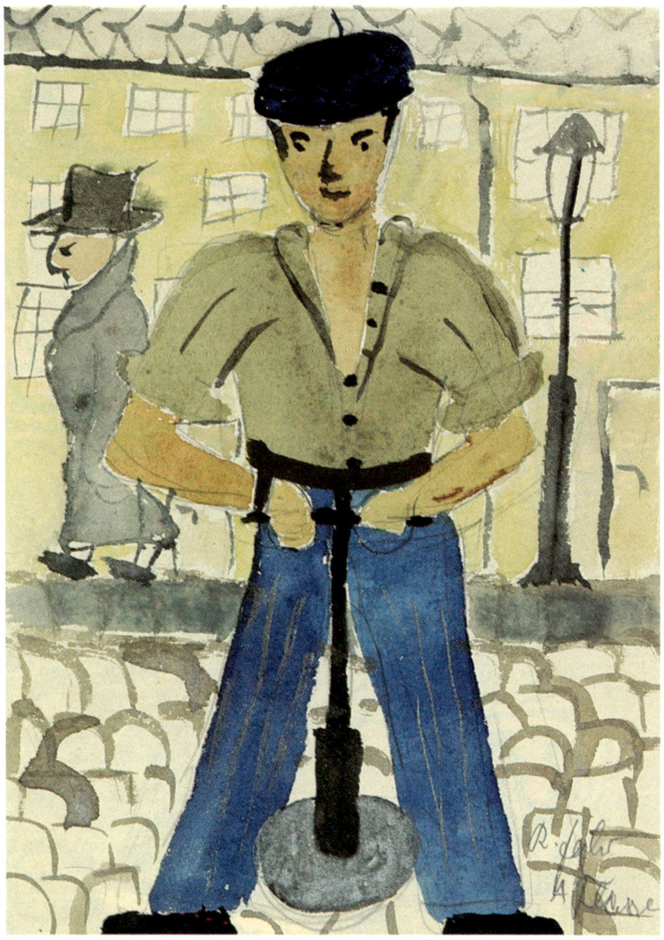

71 R. Fahr, *The Road Repairman*, undated (Cat. 97)

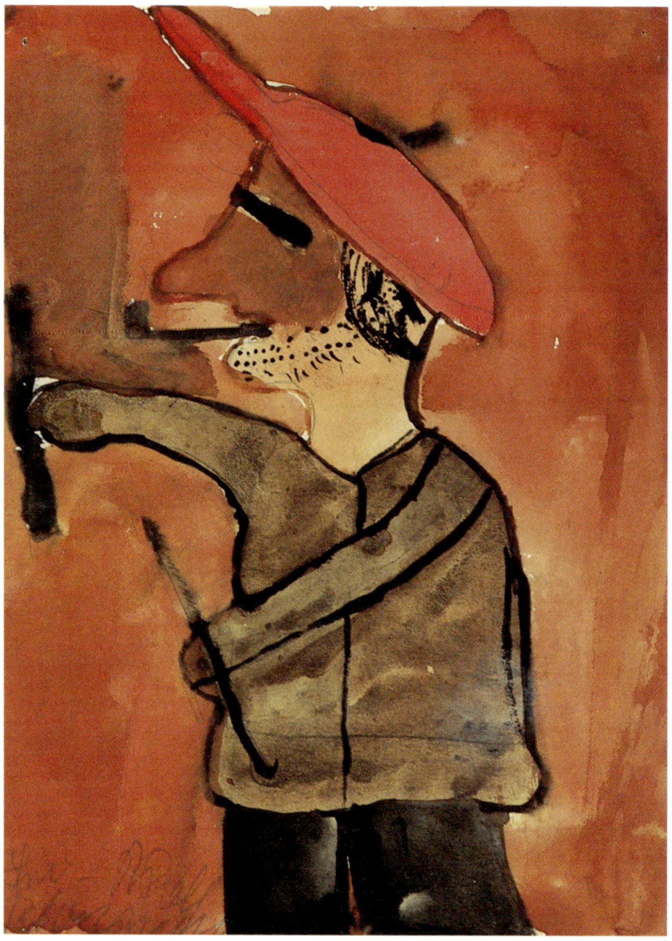

72 Leo-Wolf Klarmann, *The Thief*, Oct. 1937 (Cat. 30)

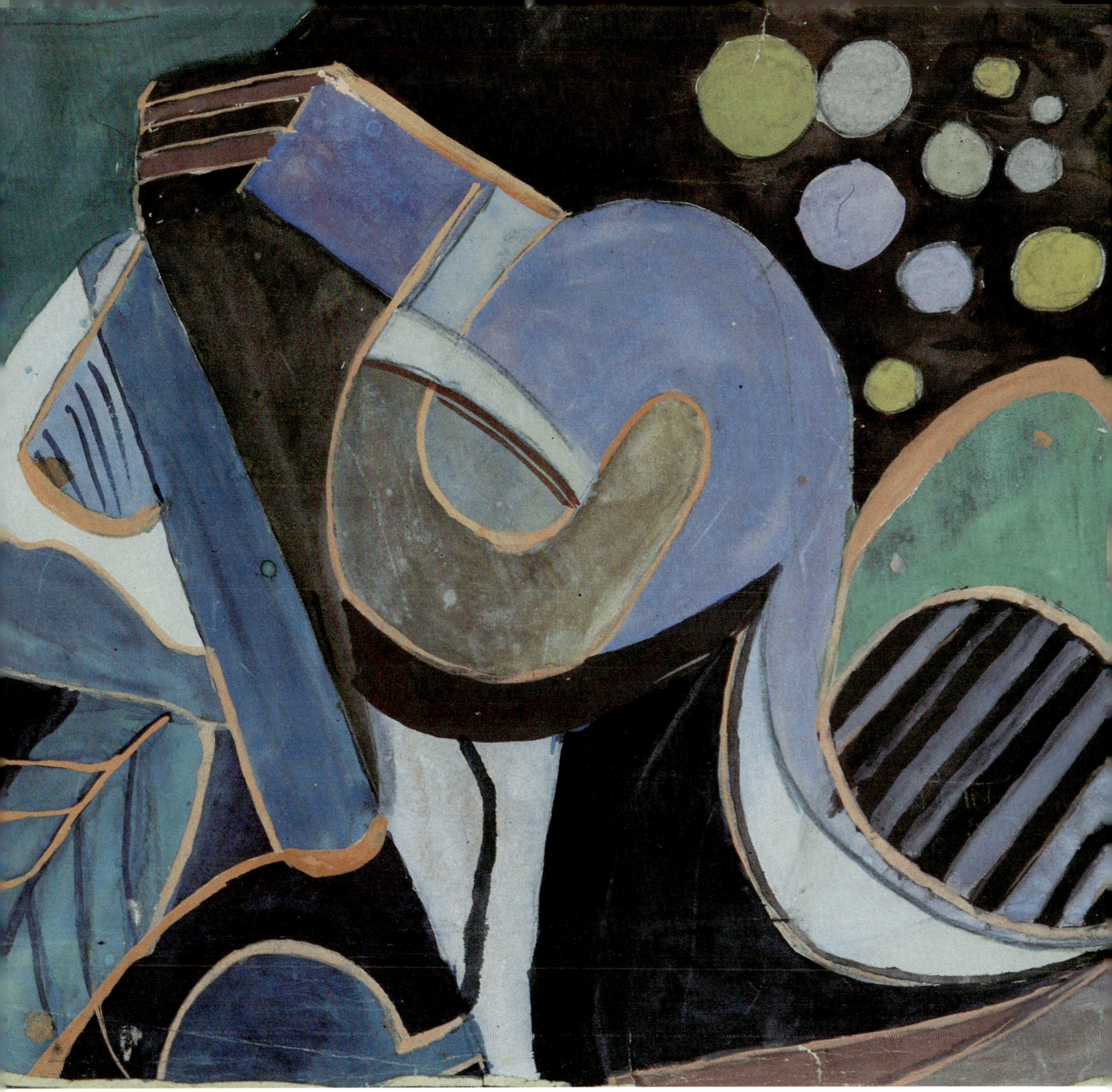

73 Ruth Pschednowek, *Pattern*, Oct. 1937 (Cat. 32)

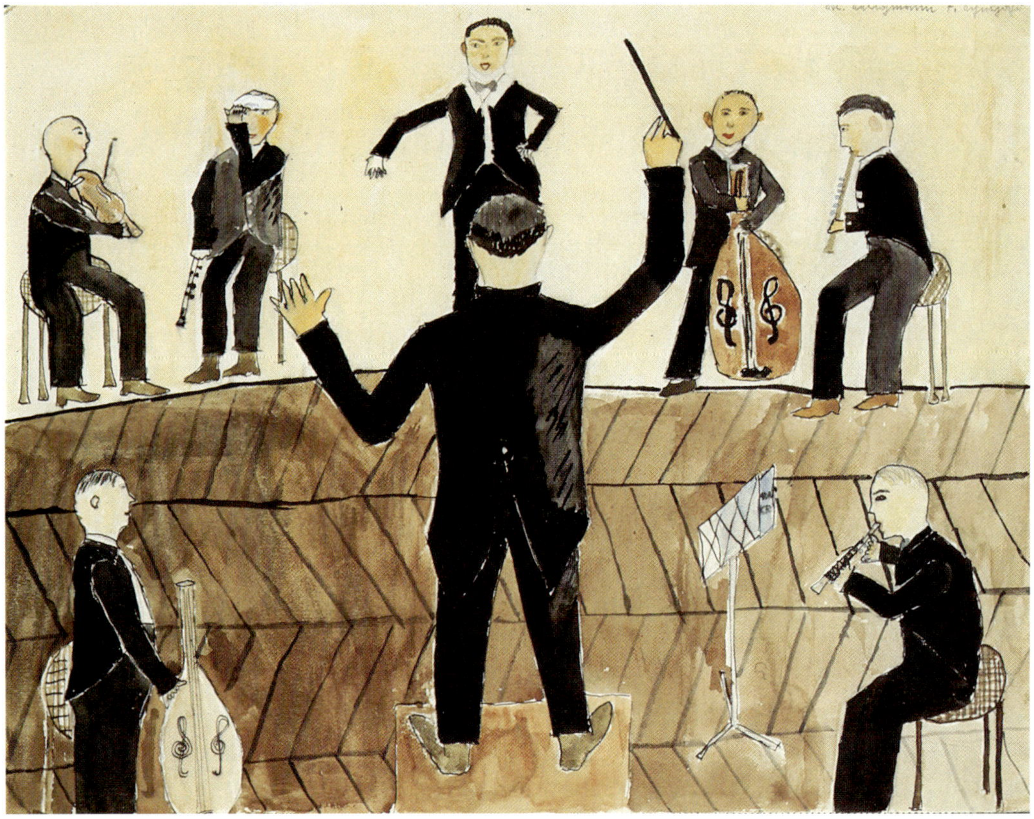

74 Marianne Seligmann,
Concert,
Oct.–Nov. 1937
(Cat. 34)

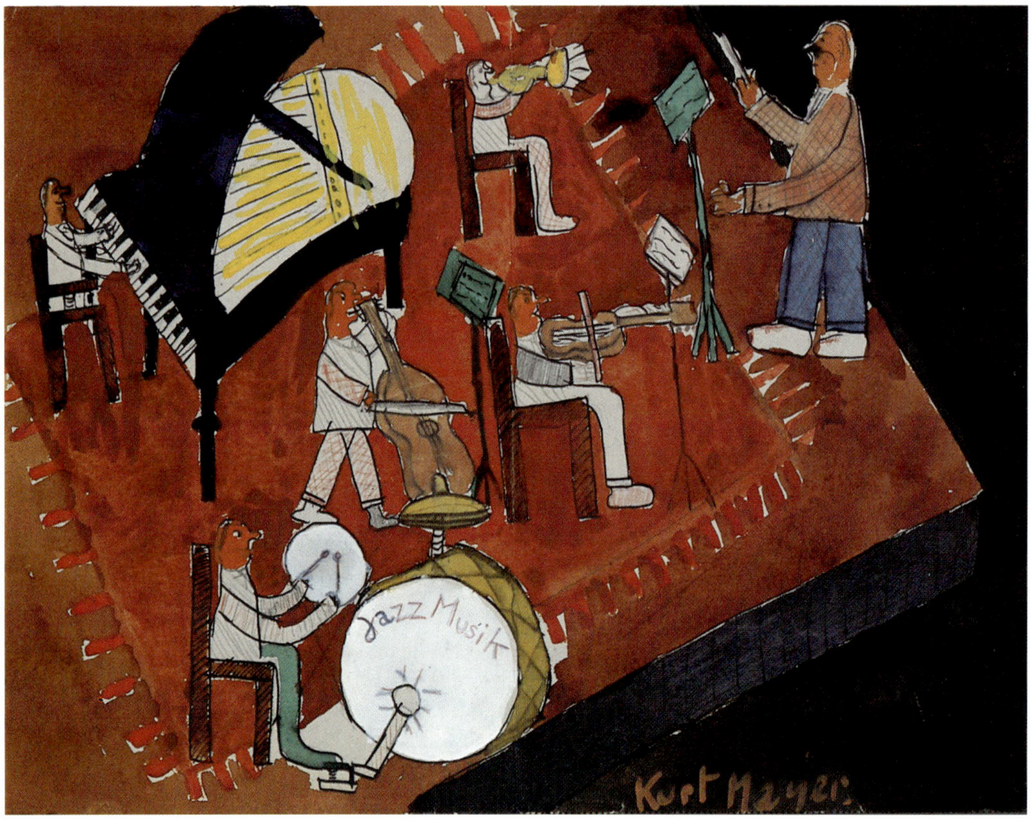

75 Kurt Mayer,
Jazz Orchestra,
Oct. 1937
(Cat. 33)

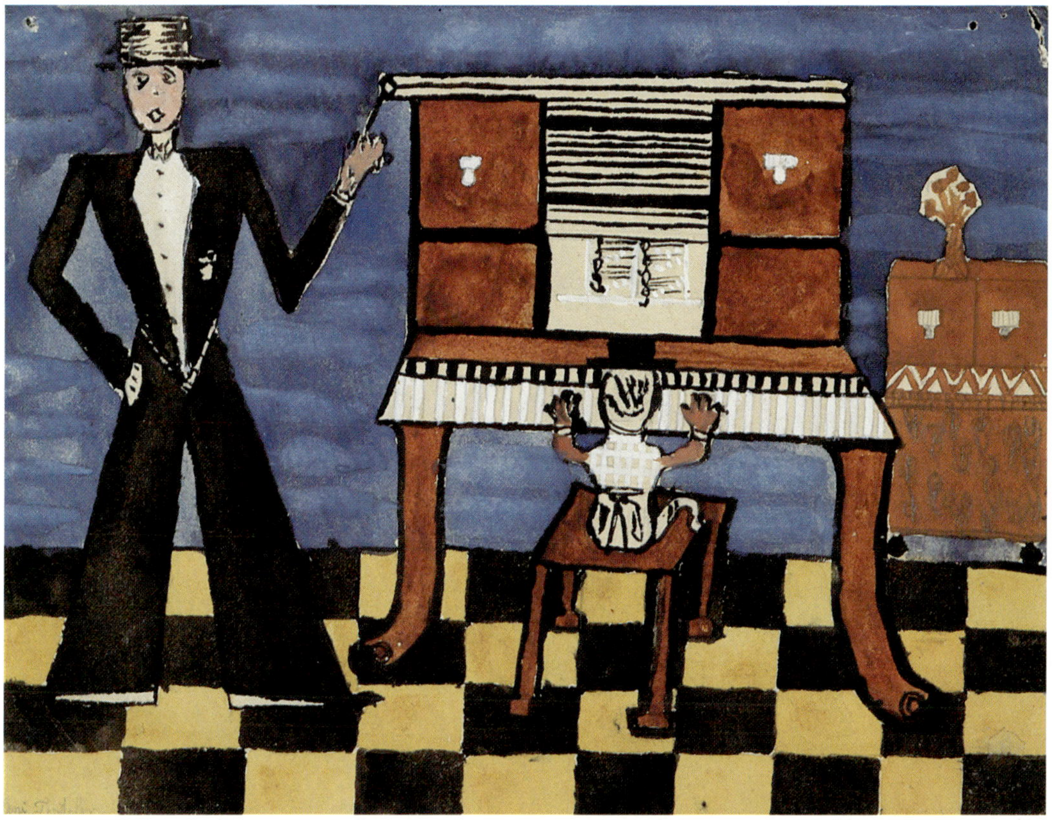

76 Helene Testiler,
Cabaret,
undated
(Cat. 35)

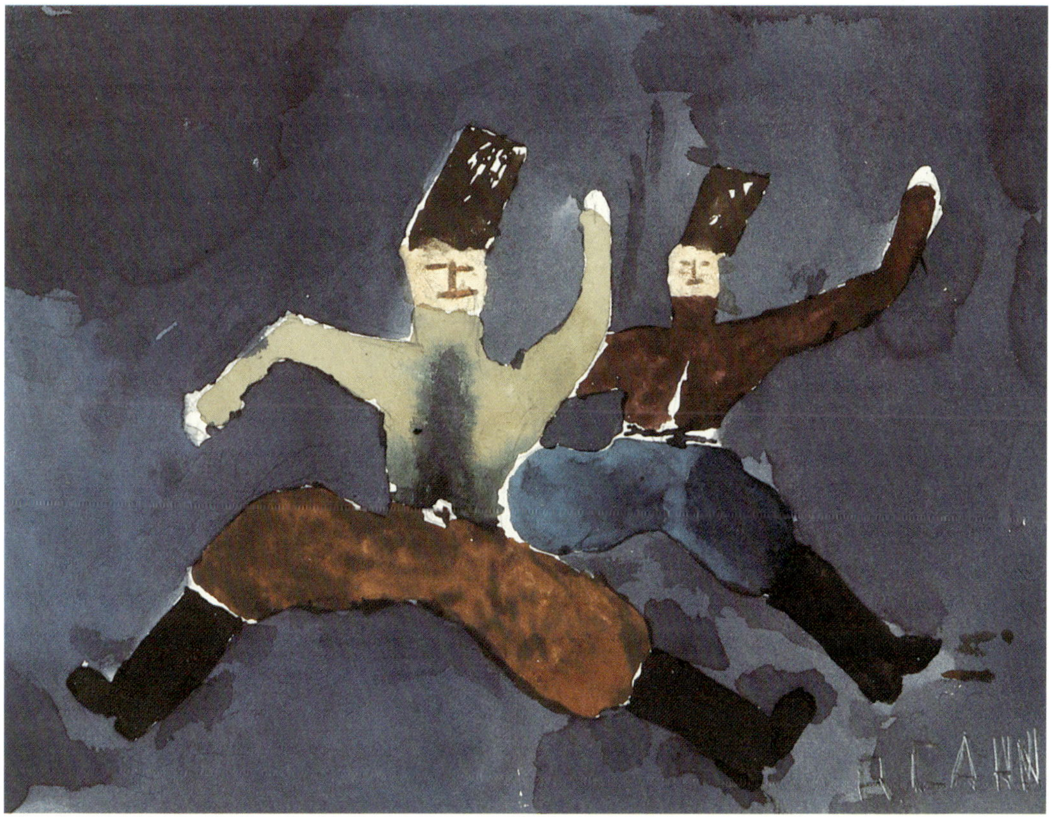

77 Rolf Cahn,
Cossack's Dance,
undated
(Cat. 94)

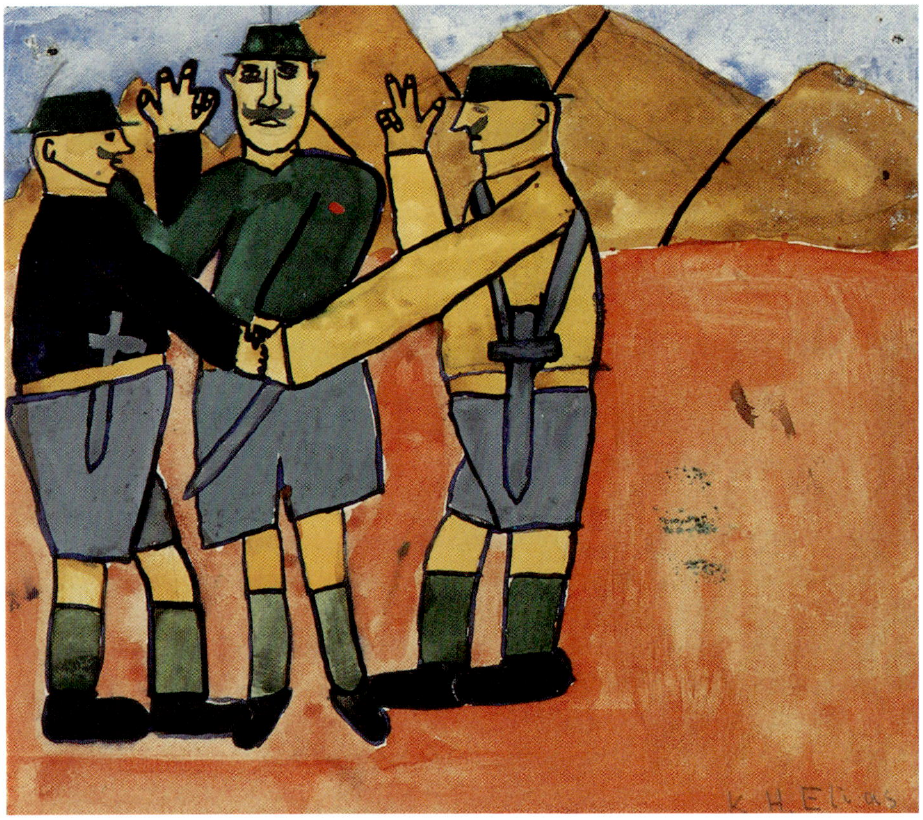

78 Kurt-Heinz Elias,
The Rütli Oath,
Oct. 1937
(Cat. 36)

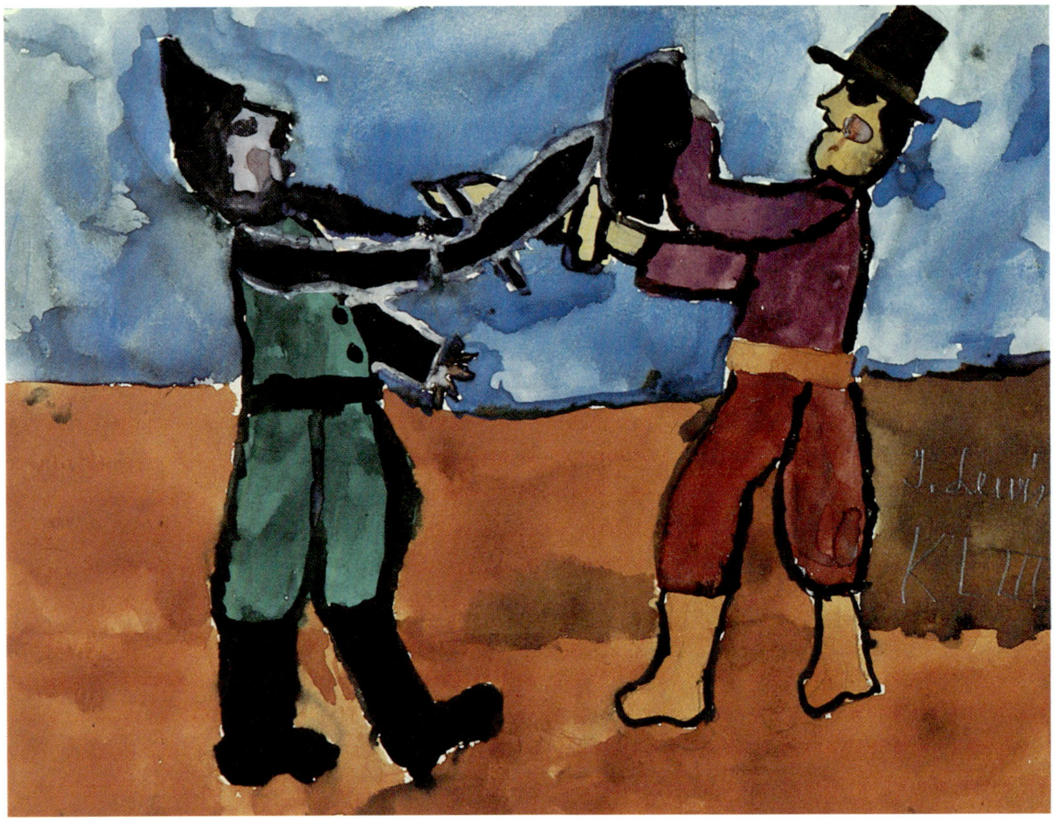

79 Inge Lewin,
The Blind King,
Dec. 1937
(Cat. 43)

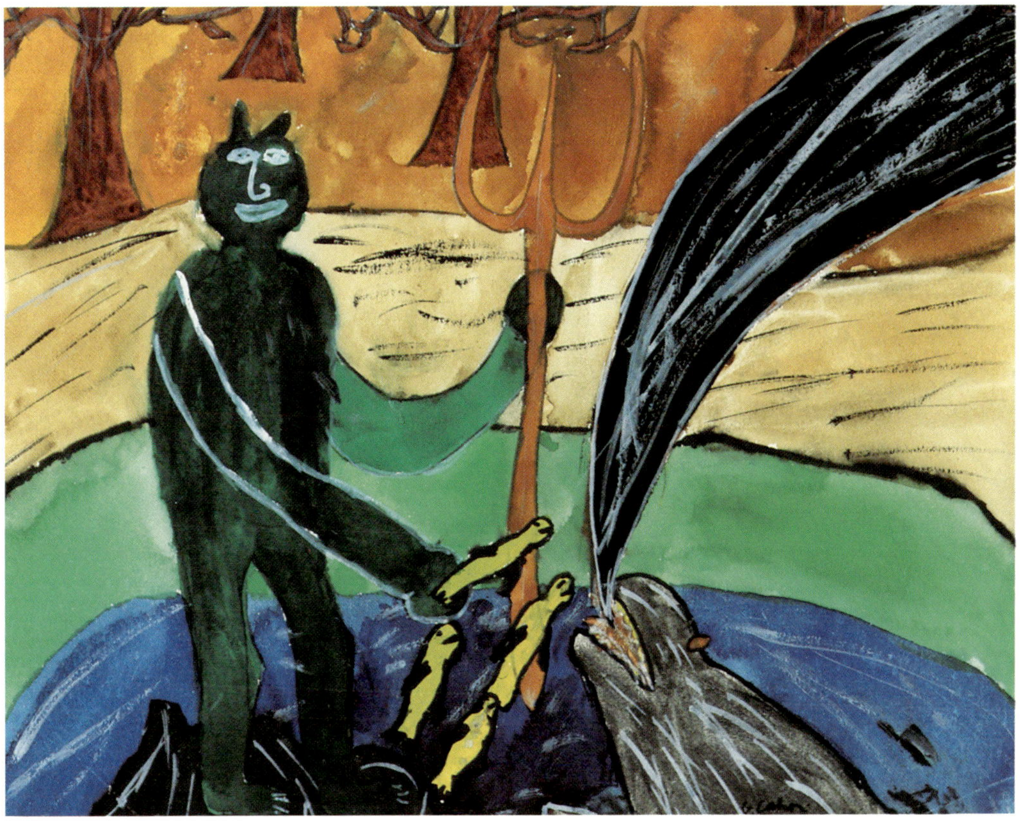

80 Günther Cahn,
The Gröne Jong,
Nov. 1937
(Cat. 38)

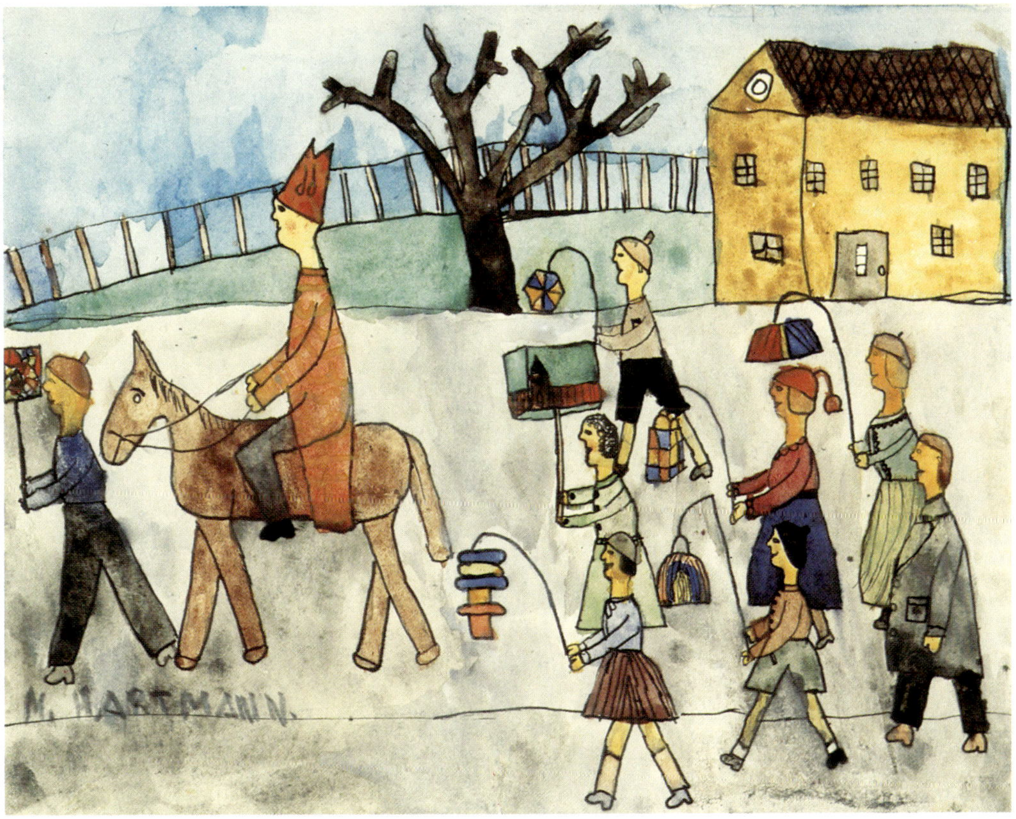

81 Margit Hartmann,
St. Martin's Day Procession,
Nov. 1937
(Cat. 37)

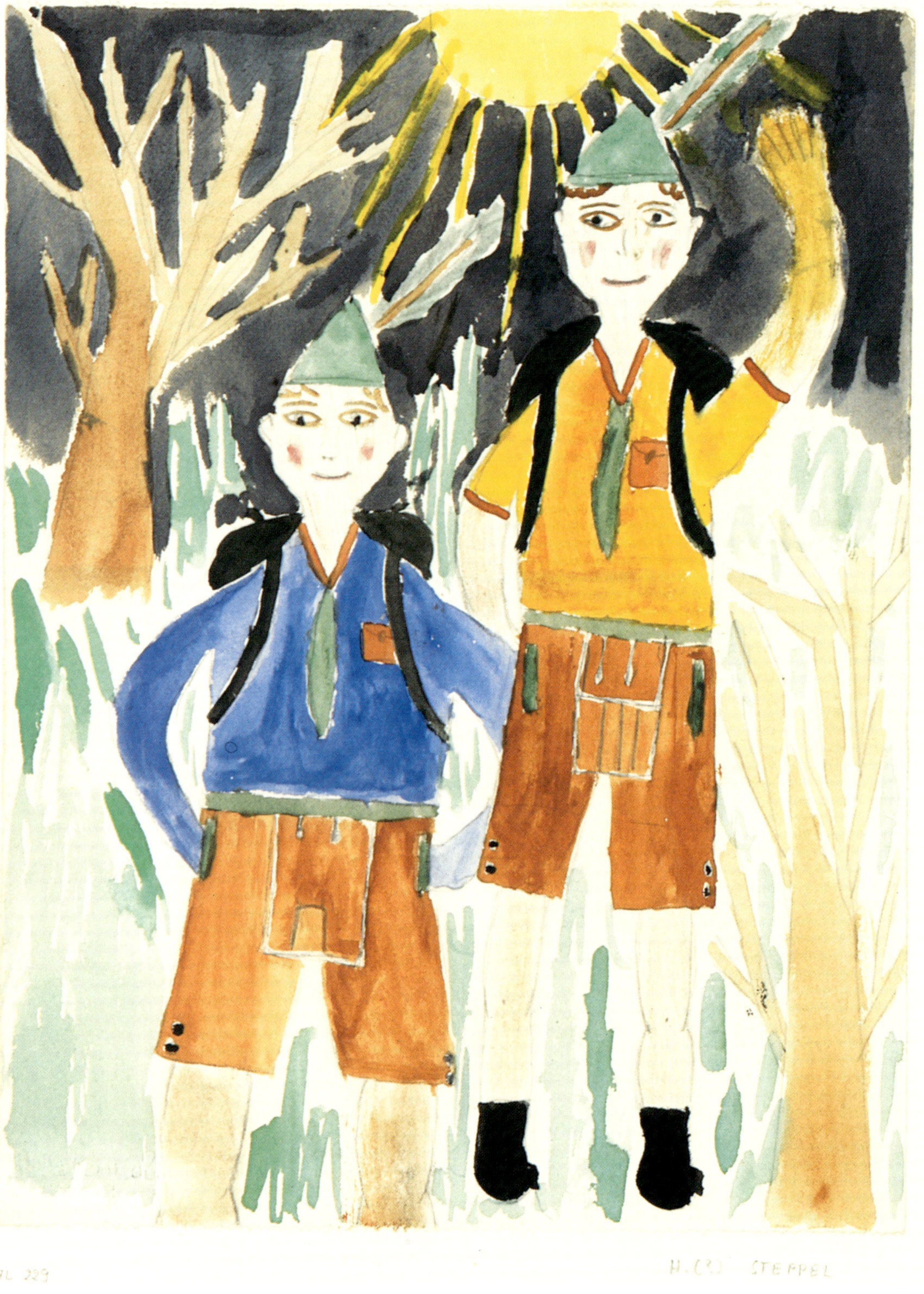

82 Henni Steppel, *The Hikers*, Nov. 1937 (Cat. 39)

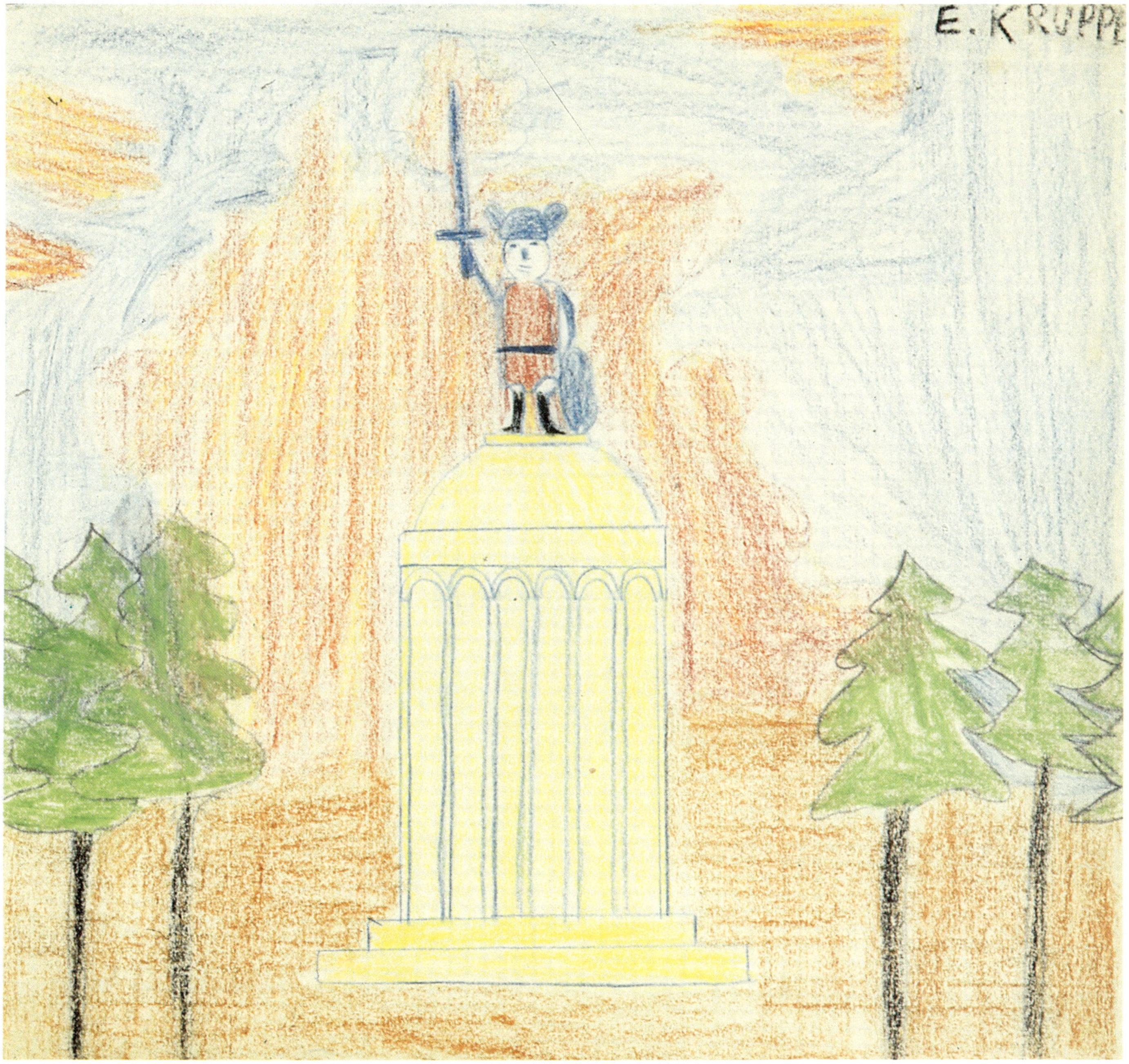

83 E. Kruppe, *The Herman Memorial in Teutoburg Forest*, undated (Cat. 102)

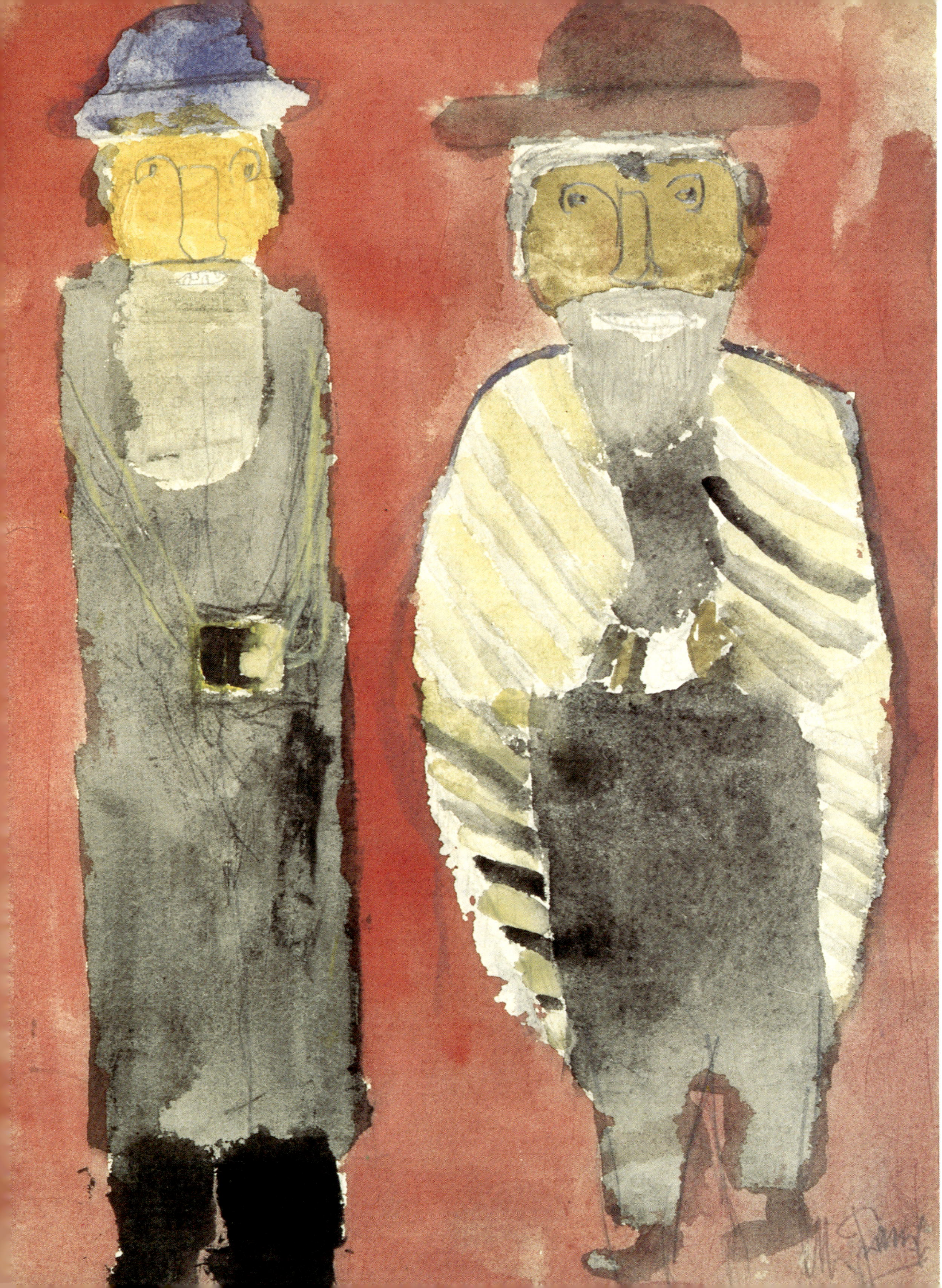

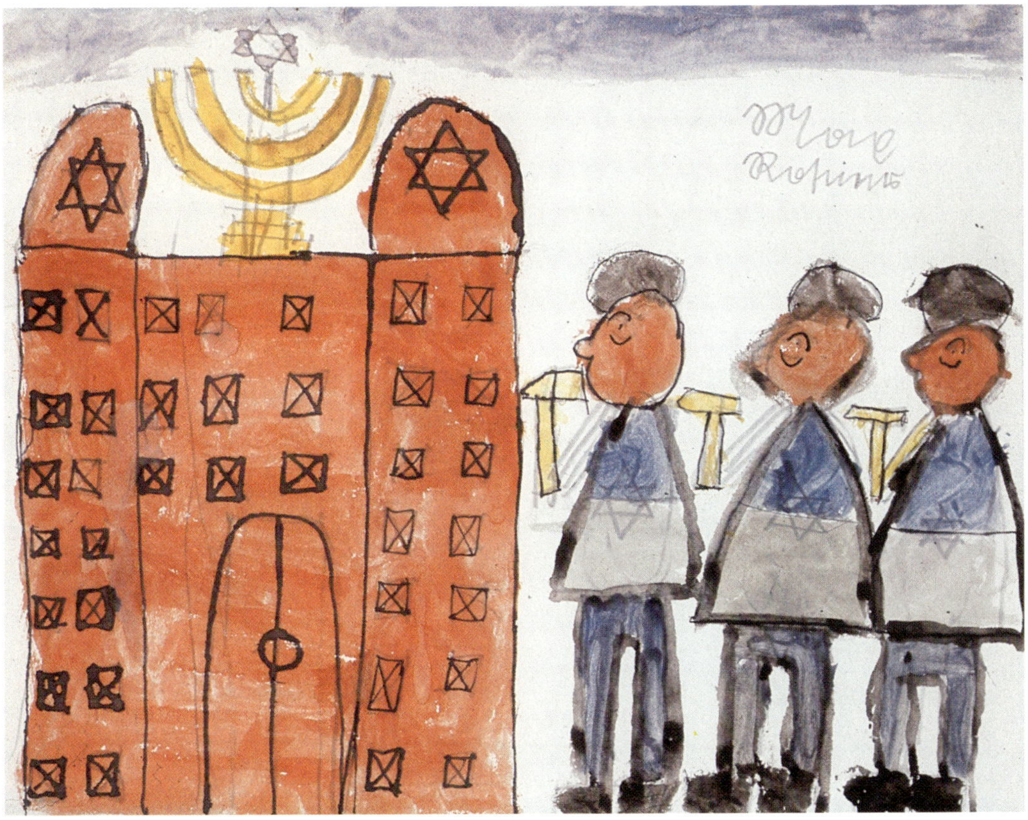

85 Max Rosner,
The Maccabees,
Dec. 1937
(Cat. 42)

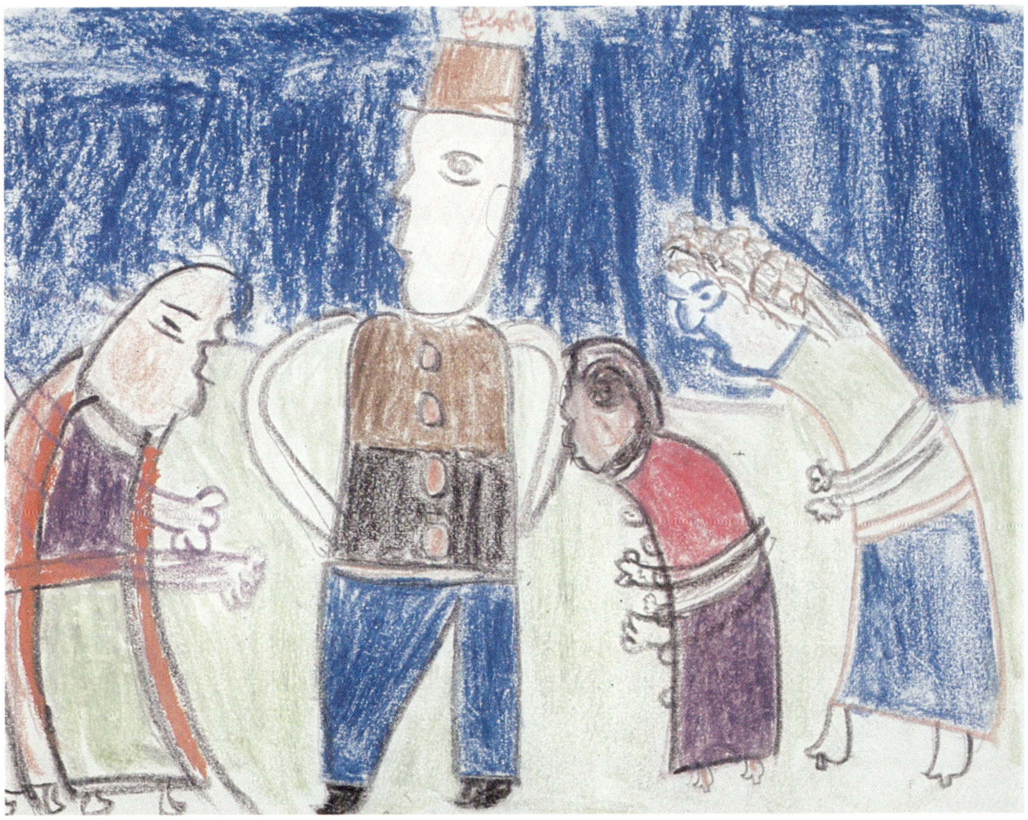

86 Name unknown,
Forced to Pay Homage,
March 1938
(Cat. 46)

◁
84 M. Franz,
Two Jews,
undated
(Cat. 91)

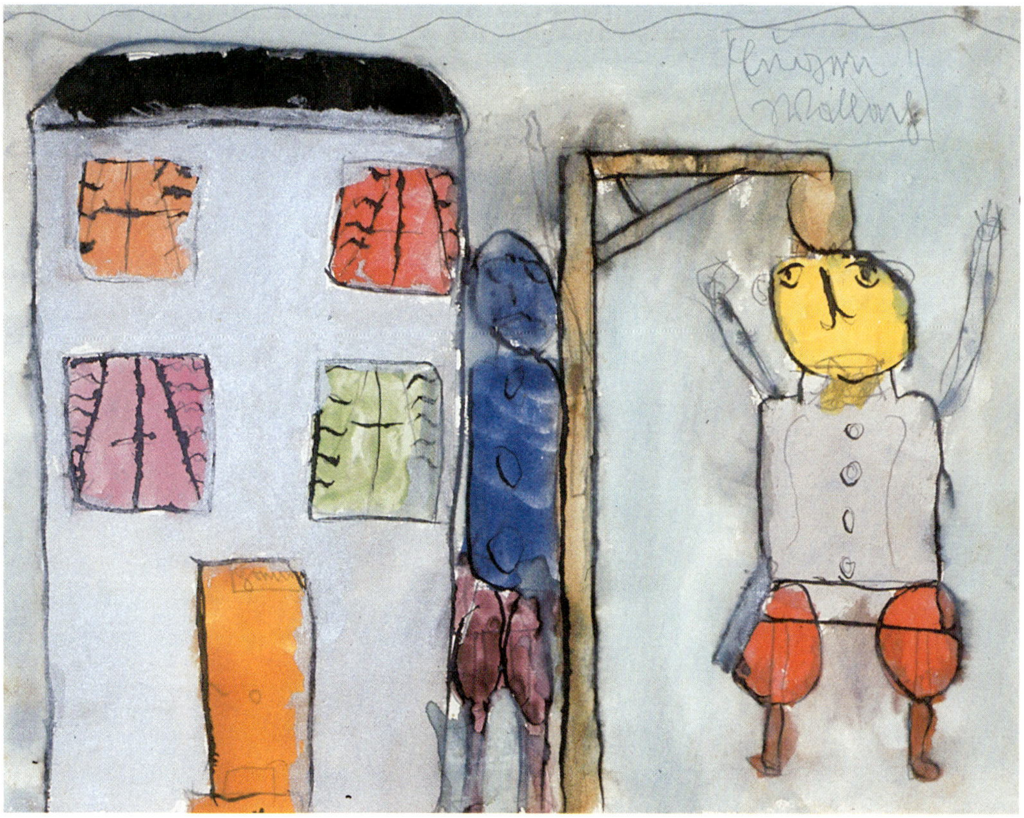

87 Eugen Wallach,
Haman on the Gallows,
undated
(Cat. 86)

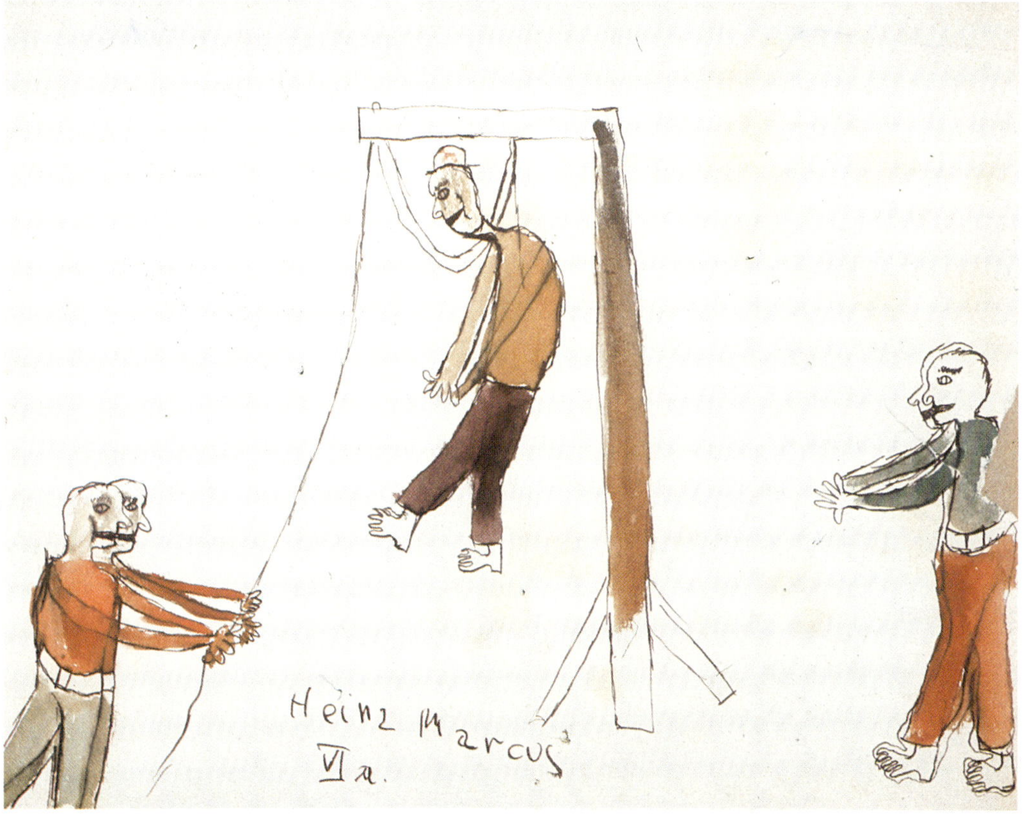

88 Heinz Marcus,
Man on Gallows,
undated
(Cat. 87)

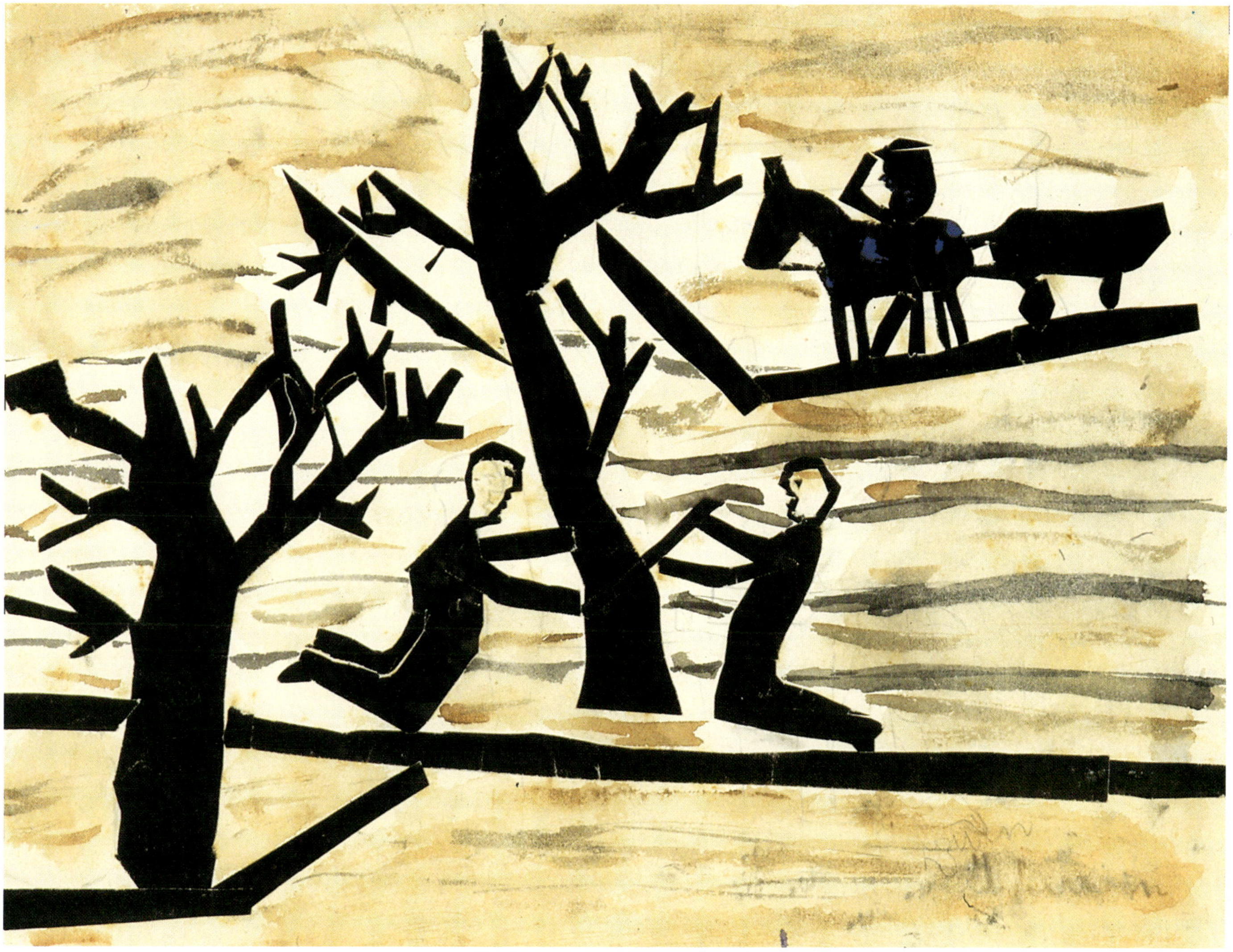

89 Inge Lewin, *The Woodcutters*, Jan. 1938 (Cat. 45)

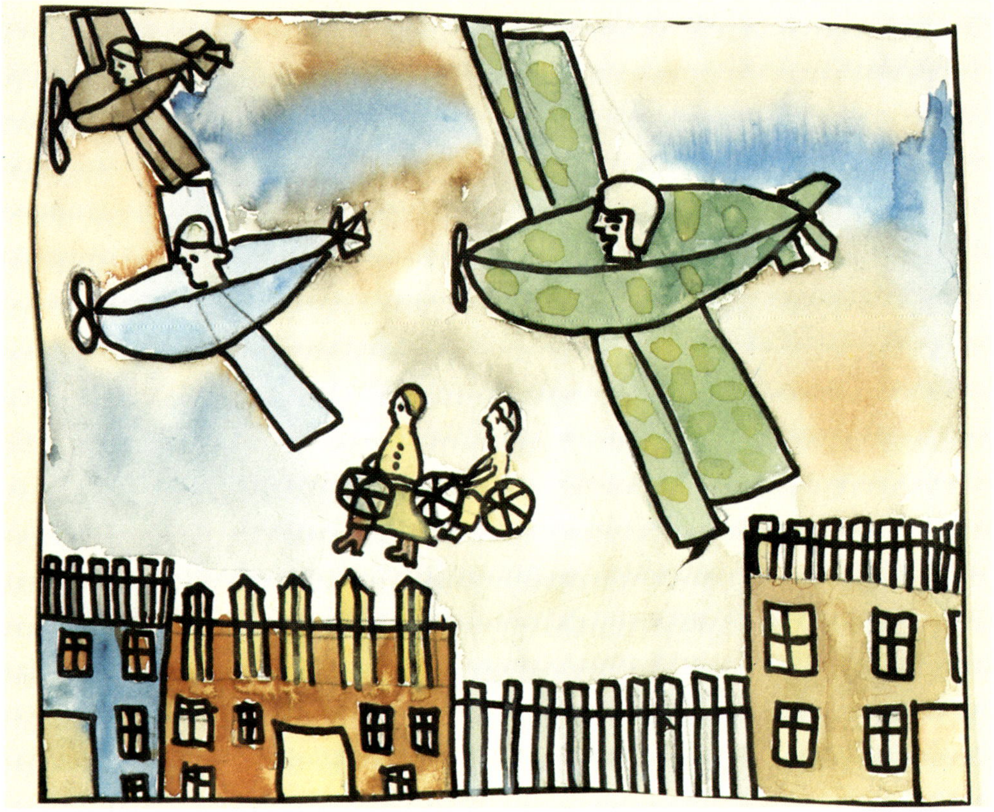

90 Name unknown,
Airplanes above the City,
undated
(Cat. 101)

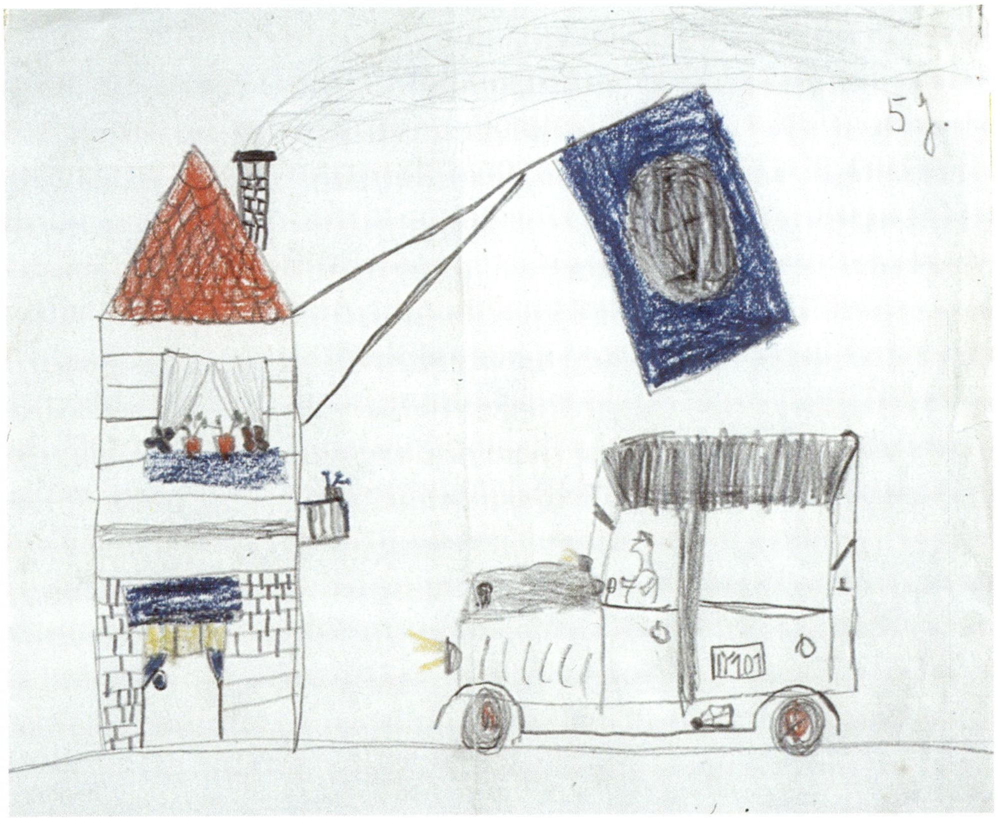

91 Name unknown,
House with Swastika Flag,
undated
(Cat. 85)

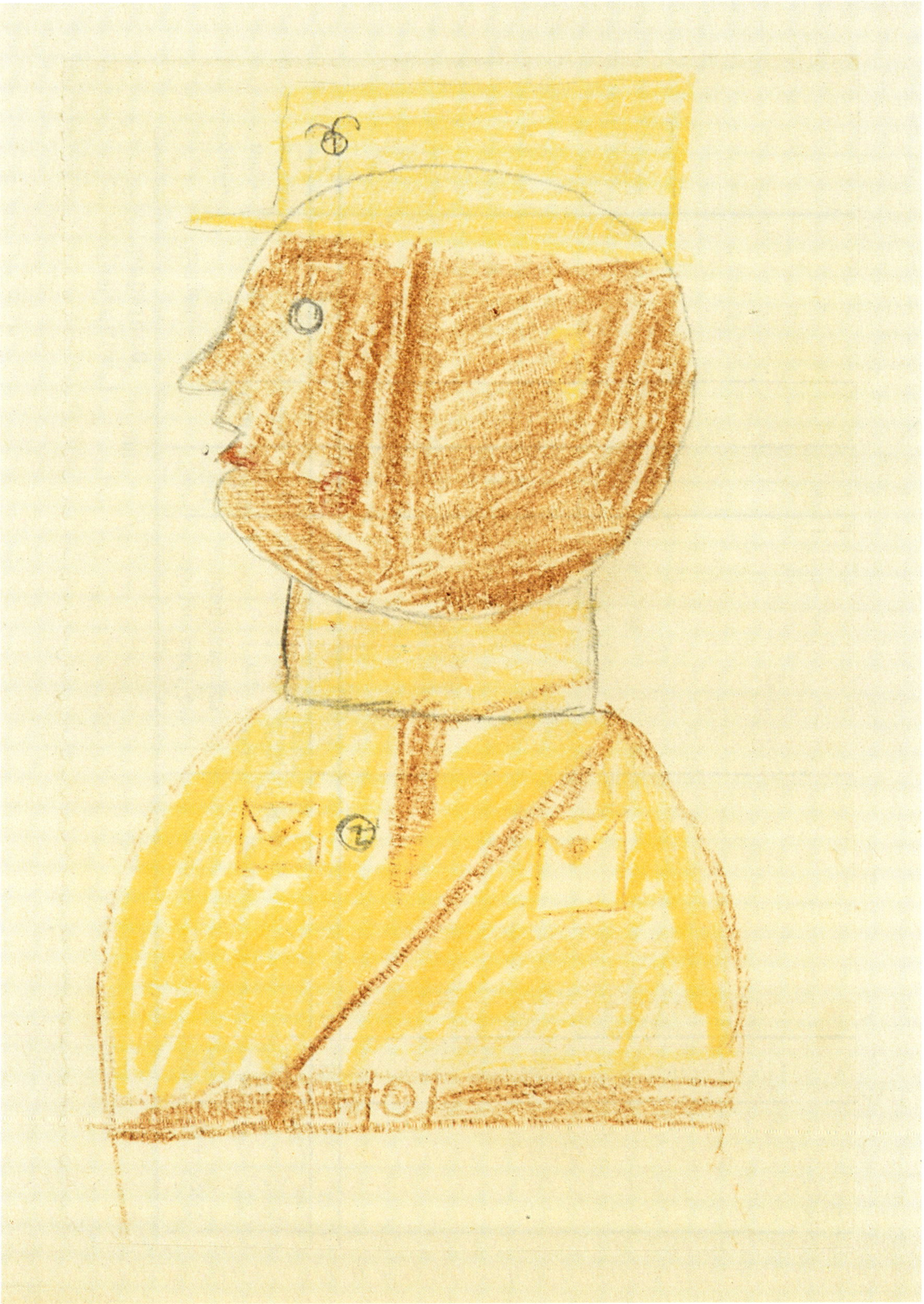

92 Name unknown, *Man in SA Uniform*, undated (Cat. 84)

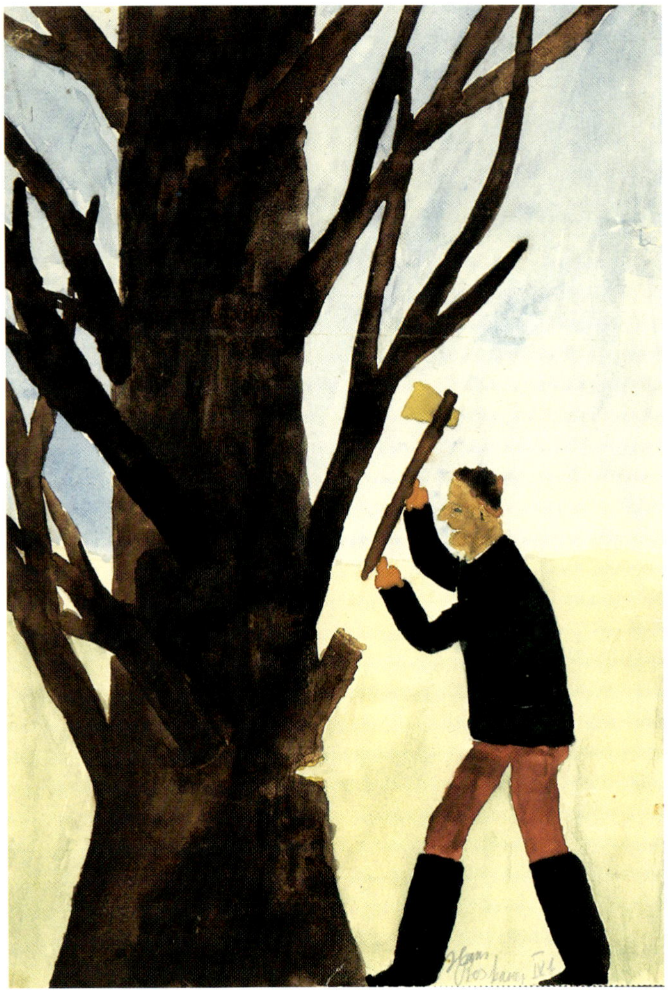

93 Hans Rosbauer, *The Woodcutter*, June 1938 (Cat. 48)

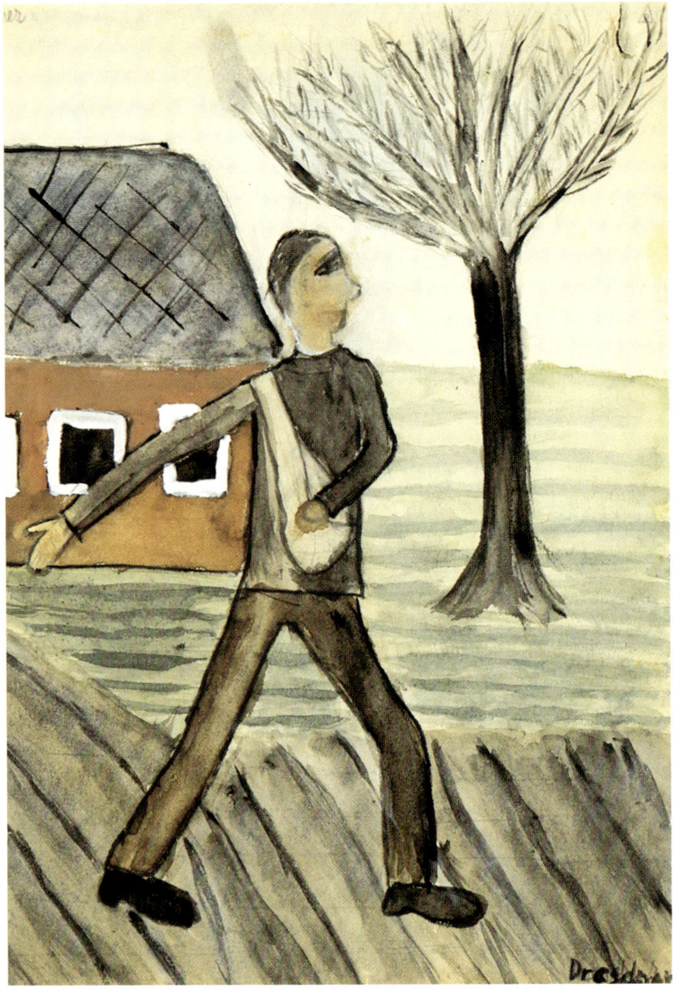

94 (?) Dresdner, *The Sower*, Aug. 1938 (Cat. 50)

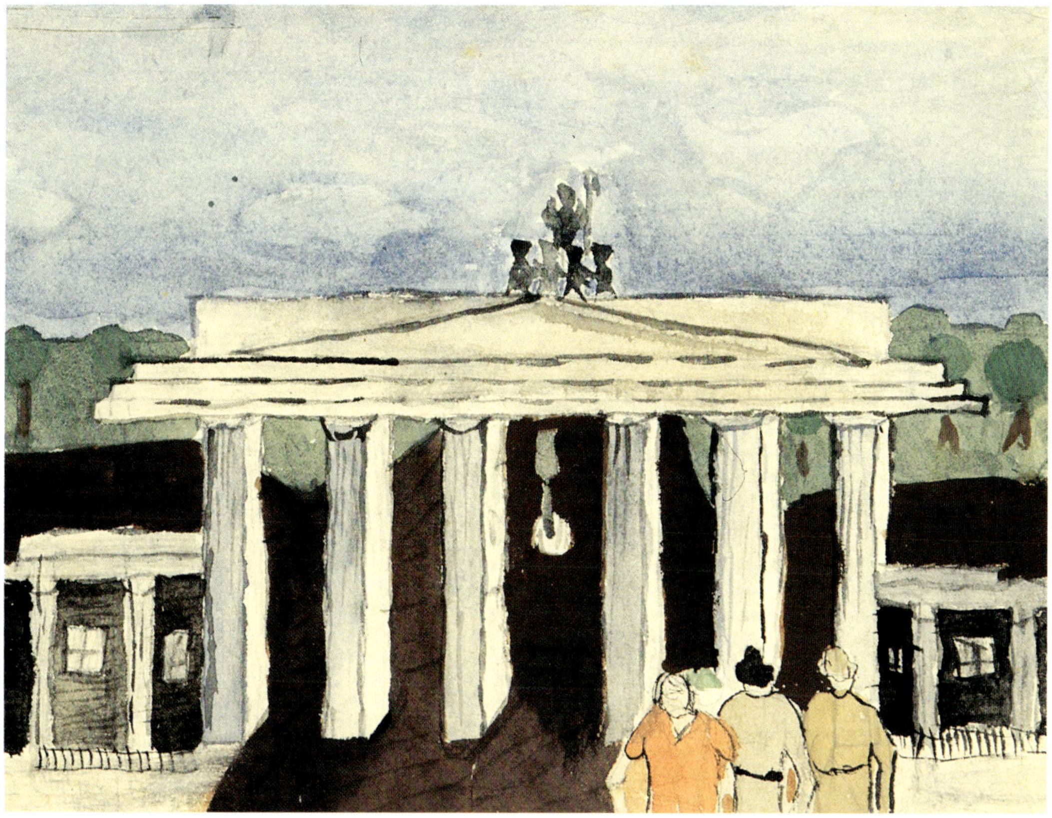

95 Name unknown,
The Brandenburg Gate in Berlin,
Aug. 1938
(Cat. 49)

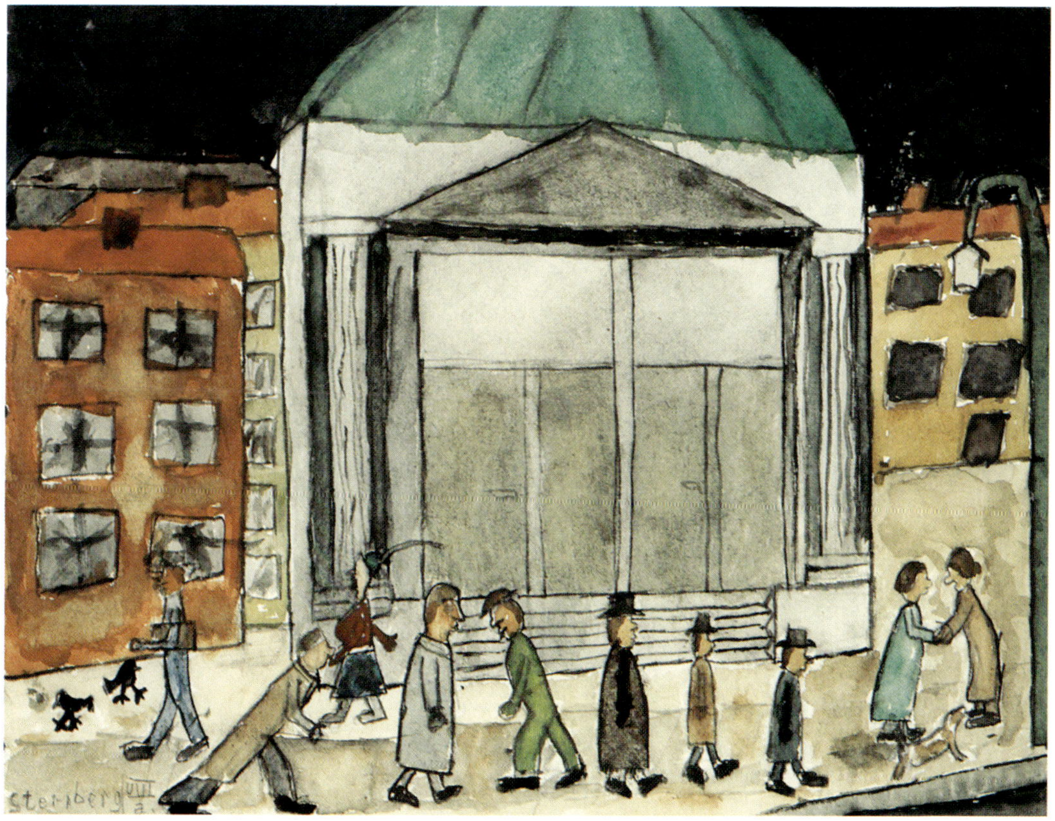

96 (?) Sternberg,
London,
Dec. 1938
(Cat. 66)

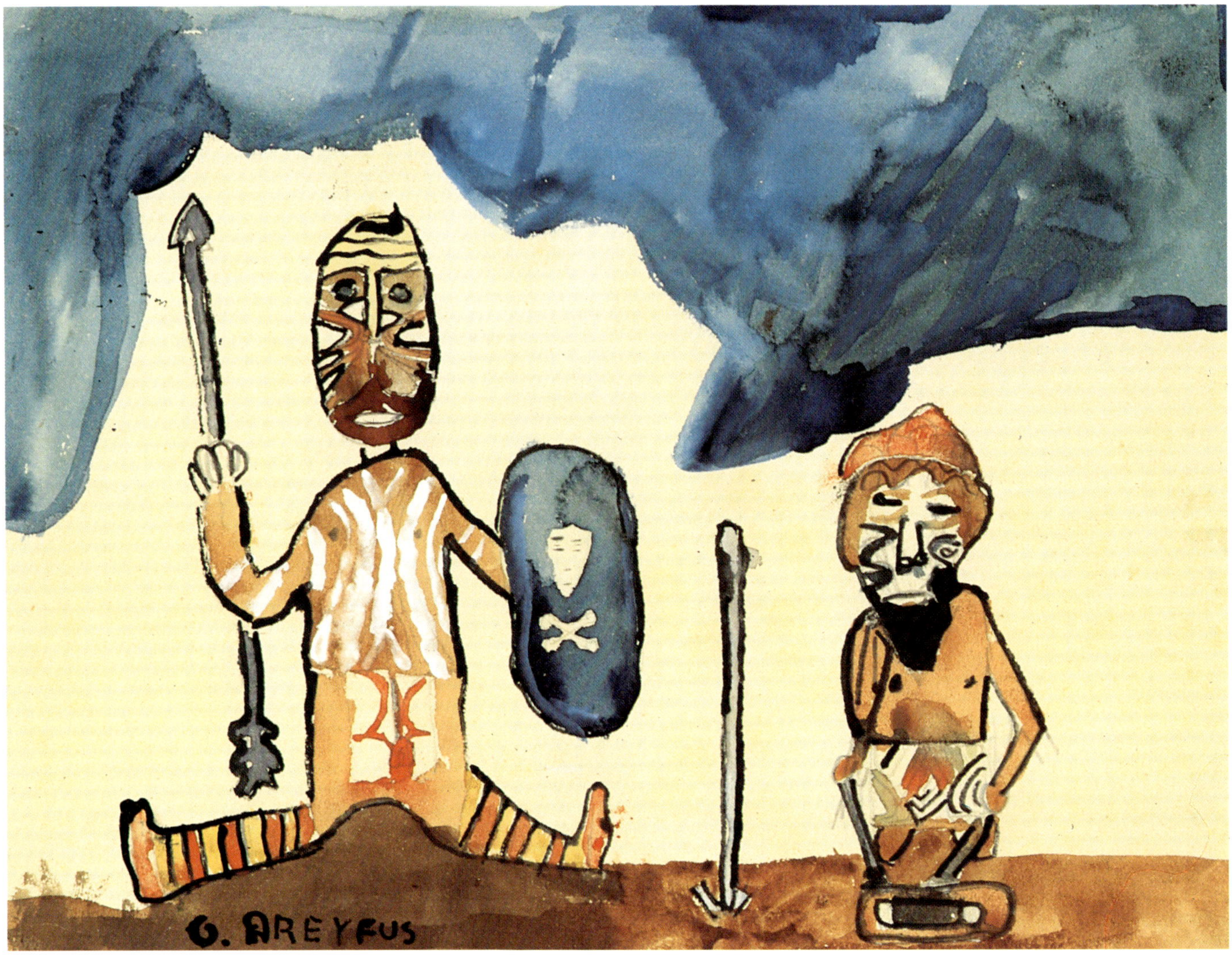

97 Georg Dreyfus, *Africa*, Sept. 1938 (Cat. 51)

98 M. Rosenstock, *Africa*, undated (Cat. 52) ▷

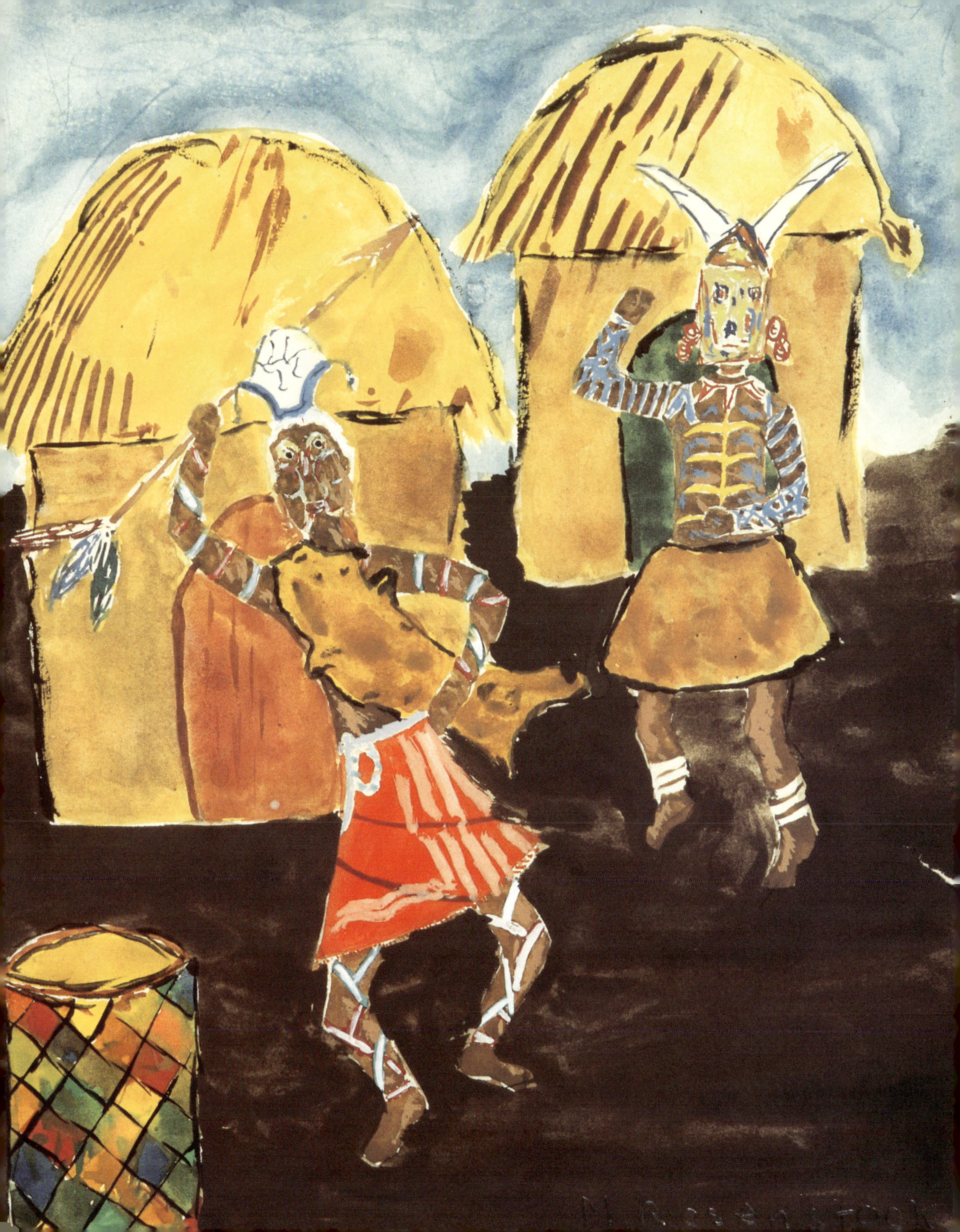

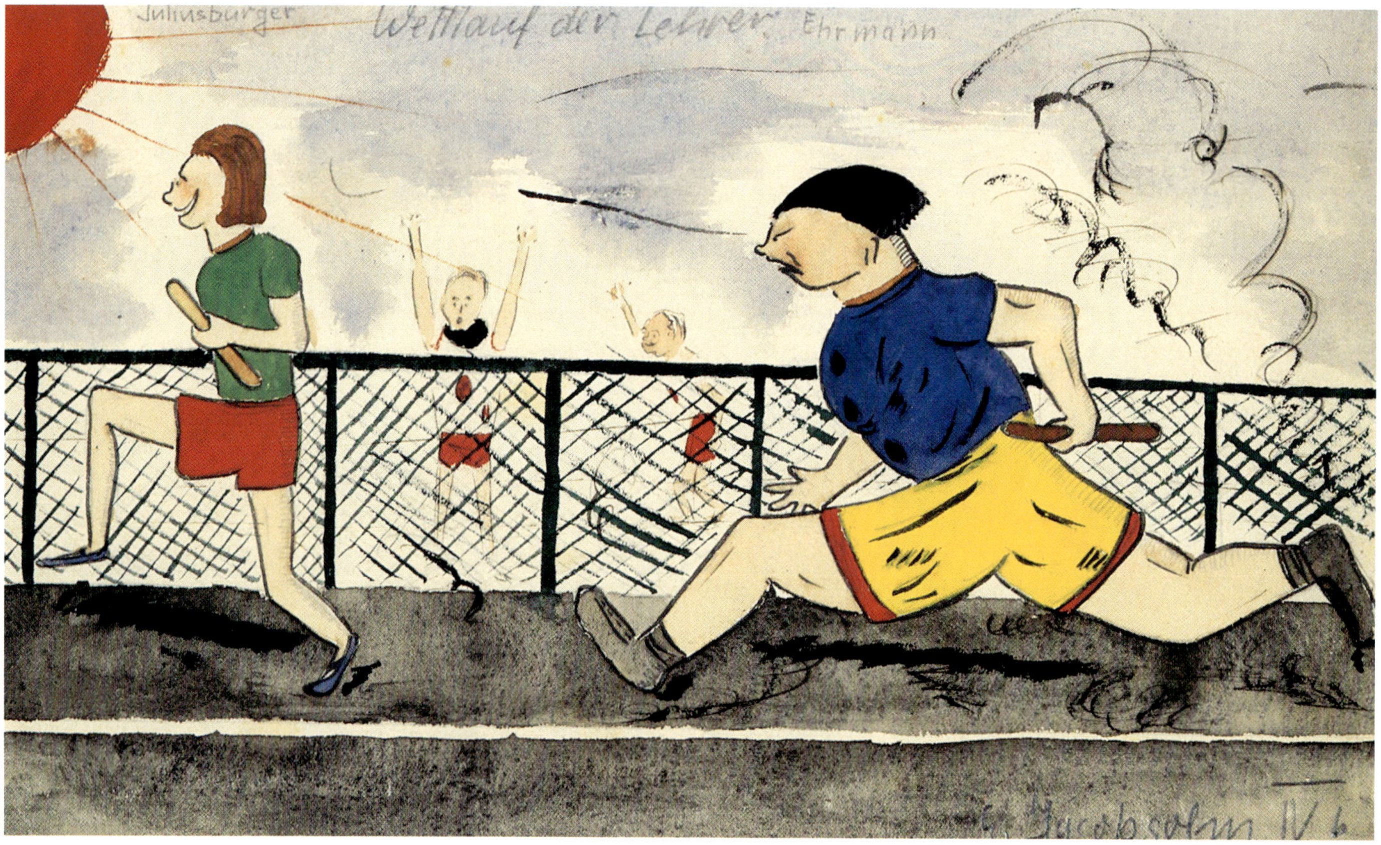

99 G. Jacobsohn, *Teacher's Track Race*, Nov. 1938 (Cat. 54)

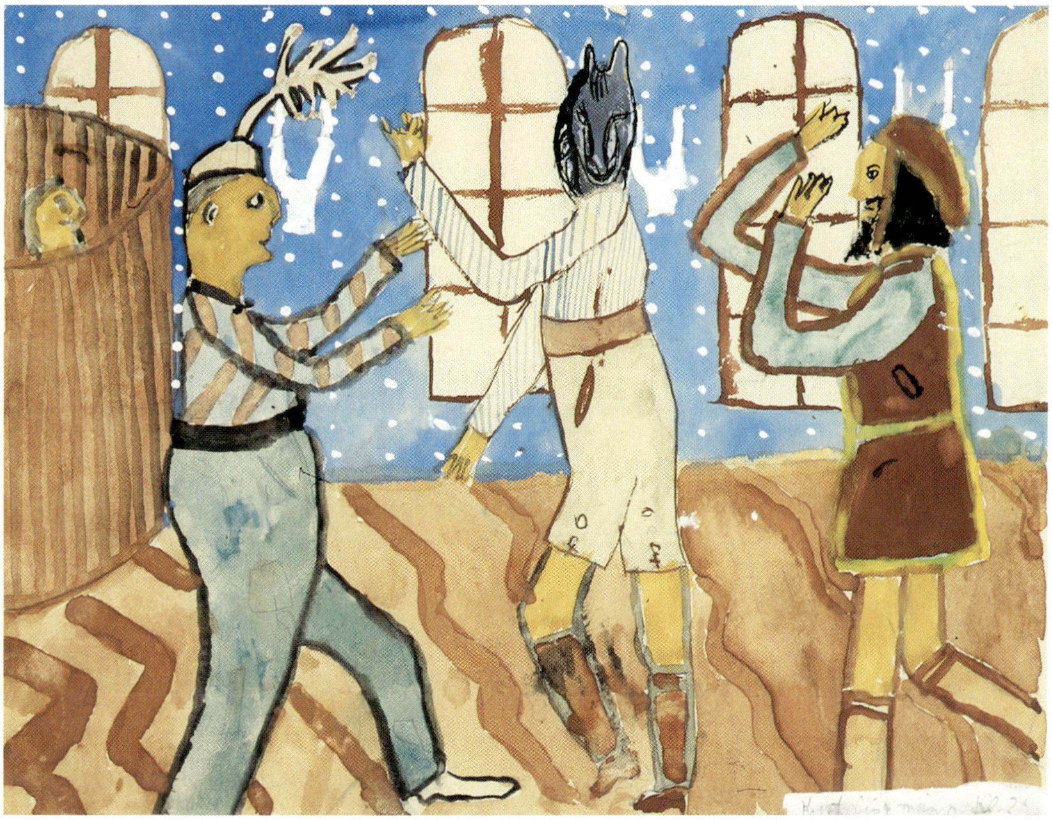

100 Kurt Lippmann, *A Midsummer Night's Dream*, Nov. 1938 (Cat. 55)

101 Albert Tell, *Battle Scene*, Nov. 1938 (Cat. 59)

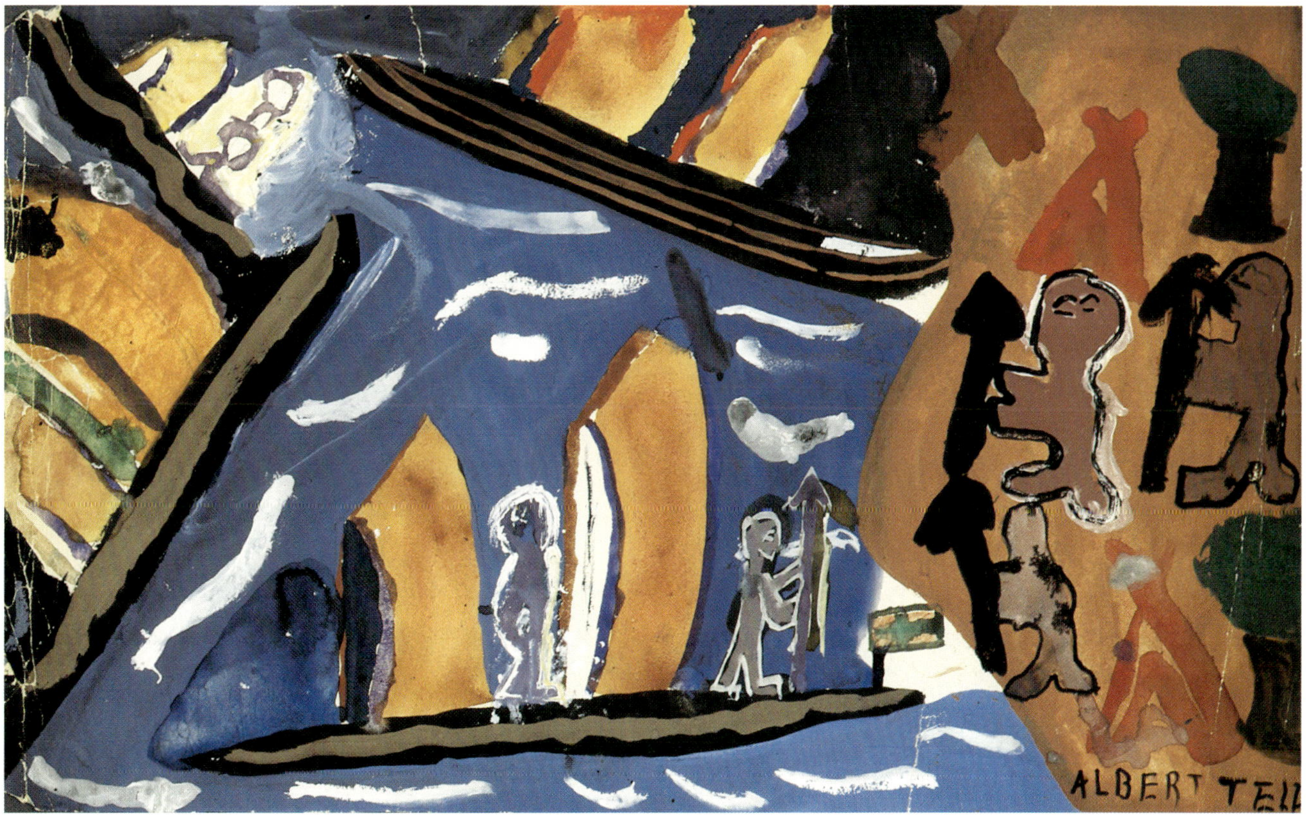

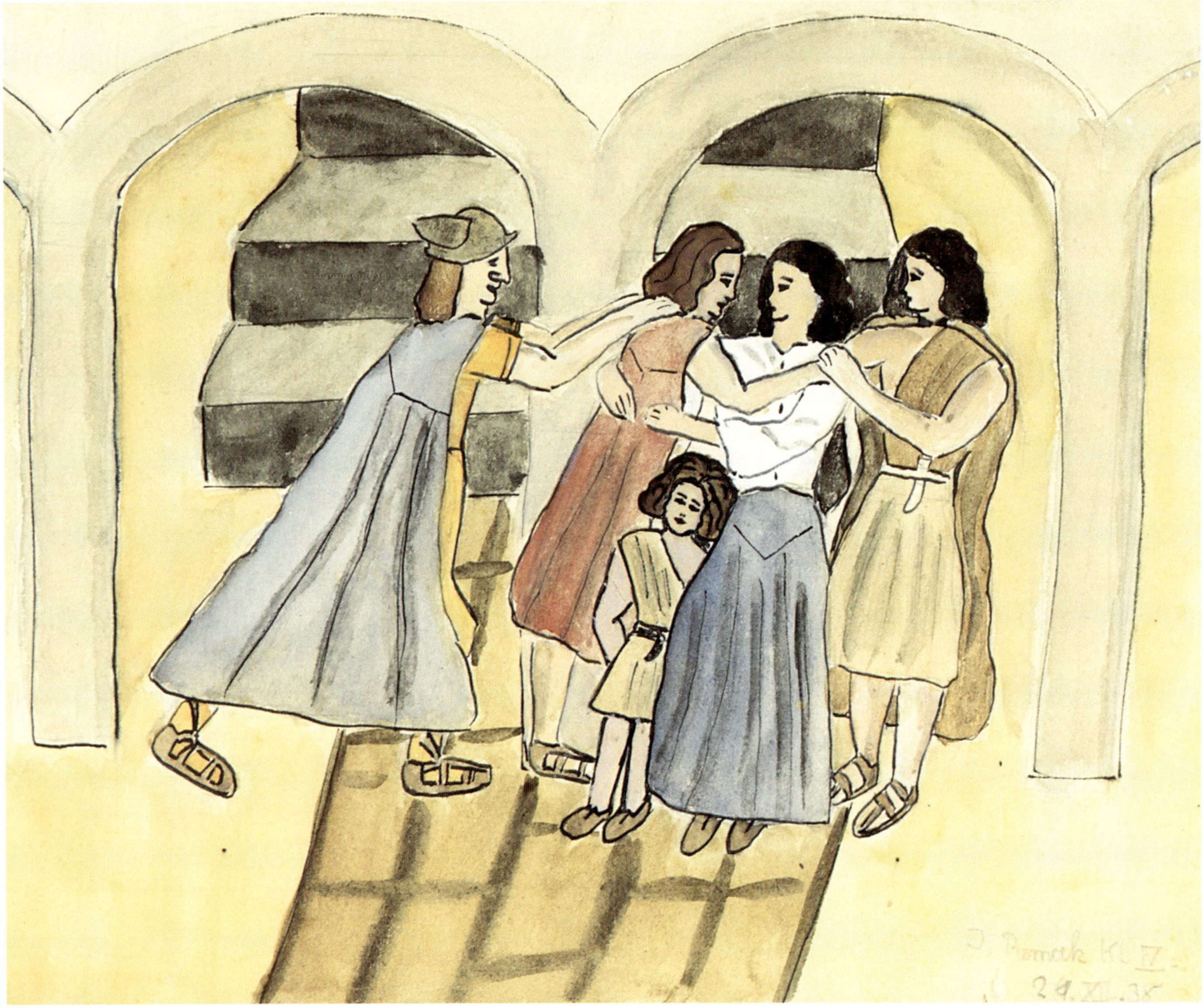

102 I. Remak, *Scene from Antiquity with the God Mercury*, 21 Dec. 1938 (Cat. 63)

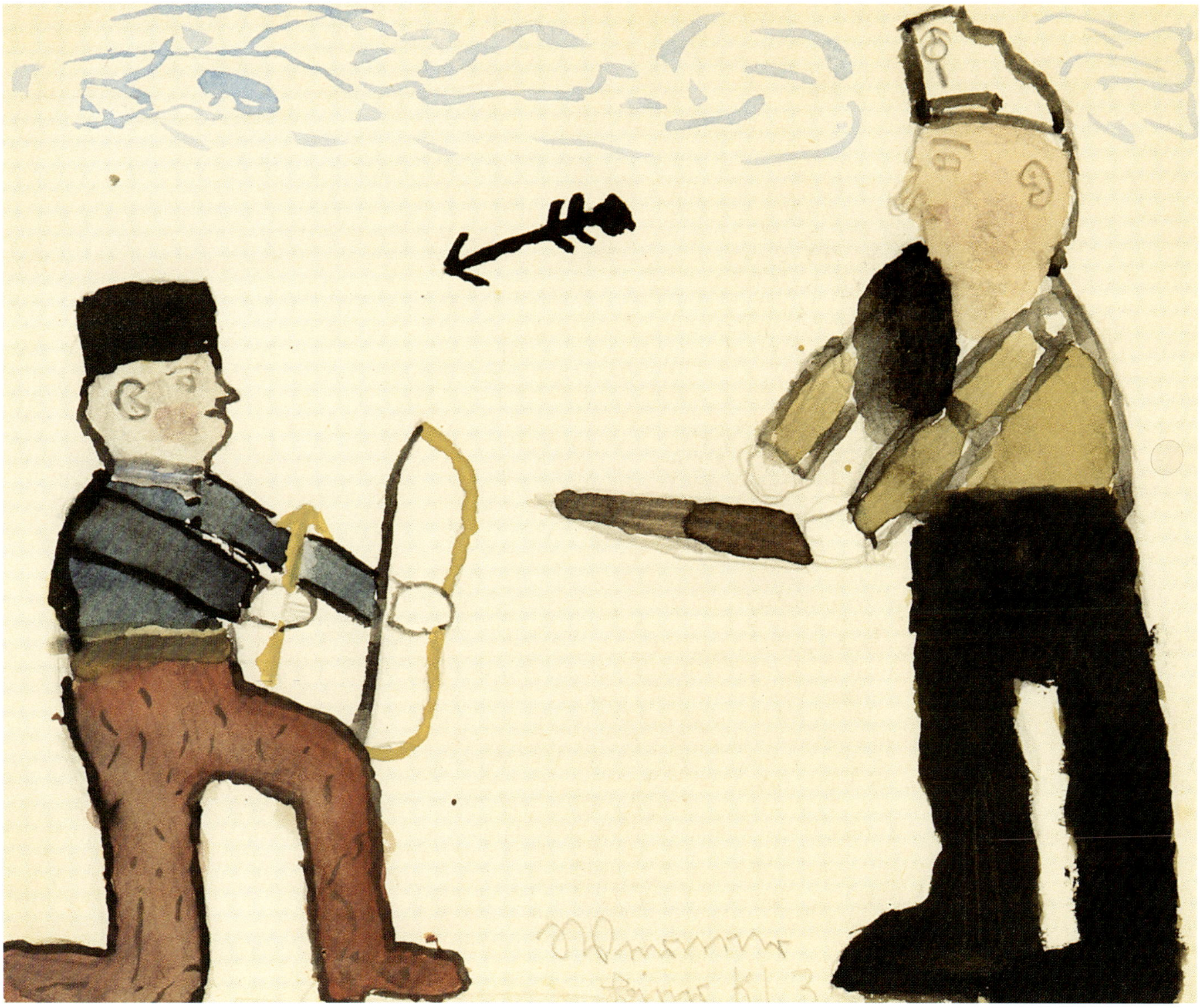

103 Werner Lier, *The Maccabean*, Dec. 1938 (Cat. 61)

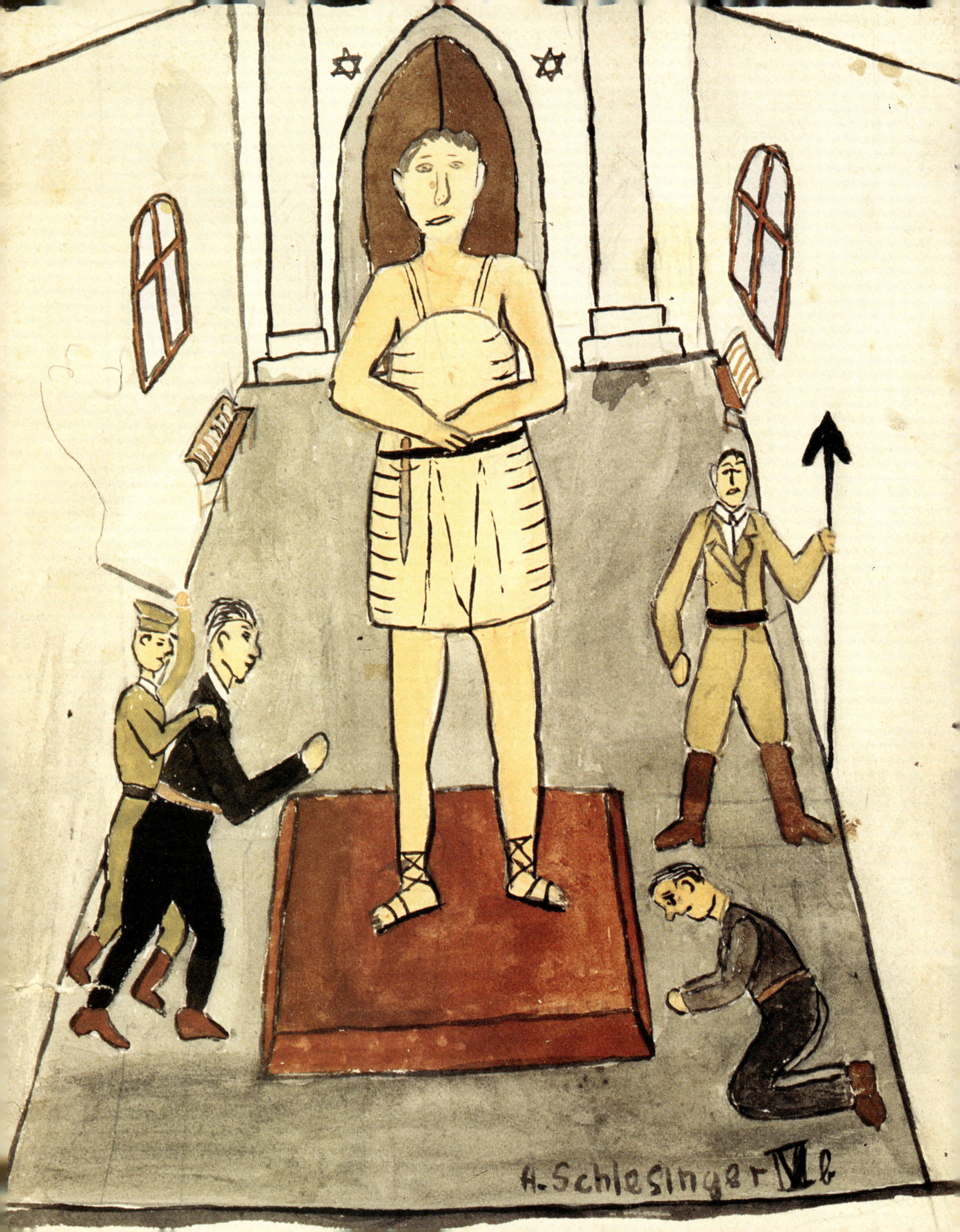
A. Schlesinger VI b

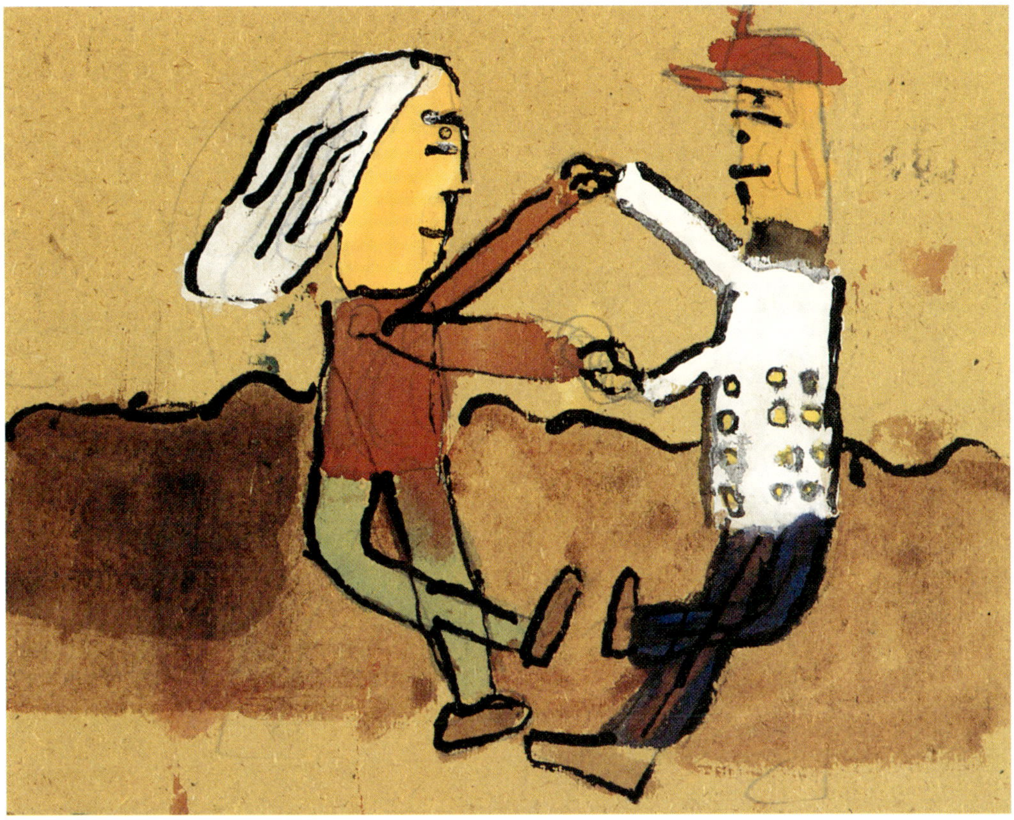

105 Georg Dreyfus,
Dancing Couple,
Febr. 1939
(Cat. 68)

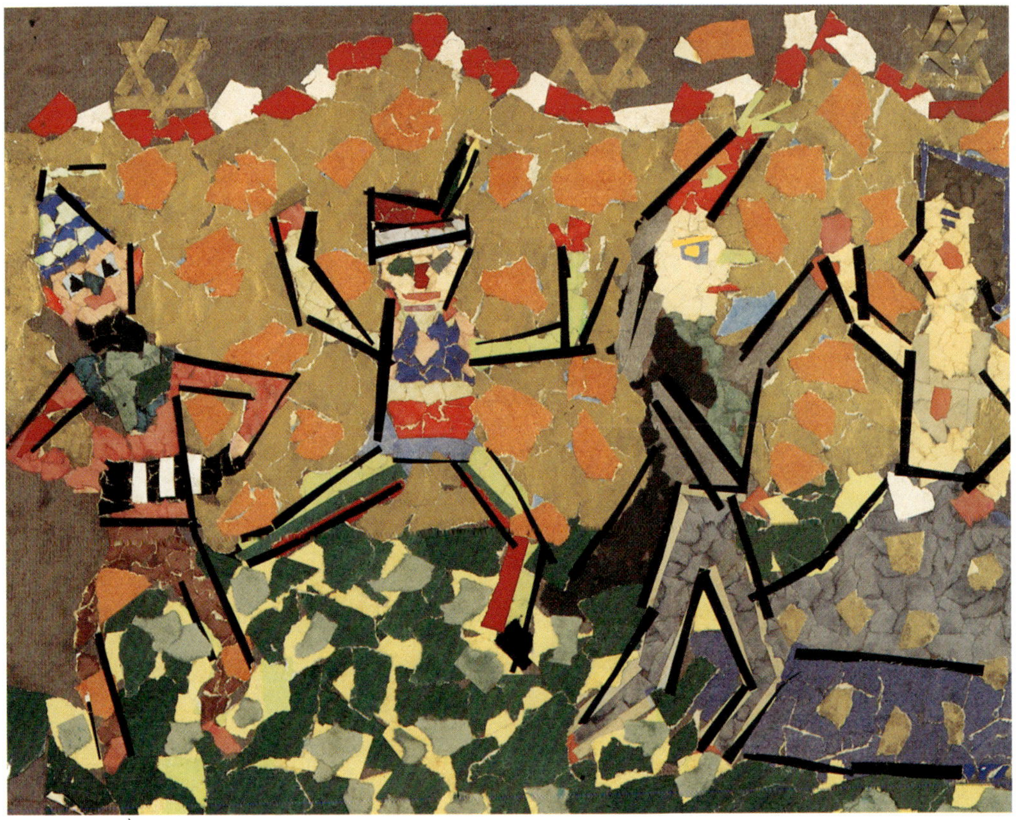

106 Name unknown,
The Costume Party,
undated
(Cat. 90)

◁
104 H. Schlesinger,
Idolatry,
Dec. 1938
(Cat. 62)

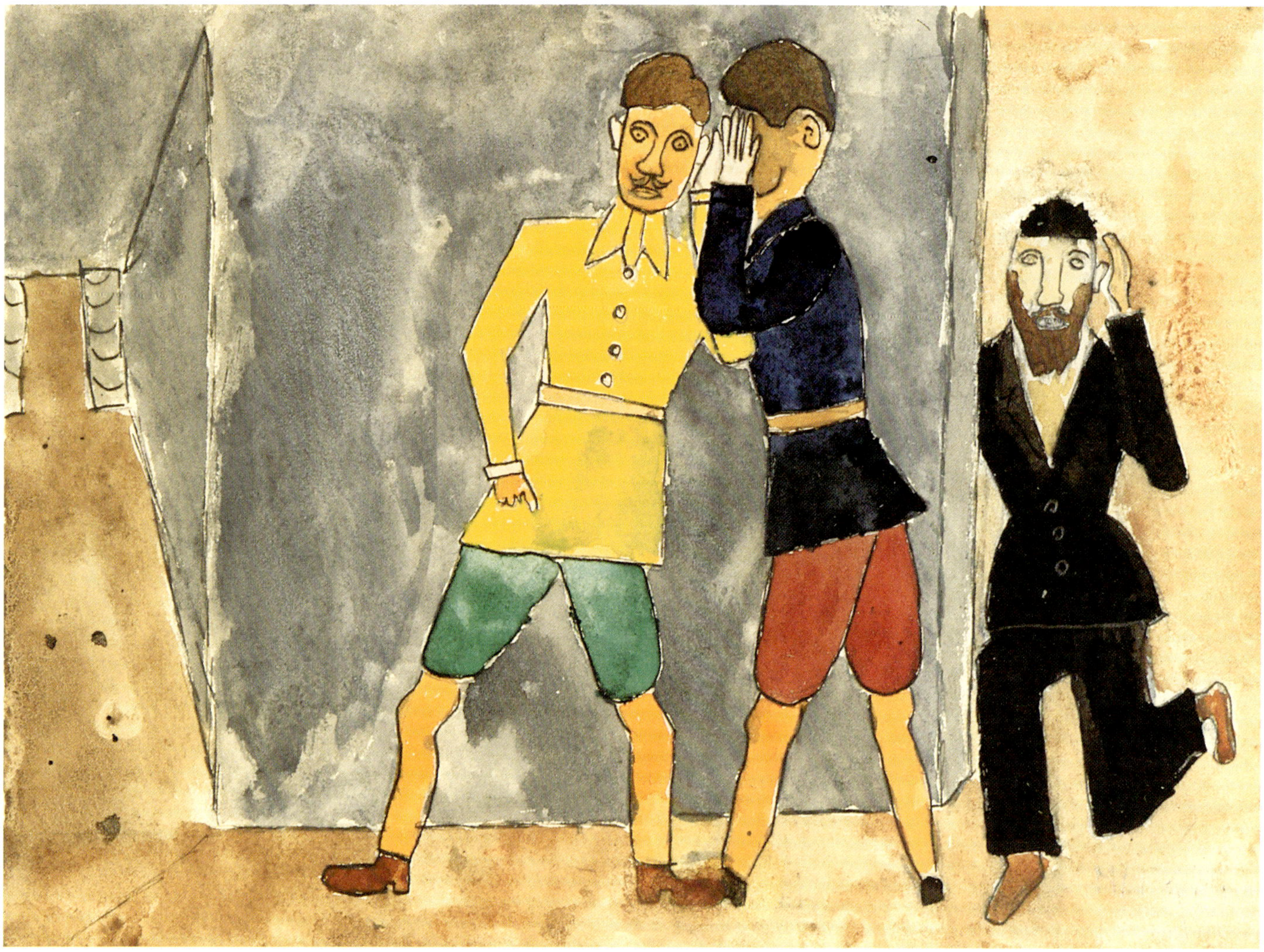

107 M. Lermann, *Purim*, Febr. 1939 (Cat. 69)

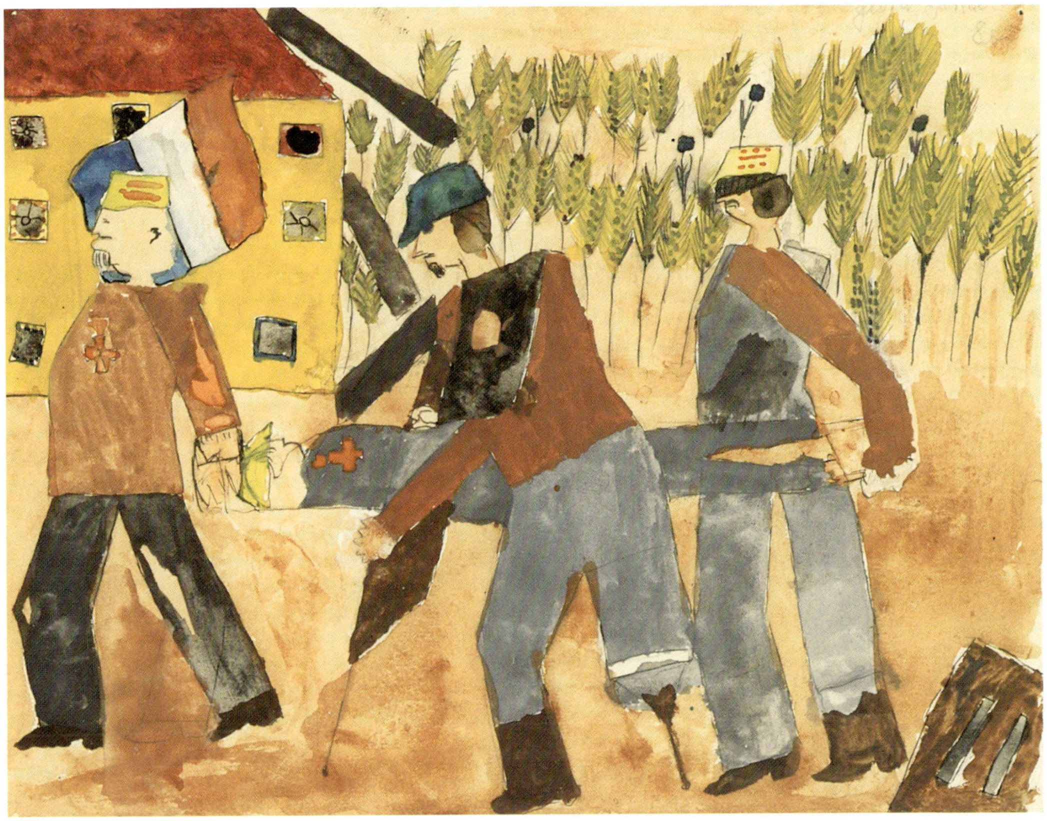

108 Flora Jentes,
Medics,
June 1939
(Cat. 73)

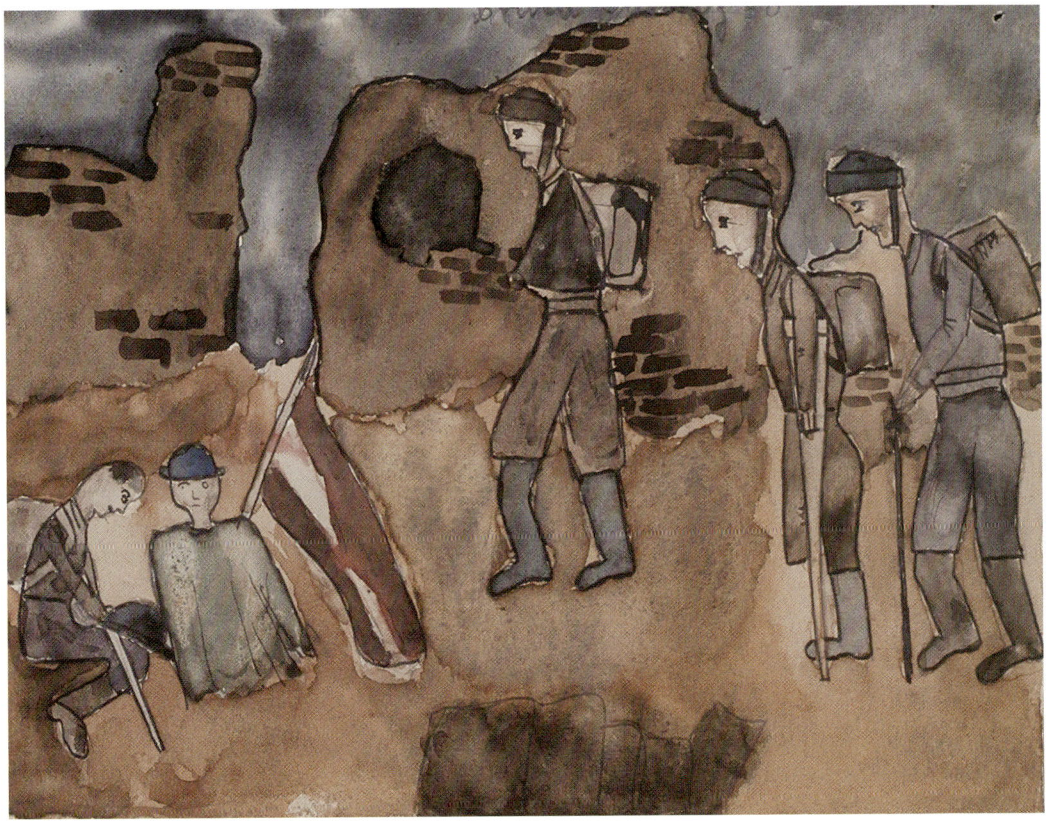

109 Anita Pukascz,
Crippled Veterans,
Sept. 1939
(Cat. 75)

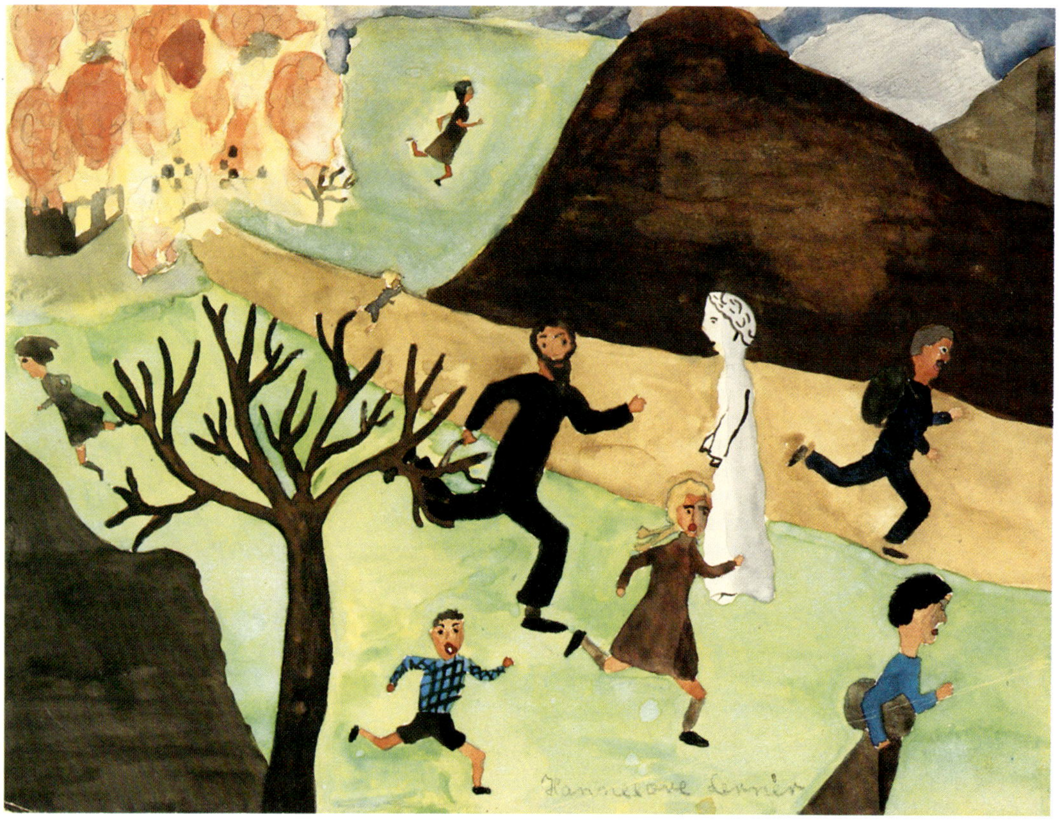

110 Hannelore Lerner,
Lot's Flight from Sodom,
Aug. 1939
(Cat. 74)

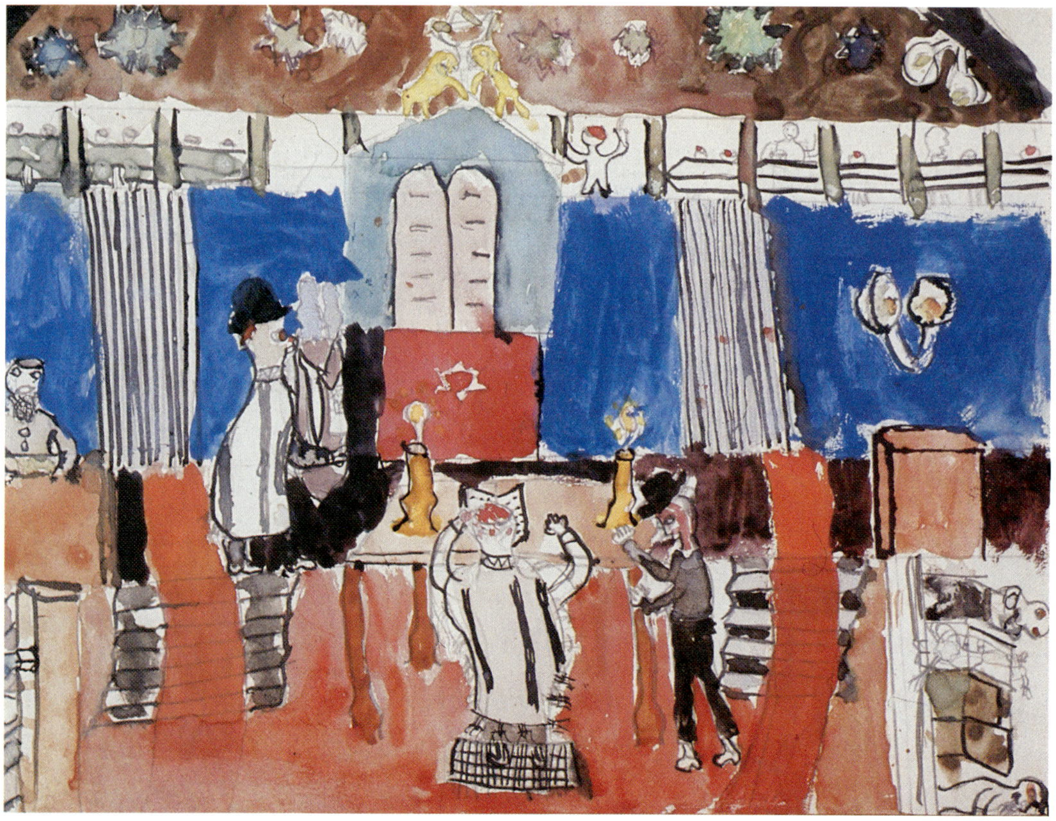

111 Gisa Blau,
In the Synagogue,
Nov. 1939
(Cat. 76)

▷
112 A. F.,
The Kiosk,
1939
(Cat. 67)

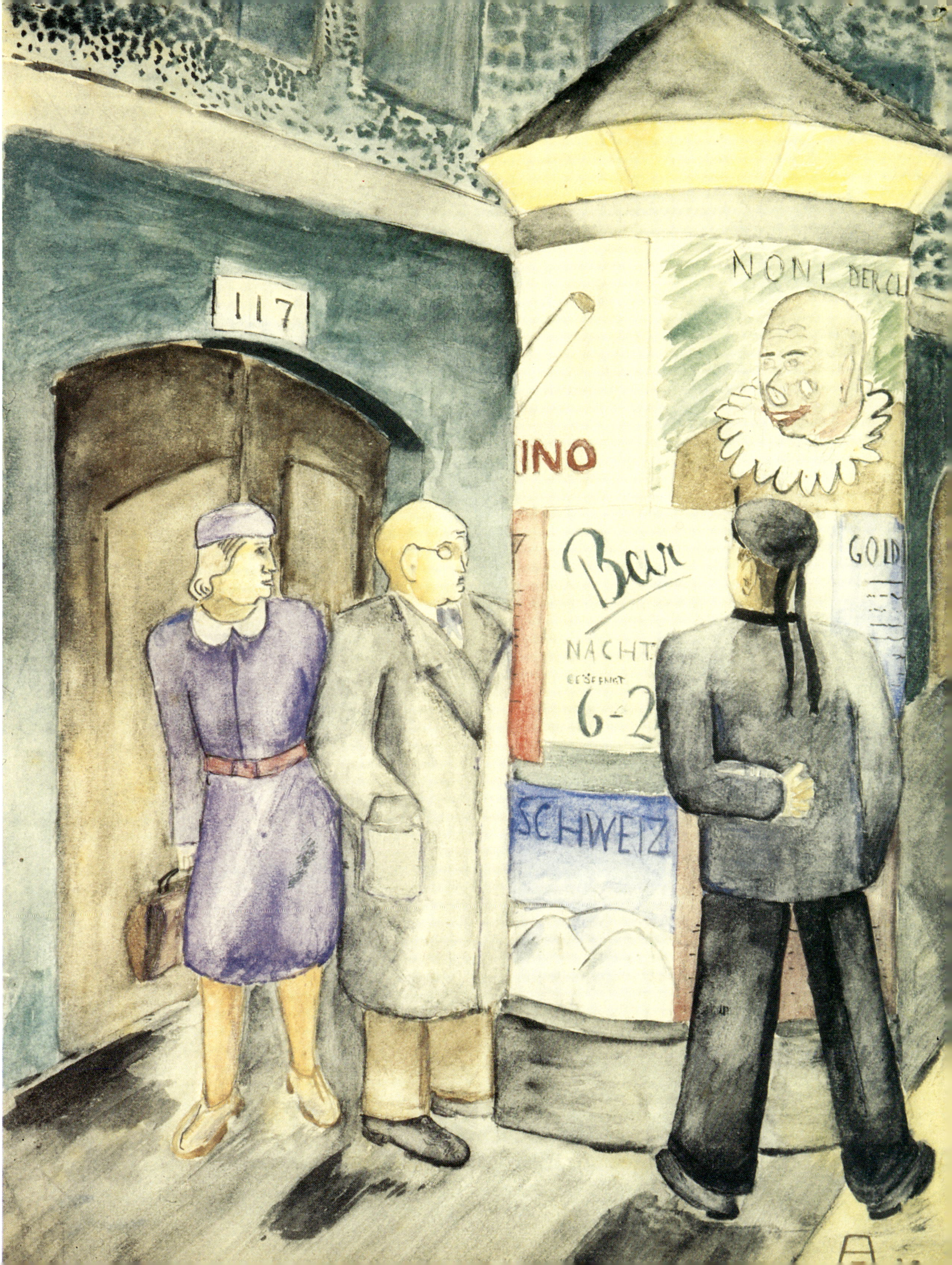
117
NONI
INO
Bar
NACHT
GOLD
SCHWEIZ

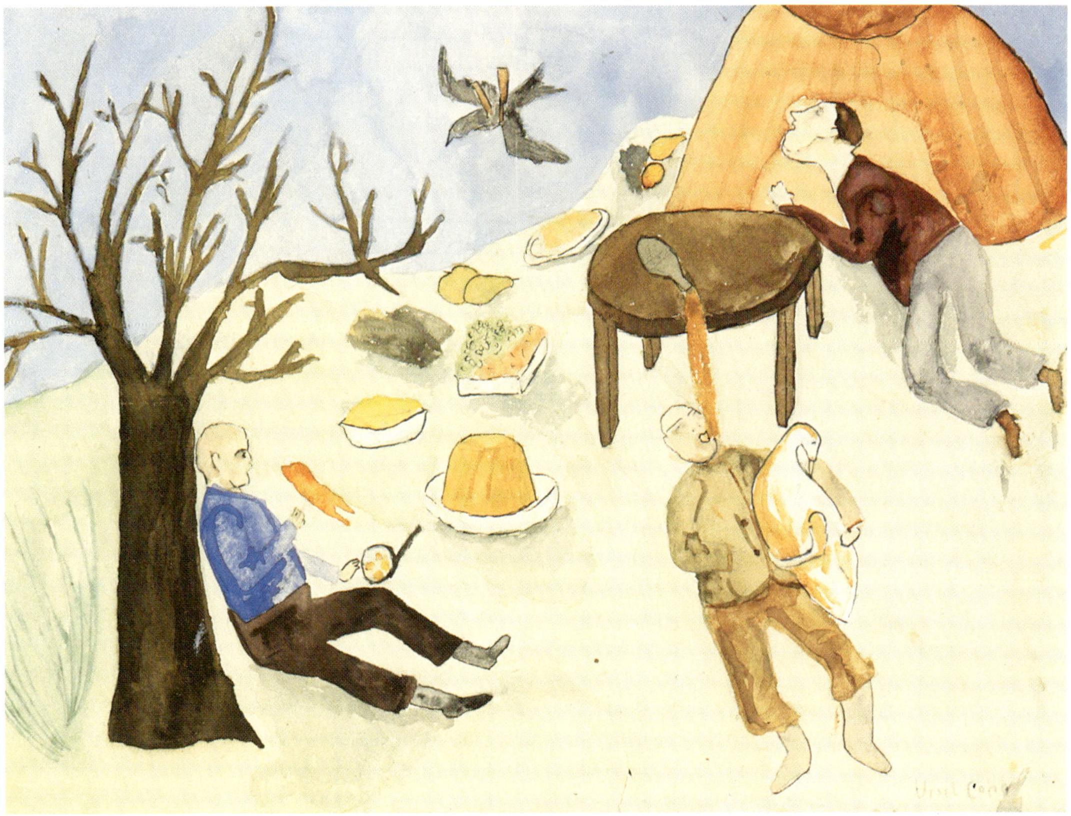

113 Ursel Cohn, *Dreams of Paradise,* Jan. 1940 (Cat. 80)

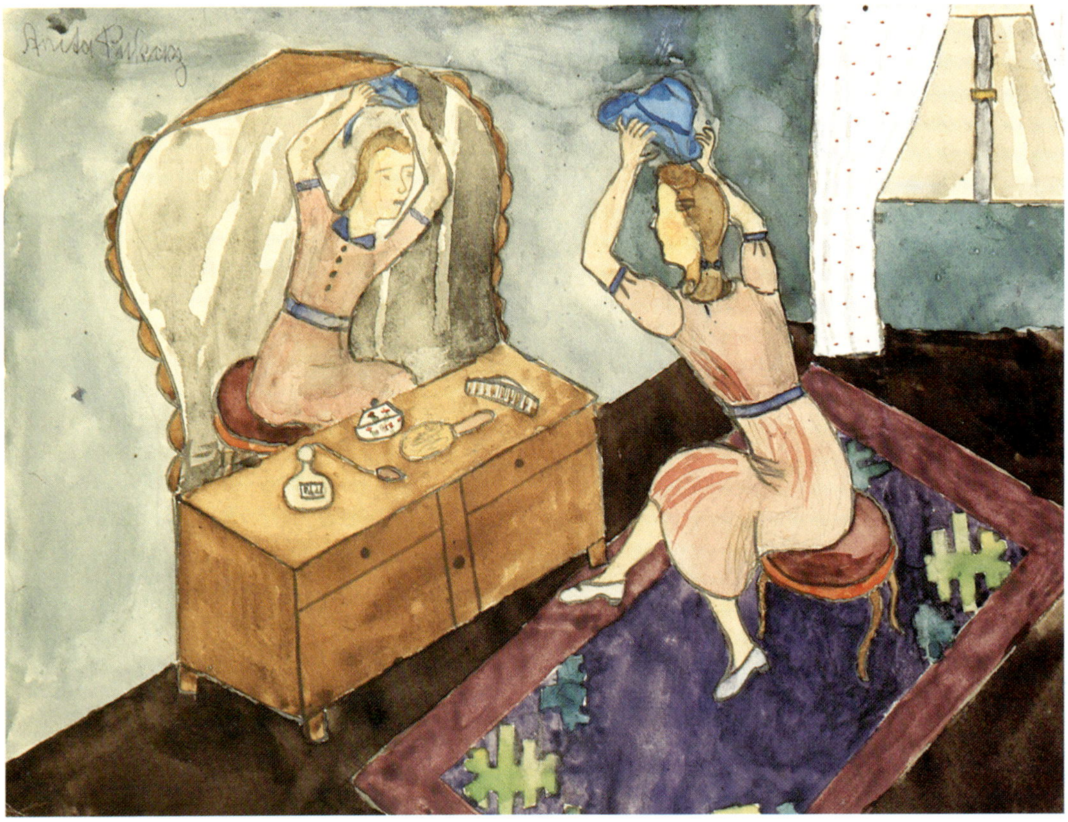

114 Anita Pukascz, *In Front of the Dresser Mirror,* Jan. 1940 (Cat. 81)

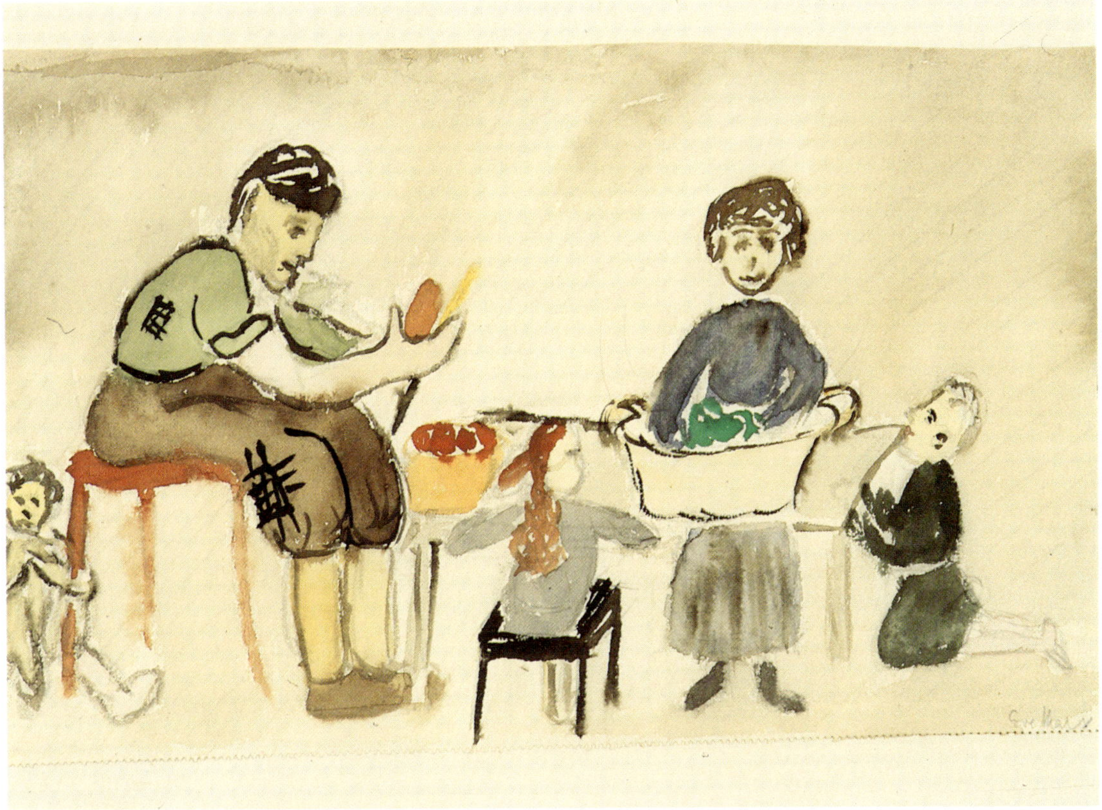

115 Eve Marx,
In the Kitchen,
undated
(Cat. 98)

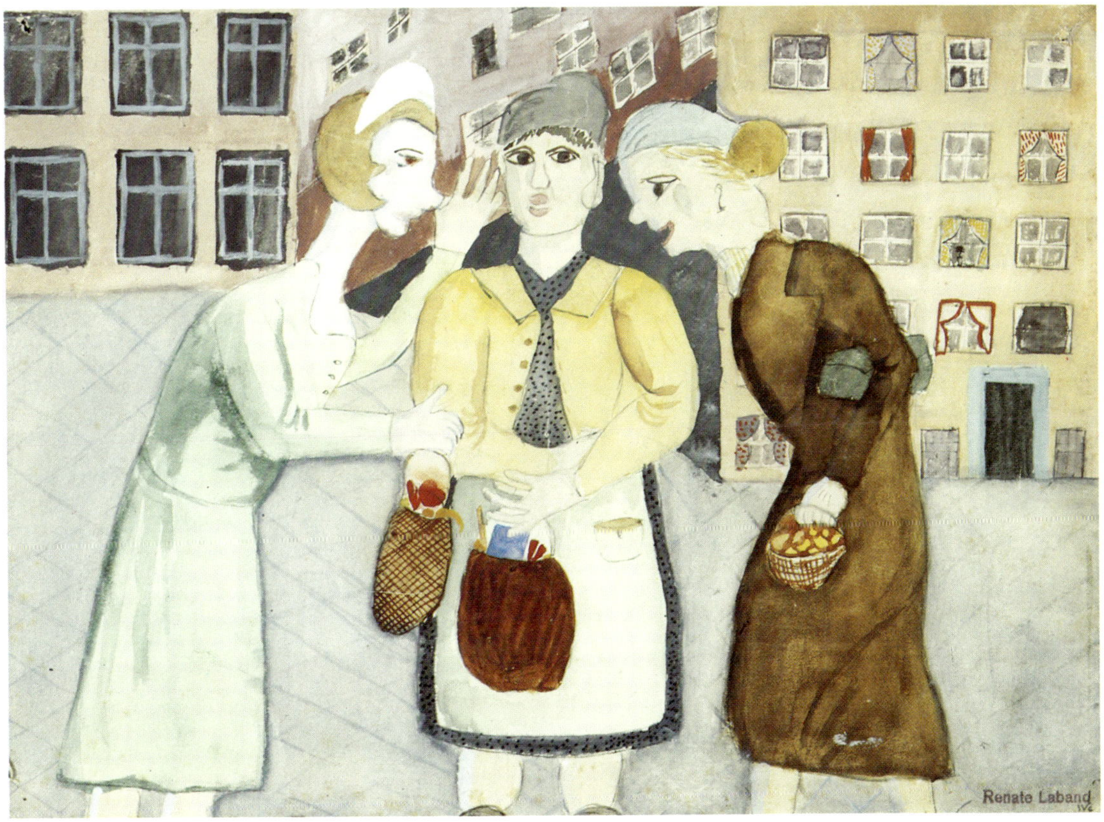

116 Renate Laband,
Rumor,
undated
(Cat. 96)

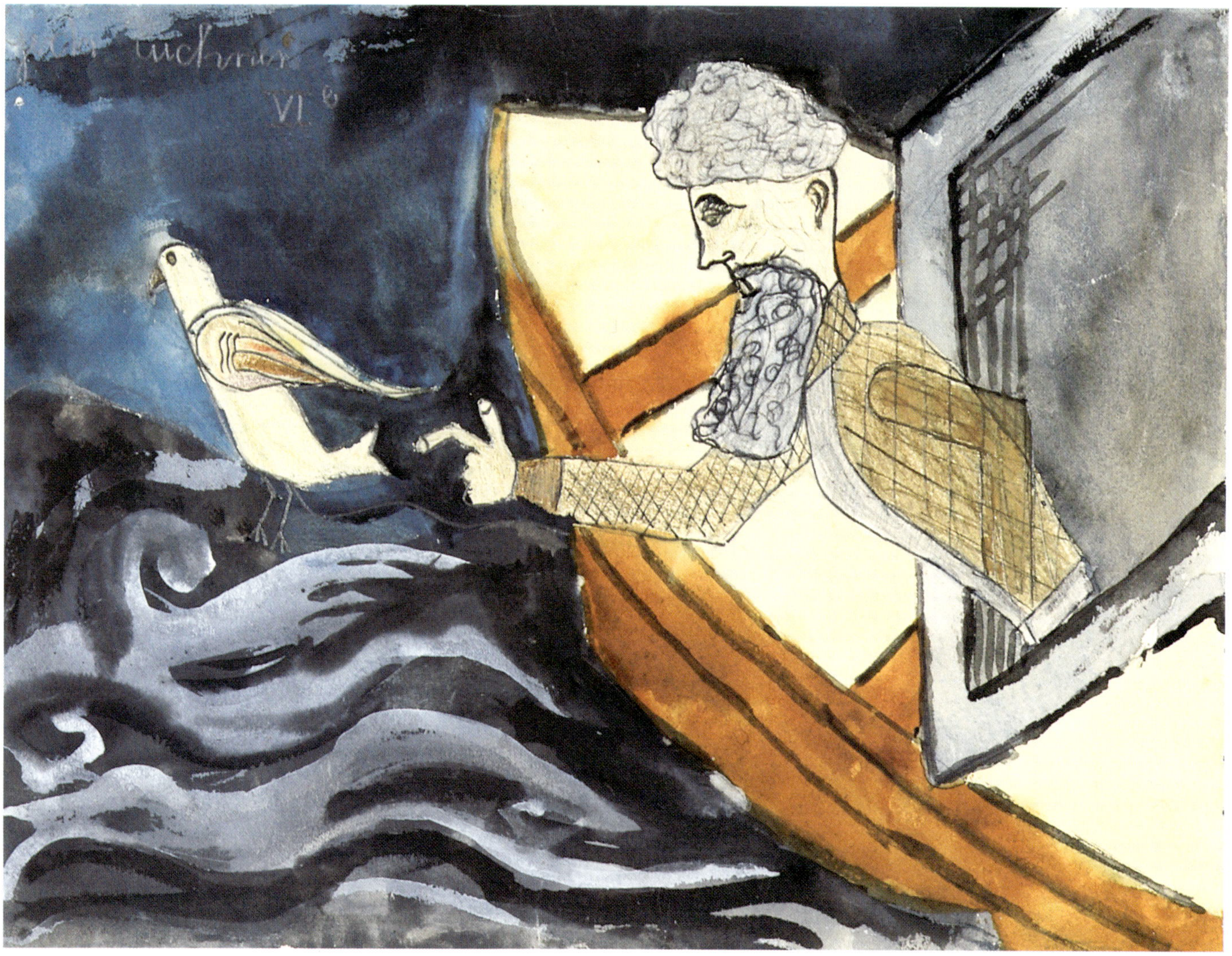

117 Gerda Tuchner, *Noah Releases the Dove,* Aug. 1940 (Cat. 82)

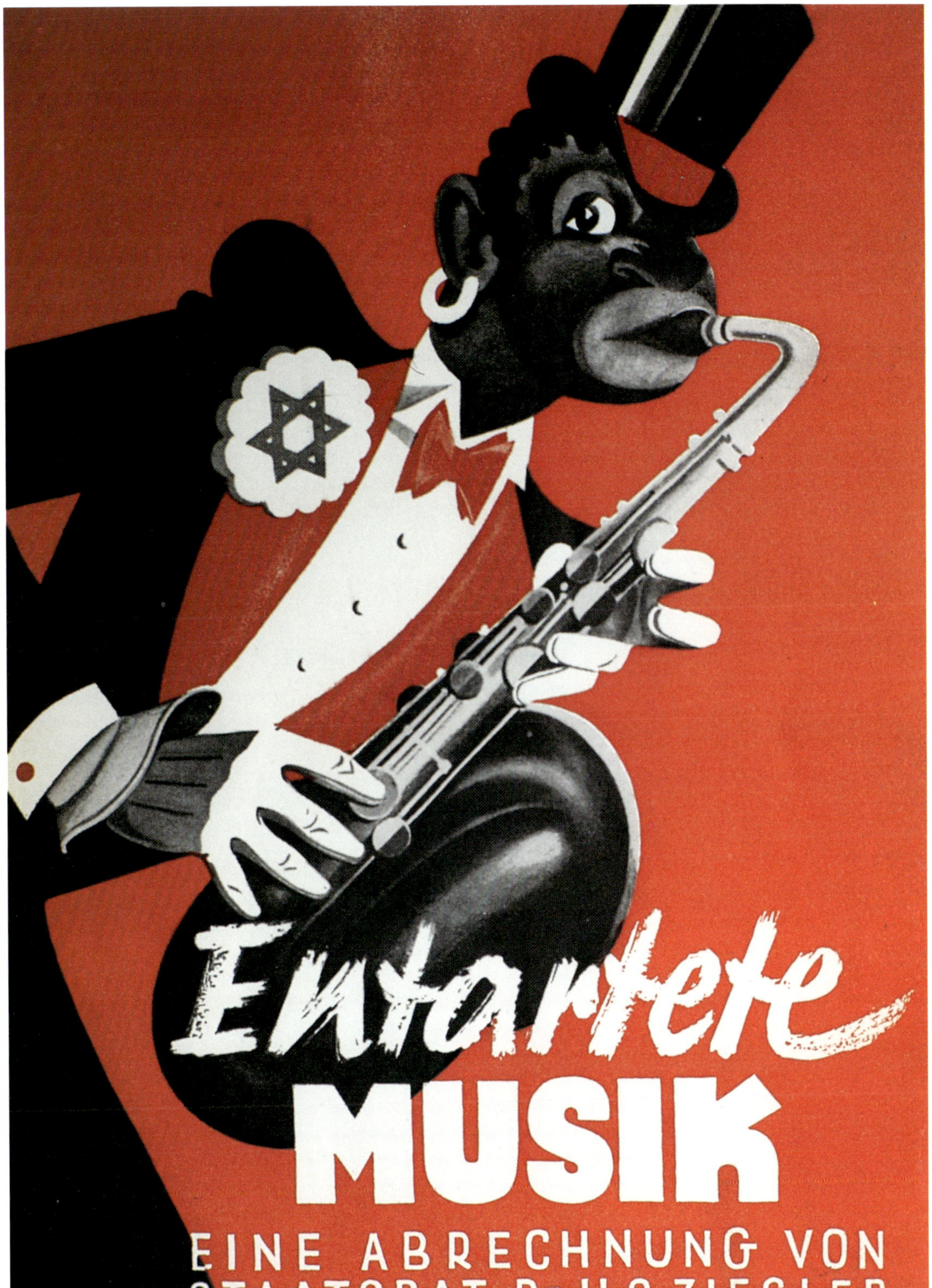

118 Cover of the catalog *Entartete Musik* ("Degenerate Music"), Düsseldorf, 1938.

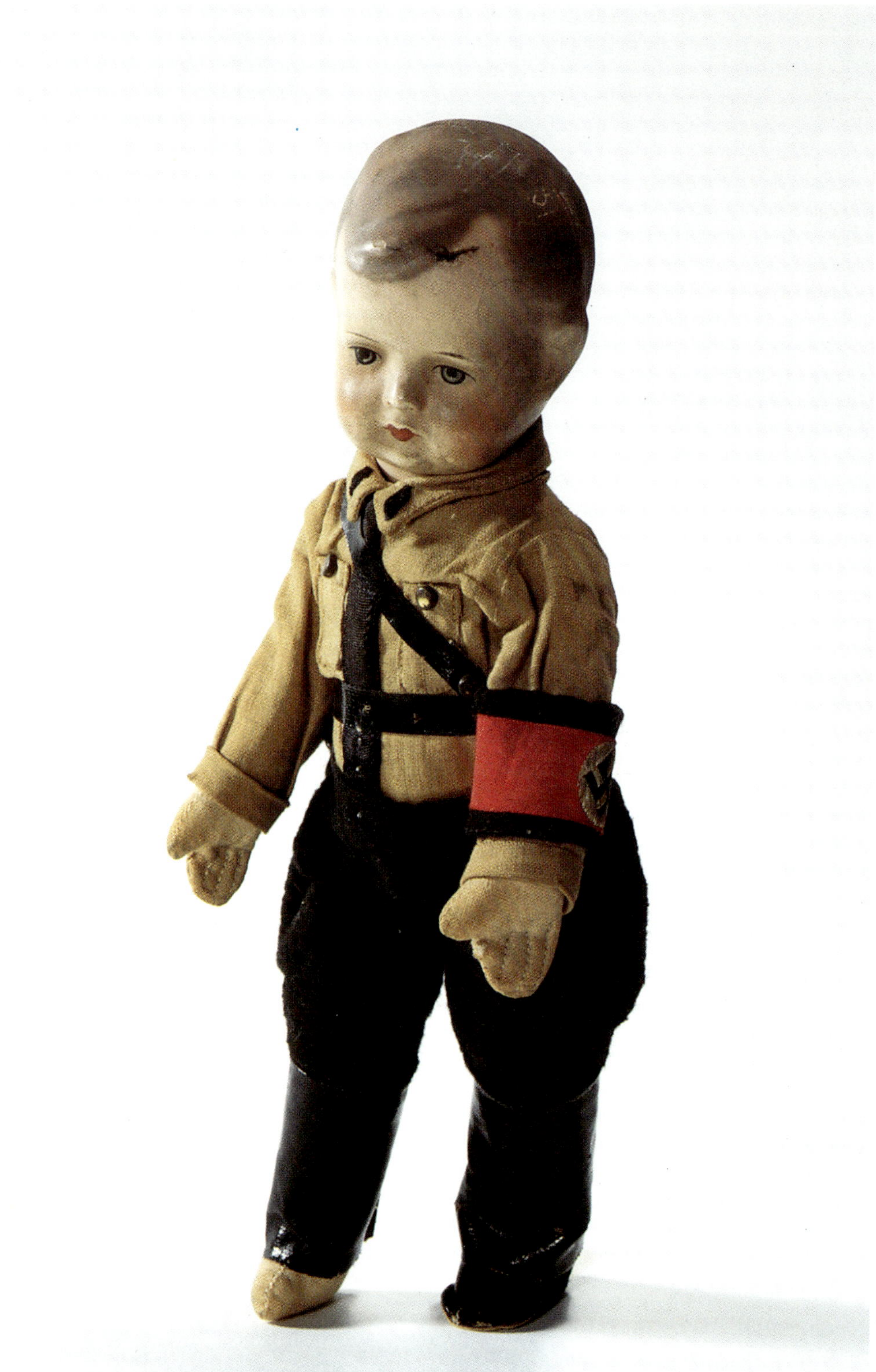

119 A doll dressed in Hitler Youth Uniform.

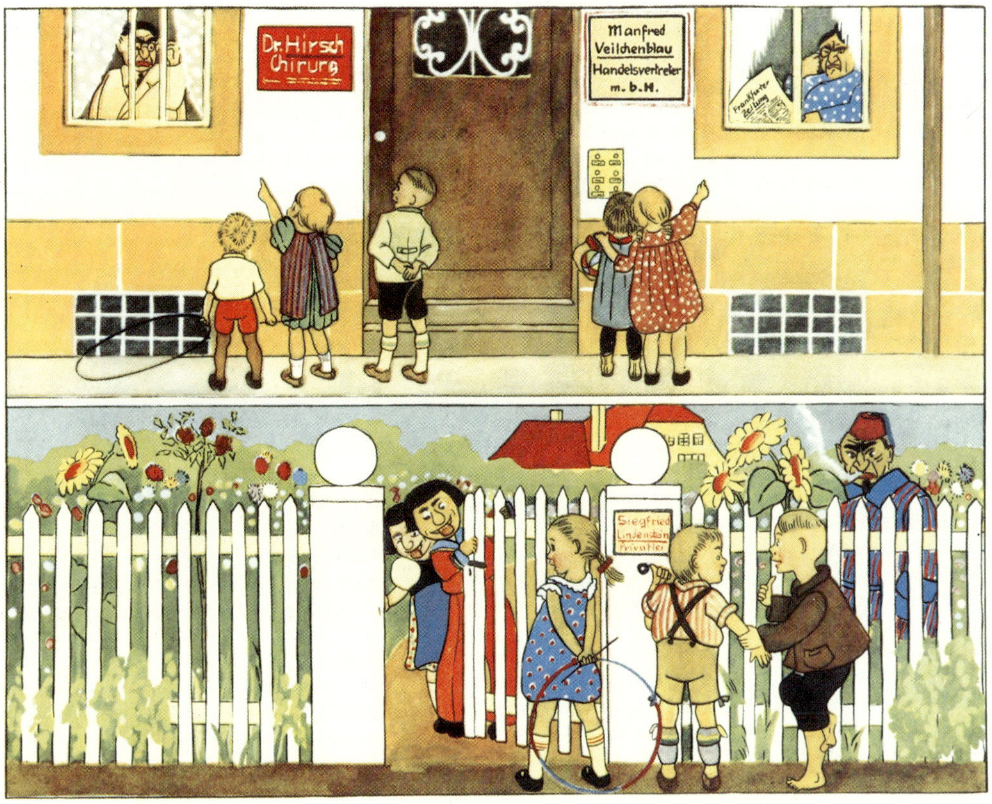

120 Elwira Bauer, *Trust No Fox in The Green Meadow and No Jew Taking an Oath*, Nuremberg: Stürmer Verlag, 1938; illustration entitled "Jewish Names."

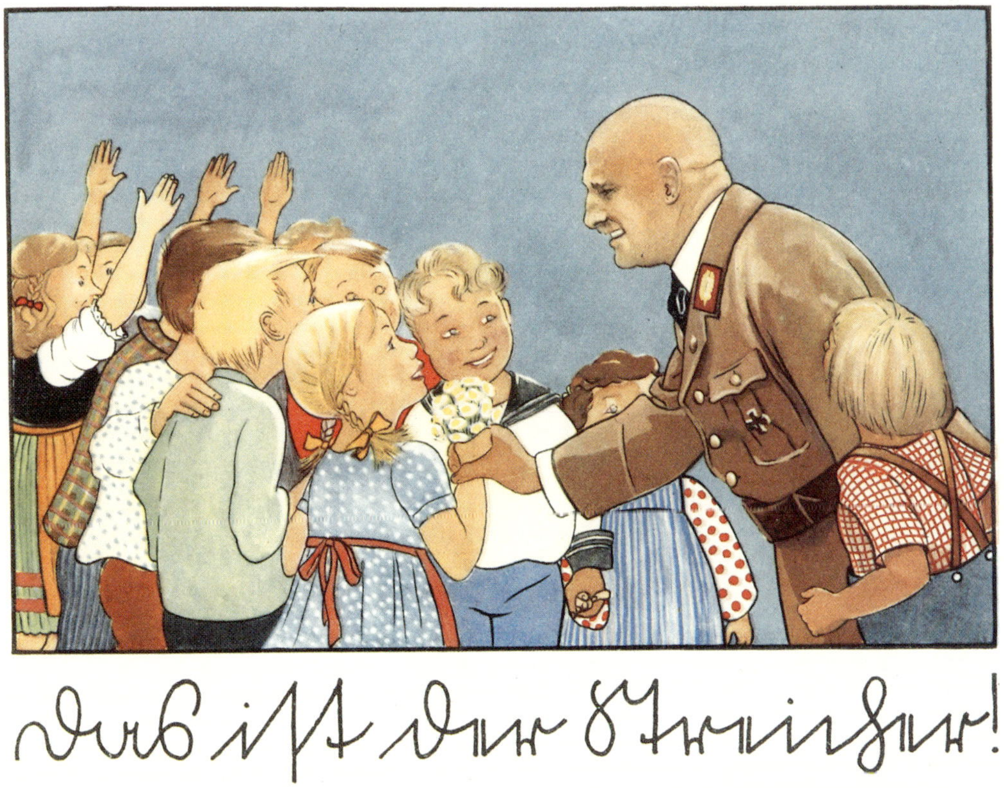

121 Elwira Bauer, *Trust No Fox . . . and No Jew*, Stürmer 1936, illustration entitled "That's Streicher!"

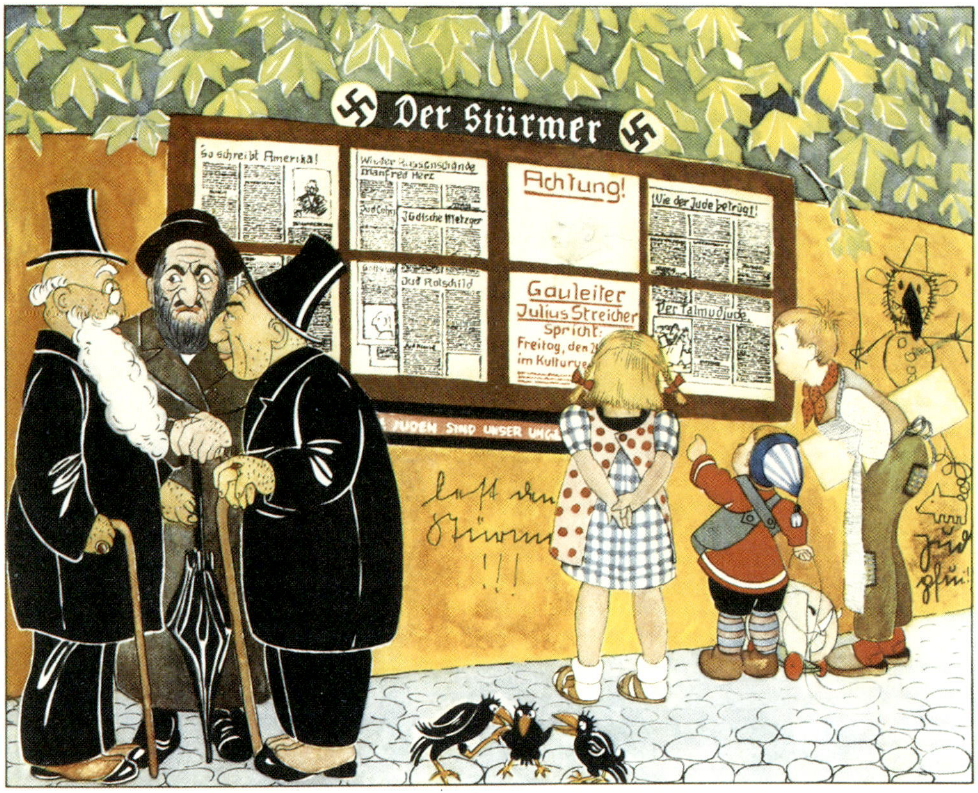

122 Elwira Bauer, *Trust No Fox . . . and No Jew*, Stürmer 1936, illustration entitled "He printed the *Stürmer*."

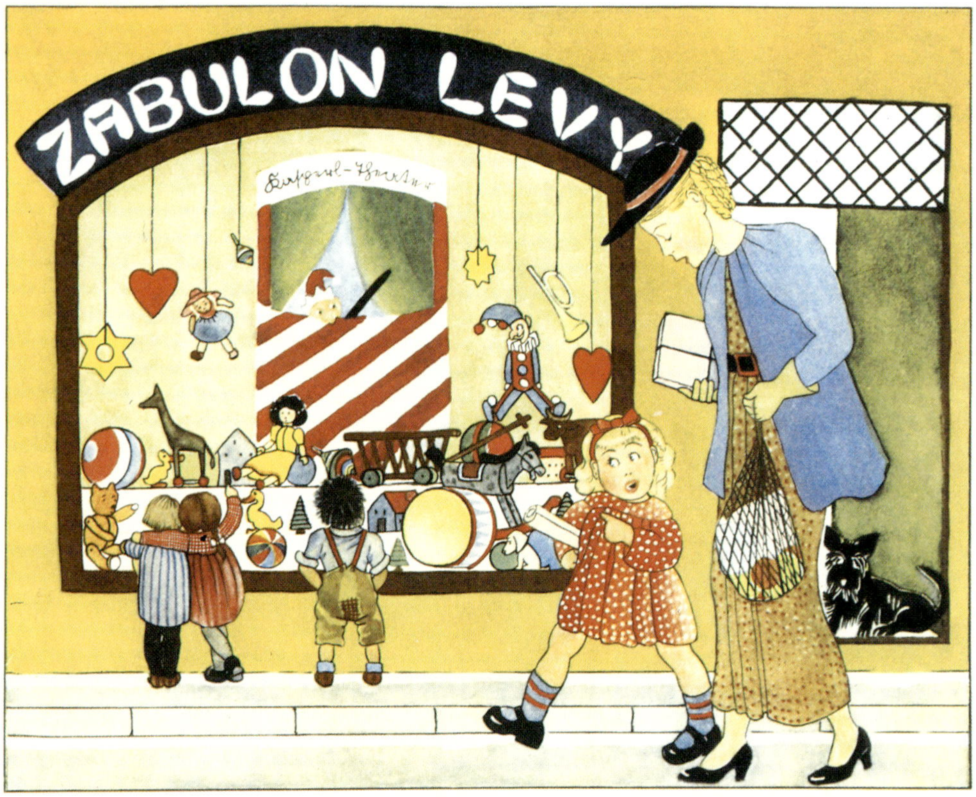

123 Elwira Bauer, *Trust No Fox . . . and No Jew*, Stürmer 1936, illustration entitled "We won't shop at the Jewish department store."

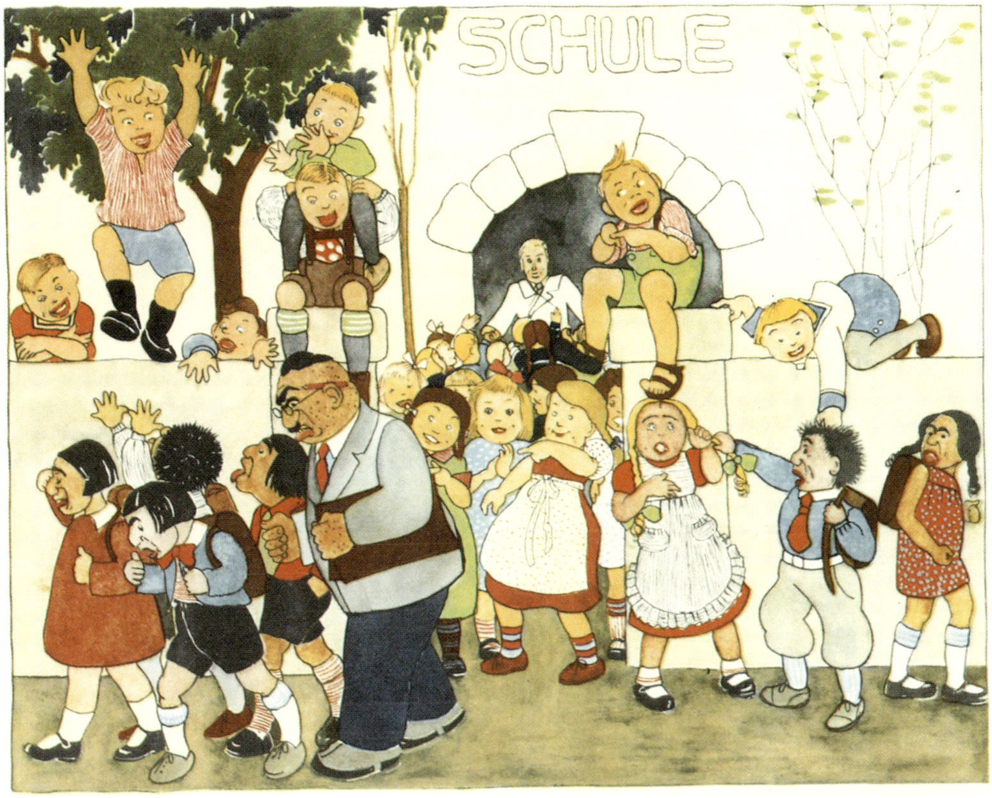

124 Elwira Bauer, *Trust No Fox . . . and No Jew*, Stürmer 1936, illustration entitled "Now school will be nice."

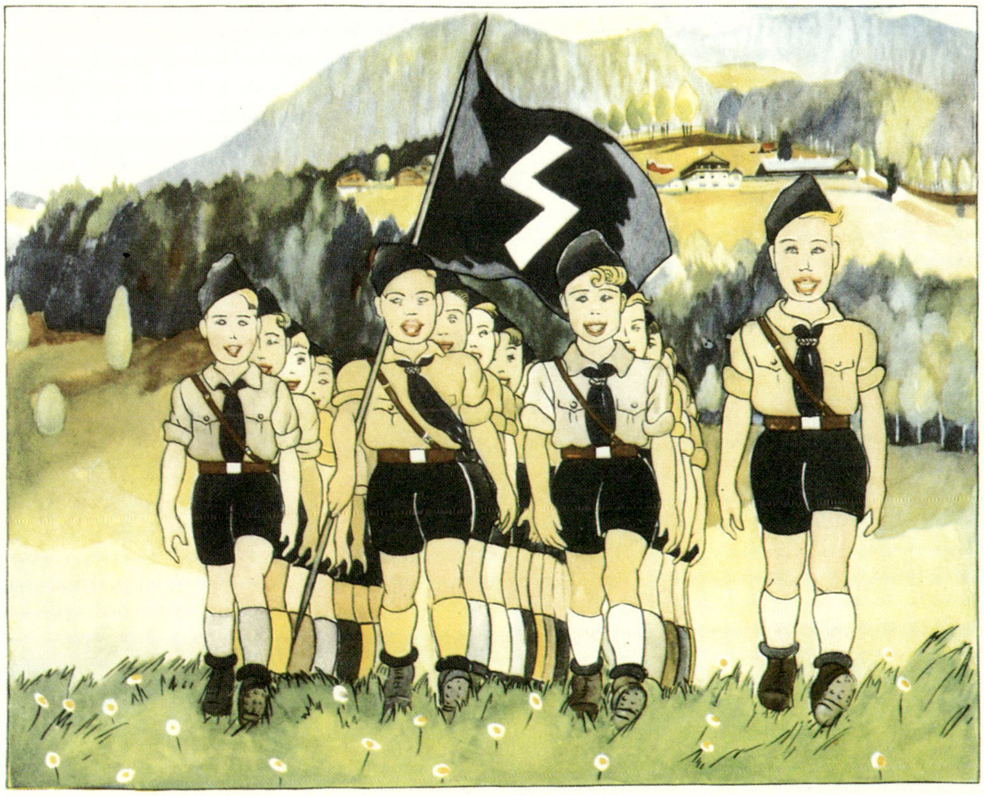

125 Elwira Bauer, *Trust No Fox . . . and No Jew*, Stürmer 1936, illustration entitled "The Führer's Youth."

Catalog of the Exhibition

The descriptive entries are arranged in the following sequence:

Catalog entry running number and, in parenthesis, the figure number for the illustration reproduced in this book.

The student's name and school year, or the artist's name and biographical data.

The title and date of the work.

The medium and size of the work.

The accession number or collection name, such as AL for Lauterbach Archive, at the Stadtmuseum Düsseldorf. Credits to other institutions or individuals for photographs are listed separately.

Titles are given in quotes if the works were titled by the artists; titles without quotation marks were provided by the museum or the editor.

The size given is the total size of paper or canvas used. It was not always possible to provide a consistent identification for the grade or school year for the Berlin schools.

1 (Fig. 55)
Ilse Marx, 9th Grade
Job, Oct. 1936
Watercolor, 30 × 26.3 cm.
Inv. No. 1983/71 (120)

2 (Fig. 56)
Name unknown, grade unknown
"The Art Class," Dec. 1936
Pencil and watercolor, 31.8 × 24.1 cm.
Inv. No. 1983/71 (593)

3
G(erd) Westfeld, 5th Grade
History Class: "Roosevelt's Victory,"
Dec. 1936
Pencil and colored chalk,
23.7 × 32.6 cm.
Inv. No. 1983/71 (168)

4 (Fig. 60)
H(elmut) Cahn, grade unknown
"Cowboy," 1937
Watercolor, 21 × 27.5 cm.
Inv. No. 1983/71 (686)

5 (Fig. 49)
M(argot) Cohn, grade unknown
"Leaving Egypt," Jan. 1937
Black wash, 32 × 24.1 cm.
Inv. No. 1983/71 (163)

6 (Fig. 52)
Name unknown, grade unknown
"Moses Parts the Red Sea," undated
Pencil, 25.5 × 31.9 cm.
Inv. No. 1983/71 (162)

7 (Fig. 51)
Sella Helga Paradies, 7th Grade
"Slave Labor in Egypt," Jan. 1937
Black wash, 19.4 × 26.1 cm.
Inv. No. 1983/71 (164)

8 (Fig. 48)
G. Sostheim, 7th Grade
"Finding Moses," Jan. 1937
Black wash and ceruse, 25 × 19.4 cm.
Inv. No. 1983/71 (148)

9 (Fig. 50)
Name unknown, 7th Grade
"Finding Moses," Feb. 1937
Pencil and black wash, 24.2 × 31.8 cm.
AL 722

10 (Fig. 57)
E(va) Alexander, 7th Grade
"Faces, Masks," Feb. 1937
Watercolor, 31.9 × 24.1 cm.
AL 244

11
M(arianne) Eckstein, 6th Grade
"Old Man in Armchair," March 1937
Watercolor, 31.3 × 23.8 cm.
Inv. No. 1983/71 (383)

12 (Fig. 59)
Margot Salomon, 7th Grade
"Africa," March 1937
Watercolor, 24.8 × 24.2 cm.
Inv. No. 1983/71 (71)

13
Hermann Feldmann, grade unknown
"Africa," undated
Watercolor, 24 × 33 cm.
Inv. No. 1983/71 (536)

14 (Fig. 58)
Name unknown, grade unknown
"Black Man," undated
Watercolor, 25.9 × 19.2 cm.
AL 791

15 (Fig. 63)
Manfred Kaufmann, 6th Grade
"Prometheus," May 1937
Watercolor, 24 × 33 cm.
Inv. No. 1983/71 (744)

16 (Fig. 61)
H(enni) Schwarz, 8th Grade
"India," May 1937
Watercolor, 24.2 × 31.8 cm.
Inv. No. 1983/71 (737)

17 (Fig. 62)
Name unknown, 8th Grade
"China," May 1937
Pencil and watercolor, 19.1 × 27.6 cm.
AL 851

18
Name unknown, 9th Grade
"The Old City," May 1937
Watercolor, 24.3 × 31.8 cm.
AL 737

19 (Fig. 64)
G(ünther) Cahn, 6th Grade
"Atlas," June 1937
Watercolor, 31.7 × 22.7 cm.
Inv. No. 1983/71 (658)

20
Inge Jordan, 6th Grade
"The Bull of Minos," June 1937
Watercolor, 11 × 27.4 cm.
Inv. No. 1983/71 (689)

21
Ellen Wallach, 4th Grade
"Blowing the Shofar" (Jewish New Year),
Sept. 1937
Colored chalk, 21 × 27.5 cm.
Inv. No. 1983/71 (523)

22
Lotti Ran, 6th Grade
"The Milker," Sept. 1937

Watercolor, 21 × 27.5 cm.
Inv. No. 1983/71 (731)

23 (Fig. 47)
Name unknown, grade unknown
Dr. Siegfried "Klein," Oct. 1937
Black wash, 27 × 21 cm.
Inv. No. 1983/71

24 (Fig. 46)
D(ora) Moritz, 6th Grade
"Rabbi," Oct. 1937
Pencil, 28.7 × 21 cm.
AL 657

25 (Fig. 65)
Eugen Wallach, 4th Grade
"The Emigrant," Oct. 1937
Pencil and watercolor, 37.6 × 28.8 cm.
Inv. No. 1983/71 (69)

26 (Fig. 66)
Hermann Feldmann, grade unknown
"Müllmer's Small Boat," undated
Pencil and watercolor, 24.1 × 32 cm.
Inv. No. 1983/71 (139)

27 (Fig. 70)
Ellen Wallach, 4th Grade
"Gypsies," Oct. 1937
Watercolor, 21 × 27.5 cm.
Inv. No. 1983/71 (551)

28
Esther Rüssler, 4th Grade
"Gypsies," Oct. 1937
Mixed media, 23.5 × 34.5 cm.
Inv. No. 1983/71 (539)

29 (Fig. 68)
H(einz) Leopold, 5th Grade (?)
"Düsseldorf: The Old City," Oct. 1937
Colored pencils and ink, 21 × 27.5 cm.
AL 245

30 (Fig. 72)
Leo-Wolf Klarmann, 6th Grade
"The Thief," Oct. 1937
Watercolor, 27.5 × 20.9 cm.
Inv. No. 1983/71 (723)

31 (Fig. 67)
Leo-Wolf Klarmann, 6th Grade
"The Mover," Oct. 1937
Watercolor, 21 × 27.7 cm.
Inv. No. 1983/71 (134)

32 (Fig. 73)
R(uth) Pschednowek, 7th Grade
"Pattern," Oct. 1937
Watercolor, 26.2 × 29.2 cm.
Inv. No. 1983/71 (374)

33 (Fig. 75)
Kurt Mayer, 7th Grade
"Jazz Orchestra," Oct. 1937
Watercolor, 24 × 31.9 cm.
Inv. No. 1983/71 (422)

34 (Fig. 74)
M(arianne) Seligmann, 7th Grade
"Concert," Oct.–Nov. 1937
Watercolor, 24.3 × 31.7 cm.
Inv. No. 1983/71 (30)

35 (Fig. 76)
Helene Testiler, 7th Grade
"Cabaret," undated
Watercolor, 21 × 27.6 cm.
Inv. No. 1983/71 (28)

36 (Fig. 78)
K(urt)-H(einz) Elias, 7th Grade
"The Rütli Oath," Oct. 1937
Watercolor, 17.8 × 20.9 cm.
Inv. No. 1983/71 (713)

37 (Fig. 81)
M(argit) Hartmann, 6th Grade
"St. Martin's Day Procession," Nov. 1937
Watercolor, 21.1 × 26.7 cm.
AL 533

38 (Fig. 80)
G(ünther) Cahn, 6th Grade
"The Gröne Jong," Nov. 1937
Watercolor, 21 × 27.5 cm.
AL 534

39 (Fig. 82)
H(enni) Steppel, 6th Grade
"The Hikers," Nov. 1937
Watercolor, 27.5 × 21 cm.
AL 229

40 (Fig. 69)
Gerhard Wahrenberg, 7th Grade
Düsseldorf: "The Old City," Nov. 1937
Watercolor, 21 × 27.6 cm.
Inv. No. 1983/71 (779)

41
Mela(nie) Lesekewitz, 8th Grade
"Pattern," Nov. 1937
Watercolor and ink, 27.6 × 21.1 cm.
Inv. No. 1983/71 (466)

42 (Fig. 85)
Max Rosner, 4th Grade
"The Maccabees," Dec. 1937
Pencil and watercolor, 21 × 27.5 cm.
Inv. No. 1983/71 (160)

43 (Fig. 79)
I(nge) Lewin, 6th Grade
"The Blind King," Dec. 1937
Watercolor, 21 × 27.6 cm.
Inv. No. 1983/71 (668)

44
Vera Winter, 7th Grade
"The Peasant Woman," Dec. 1937
Pencil, watercolor, and India ink, 27.6 × 20.9 cm.
Inv. No. 1983/71 (439)

45 (Fig. 89)
I(nge) Lewin, 6th Grade
"The Woodcutters," Jan. 1938
Mixed media, 21 × 27.6 cm.
Inv. No. 1983/71 (630)

46 (Fig. 86)
Name unknown, grade unknown
"Forced to Pay Homage," March 1938
Colored chalk, 21 × 27.5 cm.
AL 246

47
Willi Cohn (?)
"Stores," April 1938
Watercolor and ink, 16.2 × 26.5 cm.
AL 562

48 (Fig. 93)
Hans Rosbauer, Class IV
"The Woodcutter," June 1938
Watercolor, 28.5 × 20.5 cm.
Loan Mieke Monjau

49 (Fig. 95)
Name unknown, 8th Grade
"The Brandenburg Gate in Berlin," Aug. 1938
Watercolor, 20.6 × 28.5 cm.
Inv. No. 1983/71 (14)

50 (Fig. 94)
. . . Dresdner, 4th Grade
"The Sower," Aug. 1938
Watercolor, 31.9 × 24 cm.
Inv. No. 1983/71 (484)

51 (Fig. 97)
Georg Dreyfus, Class V
"Africa," Sept. 1938

Watercolor, 20.7 × 27.7 cm.
Loan Mieke Monjau

52 (Fig. 98)
M. Rosenstock, Class IV
"Africa," Undated
Watercolor, 32 × 27.5 cm.
Inv. No. 1983/71 (707)

53
Th. Schüttenberg, Class V
"Scouts (Spies) from Canaan," Oct. 1938
Watercolor, 20.8 × 27.5 cm.
Loan Mieke Monjau

54 (Fig. 99)
G. Jacobsohn, Class IV
"Teacher's Track Race," Nov. 1938
Watercolor, 16.9 × 28.1 cm.
Inv. No. 1983/71 (31)

55 (Fig. 100)
Kurt Lippmann, Class 2
"A Midsummer Night's Dream,"
Nov. 1938
Watercolor, 20.7 × 27.5 cm.
Inv. No. 1983/71 (129)

56 (Fig. 53)
Joachim Tietz, 7th Grade
"Competition for 'Die Brücke'," Nov. 1938
Black wash and ceruse, 20.5 x 27.7 cm.
Inv. No. 1983/71 (11)

57 (Fig. 54)
H. Kneller, 7th Grade
"'The Bridge': Periodical of the Kaliski School," Nov. 1938
Linocut, 27.8 × 21 cm.
Inv. No. 1983/71 (12)

58
I. Remak, Class IV
"Camel," Nov. 1938
Watercolor, 27.6 × 20.6 cm.
Inv. No. 1983/71 (53)

59 (Fig. 101)
Albert Tell, Class 5
"Battle Scene," Nov. 1938
Watercolor, 25.5 × 41.8 cm.
Inv. No. 1983/71 (575)

60
Ernst Gotthilf, Class 5
"Harvest," Nov. 1938
Watercolor, 21 × 27.5 cm.
Inv. No. 1983/71 (567)

61 (Fig. 103)
Werner Lier, Class 3
"The Maccabean," Dec. 1938
Watercolor, 18.4 × 22.6 cm.
Inv. No. 1983/71 (4)

62 (Fig. 104)
H. Schlesinger, Class IV
"Idolatry," Dec. 1938
Watercolor, 27.4 × 21 cm.
Loan Mieke Monjau

63 (Fig. 102)
I. Remak, Class IV
"Scene from Antiquity with the God Mercury," 21 Dec. 1938
Watercolor and ink, 20.6 × 27.5 cm.
Loan Mieke Monjau

64
W. Frank, 7th Grade
"Idolatry," Dec. 1938
Watercolor, 27.5 × 21 cm.
Inv. No. 1983/71 (142)

65
Name unknown, grade unknown
"The Idol," undated
Transparency, 40.3 × 30 cm.
Loan Mieke Monjau

66 (Fig. 96)
. . . Sternberg, 7th Grade
"London," Dec. 1938
Watercolor, 20.6 × 27.4 cm.
Loan Mieke Monjau

67 (Fig. 112)
A. F., grade unknown
"The Kiosk," 1939
Watercolor, 32 × 24.4 cm.
Inv. No. 1983/71 (17)

68 (Fig. 105)
Georg Dreyfus, Class 5
"Dancing Couple," Feb. 1939
Watercolor, 21 × 26.3 cm.
Loan Mieke Monjau

69 (Fig. 107)
M. Lermann, Class VI
"Purim," Feb. 1939
Watercolor, 20.8 × 28.4 cm.
AL 528

70
Ursel Berger, Class VII
"Chicken," May 1939
Watercolor, 27.6 × 20.5 cm.
Inv. No. 1983/71 (54)

71
Dora Sylbertrest, Class VIII
"Two Fishes," May 1939
Watercolor, 21.1 × 28.6 cm.
Inv. No. 1983/71 (20)

72
Nanny Horowitz, Class 7
"Zum Hasensteg" (trans.: The Rabbit's Path), June 1939
Watercolor, 15.2 × 27.2 cm.
Loan Mieke Monjau

73 (Fig. 108)
Flora Jentes, Class VIII
"Medics," June 1939
Watercolor, 21 × 27.4 cm.
Loan Mieke Monjau

74 (Fig. 110)
Hannelore Lerner, Class VII
"Lot's Flight from Sodom," Aug. 1939
Watercolor, 21.1 × 27.5 cm.
Loan Mieke Monjau

75 (Fig. 109)
Anita Pukascz, Class VIII
"Crippled Veterans," Sept. 1939
Watercolor, 20.5 × 27.5 cm.
Inv. No. 1983/71 (169)

76 (Fig. 111)
Gisa Blau, Class IV
"In the Synagogue," Nov. 1939
Watercolor, 21 × 28.6 cm.
Inv. No. 1983/71 (128)

77
I. Rothmacheg, Class V
"Gypsies," Nov. 1939
Pencil and watercolor, 20.7 × 27.7 cm.
Loan Mieke Monjau

78
Sonja Weissb. . ., Class VII
"The Harvester," Nov. 1939
Watercolor, 26.9 × 20.9 cm.
Loan Mieke Monjau

79
Ursel Cohn, Class VIII
"Working in the Garden," Nov. 1939
Watercolor, 20.5 × 26.5 cm.
Loan Mieke Monjau

80 (Fig. 113)
Ursel Cohn, Class VIII
"Dreams of Paradise," Jan. 1940
Watercolor, 20.4 × 27.4 cm.
Loan Mieke Monjau

81 (Fig. 114)
Anita Pukascz, Class VIII
"In Front of the Dresser Mirror," Jan. 1940
Watercolor, 20.6 × 27.5 cm.
Loan Mieke Monjau

82 (Fig. 117)
Gerda Tuchner, Class VI
"Noah Releases the Dove," Aug. 1940
Watercolor, 20.5 × 27.5 cm.
Inv. No. 1983/71 (8)

83
Walter Bloch, Class VI
"Frieze of Masks," Aug. 1941
Watercolor, 10.1 × 28.4 cm.
Loan Mieke Monjau

84 (Fig. 92)
Name unknown, grade unknown
"Man in SA Uniform," undated
Brown and yellow crayons, 17.9 × 12 cm.
AL 527

85 (Fig. 91)
Bubi . . ., 5 Years Old
"House with Swastika Flag," undated
Pencil and colored pencils, 16.5 × 21 cm.
Inv. No. 1983/71 (116)

86 (Fig. 87)
Eugen Wallach (Düsseldorf), grade unknown
"Haman on the Gallows," undated
Watercolor, 21 × 27.5 cm.
Inv. No. 1983/71 (117)

87 (Fig. 88)
Heinz Marcus, Class VI
"Man on Gallows," undated
Watercolor, 20.5 × 27.7 cm.
Inv. No. 1983/71 (137)

88
. . . Munderstein, grade unknown
"Elijah," undated
Watercolor, 20.7 × 27.4 cm.
Loan Mieke Monjau

89
Name unknown, grade unknown
"Carnival," undated
Pencil and pastels, 21 × 29.6 cm.
Inv. No. 1983/71 (115)

90 (Fig. 106)
Name unknown, grade unknown
"The Costume Party," undated
Collage, 27.9 × 35.9 cm.
Loan Mieke Monjau

91 (Fig. 84)
M. Franz, grade unknown
"Two Jews," undated
Pencil and watercolor, 26 × 19.4 cm.
Inv. No. 1983/71 (136)

92
Name unknown, grade unknown
"Parade," undated
Mixed media, 24.5 × 31.5 cm.
Inv. No. 1983/71 (19)

93
G(isela) Straus (Düsseldorf), grade unknown
"Weightlifter: Makkabi Sports Association," undated
Watercolor, 32 × 24.4 cm.
AL 621

94 (Fig. 77)
R(olf) Cahn (Düsseldorf), grade unknown
"Cossack's Dance," undated
Watercolor, 17.5 × 24 cm.
AL 626

95
Name unknown, grade unknown
"Wine Harvest on the Rhine," undated
Watercolor, 19.3 × 25.1 cm.
AL 584

96 (Fig. 116)
Renate Laband, Class IV
"Rumor," undated
Watercolor, 26.4 × 36.3 cm.
Inv. No. 1983/71 (15)

97 (Fig. 71)
R. Fahr, grade unknown
"The Road Repairman," undated
Watercolor, 26 × 19.1 cm.
AL 559

98 (Fig. 115)
Eve Marx, grade unknown
"In the Kitchen," undated
Watercolor, 16.5 × 27 cm.
AL 582

99
Kurt Reich, grade unknown
"Sleigh Ride," undated
Chalk pastels, 15.9 × 22.5 cm.
AL 879

100
Name unknown, grade unknown
"Lilliputian (Miniature) City," undated
Watercolor, 21.7 × 32 cm.
AL 535

101 (Fig. 90)
Name unknown, grade unknown
"Airplanes above the City," undated
Watercolor and ink wash, 18.8 × 22.8 cm.
AL 566

102 (Fig. 83)
E. Kruppe, grade unknown
"The Herman Memorial in Teutoburg Forest," undated
Colored pencils, 25 × 27.3 cm.
Inv. No. 1983/71 (130)

103
Name unknown, grade unknown
"A Black from Africa . . ." undated
Watercolor, 22.2 × 19.5 cm.
AL 241

104
Name unknown, grade unknown
"The Guarantee," undated
Pencil and watercolor, 13.3 × 24.4 cm.
Inv. No. 1983/71 (82)

105
. . .wig Kasischke, grade unknown
"The Glove," undated
Watercolor and ink, 24.7 × 32.9 cm.
Inv. No. 1983/71 (16)

* * *

Willem Jean Baptiste Stocké
(Born 1900 Beweren Waast, Belgium; Died 1945 Berlin)
1916–1918 studied archeology in Brussels; 1918 moved to Germany;

1919–1925 studied at the Munich art academy; 1926–1928 studied at the Düsseldorf art academy; 1932 appointed professor at the Düsseldorf art academy and also professor at the Fulda art academy;
1933 fired by the Nazis before assuming office; 1935 moved from Düsseldorf to Berlin; 1944 arrested; 1945 killed in an air raid on a Berlin prison.

106 (Fig. 3)
"Karlrobert Kreiten," ca. 1925
Oil on canvas, 90.5 × 65 cm.
Karlrobert Kreiten (1916–1943), a young German pianist, arrested because of anti-Nazi comments and executed at Berlin-Plötzensee on 7 Sept. 1943.

Gert Heinrich Wollheim
(Born 1894 Dresden-Loschwitz; Died 1974 New York)
Born into a wealthy Jewish family. 1911–1913 studied at the Weimar art academy; 1914–1917 severely wounded in World War I; 1919–1925 resided in Düsseldorf. One of the most prominent young avant-garde artists. In 1920s his pictures were received with hostility and protests by a bourgeois public; 1925–1933 lived in Berlin; 1933 fled Nazi Germany to Paris; 1939–1942 imprisoned in southern French transit camps (Richard, Gurs, and Septfonds); 1943 fled to Nay and survived in hiding until liberation; 1947 emigrated to New York.

107 (Fig. 44)
"Arthur Kaufmann with his Children, Miriam and Hans," ca. 1925.
Oil on canvas, 68 × 80 cm.
The artist Arthur Kaufmann (1888–1971), like Gert Wollheim, was one of the progressive artists of the 1920s. He was dismissed from the Düsseldorf commercial art school *(Kunstgewerbeschule)* in 1933. He first emigrated to Holland and in 1935 moved to the United States, living there until his death in 1971.

Mathias Barz
(Born 1895 Düsseldorf; Died 1982 Margraten, Netherlands)
1913–1922 studied at the Düsseldorf art academy; 1925 married Brunhilde Stein, who was Jewish; 1933 house searches, confiscation, and destruction of 3 paintings by the Nazis; 1936 the couple were arrested briefly; 1939 expelled from the Reich Chamber for Fine Arts and subsequently prohibited to paint or exhibit. Refused to divorce his Jewish wife despite repeated requests. 1944 fled to avert the impending deportation of his wife and survived in hiding. 1965 Brunhilde Barz died. 1973 Barz moved to the Netherlands.

108 (Fig. 1)
"Working-Class Children," 1926
Oil on canvas, 171 × 121 cm.
See also catalog entries 122 and 123.

Gerhard Keller
(Born 1905 Düsseldorf; Died 1984 Wachtberg-Oberbachen)
After 1923 studied at the Düsseldorf art academy; 1929–1933 studied at Berlin art academy and passed state examinations as an art educator. Worked as teacher until 1939. Served as a soldier during World War II. From 1945 until retirement resumed work as an art educator.

109 (Fig. 2)
"Portrait of Childhood (Ilse Studemund)," 1928.
Oil on canvas, 73 × 70 cm.
Loan

Franz Monjau
(Born 1903 Cologne; Died 1945 Buchenwald)
1920–1926 studied at the Düsseldorf art academy, subsequently enrolled in program for degree as art educator. 1933 banned from employment for political reasons, later compulsory work assignment as technical draftsman. 1944 denounced and arrested, deported to Buchenwald, where he was murdered. (See the memoirs of his widow, Mieke Monjau.)

110 (Fig. 4)
"Carnival," 1929
Oil on canvas, 95 × 75 cm.
The painting shows the artist and his future wife, Mieke, at a Carnival celebration, where they first met.

Adolf Uzarski
(Born 1885 Duisburg; Died 1970 Düsseldorf)
1906 studied at the commercial art school in Düsseldorf, employed in the advertising department of Tietz department store in Düsseldorf; 1919 founded the avant garde artists' association "The Young Rhineland" together with the artist Arthur Kaufmann (see catalog entry 107) and the poet Herbert Eulenberg. The satirist Uzarski was employed as a painter, a book illustrator, and writer. 1933–1945 unable to exhibit and after 1942 prohibited from any artistic or literary work. After 1945, satirical and critical drawings on the historical past and present.

111 (Fig. 5)
"German Family," 1932
Watercolor on paper, 67 × 48.8 cm.

Otto Pankok
(Born 1893 Mülheim an der Ruhr; Died 1966 Drevenack bei Wesel)
1912–1913 studied at the Düsseldorf and Weimar art academies. 1914 drafted into the Army and 1915 buried alive when a trench exploded. In the 1920s, close relations to the Düsseldorf art avant garde. 1935–1945 prohibited from exhibiting and constantly threatened by house searches and police visits. 1947–1958 appointed professor at the Düsseldorf art academy.

112 (Fig. 39)
"Gypsy children behind barbed wire," 1936
Woodcut, 53.5 × 76.7 cm.
AL
Pankok first became acquainted with Sinti in southern France in 1931. He intensified this initial contact with Düsseldorfer Sinti after he returned to Germany. Apart from accounts of their daily life, he also courageously attacked the persecution and expulsion of the Sinti by the Nazis. These works augment Pankok's depiction of the fate of German Jews.

Julius (Julo) Levin
(Born 1901 Stettin; Died 1943 Auschwitz)
1919–1920 studied at the commercial art

school in Essen; 1920 studied at the Munich art academy; 1923–1926 studied at the Düsseldorf art academy. After 1926 worked as an independent artist in Düsseldorf. 1936–1938 taught art at the Jewish school in Düsseldorf; 1938–1941 taught art at the Kaliski and Holdheim schools in Berlin. 1943 arrested and deported to Auschwitz, where he was murdered.

113 (Fig. 7)
"My Friend Ibrahim," 1931
Oil on canvas, 64.5 × 76.5 cm.
In 1931, Levin made a study trip to Marseilles, as did many other Düsseldorf artists and became friends with many of the dock workers there. Ibrahim Kountel, alias Breman, worked as a cook on ships sailing the route Marseilles – Casablanca – Dakar – Marseilles. Levin did several portraits of him.

114 (Fig. 8)
"Job," 1933–1934
Oil on canvas, 69 × 103 cm.
This painting was completed after Levin, along with the Monjaus, his atelier neighbor and friend Karl Schwesig, and many other friends and acquaintances were arrested and tortured in the mass arrests of suspected left-wing Düsseldorfers in 1933.

115 (Fig. 6)
"My Mother," 1939–1940
Oil on canvas, 110 × 76 cm.
Levin painted his mother, Emma Levin, née Arnfeld, after she had moved from Stettin to Berlin. Emma Levin was deported to Theresienstadt in 1942, where she was murdered.

Carl Lauterbach
(Born 1906 Burscheid; Lives in Düsseldorf)
1924–1930 studied at the Düsseldorf art academy; after 1930 worked as an independent artist. 1933 and subsequently, frequent confiscations of Lauterbach's paintings. Apart from harmless paintings completed for official exhibitions, Lauterbach continued to paint secretly and also assisted endangered and persecuted friends. Apart from this clandestine work, Lauterbach also accumulated a major archival collection of documents about the Nazi era.

116 (Fig. 44)
"Self-Portrait with Death," 1939
Ink wash and watercolor on Japanese vellum, 92 × 62 cm.
AL

117 (Fig. 43)
"Behind Barbed Wire," 1942
Charcoal and chalk on paper,
50 × 35 cm.
AL

Bernhard Sopher
(Born 1879 Safed, Israel; Died 1949 Los Angeles)
1897 started studies at the Berlin art academy; 1906–1909 studied at the Weimar art academy; after 1910 in Düsseldorf as an independent sculptor. 1914 became a German citizen, served as a soldier during World War I. Recognized as an important sculptor in the 1920s. 1935 decided to leave Germany; 1937 emigrated to the United States; 1943 became an American citizen.

118 (Fig. 9)
"Chinese Mother," 1942
Terra-cotta, height 36 cm.
Permanent Loan
This figure is part of a series with the title "Motherhood in War." Sopher completed these works in 1942 upon learning about the fate of civilians in occupied Europe and from air raids.

Paul Loskill
(Born 1899 Düsseldorf; Lives in southern France)
1917 soldier in World War I; 1918 wounded; 1919–1925 studied at the Düsseldorf art academy. Built a mosaic workshop; took control of his parents' porcelain and glass business, which he expanded into a studio for porcelain and glass painting. 1943 lost most of his works during an air raid.

119 (Fig. 10)
"Madonna of the Bombs," 1943
Tempera on canvas, 81 × 60 cm.

Hanna Fonk
(Born 1905 Göttingen; Died 1969 Düsseldorf)
1924–1928 studied at the Düsseldorf art academy. Friend of Mieke Monjau; unable to withstand the brutal interrogation techniques during her 1933 arrest, implicated the Monjaus and other friends.

120 (Fig. 20)
"Mieke Monjau," 1947
Lithograph, 57 × 42.9 cm.

Peter August Böckstiegel
(Born 1889 Arrode, Westphalia; Died 1951 Arrode)
1903–1907 apprenticed as house painter and glazier in Bielefeld; 1907–1913 studied at the commercial art school in Bielefeld; 1913–1915 studied at the Dresden art academy. 1915–1919 served in World War I and subsequently returned to Dresden. Important expressionist artist and recipient of many important art prizes. 1937 his works confiscated from German museums. 1945 numerous works lost during the bombing of Dresden; returned to Arrode, where he later died.

121 (Fig. 13)
"Refugee Youth," 1951
Pastels on dark paper, 74 × 54 cm.

Mathias Barz
See catalog entry 108 for biography

122 (Fig. 11)
"Inferno," begun in 1945, never completed
Oil on wood, 151 × 151 cm.
The work shows a crucified Christ among the Jews waiting in line for their deaths. It is an affirmation that Christ was a Jew. Adjacent to the crucified Jesus is a Star of David, saying "Jude." Barz never completed this canvas before his death, since the horrors of the past and the indifference of his contemporaries never allowed him to view this work as "completed."

123 (Fig. 12)
"SS Man," 1979
Oil on cardboard, 114 × 87 cm.

Lothar Spinn-Conradt
(Born 1911 Braunschweig; Lives in Düsseldorf)

Studied architecture at the Aachen and Düsseldorf art academies; self-taught photographer. Participant in numerous exhibitions.

124 (Fig. 18)
"City Scene: Deported from Here," 1985
Photomontage, 40.5 × 30.5 cm.
Deportation trains had departed from the Düsseldorf-Bilk train station; superimposed portrait of an old Polish-Jewish woman from well-known Auschwitz photographs.

125 (Fig. 19)
"City Scene: Mühlenstrasse, the Maidanek Trial," 1985
Photomontage, 40.5 × 30.5 cm.
The exterior of the district court at Mühlenstrasse 34, where the Maidanek trial was held over several years, with a corpse superimposed over the building.

Matthias Koeppel
(Born 1937 Hamburg; Lives in Berlin)
1955–1961 studied at the Hochschule für bildende Kunst in Berlin; since 1961 an independent artist with numerous prizes. 1972–1981 taught at the State School for Fine Arts in Berlin; since 1981 Professor for Drawing and Painting at the Technical University, Berlin. Numerous one-man shows and represented in many group exhibitions.

126 (Fig. 14)
"Looking Backwards": The Führer's Tea House in Berchtesgaden, 1985
Oil on canvas, 150 × 200 cm.

The painting is part of the series "German Landscapes." In the right background is the Führer's Tea House, still a tourist attraction. The man looking through a telescope towards Watzmann is a self-portrait of the artist.

Youval Yariv
(Born 1942 Kibbutz Dafna, Israel; Lives in Düsseldorf)
Studied at the Avni Institute, Tel Aviv; the Academy for Fine Arts, Brussels; the Central School of Art, Morley College, and Sir John Cass College, London; and at the Düsseldorf art academy. Numerous one-man shows and participant in many group exhibitions.

127 (Fig. 15)
"The Artist on his Way to Work," based on a painting by Vincent van Gogh and from Yariv's cycle "In Homage to Dinah Gottliebova, No. 1," 1985
Oil on canvas, 200 × 300 cm.

128 (Fig. 16)
"The Artist on his Way to Work," based on a painting by Vincent van Gogh and from Yariv's cycle "In Homage to Dinah Gottliebova, No. 4," 1986–1987
Oil on canvas, 214 × 300 cm.

Sandra Ikse
(Born 1945 Lübeck; Lives in Göteborg, Sweden)
1964–1968 studied at the commercial art school Göteborg; 1968–1973 at the Valand art academy. A Swedish textile designer, whose parents were expelled from Latvia, she created after graduation large Gobelin-like tapestries on social and political themes.

129 (Fig. 17)
"In Memory of Anne Frank," 1985
Gobelin, 150 × 200 cm.

Acknowledgments

The Stadtmuseum Düsseldorf and the authors would like to thank the following institutions and individuals for their generosity and assistance:

Prof. Dr. Kurt Bergel, Orange, CA;

Inge Bodesohn-Vogel, Cologne, FRG;

Prof. Dr. Michael Daxner, President, Oldenburg University, FRG;

Prof. Dr. Friedrich Kahlenberg, Director, Bundesarchiv, Koblenz, FRG;

Lotte Kaliski, New York;

Dr. Roland Klemig, Director Emeritus, Bildarchiv Preussischer Kulturbesitz, Berlin, FRG;

Gloria Lachmann, Houston, TX;

Hermann Langbein, Comité International des Camps, Vienna, Austria;

Carl Lauterbach, Düsseldorf, FRG;

Else Levin, London;

Dr. Yitzhak Mais, Director, Yad Vashem Museum, Jerusalem;

Mieke Monjau, Düsseldorf, FRG;

the Oberfinanzdirektion, Berlin, FRG;

the Pädagogisches Zentrum, Berlin, FRG;

Eva Pankok, Otto Pankok Archive, Hünxe-Drevenack, FRG;

Dr. Karl-Heinz Pütz, Director, Bildarchiv Preussischer Kulturbesitz, Berlin, FRG;

Dr. Hans J. Reichhardt, Director, Landesarchiv Berlin, FRG;

Daniel P. Simon, Director, Berlin Document Center;

Dr. Hermann Simon, Jüdische Gemeinde von Berlin, GDR;

Dr. Kazimierz Smolen, Director, Panstwowe Muzeum Oświęcim, Poland;

Dr. Diane Spielmann, Archivist, Leo Baeck Institute, NY;

Stadtarchiv Düsseldorf, FRG; and

Hans Winkens, Claassen Verlag, Düsseldorf.

The Authors

Dr. Annette Baumeister, art historian, staff member of the Stadtmuseum Düsseldorf.

Dr. Wieland Koenig, Director, Stadtmuseum Düsseldorf.

Carl Lauterbach, artist, member of the Young Rhineland and Mother Ey groups and a friend of Julo Levin in Düsseldorf.

Dr. Sybil Milton, historian, Research curator of the United States Holocaust Memorial Museum, Washington, D. C.; co-curator and North American coordinator of this exhibition.

Mieke Monjau, widow of the artist Franz Monjau and friend of Julo Levin; executrix of the Monjau and Levin estates.

Dr. Barbara Suchy, historian, commissioned by the city of Düsseldorf to write a history of the Düsseldorf Jewish community.

Photo Credits

Landschaftsverband Rheinland and Landesbildstelle Rheinland, Düsseldorf (if not otherwise indicated);

Bildarchiv Preussischer Kulturbesitz, Berlin; and Walter Klein, Düsseldorf.